Medicolegal Reporting in Surgery

For Churchill Livingstone

Commissioning Editor Miranda Bromage
Project Editor Deborah Russell
Copy Editor Nicola Wood
Indexer Monica Trigg

Medicolegal Reporting in Surgery

Edited by

Barry J. Jones MCh FRCSI DLS(King's Inns)
Consultant Surgeon, International Missionary Training Hospital, Drogheda, Aut Even Hospital, Kilkenny and Charlemont Clinic, Dublin

CHURCHILL LIVINGSTONE

NEW YORK EDINBURGH LONDON MADRID MELBOURNE SAN FRANCISCO AND TOKYO 1997

CHURCHILL LIVINGSTONE
Medical Division of Pearson Professional Limited

Distributed in the United States of America by Churchill Livingstone Inc., 650 Avenue of the Americas, New York, N.Y. 10011, and by associated companies, branches and representatives throughout the world.

First published 1997

ISBN 0 443 051607

British Library Cataloguing in Publication Data
A catalogue record for this book is available from the British Library.

Library of Congress Cataloging in Publication Data
A catalog record for this book is available from the Library of Congress.

Note
Medical knowledge is constantly changing. As new information becomes available, changes in treatment, procedures, equipment and the use of drugs become necessary. The editor and contributors and the publishers have, as far as it is possible, taken care to ensure that the information given in this text is accurate and up to date. However, readers are strongly advised to confirm that the information, especially with regard to drug usage, complies with latest legislation and standards of practice

The publishers have made every effort to trace holders of copyright in original material and to seek permission for its use. Should this have proved impossible, then copyright holders are asked to contact the publishers so that suitable acknowledgment can be made at the first opportunity.

Produced by Longman Singapore Publishers Pte Ltd
Printed in Singapore

Contents

Preface

The management of trauma and injury has always been an integral part of surgical practice regardless of speciality. The outcome of trauma management has improved pari passu with general developments in medicine. In addition trauma and injury have become closely associated with litigation in recent years. This is an additional perspective which the practising clinician has to take into account. Busy trauma surgeons resent the imposition on their time caused by the preparation of legal reports and subsequent court attendance.

The purpose of this book is to provide easy access to hard data. There is an emphasis on the precise classification of injuries which are, where possible, correlated with their outcome. I believe that where such classification can be applied the scope for conflicting medical reports from different sources is thereby narrowed. It seems likely that where reports are carefully prepared relying on objective classification and objective data that the opposing parties will agree the reports in advance of the court hearings. This would reduce the amount of time that would be spent on stand-by and giving evidence.

This book is not intended to be a textbook on the management of trauma. Where different management options exist for a given injury, they are described and where there is a difference in outcome, this is mentioned and discussed.

I should like to thank the contributors for their scholarship and application which made my task in compiling this text less difficult than it might have been.

Dublin 1997 B.J.J.

Contributors

Orla M. B. Austin MB FRSCI
Registrar, Department of Plastic and Reconstructive Surgery, St James's University Hospital, Leeds, UK

Aongus J. Curran MB FRCSI
Registrar in Otolaryngology – Head and Neck Surgery, St James's Hospital, Dublin, Ireland

Patricia A. Eadie FRCSI(Plast)
Consultant Plastic and Hand Surgeon, Department of Plastic Surgery, St James's Hospital, Dublin, Ireland

Christopher J. Glynn MA MB BS DCH FRCA MSc
Consultant – Pain Relief Unit, Churchill Hospital, Headington, Oxford; Honorary Senior Lecturer, Nuffield Department of Anaesthetics, Oxford University, Oxford, UK

Pierce A. Grace MCh FRCS FRCSI
Professor of Surgical Science, University of Limerick; Consultant Vascular Surgeon, Regional General Hospital, Limerick, Ireland

Yunus A. Gul MB FRCSI
Surgical Tutor Registrar, Department of Surgery, Our Lady of Lourdes Hospital, Drogheda, Ireland

Barry J. Jones MCh FRCSI DLS(King's Inns)
Consultant Surgeon, International Missionary Training Hospital, Drogheda, Aut Even Hospital, Kilkenny and Charlemont Clinic, Dublin, Ireland

John E. de Burgh Norman MBChB(Leeds) FRCS(Ed) FRACS MDS(Sydney) FDSRCS(Eng) FRACDS
Maxillofacial Surgeon, Department of Maxillofacial Surgery (Head and Neck Oncology), The St George Hospital, Sydney; Clinical Professor, University of Sydney; VMO, Mater Misericordiae and Royal North Shore Hospitals, Sydney; Consultant to the Royal Australian Navy; Hunterian Professor Royal College of Surgeons (England)

Daniel J. R. Rawluk MBChB FRCS
Consultant Neurosurgeon, Beaumont Hospital, Dublin, Ireland

H. Paul Redmond BSc MCh FRCSI
Senior Lecturer/Hon. Consultant Surgeon, RCSI, Beaumont Hospital, Dublin, Ireland

Peter Somers BA Barrister-at-Law
Lecturer in Tort, King's Inns, Dublin; Practising Barrister, Law Library, Dublin, Ireland

Alastair R. L. Stevenson MDSc(Syd) FDSRCS FRACDS AKC
Consultant Oral Surgeon, Staff Specialist, United Dental Hospital; Clinical Senior Lecturer, University of Sydney, Sydney, Australia

Conrad V. I. Timon MB FRCSI FRCSORL MD
Professor of Otolaryngology/Head and Neck Surgery, St James's Hospital, Dublin, Eye and Ear Hospital, Dublin and Trinity College, Dublin, Ireland

1. Preparation of reports and overview of the law

Barry Jones   Peter Somers

Medicolegal reporting is regarded by many clinicians as a nuisance which is peripheral to their main field of practice and may, at times, be highly disruptive of it. Nevertheless, a well-prepared report can be a source of satisfaction and education to its author. It is an unavoidable aspect of clinical practice and without obvious signs of abatement in civil litigation rates is likely to remain so for the foreseeable future.

Reports are requested for different reasons and it is important to understand how the report is to be used. The principal types of reports are:

Plaintiff report. The author will often be the principal clinician in the management of the patient's injury. Part of this report may be quoted verbatim in the plaintiff's statement of claim against the defendant.

Defendant report. These are usually requested by the insurance underwriters by way of an independent assessment. It is important to be objective. It is also important to remember that your contractual obligation is to the insurance company so that unless there is an overriding medical imperative, it is unwise to get involved in the patient's treatment.

Criminal injury report. Your report should be designed to assist the court in distinguishing 'actual bodily harm' from 'grievous bodily harm'. Precise times, ambulance pick-up, arrival in the Accident and Emergency department may also be of great help.

Disability pension report. These are requested by insurance companies to determine if the beneficiary remains unfit for work. Since this type of case rarely goes to court, the author can be less circumspect in expressing his opinions.

Medical negligence/malpractice report. These should be approached with great caution. They are very demanding and are rarely as straightforward as they seem. If, however, you were the main clinician in repairing the damage they are difficult to avoid and in many such situations there is an ethical obligation to the patient to provide a report.

It is important to have a format to which one should adhere throughout the consultation and the preparation of the report. In many cases there is no therapeutic input to the consultation so there is a danger that the clinician may become detached. Adhering to a well honed format ensures that important omissions are avoided. In some ways the preparation of a report is similar to a clinical examination and presentation prepared by a final medical student with the difference that an expert opinion is formulated at its conclusion. Details concerning the patient's social life and family history etc. help formulate an accurate overall picture and may be of assistance to the legal representatives of both parties in coming to an out-of-court settlement. There are no legal stipulations as to how a report should be structured, indeed it has been held that this should be left to the discretion of the expert witness (*Whitehouse* v. *Jordan* [1981] 1AER. 267). Nevertheless experience and good sense recommend some degree of uniformity in the layout of reports.

The title page should be on the headed notepaper of the specialist and include name, title, qualifications, position(s), address, telephone and fax numbers. The remainder of the title page is usually taken up with the case details as follows:

Name:
Address:
Date of birth:
Occupation:
Date of injury:
Date of examination:
Date of previous examination(s):
Report requested by: Name and address of law firm/insurance company.
Your ref.:
Our ref.:
Reports available: Name, address and date of other expert
Hospital notes, dates
Radiology reports, name of radiologist.

If reports have been requested but not received, state date of requisition and date and number of reminders.

Current complaint

It is useful to start with a short overview statement based on the subjective complaint of the patient: Mr X. said that due to an injury to his neck which occurred on 4.5.95 he has suffered and continues to suffer pain and disability causing him to be unfit for work etc.

Although a medical report becomes a legal document when entered in evidence, the medical expert should avoid the use of legal terminology except where it is definitely appropriate bearing in mind, also, that such terminology varies according to location. Where the causation of an injury and the liability for same has not been established it is not necessary for the medical expert to refer constantly to the 'alleged injury' or 'alleged accident'. It is sufficient that the doctor has clearly distinguished the subjective complaints from the objective findings. Referring merely to the injury or the accident will not be taken as an endorsement by the doctor of the patient's version of events.

Trauma history

A detailed description of the trauma event is required. An understanding of the mechanism of injury is helpful. Again, in reporting this, the doctor will be relying on the patient'/plaintiff's version of events and should indicate this accordingly. As before, the doctor should not be overconcerned with the issue of liability as this will not be decided on the medical report. It is worth spending some time with the patient documenting the precise chronology of events from the time of the trauma event to the time that the patient first sought treatment.

Treatment history

This should be compiled based on the account and the available medical documents. It is important to distinguish the source of the treatment information. Again a detailed account is required explaining where appropriate the nature and rationale of treatment modalities. The interval between injury and first medical consultation is important to record and if there has been a delay in seeking medical attention, the reason should be explained.

In addition to documenting the medical input, you should also record other treatments such as physiotherapy or occupational therapy. This should include the number of treatment sessions and their duration. It is sometimes appropriate to recommend a separate paramedical report.

In most personal injury cases, if the course of treatment has been reasonable it is not appropriate to comment critically even if you believe a different course of action would have been preferable. Obviously if the action is one of negligence or malpractice against another doctor this does not apply. However, in cases where the course of treatment has not been reasonable this should be stated. If failure to pursue a reasonable course potentially compromises the outcome of rehabilitation, this should be discussed together with reasons why you have formed such an opinion. Caution should be exercised if you feel obliged to adopt such an approach and any negative comment must have a sound basis in fact. The author of a report containing negligently formulated opinion may himself become a target for damages.

The treatment history will also include an account of investigations performed. Where radiographic or pathological reports are relied on, their authors must be cited.

Present status

This should entail a detailed account of the patient's condition at present including the effect such symptoms have on daytime activities: work, sleep etc.

Examination

Comment on the patient's demeanour and general movements. If a third party is present record their name and status. The examination should be as comprehensive as possible. There is no need to explain common medical terms such as 'spasm' or 'tenderness' although if there is a disparity between signs, this will need elaboration. Eponymous clinical signs and unusual terms should always be explained.

Where there is a limitation in the range of movement, state whether the restriction is due to pain, stiffness or apprehension. Always cover active, passive and resisted movements for musculoskeletal injuries.

Social and occupational history

It is important to document precisely the impact of the injury on the patient's occupational and leisure activities. Record the amount of time missed from work. Where possible state if the reported restrictions in occupational activities tally with your findings.

Past medical history

Previous injuries, previous X-rays and other significant surgical and medical events should be documented, irrelevant medical facts may be ignored. Current and previous medications should be listed explaining their function.

Opinion and conclusion

The author should strive to diagnose and classify accurately the injury. Where possible internationally accepted classification systems, such as the AAST system, should be used. This enables like to be compared with like. You should comment as to whether the apparent injury is compatible with the original trauma and whether the objective findings tally with the subjective complaints.

A clear but concise explanation of the condition in non-medical terminology is helpful.

The use of a standardized classification should enable an accurate expectation of outcome to be stated based on the medical literature. Mainstream references where applicable should be cited. The use of references in medical reports has elicited mixed feelings in the medical sphere as there is a fear of being ambushed in court by the adversary's expert quoting obscure references which are not readily contestable. There is a lobby in favour of disclosing references before the hearing.

A reasonable compromise is to use mainstream references, particularly where the injury is not especially rare. With data being so readily accessible on CD Rom it is not too much to expect an expert to appraise himself of the recent literature prior to taking the stand.

In some cases where it is not possible accurately to define the injury or where injuries are multiple and complex, it is not reasonable to give an exact prognosis. It is acceptable to state this, perhaps recommending re-assessment in 6 to 12 months.

It is helpful to conclude as you started, with an overview of your assessment and conclusions.

Discovery of medical reports and records

In civil litigation a process exists whereby the parties to the action are able to obtain from each other a list of all documents which are relevant to the proceedings. The court may make an order obliging one or both parties to the action to make discovery of such documents upon oath. Ultimately the party making discovery must make available for inspection by the other party all such documents, unless a valid objection to production is properly made. The court has control of the discovery process and, if necessary, will rule on the validity or otherwise of the objection.

The objection will usually be based on a claim that a particular document is privileged or is confidential. Documents which are created for the purpose of use in legal proceedings, or for the purpose of obtaining or collecting evidence to be used in such proceedings attract a privilege known as 'legal professional privilege'. It follows that medicolegal reports, which are prepared when litigation is either contemplated or commenced, attract such a privilege and the party who has commissioned the medical report will not be forced to discover it to his opponent.

In addition to the discovery procedure which enables the parties in a civil action to obtain disclosure of relevant documents from each other, there is also a procedure which is sometimes referred to as 'third party discovery'. This enables a party to an action to obtain disclosure of documents which are relevant to the facts in issue between the parties, but which are in the possession or control of a third party – that is, someone who is not a party to the legal proceedings in question. This procedure will usually have no relevance to the medicolegal report which has been prepared for either party in an action.

Firstly, such a report is privileged, and since the report has been commissioned by one of the parties to the action it will clearly be in the possession, power or control of that party and there is no need to involve a third party (the medical practitioner). However, if the plaintiff in a personal injuries action had a pre-accident injury which is in any way relevant to, or connected with, the injuries complained of in the proceedings, then the defendant is entitled to know full particulars of the plaintiff's prior injury, and may seek discovery of medical records which were created prior to the contemplation of the legal proceedings. These records may be in the possession or control of the author of the medicolegal report, but more commonly they will be in the possession of the plaintiff's general practitioner, or of the hospital in which he was treated for his previous injury. Applications for discovery of such prior medical records are now commonplace in the courts. If a medical practitioner receives a request to disclose any medical records from any party other than his patient (or former patient), or from his patient's legal advisers acting with the authority of his patient, then the safe course of action is to refuse to disclose or release such records on the grounds of confidentiality. The party seeking such disclosure is then obliged to bring an application for discovery of the records to court. Both the medical practitioner and his patient's legal advisers will be served with notice of the application to court which will facilitate the making of any objections to the discovery of the medical records. Except in unusual circumstances, the medical practitioner's role in this application will be passive and he will simply comply with whatever order the court makes. Such a circumstance might arise where the medical practitioner believes that the records contain information which, if released, would be detrimental to his patient's health. The judge may examine the records and decide whether or not to make the order for discovery.

Finally, the court will usually order that the medical practitioner's legal and incidental costs in respect of the application should be paid by one of the parties actually involved in the litigation.

Exchange of reports

Although the general rule is that medicolegal reports are privileged from disclosure, it is common practice for the parties in personal injury litigation to exchange such reports in advance of either settlement negotiations or the hearing of the action. This practice has been encouraged and in many jurisdictions there is a growing trend towards restricting the rights of parties to adduce oral expert evidence in civil proceedings as a matter of course. In most jurisdictions procedures have been developed, or rules of court have been introduced, to enable pre-trial disclosure by each party to the other of the medical and other expert evidence upon which it is intended to rely at the trial. The benefit of this policy is self-evident. It reduces costs and also lessens the incidence of what is sometimes referred to as 'trial by ambush' – where the expert acting on behalf of one party is taken completely by surprise by some aspect of the opposing expert's evidence.

In England the policy has been developed to such an extent that the Rules of the Superior Courts (RSC [1995] 0.12. [1A]) now impose an obligation on a plaintiff in an action for personal injuries to serve a medical report with a statement of claim. The Rules define medical report as:

a report substantiating all the personal injuries alleged in the statement of claim which the plaintiff proposes to adduce in evidence as part of his case at the trial.

A medical practitioner who is asked to prepare a medicolegal report should bear in mind that there is every likelihood that the report will be seen by the opposing side in the litigation. However, it should also be borne in mind that a plaintiff can never be obliged to exchange or disclose a medicolegal report upon which he does not intend to rely at the hearing of his action. He is entitled to seek a second, or third, opinion and to use the medical report from that source if it is considered more favourable from the plaintiff's perspective. Clearly, if an exchange of reports has been agreed between the parties, he will be obliged to disclose any report upon which he wishes to rely. The decision to exchange or disclose any report is a matter for that party's legal advisers and it follows that a medical practitioner should not send a report to the opposite side without the express instruction, or authorization, of the legal advisers for the party who has commissioned the report in question.

Change of diagnosis/prognosis

What then if the author of the medicolegal report subsequently changes his mind, either as to the nature of a particular injury or as to the prognosis which had previously been indicated in his report? If this situation does arise, the practitioner should contact his client's legal advisers at the earliest possible date, and indicate that he will write a further report which may contain material changes.

As far as the litigation is concerned, a party will only have been prejudiced if the case has actually been heard, or has been compromised. Such an event is unlikely to have transpired unless the previous medicolegal report contains something akin to a final prognosis. If the report has been prepared for a plaintiff then it is a relatively simple matter for that party's legal advisers to amend the document known as the 'statement of claim', which sets out in detailed form the nature and extent of the plaintiff's claim. The general principle underlying the amendment of legal pleadings is that all such amendments should be allowed for the purposes of determining the real question of controversy between the parties. The vast majority of such amendments are consented to by the opposing party to avoid the necessity of applying to court which will invariably permit the amendment and will only incur further legal costs. If the pleadings are not closed, that is to say that the matter has not been set down for hearing, an amendment is easily effected by serving an amended statement of claim on the defendant. In turn, the defendant, if he so wishes, may serve an amended defence.

Where medical reports have been exchanged between the parties, it is less likely that the claim will go to court without the parties being aware of the full extent of the plaintiff's injuries – unless, of course, both medical practitioners have misreported the extent or nature of the plaintiff's injury.

Civil and criminal litigation

There are important differences between the civil and criminal judicial processes. Firstly, the standard of proof is far greater in a criminal prosecution. In civil cases the plaintiff, or claimant, merely has to prove his case 'on the balance of probability'. The prosecution in criminal proceedings must prove the charge 'beyond reasonable doubt'. In a civil claim for damages for personal injury, a plaintiff will succeed if the medical evidence adduced on his behalf indicates that the symptoms complained of were probably caused by the incident unless of course more convincing conflicting expert evidence is adduced on behalf of the defence. Conversely, if a medical report merely indicates that the plaintiff's symptoms were possibly caused by the incident the appropriate standard of proof will not have been met.

In keeping with the lower standard of proof required in civil actions, the civil courts have by and large no function in respect of meting out punishment. The remedies available to a plaintiff in civil litigation are primarily damages or an injunction restraining the defendant from committing the act in question. Most civil claims will either allege a breach of contract or the commission of a tort, such as negligence, nuisance or defamation. Actions founded on tort or on breach of contract are inevitably based on disputes between private individuals.

A criminal action has a wider public dimension. A crime may be regarded as an offence against society and the criminal court has to concern itself with the maintenance of public order and safety. The focus in a criminal court is the punishment of the accused person, rather than the compensation of the injured party. Sometimes a single act will constitute both a crime and a tort. The most obvious example is the crime of rape, which also gives rise to an action in tort for trespass to the person. The lower standard of proof required in civil courts can mean that an accused person, who successfully defends a criminal charge of rape, may be unsuccessful in defending an action for damages subsequently brought in the civil courts, based on the same complaint.

The vast majority of civil actions which involve medical personnel as expert witnesses are claims in tort, or more specifically the tort of negligence. A tort is defined as a civil wrong, independent of contract, which arises from a breach of duty imposed by law, the main remedy for which is an action for unliquidated damages. The principal torts are: trespass, nuisance, defamation and negligence.

To succeed in an action for damages for breach of contract, the plaintiff must firstly show the existence of a contract between the parties. A contract is a legally binding agreement. A simple contract is one which is not made under seal (i.e. formally). All simple contracts require consideration (i.e. payment of some kind) to support them. A doctor who provides a service for a fee enters into a contractual relationship with his patient. Such a contract will contain few, if any, express terms but will contain many implied terms. For example, it would be an implied term that the doctor will exercise reasonable care when treating the patient, or that he would warn the patient of the possible side effects of medication which he has prescribed. Where a doctor breaches such an implied term, he may be liable to the patient in an action for damages for breach of contract. Arising out of the same act or omission, there may well be a liability also in tort, specifically in negligence. The claim brought on behalf of such a patient will be based both on negligence and breach of contract.

Damages

The function of damages is to restore, as far as possible, the plaintiff to the position he was in prior to his 'injury' whatever that might be. Whereas there are technical differences in the manner in which damages for breach of contract are calculated, as distinct from damages in tort, the practical effect is not significant, and this is particularly so in claims for damages for personal injuries.

Except for the extremely rare occasion where the court awards punitive damages – in order to punish the defendant – damages are said to be compensatory in nature. It will be obvious that in some instances, such as the loss of a limb, it would be impossible for the court to restore the plaintiff to his pre-accident position and any award must, to some extent, be arbitrary. Indeed the value placed on such an injury varies greatly from jurisdiction to jurisdiction. However, certain aspects of a claim for damages can be calculated with a degree of certainty, for example, the amount of income lost by the plaintiff to date, and which will be lost in the future. In personal injury claims, damages are awarded under the following headings:

- pain and suffering to date
- pain and suffering in the future
- actual pecuniary loss to date (such as loss of income and medical expenses)
- estimated future pecuniary loss.

The role which the medicolegal report plays in the assessment of damages in personal injury claims cannot be overestimated. The majority of such claims are settled without going to court and, assuming that there is no real contest on liability, the medicolegal report has a pivotal position in settlement negotiations. A personal injuries lawyer will look to the reports to answer the following:

1. Has the causal link between the accident, or incident, complained of and the plaintiff's injuries and symptoms been established at least as a matter of probability?

2. Are there injuries or symptoms indicated by the plaintiff to his lawyer which are not reflected in the medicolegal report?
3. Is there a sufficient degree of finality, or certainty, indicated in the prognosis?

Causation

Causation is a vital concept within the tort of negligence. Causation is concerned with the physical connection which links the defendant's negligent act or omission with the plaintiff's damage. Ultimately, it is for the court to decide whether the causal link has been established, but it does so with the assistance of the opinion of a relevant expert. In simple terms, the court has to consider whether the harm caused to the plaintiff would not have occurred 'but for' the defendant's negligent act. If the answer is in the affirmative, then the causal link has been established. Lawyers sometimes refer to this as the 'but for test'. A case law example illustrates this test. In *Barnett* v. *Chelsea & Kensington Hospital Management Committee* [1969] 1QB.428, a doctor in a casualty department attended a night-watchman who vomited after drinking tea. The doctor sent him away without treating him, suggesting that the patient should see his own doctor. The patient died of arsenic poisoning. The court, while holding that the doctor's conduct was negligent, did not find the doctor liable for damages in negligence because expert evidence was adduced and accepted to the effect that the patient was beyond help and would have died in any event.

Another example of a plaintiff failing to establish the causal link is to be found in *Smith* v. *Barking, Havering and Brentwood Health Authority* [1989] N-J&B.318. Here the plaintiff proved that the defendants had been negligent in failing to warn her adequately of the risks associated with a serious operation on the cervical spine. The risk materialised, but the plaintiff failed in her action for damages because the court decided that even if warned she would still have agreed to the operation as it was her only chance of avoiding the onset of quadriplegia.

In respect of loss of income, it is a great help if the report records periods of hospitalisation and recuperation, and the date upon which the patient was considered fit to return to work. Or, if he is still incapacitated, the probable duration of the incapacity. If the patient is unable to return to his regular work, then it is helpful if the medical practitioner can indicate whether or not he believes that the patient is fit to carry out some other type of work. Ultimately the plaintiff may have to be assessed by a vocational assessor.

The expert witness

Strict legal rules exist concerning the admissibility of evidence in a court hearing. The general rule is that a witness is permitted only to state what he has observed with his own senses, and he is not permitted to draw inferences or conclusions from his observations, because that is a role reserved for judge or jury.

However, an exception to this general rule is made for the expert witness – such as the doctor, engineer or architect. The expert is allowed to give opinion evidence. It should be noted that the burden of proof with regard to proving the expertise of the witness rests upon the party calling such a witness in evidence. At the commencement of such evidence counsel is therefore obliged to lead the witness through his qualifications and experience. In the majority of cases this evidence of expertise will be non-contentious, and cross-examination of the medical witness will only be engaged in where the opposing party is hoping to show that the particular medical procedure, or injury, is outside of the range of the witness's experience. For obvious reasons, the scrutiny of an expert's qualification and expertise will be much greater in a criminal trial than in a civil case. The Canadian case, *R* v. *Cusmack*, provides an example. Here the accused person was charged with murder. In his defence he alleged that the victim had a knife when he grabbed her and, consequently, that the killing had been accidental. A doctor gave evidence on behalf of the prosecution to the effect that the wounds on the victim's hands were sustained while defending herself. This evidence was not accepted because the doctor was not an expert on wounds or forensic evidence.

Consent

The issue of consent frequently arises in the medicolegal field. Acting without consent can have a variety of effects including criminal actions for assault and battery, civil actions for the tort of battery, negligence or defamation. An awareness of consent should pervade all interactions between clinician, patient and third parties. It is helpful to reconsider the meaning of the word consent in terms of the original phrase 'consensus ad idem' – an agreement of minds. When viewed in this light it becomes clear that for consent to be valid a patient may require a considerable amount of information in order for there to be a genuine agreement of minds.

Consent should also be viewed as being similar in many respects to a contract. It should be clear therefore, that when consent is required to a complex and serious procedure greater attention should be paid to the 'small print' than for a simple, routine procedure. Notwithstanding this approach a doctor must take full cognizance of individual requirements as to differing levels of information.

The categories of consent are usually distinguished as express or implied. When a patient attends a doctor and complains of abdominal pain there is implied consent to a standard abdominal examination. Similarly, by telling a patient that blood tests are required there is implied consent when the patient presents himself to the phlebotomist. It can be reasonably suggested that when a woman attends a gynaecologist with a gynaecological problem that there is implied consent to a pelvic examination. The accepted current practice, though, is not to rely on implied consent for pelvic or rectal examinations even when they are clearly indicated and would be expected by any reasonable patient. Similarly, examination of the breast or scrotum as part of a routine clinical examination should be based on express oral consent.

The legal guidelines as to what level of information is necessary for consent to be valid are deliberately vague. The general interpretation of the leading case of *Sidaway* v. *Governors of Bethlem Royal Hospital* [1985] AC. 871 is that the level of disclosure of risks to an individual patient is a matter of medical judgement and discretion.

This judgement reinforced the so-called Bolam principle (*Bolam* v. *Friern Hospital* [1957] 2 AER.118) where it was held that variations in accepted practice were not negligent provided support for such practice was available from some responsible members of a given specialty.

Reading the judgement in *Sidaway*, however, it is clear that there was considerable variation amongst the judges as to what constituted an acceptable degree of disclosure. Lord Diplock appeared to support the principle that the degree of disclosure was fundamentally a matter of medical discretion. Lord Scarman, however, tended towards the American position which states that a patient must be supplied with 'the material facts the patient will need in order to intelligently chart [his] destiny with dignity' (*Miller* v. *Kennedy* [1975] 85 Wash 2d 151 530P. 2d 334). An intermediate position seemed to be taken by Lord Keith and Lord Bridge which supports the 'medical discretion' concept except where disclosure of a particular risk is obviously necessary for the patient to make an informed choice, i.e. 'no reasonably prudent medical man would fail to make' [such disclosure]. It is generally believed that this latter intermediate approach is the most relevant at the present time.

Consent to Treatment Act 1995 (Canada)

Canada has recently passed the Consent to Treatment Act 1995. This states that consent is informed if, before giving it, the patient received sufficient information about the treatment, alternative courses of action, the material effects, risks and side-effects in each case and the consequences of not having the treatment, for a reasonable person in the same circumstances to be able to make a decision. Additionally the doctor must respond to the patient's requests for other information about treatments, alternative courses of action, material effects, risks and side-effects and the consequences of not having treatment.

The definition of 'treatment' in this Act includes X-rays, pelvic and rectal examinations, blood tests and other invasive diagnostic procedures. In establishing criteria for capacity to consent it states that the patient must be able to acknowledge that the treatment which is recommended may affect him and what the effect of having or not having treatment could have upon his life and quality of life.

The Act defines 'substitute decision makers' in the event of lack of capacity to consent and lists them in order of authority as:

1. Validated attorney for personal care if authorized to act for the particular circumstance
2. Unvalidated attorney for personal care if authorized
3. Representative of the Consent and Capacity Review Board which has a statutory basis in the Act
4. Spouse/partner
5. Child
6. Parent/guardian
7. Brother/sister
8. Other relative.

Categories 1 and 2 will often be drawn from categories 4 to 8.

The Canadian Act is not applicable in other jurisdictions but the influence of the Act on judicial decisions in Canada could filter through to the UK and Ireland where the judiciary sometimes refers to precedents set in the Canadian courts.

Age and capacity

The Family Law Reform Act 1969 changed the age of majority from 21 years to 18 years (The Age of Majority Act 1985 achieved equivalent effect in Ireland). However, section 8(1) of the Act stipulated specifically that persons aged 16 years and over could give valid consent to medical treatment regardless of parental wishes. The Act also empowered the judiciary to interpret whether a person under the age of 16 years could give valid consent.

The Act did not expressly confer on persons aged 16 years and over the right to refuse medical treatment or the right to consent to non-therapeutic medical procedures such as cosmetic surgery or kidney live donation.

The House of Lords determined in *Gillick* v. *West Norfolk and Wisbech Area Health Authority* [1986] AC.112, that a person under the age of 16 years who is of sufficient intelligence and comprehension has the capacity to give valid consent to medical treatment. Furthermore Lord Scarman stated that when a minor is deemed to have attained such capacity the authority of the parents in this regard is negated.

This was qualified by Lord Donaldson in Re R (a minor) [1991] 3 WLR.592. At issue in this case was the refusal by a 15-year-old girl to consent to treatment for a psychiatric condition. Donaldson stated that the power of a minor who was deemed competent, as per *Gillick*, to consent was concurrent with, as distinct from independent of, the consent of a parent or guardian. Consequently if the minor refuses treatment the consent of parents or guardians may be relied on with impunity. This was reaffirmed to a point in Re J [1992] The Independent LR (14.7.92) where the Court of Appeal held that conferring capacity on a 16-year-old child did not automatically deprive the parent or guardian of their capacity. However where a *Gillick* competent minor has given positive consent to treatment, parental authority cannot be accepted to override that consent except by authority of the court. A minor has no absolute power to refuse medical treatment and can be overruled by parental positive consent.

Where both the minor and the parents/guardian refuse consent to treatment, this can be overridden where appropriate by the court. Obviously the court will only use such a power (known as parens patriae) in serious and extreme circumstances.

In an emergency life-threatening situation there is a presumption of consent. Clearly informed consent, however, is desirable and should be obtained from the patient or their nearest legal substitute at the earliest possible time.

Treatment and procedures should be confined to those necessary to maintain life and prevent further injury.

NEGLIGENCE

Every medical practitioner is acutely aware of the term ‘negligence’. This is the most common cause of civil action against doctors. Four elements must be present to constitute the tort of negligence:

1. *Duty of care.* The plaintiff must establish that the defendant has a legally recognised obligation or duty of care towards the plaintiff.
2. *Standard of care.* It must be established that the defendant failed to conform to a recognised standard of care.
3. *Damage.* It must be established that there was actual loss or damage suffered by the plaintiff.
4. *Causation.* There must be a sufficiently proximate causal link between the actions or failure to act of the defendant which resulted in injury or damage to the plaintiff.

A legal action on the foot of a claim of negligence is usually pursued as a civil action. Occasionally the degree of negligence is so severe or the nature of the damage or injury to the patient so severe that negligence results in a criminal prosecution. This, typically, would ensue where an act of gross negligence on the part of the doctor resulted in death or severe injury to the patient.

Civil actions for damages will often attach as many defendants as possible to the suit. This is based on the legal practice of pursuing the defendant with the deepest pockets. It is common, therefore, to see the doctor, the hospital and the relevant health authority named in such an action.

Duty of care

It has been stated in *Le Lievre* v. *Gould* [1893] 1QB.491 that a person is entitled to be as negligent as he pleases towards the whole world if he owes no duty of care to them. The concept of duty of care has evolved through the common law, even to the point where an owner/occupier has been found to have a duty of care towards trespassers on his property. (*O'Hanrahan* v. *The ESB* [1969] IR.75).

In the medical sphere it is not normally difficult to establish a duty of care on the part of the doctor towards the patient.

Standard of care

What constitutes an acceptable standard of care has been developed through case law over the years. In *O'Donovan* v. *Cork Co. Council* [1967] IR.173) the judgement held that a medical practitioner cannot be held negligent if he honours a general and approved practice in the situation with which he is faced. This however was qualified by the statement that if a common medical practice has obvious inherent defects, the fact that it can be shown to be widely and generally adopted over a period of time would not necessarily redeem it from an allegation of negligence.

In another Irish case (*Daniels* v. *Heskin* [1954] IR.73) the Supreme Court held that a practitioner is liable if he fails to possess that amount of skill which is usual to his profession, or if he neglects to use this skill which he possesses or the necessary degree of care demanded. It was further stated that the medical practitioner must possess such knowledge and skill as conforms to recognised contemporary standards of his profession, and that if he is a specialist he is obliged to possess the further and particularized skill and knowledge which would be expected of him.

Lord Denning in *Roe* v. *Minister for Health* [1954] 2QB.66 cautioned against being wise after an event and against condemning as negligence that which might only be a misadventure. He drew attention to the fact that medical science has conferred great benefits on society and that every surgical operation must be attended by certain risks.

Lord Denning attempted to pursue the same lenient course in *Whitehouse* v. *Jordan* [1981] AER.658 when he stated that a medical practitioner could not be held negligent because of an error of judgement. However, this was criticised on appeal to the House of Lords where Lord Frazier stated that an error of judgement may or may not be deemed negligent and it would have to be decided on the facts of the individual case. He said that if the error of judgement was one that would not be made by a reasonably competent doctor practising with ordinary care, it could be held negligent. If, however, the error of judgement was such that the competent medical practitioner acting with ordinary care might reasonably have made, then it would not be held to be negligent.

The issue of differing approaches to a particular clinical problem was discussed in *Bolam* v. *Friern Hospital* [1957] 2AER.118. In this case a patient undergoing electroconvulsive therapy (ECT) without an anaesthetic suffered a number of fractures, and the issue was whether it was an acceptable practice to administer ECT without an anaesthetic. It was held that the doctor administering ECT without an anaesthetic could not be held negligent if he was acting in accordance with the practice acceptable by a responsible body of medical practitioners practising in that area. This has subsequently been termed the Bolam Test and has been approved in numerous subsequent cases with respect to the following areas:

Treatment: *Whitehouse* v. *Jordan* [1981] 1AER.267.
Diagnosis: *Maynard* v. *West-Midlands R.H.A.* [1985] 1AER.635.
Advice: *Sidaway* v. *Governors of Bethlem Royal Hospital* [1985] AC.871.

There is an obligation on medical practitioners to keep abreast of developments in their field. In *Hunter* v. *Hanley* [1955] SLT.213 the Scottish court held a practitioner must not obstinately carry on with the same technique if it has been proved to be the contrary of what is substantially the whole of informed medical opinion. This does not mean that every new technique must be instantly implemented into one's practice.

In *Roe* v. *Minister for Health* [1954] 2QB.66 an anaesthetist was held not to be negligent for administering a spinal injection which resulted in paralysis. The injection involved Nupercaine which had been stored in glass bottles and had become contaminated. In the previous year two American journals had drawn attention to this danger. However, these publications were held to be outside the spectrum of journals which an ordinary anaesthetist practising with reasonable care could be expected to read.

The Irish Supreme Court recently set down guidelines for what could be considered an acceptable standard of care in *Dunne* v. *National Maternity Hospital* where Chief Justice Finlay said that a true test 'for establishing negligence in diagnosis or treatment on the part of the medical practitioner, is whether he has been proved to be guilty of such failure as no medical practitioner of equal specialist or general status would be guilty of if acting with ordinary care.'

Furthermore he said that if the allegation of negligence against the doctor is based on proof that he deviated from a general and approved practice that will not establish negligence unless it is also proved that the course he did take was one which no practitioner of like specialization and skill would have followed if he had been taking ordinary care required from a person of his qualification.

This was again, however, qualified by a reiteration of the decision in *O'Donovan* v. *Cork Co. Council* [1967] IR.173 stating that even if a practice has been demonstrated to be established, if the plaintiff can prove that the practice contains inherent defects which ought to be obvious, negligence can be established.

The issues of damages and causation are discussed in a previous section.

Confidentiality

In the preparation of medicolegal reports it is essential to have an awareness of the constraints of confidentiality.

As previously stated, reports may be solicited by various sources. Where the clinician has been involved in the management of the plaintiff and an action for damage due to personal injury is subsequently taken, the plaintiff's solicitor will normally request the doctor to prepare a report. The Medical Council's guidelines place an obligation on the clinician to comply to such a request. This is because failure to do so may deny the patient certain benefits and compensation to which he may be entitled.

The Medical Council suggests that such a report should be prepared and issued within a 2-month period. Where the report has been requested by the plaintiff's solicitor, it will sometimes be accompanied by a consent form signed by the plaintiff granting permission to release his personal information to a third party, i.e. his legal representative. If there is no accompanying consent there is implied consent based on the fact that the solicitor is acting on behalf of the patient.

The situation is different, however, where a request comes from the legal adversaries of the plaintiff. If the clinician has been treating the plaintiff for his injuries and such a request is received, it should be denied without the express written consent of the patient. Issuing a report without the patient's consent in such circumstances would be regarded as a breach of confidentiality and could result in an action for defamation.

The report being prepared by the plaintiff's doctor should be comprehensive and include clinical data such as previous injuries and other relevant medical history.

Disclosure of information concerning patients to a third party without the patient's consent needs to be approached with great caution. There are limited circumstances in which it is justifiable to do so.

The first of these concerns the notifiable diseases, where the doctor has a statutory obligation to notify certain diseases to the relevant authorities. The second situation is where the disclosure is covered by what is known as 'qualified privilege'. This means that the person making the disclosure is doing so with good intent and without malice and is confining the disclosure to a third party who has a clear and justifiable interest in receiving the information. An example of this is notifying the general practitioner or sexual partner of a patient who has recently been diagnosed to be HIV positive.

Under no circumstances should such disclosure be undertaken without first consulting the patient, properly counselling them and making every effort to obtain their willing consent. It is only when such channels have been exhausted and the patient persists in refusing consent that there is an obligation to notify persons whose own well-being is likely to be seriously compromised should the disclosure not be made.

A similar situation would apply to a child who is the victim of physical or sexual abuse where under normal circumstances parental consent would be required before disclosure of such information to the social services and general practitioners.

Electronic transmission of patient information

The advent of technology such as fax machines and E-mail greatly facilitates the transmission of information. Both, however, carry the potential of inadvertent disclosure of information to non-interested third parties. It is recommended that where such technology is being used the degree of disclosure should be kept to a minimum, and where possible should be preceded or followed by direct personal contact such as telephoning to ensure that the interested party receives the documentation immediately.

2. Soft tissue injuries

Barry Jones

The term ‘soft tissue injury’ is one of the most frequently used terms in medicolegal reporting. In many cases this term could be justifiably replaced with phrases such as ‘non-specific injury’ or ‘undefined injury’ The vagueness of the terminology is deliberate caused, in some cases, by an inability on the part of the medical expert to establish a specific pathological abnormality combined with an understandable reluctance to dismiss the plaintiff's claims as trivial or spurious.

Great care must be taken in the formulation of an opinion which is clearly dismissive of the plaintiff's claims. It is increasingly difficult to proffer a negative opinion based on clinical criteria. In recent years resorting to elaborate diagnostic procedures such as CT scanning, MRI and isokinetic testing has become commonplace in cases where under normal clinical circumstances such tests would be considered unjustified and wasteful. The proliferation of diagnostic tests is largely evidence-driven and for the foreseeable future looks set to continue.

The scope of this chapter has been deliberately curtailed. To cover each type and grade of soft tissue injury as applied to each part of the musculoskeletal system would require a separate textbook. Equally one is conscious not to impinge on the orthopaedic field of expertise. This chapter concentrates on a number of areas in detail and the remainder of the chapter serves as a guide or reminder of specific pathological entities affecting various regions and joints which could be overlooked or ignored by resorting to a catch-all phrase such as ‘soft tissue injury’.

The majority of soft tissue injuries are simple affairs. They can be divided into injuries affecting muscles, ligaments, tendons and subcutaneous tissues. A smaller group of soft tissue injuries can be extremely complex and pose difficult management problems.

Mechanism of injury

Determining the mechanism of injury is of utmost importance in understanding soft tissue injuries. The mechanisms can be loosely categorised into:

- Direct injury

- Indirect injury.

Direct injuries consist of direct application of physical force, either blunt or penetrating. Blunt trauma will often result in contusions and haematomas where penetrating trauma will result in lacerations plus or minus infections.

Indirect trauma will normally be caused by an abnormal or forced movement. Injuries due to indirect trauma are usually more complex as they will invariably involve soft tissues surrounding one or more joints. Important factors in indirect trauma include the velocity of trauma, the movements involved, e.g. flexion extension, whether or not there is an added torsion component, and apprehension of injury by the subject. The velocity of the trauma does not always correlate directly with the severity of the injury (Evans 1992).

Examination

Clearly a detailed history is essential with specific reference to the site of the pain, the radiation of the pain and the quality of the pain. Temporal patterns are important. Soft tissue pain is often worse at night causing sleep disturbance. Pain at night also may reflect underlying inflammatory conditions such as arthritis, nerve entrapments, Sudeck's atrophy or reflex sympathetic dystrophy. A new pattern of joint involvement is important as the injury may affect several joints.

On examining the patient it is important to look at the normal side first. In assessing movement one should assess active and passive isometric and accessory movements. Limitations of movement may be caused by stiffness, pain or apprehension and should be documented as such. Clearly the impact of the injury on occupational and social activities should be accurately documented.

MUSCLE

Direct injury

Muscle has an extensive vascular supply which increases with exertion. Direct trauma to muscle will often result in contusion or, more severely, haematoma. This is often associated with bruising which tracks along fascial planes. There is pain and loss of function, tenderness and swelling. Active and passive movements are limited by pain. Management is elevation and compression initially for the first 24 hours followed by active rehabilitation. Early active rehabilitation results in preservation of muscle mass and facilitates reabsorption of haematoma and contusion.

Complications

Complications of direct muscle trauma include fibrosis, muscle rupture, calcification and myositis ossificans and cyst formation.

Fibrosis occurs with the deposit of fibrotic tissue both within the muscle fibres and between muscle bundles resulting in adhesions and loss of muscle flexibility. The risk of this is reduced by early active rehabilitation.

In myositis ossificans there is osteoblastic invasion of the muscle haematoma. This can result in the development of a bony mass which will often display characteristic bone architecture. This is not to be confused with calcification of haematoma which can also occur as a complication of the same.

Indirect injury

Indirect trauma usually results in tearing of muscles. This will commonly affect a muscle that spans two joints. The cause of injury is usually an unexpected accelerative force. Tearing is most likely to occur in the middle of the muscle belly.

Grades of tearing include:

Grade I: Tearing within the bundle but without disruption of same.
Grade II: Partial tearing of bundles but without complete disruption of the muscle.
Grade III: Complete disruption of muscle.

Complications

Complications of indirect muscle trauma include fibrosis, haematoma and myositis ossificans.

LIGAMENTS

For specific ligamentous injuries please refer to *Medicolegal Reporting in Orthopaedic Trauma* (Foy & Fagg 1990). Ligaments consist of collagen fibres, fibrocytes, nerve fibres and a small number of blood vessels. Ligaments are usually injured by indirect trauma which may cause them to tear to a variable degree.

Grades of tearing include:

Grade I: Tearing of a few ligament fibres with preservation of the integrity of the ligament overall. The stability of the joint is not compromised.
Grade II: Tearing of a greater number of ligamentous fibres, resulting in some degree of instability to the joint.
Grade III: Complete destruction of the ligament complex with joint instability.

Grade I and II injuries are usually associated with pain, swelling and sometimes muscle spasm. Grade III injuries are associated with a considerable swelling often with haematoma, although pain may not be as pronounced as in Grades I and II.

Specific clinical signs include swelling, bruising, painful stress test often with clear joint laxity. There may be a palpable gap in the ligament.

TENDONS

Tendons consist of parallel bundles of collagen fibres, fibrocytes and blood vessels. At either end of a tendon there is a network of fibres that penetrates the cortex of the bone to form an attachment known as the enthesis. Blood supply of the tendon derives from the muscle periosteum and from the tenosynovium. Injury typically occurs either by avulsion, direct laceration or the indirect application of force. (For further detail refer to Chapter 7 (Plastic surgery).)

Complications

- Tendon rupture, partial or complete
- Tendon avulsion from insertion to bone
- Calcification: This is a complication of the repair process and may compromise tendon movement
- Tenovaginitis: Examples include de Quervain's, involving the long abductor and short extensor tendons of the thumb or affecting the tibialis posterior tendon
- Dislocation of tendon from its groove which will result in diminished function and a clicking sensation typically affecting the peroneal tendons in the ankle.

The purpose of the following sections is to draw attention to specific conditions relating to soft tissue injuries affecting specific joints. It is beyond the scope of this book to examine in detail the diagnosis and management of the multiple articular and periarticular lesions that can occur.

NECK

Neck injuries are among the most common class of injury encountered in personal injury civil litigation. The majority of these injuries are sustained in motor vehicular collisions (SUVA Review 1991) of which 90% are due to rear-end impacts (Gay & Abbott 1953).

The mechanism of the injury here is acceleration of the trunk and lower neck away from the head and upper neck resulting in hyperextension of the cervical spine and surrounding structures and succeeded by acceleration of the head as it catches up following through into forced flexion. The fact that the trunk moves first rather than the head partially explains why head-

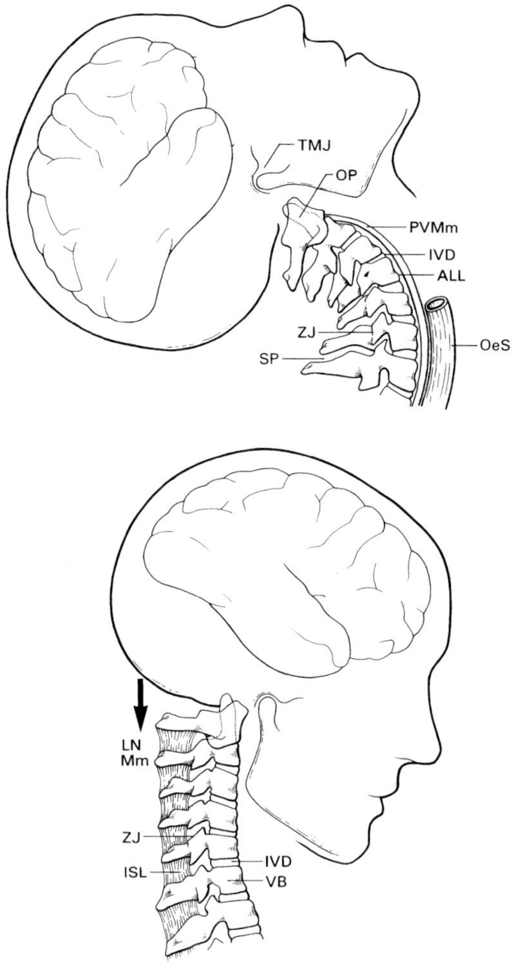

Fig. 2.1 Anatomical structures in the neck subject to injury: TMJ-temporomandibular joint; OP-odontoid process; PVMm-prevertebral muscles; IVD-intervertebral discs; ALL-anterior longitudinal ligament; ZJ-zygapophysial joint; SP-spinous processes; Oes-oesophagus; ISL-interspinous ligament; VB-vertebral body (after Bogduk).

rests have not had more effect on the incidence of neck injuries, although there is evidence that properly adjusted head restraints can reduce neck pain (Evans 1992).

Precise definition of the injury has remained problematic. Figure 2.1 illustrates the structures which could be damaged either individually or in conjunction with other structures. It is difficult to recommend an accurate grading system other than division into mild, moderate and severe. Where possible the catch-all term 'whiplash' should be avoided. The tendency to regard all 'non-serious' neck injuries as belonging to the same category is unhelpful. Undoubtedly many neck injuries are either spurious or exaggerated due to the attendant litigation. Equally, serious injuries such as cervical disc herniations, may sometimes be overlooked (Jonsson 1994).

Symptoms:

1. Pain is inevitable. The exact chronology in the evolution of the pain is important and the location and radiation of the pain should be documented. The pain commonly radiates to the occiput, shoulders or to the intrascapular region. Radiation to these areas is associated with a slower rehabilitation.
2. Headache is common in the acute phase, occurring in 82% of cases (Evans 1992) and is usually localised in the occipital area. This type of headache normally improves and relapses along with neck pain. Less frequently a migrainous headache may occur and this is more likely to be associated with a prolonged clinical course (Bring & Westman 1991).
3. Visual blurring is commonly reported yet poorly understood. Hildingsson and colleagues identified oculomotor abnormalities in almost 30% of 'whiplash' patients evaluated. These had corresponding visual symptoms. However 20% of patients with visual symptoms had normal oculomotor tests (Hildingsson et al 1990).
4. Vertigo and tinnitus may occur in the acute phase. Examination must include inspection of the tympanic membrane to exclude middle ear haemorrhage. Dizziness is associated with more severe muscular sprains (Hohl 1984). The mechanism of prolonged vertigo is not understood. Theories relating to vertebral artery impingement have not been validated.
5. Temporomandibular joint (TMJ) related symptoms are increasingly reported following hyperextension/hyperflexion injuries to the neck. The various theories as to mechanism of injury are dealt with in Chapter 3. Pressman identified MRI abnormalities in the TMJ in 88% of symptomatic patients who had no prior history of TMJ problems or evidence of direct TMJ injury at the time of trauma (Pressman et al 1992).

   The most frequent finding was displacement of the intra-articular meniscus which was identified in 56% of cases. Oedema and TMJ effusion were seen in 65% of cases. Why these lesions should occur is not clear, but it has been suggested that sudden contraction of the pterygo-masseteric and temporalis muscles may cause a rapid fluctuation in stress on the TMJ with consequent capsular or meniscal injury (Weinberg & Lapointe 1987).
6. Sensory tests have demonstrated trigeminal nerve impairment suggesting injury to the central trigeminal system in the upper cord and pontomedullary areas (Knibestol et al 1990).

7. Dysphagia is occasionally reported following soft tissue neck injury. This may be due to stretching of the oesophagus over the vertebral bodies and osteophyte formation on the cervical spine appears to be a risk factor (Kissel & Youmans 1992).
8. Cognitive dysfunction following soft tissue injury to the cervical spine has been documented by Radanov (Radanov et al 1992).

They described two distinct syndromes:

- Cervicoencephalic: Headache, fatigue, dizziness, poor concentration and disturbed ocular accommodation
- Lower cervical spine syndrome: Cervicobrachial pain and reduced speed of information processing. Cognitive impairment is less pronounced in this group.

Outcome

Predicting the outcome in individual cases is fraught with difficulties. It goes without saying that specific abnormalities such as subluxed facet joints, instability due to disrupted anterior longitudinal ligament etc. must be ruled out. This applies especially to those with persistent symptoms where occult abnormalities may have been missed (Jonsson et al 1994).

Hildingsson & Toolanen found that 2 years after the injury 42% had recovered completely, 15% had minor discomfort, but 43% continued to have sufficient pain to interfere with work. Disappointingly, there was no correlation between various 'prognostic' factors such as sex, physical findings, radiographic findings, acute symptoms, headrests, etc. and the actual outcome (Hildingsson & Toolanen 1993). This is at variance with the findings of others who have identified the following as negative prognostic factors: female gender, pre-existing arthritis, loss of cervical lordosis, multiple symptoms (vertigo, paraesthesia, etc.), interscapular pain (Evans 1992, Hohl 1984).

Most clinicians would add litigation to this list. Undeniably, 'whiplash' and litigation are inextricably connected but it is worth noting that many patients are not cured by a settlement (Evans 1992).

SHOULDER

Pain relating to the shoulder is notoriously difficult to pinpoint. The shoulder joint is highly complex and inherently unstable. Articulating areas include the glenohumeral, subacromial joint, the scapulothoracic 'joint', and the acromioclavicular and sternoclavicular articulations.

Movement is a complex combination affecting all of these. Impairment of movement in one of these joints can be masked and compensated for by the other joints, in particular reduction in glenohumeral movement is usually compensated for by scapular rotation.

Shoulder pain may be referred from other areas:

1. A patient may have shoulder pain without any neck pain, but it should be possible to reproduce the pain by neck movement. This will commonly affect the cervical vertebra at C4/5 and C5/6 levels.
2. Pain may be referred from intrathoracic or intra-abdominal diseases affecting areas in the phrenic nerve distribution at the C3/4 and C5 levels.

Common causes of shoulder pain

1. Impingement syndrome: impingement within the subacromial space of either supraspinatus or biceps tendon. A persistent impingement may result in calcification or ultimately tendon rupture.
2. Tendon lesions: (a) rotator cuff tendinitis, (b) incomplete rupture, (c) complete rupture, (d) calcification, (e) biceps tendon, (f) tendinitis, (g) tenosynovitis rupture.
3. Bursitis: subacromial bursitis, acute or chronic. Subcoracoid bursitis.
4. Capsulitis.
5. Instability of shoulder joint: complete dislocation, subluxation, recurrent or transient. Dislocation and subluxation usually occur anteriorly but occasionally may occur posteriorly.
6. Supraspinatus tendinitis: chronic irritation of the tendon within the subacromial space results in degeneration and sometimes rupture of same. This is often associated with chronic subacromial bursitis where complete rupture occurs and the superior stability of the glenohumeral joint may be compromised.

Calcification

Calcification is a common radiological finding with chronic shoulder conditions. It is present in about 8% of routine shoulder X-rays. Calcification may be asymptomatic and incidental finding or may be associated with supraspinatus tendinitis. Occasionally there may be sufficient calcification to cause mechanical impairment to shoulder abduction.

Capsulitis

Capsulitis (in the case of the shoulder, inflammation affecting the capsule of the glenohumeral joint) results in pain and stiffness for both active and passive movement of the shoulder. The term 'frozen shoulder' is often used in medicolegal reports but it is so non-specific that the use of this term is not recommended.

Progression of the condition results in thickening and shortening of the capsule fibres (Johnson 1987). It most commonly affects middle-aged females and although its precise aetiology is unknown, its history will often contain a fall or stumble which produced a non-specific soft tissue injury to the shoulder area (Murnaghan 1988). The condition may also result from anything that results in immobilisation of the shoulder for an intermediate length of time, such as mastectomy, myocardial infarction or intrathoracic disease.

Grades of capsulitis include:

Grade I: Mild synovitis over the entire joint. Active and passive movement approach full range, but pain is reproduced at the extremes of movement.

Grade II: Fibrosis and thickening of the capsule. Pain is more severe and often nocturnal. There is limitation of both active and passive movement due to pain. Resisted movements remain relatively painless. Considerable disability and activities such as dressing, brushing hair, etc. become difficult.

Grade III: Pain at rest becomes less pronounced although stiffness becomes more marked due to contraction and thickening of the capsule. There may be wasting of the supraspinatus and infraspinatus muscles. The range of active and passive movements of the glenohumeral joint is greatly restricted. Scapular movement remains although it may be reduced.

The outcome is highly variable and depends on the age and motivation of the patient. Treatment consists of judicious non-steroidal anti-inflammatory medication and aggressive physiotherapy. Prevention is important so that vigorous physiotherapy is instituted for patients with soft-tissue injury, or immobilisation due to ancillary diseases or procedures.

Instability of the shoulder joint

The shoulder joint is intrinsically unstable. Instability is a common cause of shoulder pain which may easily be overlooked (Jobe & Kvitne 1989). Subluxation may be recurrent, transient, acute or chronic (Garth et al 1987).

Subluxation is usually anterior but less frequently may occur posteriorly or in other directions (Schwartz et al 1987). Instability of the shoulder joint is usually secondary to defects in the surrounding soft tissues, muscles, tendons or capsule. A patient who has suffered an acute anterior dislocation is more likely to suffer recurrent anterior dislocation (Kieft et al 1988). Diagnosis of subacute subluxation is often difficult and may require a CT or MRI scan to establish the diagnosis.

Acromioclavicular joint

The acromioclavicular joint may be injured following trauma often due to a fall directly onto the shoulder. Commonly, tears occur in the acromioclavicular ligaments but injuries may also occur in the intra-articular meniscus.

Grades of injury to the acromioclavicular ligament:

Grade I: Partial tear in the fibres of the acromioclavicular ligaments without any dislocation. Pain and tenderness are usually well localised.

Grade II: Disruption of the acromioclavicular ligament fibres and capsules with subluxation of the joint and upper displacement of the clavicle.

Grade III: Disruption of the acromioclavicular ligament and the coracoclavicular ligament and attachment of the trapezius muscle. There is more marked upper displacement of the clavicle. Less painful than Grade II.

Grades I and II are best managed conservatively whereas Grade III injuries are most commonly treated by means of surgery. It is not clearly established that surgical reduction and fixation is the best option in all cases, in terms of functional outcome.

ELBOW

Soft tissue lesions affecting the elbow include:

1. Musculotendinous lesions:
   a. lateral epicondylitis
   b. medial epicondylitis
   c. bicipital tendinitis
2. Ligament sprains
3. Disruption – pulled elbow
4. Nerve lesions
   a. ulnar nerve
   b. median nerve
   c. radial nerve.

Lateral epicondylitis

This is a common source of pain in the elbow region. It commonly affects the dominant hand and most frequently affects middle-aged females. Pain may radiate down the forearm but tenderness is often localised. Trigger movements will stimulate the pain. X-rays may show ectopic calcification over the area. Collateral changes may result from overuse or repetitive wrist movements which would commonly affect the origin of the extensor carpi radialis brevis muscle.

A lateral epicondylitis will often follow a pattern of exacerbation and a remission. Most cases will, however, eventually resolve within a 2-year period (Gerberich & Priest 1985).

Treatment consists of rest, anti-inflammatory medication, local injections with steroids and analgesic agents, physiotherapy or surgery. Surgery is only indicated following failure of conservative measures and usually consists of tenotomy or mobilisation of the muscle origin.

Medial epicondylitis

This condition is less common than lateral epicondylitis but again occurs most frequently in middle-aged females and is frequently related to overuse.

Treatment is similar to that for lateral epicondylitis.

Nerve lesions

Ulnar nerve

The ulnar nerve is vulnerable to injury or impingement in the following ways:

- Acute trauma: in the anaesthetised patient undergoing major surgery
- Repetitive trauma: may be related to occupation
- Cubitus valgus: either traumatic or degenerative.

Radial nerve

Radial nerve syndrome may produce elbow pain and should not be confused with lateral epicondylitis.

WRIST AND HAND

Hand injuries are often complex and are beyond the scope of this chapter. The common conditions need to be borne in mind in dealing with this area, namely: tendinitis, tenosynovitis, de Quervain's disease, trigger finger, tendon rupture, ligament injuries, Dupuytren's contracture, arthritis, fracture of scaphoid or hamate bones, nerve entrapments.

HIP

Hip pain may be referred from more proximal parts of the spine and pelvis. A common pitfall in dealing with non-specific hip pain is to overlook a referred pain from the spine and the juvenile pathologies.

Causes of referred pain to the hip

- Spinal diseases: hip pain may be referred from the lumbar spine, particularly from L2/3. The commonest causes of referred pain are prolapsed intravertebral disc, metastatic secondary deposits in the lumbar spine and, rarely, spinal or psoas abscess.

- Intra-abdominal conditions: pelvic masses, appendicitis (pelvic), obturator or femoral hernia.
- Posterior pain: this may be referred from the sacro-iliac joint due to strain or inflammation.

Classification of diseases affecting the hip

1. **Soft tissue lesions:**
   a. tendinitis commonly affects abductor hamstring, gluteal and psoas tendons
   b. capsulitis
   c. bursitis
2. **Articular lesions:**
   a. osteoarthritis
   b. rheumatoid arthritis
3. **Bone pathology:**
   a. Paget's disease
   b. osteoporosis
   c. stress fracture
   d. steroid-related avascular necrosis
4. **Juvenile condition:**
   a. congenital dislocation of the hip or acetabular dysplasia
   b. Perthes' disease
   c. slipped femoral epiphysis
   d. transient synovitis (irritable hip)
5. **Entrapment neuropathy:**
   Lateral cutaneous nerve of the thigh.

Pain to the anterolateral aspect of the thigh may be due to pathology in the lateral cutaneous nerve. This is sometimes confused with hip pathology in that extension of the hip can cause an exacerbation of the pain. The nerve derives from the L2/3 nerve root and commonly becomes entrapped as it passes through its tunnel in the inguinal ligament near the anterior superior iliac spine.

Causes include overactivity, direct trauma commonly as a result of surgery in this region, and activity after prolonged immobilisation.

Treatment includes conservative measures such as deep tissue massage, local injection of local anaesthetic and steroids or surgical release of the entrapped nerve.

KNEE

For such a large synovial joint which is intrinsically unstable and which relies completely on its surrounding soft tissue for stability, it is perhaps surprising that soft tissue injuries to the knees are not seen more often in the medicolegal context.

Although much can be gained from accurate clinical examination, ultimately endoscopic evaluation is often required to exclude specific intra-articular lesions.

Common conditions affecting the knee include:

- *Ligaments:* collateral, anterior and posterior cruciates
- *Musculotendinous lesions:* quadriceps muscle tear, quadriceps tendon tear, gastrocnemius tendinitis, gastrocnemius head tear, popliteal tendinitis, iliotibial translateral femoral epicondylitis
- *Bursitis:* prepatellar, infrapatellar, semimembranosus
- *Meniscal lesions*: tears and cysts
- *Cartilaginous lesions*
- *Osteoarthritis*
- *Patellar lesions:* Fractured patella, disrupted patella tendon, chondromalacia patellae.

Ligament injuries

Collateral ligament injuries in the knee are common especially in the area of sports. An accurate assessment of the mechanism of injury is useful. There is virtually always a varus or valgus force, but the addition of torsion to this can complicate the injury significantly. In particular, the injury which can occur with varus or valgus plus torsion force to the knee with a foot stuck in the ground can result in a complex injury involving the collateral ligament, the menisci and the cruciate ligaments.

Classification

First degree These ligament sprains are associated with tearing of a number of fibres which will result in pain and tenderness localised to the point of tearing. There will usually be tenderness along the joint line when the knee is examined in the flexed position. Stretching the ligament will reproduce the pain. The knee joint is stable however, and the condition will usually resolve within 3 or 4 weeks without any adverse long-term effects.

Second degree These will often be associated with haemarthrosis or effusion. There may be subcutaneous bruising and on clinical examination there will be evidence of laxity of the ligament or joint instability. These injuries normally take 6–8 weeks to resolve. It is important to rule out associated injuries to the menisci or cruciate ligaments. Vigorous physiotherapy in the interim is essential to maintain a quadriceps muscle. These injuries are more vulnerable to repeat injury in the future.

Third degree Complete rupture of the collateral ligaments. There is marked pain and disability is usually quite significant. There is also swelling, although joint fusion may not be marked as these will often track into the surrounding tissues.

Treatment options include conservative management by means of immobilisation in cast, or surgical repair. It is not clear which method is superior in the general sense although surgery is preferable in younger active people or where there is a suspicion of associated injury to other structures. The risk of repeat injury is increased in the future.

Differential diagnosis of knee swellings

- Effusion: haemarthrosis
- Meniscal cysts: tender swelling along the joint line, usually lateral meniscus
- Bursitis: soft swelling, most commonly in the prepatellar area. Also infrapatellar or semimembranous
- Osgood-Schlatter disease: tender swelling over tibial tubercle
- Osteochondromatosis: bony swelling within the synovial cavity
- Soft tissue swellings in the synovial cavity, e.g. ganglion fibroma or tumour
- Synovial cyst, Baker's cyst
- Pellegrini-Stieda lesion: ossification of medial collateral ligament as a complication of haematoma formation. This is usually due to direct blunt trauma or may complicate a first or second degree sprain of the collateral ligament.

Post-traumatic conditions affecting the patellofemoral joint

— Fracture
— Stress fracture
— Dislocation
— Ruptured patella tendon
— Patellar tendinitis of Osgood-Schlatter disease
— Injuries to the infrapatellar pad
— Reflex sympathetic dystrophy.

LOWER LEG

Compartment syndrome

Because the lower leg is circumscribed with strong fascia, increase in pressure in the relevant muscle compartments can have profound implications with respect to ischaemic necrosis. There are four fascial compartments: anterior, posterior, medial and lateral.

Compartment syndrome can occur either acutely, as in a typical crush injury to the lower limb, or chronically. There is a high probability that this will occur in a traumatised leg. Diagnosis is usually made clinically but may be supported by positive MRI findings (Amendola et al 1990) or by measuring intracompartmental pressure (Allen et al 1985).

Appropriate treatment is an emergency fasciotomy to decompress the relevant compartment.

Conditions of the Achilles tendon

— Partial rupture
— Complete rupture
— Acute tendinitis
— Chronic tendinitis
— Nodule formation (rheumatoid, gout).

ANKLE

Ankle joint injuries are amongst the most common reasons for presenting to Accident and Emergency departments following musculoskeletal trauma. The ankle joint is a modified hinge joint and is intimately related to the inferior tibiofibular or talofibular joint and to the subtalar joint.

The commonest injuries affecting the ankle joint are inversion injuries resulting in sprains to the collateral ligaments. The collateral ligaments comprise:

- Anterior talofibular ligament: this is a relatively weak ligament and is commonly injured in a combination of inversion and forced plantar flexion
- Fibulocalcaneal ligament
- Posterior talofibular ligament: this is the least vulnerable to injury.

Grades of sprain:

Grade I: Partial tear, with tenderness, pain, swelling but usually no bruising.
Grade II: Incomplete tear, with evidence of ankle joint instability, swelling, pain and usually bruising.
Grade III: Complete rupture, with marked instability, often less painful at rest than a Grade II injury and often associated with additional pathology on the medial side.

Management depends on the patient. It is not clear whether surgical repair of the higher grade of ligamentous injury is superior to conservative management. Rehabilitation consists of vigorous physiotherapy including proprioceptive exercises. There is an increased risk of repeat injury. Rehabilitation usually takes a minimum of 6 weeks.

REFERENCES

Introduction

Foy M A, Fagg P S (eds) 1990 Medicolegal reporting in orthopaedic trauma. Churchill Livingstone, Edinburgh

Neck

Bring G, Westman G 1991 Chronic post-traumatic syndrome after whiplash injury. Scandinavian Journal of Primary Health Care 9(2): 135

Evans R W 1992 Some observations on whiplash injuries. Neurologic Clinics 10(4): 975

Gay J R, Abbott K H 1953 Common whiplash injuries to the neck. Journal of the American Medical Association 152: 1698

Hildingsson C, Wenngren B L, Toolanen G 1990 Eye motility dysfunction after soft-tissue injury of the cervical spine: a prospective study. Acta Orthopaedica Scandinavica 61(4): 357

Hildingsson C, Toolanen G 1993 Outcome after soft tissue injury of the cervical spine. Acta Orthopaedica Scandinavica 64(2): 129

Hohl M 1984 Soft tissue injuries to the neck in automobile accidents. Journal of Bone and Joint Surgery 56A: 1675

Jonsson H, Cesarini K, Sahlstedt B 1994 Findings and outcome in whiplash type neck distortions. Spine 19(24): 27–33

Kissel P, Youmans J R 1992 Post-traumatic anterior cervical osteophyte and dysphagia. Journal of Spinal Discord 5(1): 104

Knibestol M, Hildingsson C, Toolanen G 1990 Trigeminal sensory impairment after soft-tissue injury of the cervical spine. Acta Neurologica Scandinavica 82(4): 271

Pressman B D, Shellock F G, Schames J et al 1992 MRI of TMJ abnormalities associated with cervical hyperextension/hyperflexion injuries. Journal of Magnetic Resonance Imaging 2(5): 569

Radanov B P, Dvorak J, Valach L 1992 Cognitive deficits in patients after soft-tissue injury of the cervical spine. Spine 17(2): 127

SUVA review 1991 Acta Radiologica 84(2): 101

Weinberg S, Lapointe H 1987 Cervical extension-flexion injury and derangement of the TMJ. Journal of Oral and Maxillofacial Surgery 45: 653

Shoulder

Garth W P, Allman F L, Armstrong W S 1987 Subluxation of the shoulder joint. American Journal of Sports Medicine 15: 579–585

Gerberich S G, Priest J D 1985 Treatment for lateral epicondylitis; verables related to recovery. British Journal of Sports Medicine 19: 224–227

Jobe S W, Kvitne R S 1989 The relationship of anterior instability and rotator cuff impingement. Orthopaedic Reviews: 963–975

Johnson L L 1987 The shoulder joint. Clinical Orthopaedics and Related Research 223: 113–125

Kieft G J, Satoris D J, Bloem J L et al 1988 MRI of the glenohumeral joint. Skeletal Radiology 16: 285–290

Murnaghan J P 1988 Adhesive capsulitis of the shoulder. Orthopaedics 11: 153–158

Schwartz E, Warren E F, O'Brien S J et al 1987 Posterior shoulder joint instability. Orthopaedic Clinics of North America 18: 409–419

Lower leg

Allen M J, Stirling A J, Crawshaw C V 1985 Intracompartmental pressure monitoring of leg injuries: an aid to management. Journal of Bone and Joint Surgery 67B: 53

Amendola A, Rorabeck C H, Bellett D 1990 The use of magnetic resonance imaging in exertion compartment syndromes. The American Journal of Sports Medicine 18: 29

3. Neurosurgical injuries

Daniel Rawluk

Following any neurological injury, there is a capacity for recovery and some restoration of neurological function, however, this is dictated by the extent of the primary injury. This recovery may be hindered by the development of secondary complications which might compromise the chances of the potential further recovery.

Injury to the nervous system can be divided into those affecting the brain, spinal cord and peripheral nervous system and while some patients may have injuries to all three aspects of the nervous system, these injuries more frequently occur in isolation usually with concomitant injuries to surrounding soft tissues or the skeletal system.

HEAD INJURIES

Estimates of the incidence of traumatic brain injury vary quite widely from different centres throughout the world depending on how data is collected, but current approximations suggest that 10.5 cases per 1000 of the population suffer a head injury every year in the western world (Hickey 1992). Only a fraction of these patients are admitted to hospital: Kraus (1993) has estimated that the annual incidence of patients hospitalised for traumatic brain injury is approximately 2 per 1000 population.

Jacobs (1988) found head injury to be the leading cause of death and disability in persons under the age of 35, and more than 50% of fatal and severe head injuries are due to road traffic accidents (Jennett & MacMillan 1981). According to Gentleman et al (1986), 65% of head injury admissions to a neurosurgical unit are due to road traffic accidents. Assaults and falls are the next most significant cause of head injury, with occupational or recreational injuries being responsible for only 8% and 7% respectively of those hospitalised with severe head injury.

Approximately one-fifth of patients with traumatic brain injuries will die as a consequence of their injuries with up to 20% of patients having significant deficits which render them incapable of sustaining an independent existence. A further 40% will have continuing problems which will interfere with some aspects of their everyday activities at work, school or in social activities (Jacobs 1988).

Classification

Worldwide, the most commonly used classification of head injuries is that of Teasdale & Jennett (1974) who first described the use of the Glasgow Coma Scale.

This defines a severe head injury being present in a patient whose Glasgow Coma Score is 8 or less on admission or 6 hours following the injury. A patient with a Glasgow Coma Score of 9–12 is defined as having a moderate head injury, while a patient with a Glasgow Coma Score of 13–15 is described as having a minor head injury.

Jennett & Teasdale (1981) have used other definitions of head injuries, looking at the duration of post-traumatic amnesia (PTA), where a PTA of less than 5 minutes would correlate with a very minor head injury and a PTA of more than 4 weeks would be described as an extremely severe head injury. Four other descriptive terms of severity are used which include mild, moderate, severe and very severe correlating with PTAs of 5–60 minutes, 1–24 hours, 1–7 days and 1–4 weeks respectively. This second scale may be more appropriately used in those patients who initially present with a good Glasgow Coma Scale, but who subsequently deteriorate from complications, where a definition based on a Glasgow Coma Score at presentation or within 6 hours of the injury might be inappropriate.

Complications

The outcome following a head injury is dependent on the extent of damage which is sustained by the brain and this damage can be subdivided into primary damage and secondary damage.

Approximately 50% of severely head injured patients will remain in a coma in the absence of any intracranial mass lesion and patients presenting in this condition are responsible for 35% of deaths following a head injury (Genarelli et al 1982).

In these patients, diffuse injury to the brain is responsible for the coma and for neurological disturbance, which was first described by Strich (1956), and has subsequently become recognised and accepted as the definition of the diffuse form of head injury.

The most extreme form of this type of brain injury comprises a focal lesion in the corpus callosum, a focal lesion within the brain stem and microscopic evidence of diffuse injury to axons throughout the brain. This form of injury can be graded depending on the extent of the injury, with the presence of microscopic injury by itself being classified as Grade I. If a focal lesion is also present in the corpus callosum, then the injury is described as Grade II and if a further lesion is present in the dorsal lateral rostral brain stem, then the injury is described as Grade III (Adams et al 1989).

Studies have shown some correlation between the severity of the injury and the patient's clinical condition, recognising that Grade I diffuse axonal injury is compatible with patients being unconscious for a time as short as 5 minutes following the injury (Pilz 1983).

Other primary injuries to the brain comprise surface contusions and lacerations and cerebrovascular injuries which can initiate complicated processes with progressive deterioration. This can result in intracerebral haemorrhage, brain swelling and areas of ischaemic and hypoxic brain damage.

There has been a reduction in the mortality from head injury as a consequence of intensive treatment coupled with recognition and treatment of the complications. Despite this, many patients who present initially with moderate to severe head injuries go on to deteriorate and die either from the cascade mechanisms following injury which cannot be reversed, or alternatively due to delays in recognising complications following a head injury.

Intracranial haematomas in the extradural or subdural space can compound the injury to the brain and if they are allowed to expand, can result in the development of secondary brain damage from local areas of hypoxia, ischaemia and brain swelling.

Teasdale et al (1990) found that more than 90% of patients attending Accident and Emergency departments following head injury will be orientated without a skull fracture, and they calculated that the risk of any patient in this group developing a traumatic intracranial haematoma is greater than 1 in 30 000. If a skull fracture is present, the risk is 1 in 81 and in those patients who have a history of an altered state of consciousness, the risk is greater than 1 in 6000 if no skull fracture is present, but falls to 1 in 29 if a skull fracture is present.

Intracranial haematomas can occur either extradurally, subdurally or intraparenchymally, with the extradural haematomas being the least common. The incidence of an extradural haematoma following a head injury has been reported as 0.2% in independent surveys (Galbraith 1973, Sandeman 1986), with other estimates ranging from 1.5% (Jamieson & Yelland 1968) to incidences as high as 9% in severely injured or comatose patients (Seelig et al 1984). These haematomas are uncommon in patients over the age of 60 (Jamieson & Yelland 1968) or younger than 2 years of age (Hooper 1959). The outcome can vary with a mortality of between 5% and 41% depending on the age of the patient and the duration and severity of symptoms. Mendelow et al (1979) found that the outcome of evacuation of extradural haematoma where no intradural lesion was present was related to any delay in surgery, with a mean delay of more than 15 hours found in those patients dying of their extradural haematoma.

Subdural haematomas are more common than extradural haematomas with a reported incidence of 5–22% (Jamieson & Yelland 1972a, Seelig et al 1981). Acute subdural haematomas are associated with higher mortalities compared to other intracranial mass lesions with a mortality of 50% or greater and a high incidence of disabled survivors (Cooper 1993).

Chronic subdural haematomas are those subdural collections which present at least 3 weeks or more following a head injury and those haematomas that present between 3 days and 20 days following head injury are classified as being subacute. The overall incidence of chronic subdural haematomas is thought to be 1–2 per 100 000 population per year with the vast majority of patients being elderly or in their late middle age. The age-specific incidence, therefore, increases with age, and is approximately 7.4 per 100 000 per year for the population in their 70s. The vast majority of patients will probably only recollect a very minor head injury and 25–48% of patients will not recollect any head injury. The outcome after drainage is usually related to the patient's neurological condition at the time of operation, with the average mortality rate approximately 10% with a 14% incidence of minor morbidity and a 17% incidence of more serious disability following treatment (Luxon & Harrison 1979). Some have reported a 75% return to normal function following treatment for chronic subdural haematomas (Raskind et al 1972).

Intracerebral haematomas have been reported in up to 23% of patients who had CT scans following head injury (Zimmerman et al 1978), but the true incidence might be higher than this. Surgical evacuation is associated with a mortality as high as 45% in patients who are unconscious at the time of surgery, or as low as 6% in those patients who are lucid prior to surgery (Jamieson & Yelland 1972b). Miller et al (1981) found that their series of comatose patients with intracerebral haematomas had a mortality of 58% and slightly more than 25% of all of their subjects had a good or satisfactory outcome.

Cranial nerve injury

Any of the intracranial nerves is liable to damage following a head injury, with the most common nerve injury probably to the olfactory nerve, which occurs in approximately 7% of all head injuries (Sumner 1962). This could represent an underestimate given the difficulty in testing for sense of smell in an unconscious patient. Approximately 50% of patients will show some recovery of their sense of smell and the time taken can vary from a few days to 5 years, with a more rapid increase in recovery at approximately 10 weeks following the injury.

Optic nerve and chiasmatic injury occurs in up to 5% of patients following head injury and in general, the prognosis for return of vision is very poor, with 40–50% of patients remaining blind following such an injury (Mahapatra & Tandon 1994). Those patients who do improve will do so within the first 3–4 weeks of the injury and this can continue for up to 6 weeks, but following this, there is little chance of further improvement in vision.

Management

Surgery to decompress and explore the optic nerve has been studied and the overall suggestion is that the results of surgery are unimpressive. However, surgery does have a place in those patients who have good vision immediately following the head injury, but who deteriorate thereafter. The use of steroids in optic nerve injury has not been proven, although some do advocate their use (Anderson et al 1982).

Direct injury to the 3rd, 4th and 6th cranial nerves can occur in up to 3% of head injuries, with the 3rd and 6th nerves the most commonly affected and the 4th cranial nerve very rarely affected by itself (Russell 1960, Hughes 1964).

Provided the nerve has not been sectioned, then there is usually a spontaneous recovery within 3–6 months, although recovery of a 4th nerve palsy is not as good as recovery in the other nerves, as a consequence of its slenderness and the fact that it is more often avulsed following trauma. If recovery does not occur after approximately 6 months following the head injury, then local procedures on the ocular muscles can be carried out in order to help troublesome diplopia (Rovit & Murali 1993).

Injuries to the trigeminal nerve and trigeminal ganglion most often affect the peripheral branches, with the supratrochlear and supra-orbital branches damaged or divided in 4.5% of head injuries. If the injury is partial, then this can lead to hypersensitivity which might justify exploration and resection of contused irritable nerve. The infra-orbital nerve can frequently be involved following maxillary fractures, and injury to the ganglia following blunt head injury is often associated with injury to adjacent cranial nerves or the development of carotid cavernous fistulas. The mechanism is probably due to backward and medial rotation of the tip of the petrous bone which causes opening of the foramen lacerum, traumatising the trigeminal root and its ganglia (Russell & Schiller 1949).

Injury to the 7th and 8th cranial nerves usually occur in association with fractures through the temporal bone with approximately 50% of such fractures associated with damage to either of these cranial nerves. Most patients with damage to the 7th cranial nerve will undergo spontaneous recovery and the place for surgical decompression or repair is controversial. Where the 8th nerve has suffered damage resulting in deafness, the prognosis is poor, although improvement can occur with partial lesions. Tinnitus usually improves spontaneously, but can become a disabling long-term symptom, and persisting vertigo and dizziness might require symptomatic treatment with labyrinthine sedatives. If the cause of loss of hearing is due to haemotympanum or disruption of the ossicular chain, then the prognosis is much better for restoration of hearing with spontaneous improvement following haemotympanum or correction of any ossicular chain disruption by surgery (Rovit & Murali 1993).

Injuries to the lower cranial nerves tend to occur more often following penetrating injuries such as gunshot wounds, although they have been described after minor head injury (Hashimoto et al 1988) and the treatment of these cases is usually expectant of some spontaneous improvement.

Post-traumatic epilepsy

The overall incidence of post-traumatic epilepsy in any series which contains the average spectrum of head injuries presenting in peacetime is approximately 3–5% where most of the damage is due to closed head injuries (Jennett 1975). Following injuries which occur during war, the incidence is higher (12–24%) where non missile injuries are involved and can be as high as 50% where penetrating brain injuries are reported (Salazar et al 1985).

Epilepsy can be described either as early, where the fit usually occurs within the first week of the injury, or late, where the seizure occurs any time after a week following the injury. This distinction does have implications with regard to decisions on management, especially from the point of view of considering prospects of returning to driving or to an individual person's occupation.

Early epilepsy occurs more frequently in children. Its incidence is increased with loss of consciousness where the risk will rise from 2–6% to 11–14% if the period of loss of consciousness is more than 24 hours. There is also an increased risk of having early epilepsy following prolonged periods of post-traumatic amnesia without major cerebral injury, but in these cases the risk of late epilepsy is not increased. A fracture will also increase risk, with approximately 7% of patients with linear fractures having early epilepsy. The presence of a depressed fracture can increase the risk of early epilepsy still further to 11%. If a subdural or intracerebral haematoma or haemorrhagic contusion with laceration is present, then the rate of early epilepsy can vary between 20% and 45%. Early epilepsy does increase the risk of developing late post-traumatic epilepsy and this association is particularly significant following depressed skull fractures or where an early fit occurs following a relatively trivial and uncomplicated head injury, which is normally associated with a low risk of late post-traumatic epilepsy.

Those fits which occur immediately following a relatively minor head injury are not usually significantly associated with the occurrence of late post-traumatic epilepsy.

The overall incidence of late post-traumatic epilepsy varies between 1.85% (Annegers 1980) and 25% (Guidice & Berchou 1987) depending on the patient population studied. Pagni (1990) identified certain factors as relatively more important in generating late epilepsy, with a penetrating missile injury resulting in late epilepsy in 53% of patients.

The presence of an intracerebral haematoma or laceration results in late epilepsy in 39% of patients and if a depressed fracture has resulted in tearing of the dura, then the incidence is approximately 25%. The incidence of late epilepsy is 20% following extradural or subdural haemorrhage without any additional complications, and those patients who have focal neurological signs in the absence of any other pathology which would increase the risk also have a risk of 20%. Where the extent of cerebral injury is much less, such as in an uncomplicated depressed skull fracture, then the incidence falls to 15% and if the period of loss of consciousness is more than 24 hours or if a linear fracture is present, then the incidence is approximately 5%. Mild concussion by itself is associated with a 1% risk of developing late post-traumatic epilepsy.

50% of late seizures occur within the first year following the injury and up to 80% have usually occurred within 2 years of the head injury. Following this time, the annual incidence is 3–5% per year (Feeney & Walker 1979).

Annegers et al (1980) compared head injured patients with matched controls and found an overall relative risk of developing late post-traumatic epilepsy of 3.6% and put the risk in the first year at 12.6% with a steady decrease thereafter.

Seizures occurring after head injury can result in secondary injury to the brain from hypoxia and require to be controlled, although a seizure which occurs immediately after a head injury may not require any long-term treatment unless further seizures occur at a later date. If seizures do develop within a week following a head injury, then there is a strong indication for long-term anticonvulsant treatment, although opinions vary whether such treatment should be started after a single seizure or whether one should await the development of repeated seizures.

Management

Diazepam is best avoided in the acute management of post-traumatic seizures due to the central depressant effect on ventilatory function, and it is probably preferable to treat seizures in the head injured patient with parenteral anticonvulsants such as phenytoin, paraldehyde or phenobarbitone. Bearing in mind the side-effects of anticonvulsants, however, it is desirable to wean patients off anticonvulsants at some point. Approximately 50% of patients who are defined as having late post-traumatic epilepsy will be in complete remission 15 years following the head injury. If patients have remained well controlled and free from any seizure activity, then it might be reasonable to consider withdrawing anticonvulsants at this stage. However, this decision needs to be made on an individual basis due to potential effects on the patient's employment opportunities and his/her fitness to drive. There is no convincing evidence that prophylactic anticonvulsants reduce the incidence of late post-traumatic epilepsy.

Intracranial infection

Following a penetrating head injury, there is an obvious risk of infection occurring at the site of the injury with possibly an abscess or empyema developing. The risk of this is magnified if debris and necrotic material is not evacuated, hence the need to explore and débride all compound depressed skull fractures. Any organisms gaining entry to the meninges through an open wound may also result in the development of meningitis, which is most often due to infection with Gram-negative organisms or Staphylococcus aureus, especially if the infection occurs several days following the injury. Since such injuries are readily recognised and treated aggressively, the incidence of such infections is quite low.

The overall incidence of traumatic cerebrospinal fluid (CSF) fistula is approximately 2% in adults, but following basal skull fracture, the frequency does rise to 11% (Lewin 1954, Brackman 1971, Calcaterra 1980).

Management

If a CSF fistula develops after a skull base fracture, meningitis can also occur and lead to other infective complications. More than 80% of patients will leak CSF within the first 48 hours of the head injury, but 80% of patients developing a leak show spontaneous resolution within a week of its onset (Eljamel & Foy 1990). Despite the apparently spontaneous closure of the CSF leaks, the risk of subsequently developing meningitis if no dural repair is performed does continue and 6 months following the head injury, the annual risk of developing meningitis is 8.4% per year. The use of prophylactic antibiotics following the development of a CSF fistula is controversial and if it is felt that an antibiotic is necessary, then penicillin would probably be the preferred choice. Any advantage in the use of antibiotic prophylaxis may only be of benefit in the early stages after the onset of the fistula.

The CSF fistula is usually diagnosed by identifying CSF leaking from the nose, with the most reliable assay the detection of Beta-2 transferrin in the secretions which is always present in cerebrospinal fluid (Rouah et al 1987). This assay is much more specific than testing for glucose which can be contaminated by nasal or lacrimal secretions which contain glucose. The precise site of the dural tear resulting in the leak of CSF can be seen on CT scanning although MRI scanning may be even more accurate in demonstrating the brain hernia which plugs the dural defect through which CSF may have escaped.

Where a CSF leak persists, or if an episode of meningitis has occurred, then surgery via either an intracranial or extracranial approach is usually advocated to close the fistula and thereby abolish the risk of meningitis occurring. Given the extent of the fracturing of the skull base, re-operation may be required in about 30% of cases, regardless of whether an extracranial or intracranial approach is used to repair the fistula initially.

Sequelae

The neurological consequences of brain damage in those patients surviving a head injury can be all too obvious with patients exhibiting focal neurological deficits or other manifestations of the extent of their head injury.

It is well known that recovery after a head injury can take a long time; approximately 65% of patients will reach their final outcome 3 months following their injury. Jennett & Bond (1975) described an outcome score which has gained wide acceptance in neurosurgical literature. This scale contains five categories which use the descriptive terms of death; persistent vegetative state; severe disability where a patient is not independent for all activities of daily living; moderate disability where patients are independent for activities of daily living, but are not able to return to normal activities; and finally a good recovery where the patient returns to their previous level of function. There is usually little difficulty in defining the outcomes of death, persistent vegetative state and severe disability, these conditions being quite easily recognised. However, those patients who are moderately disabled or who are described as having a good recovery from the head injury can pose a greater problem in recognising precisely into which category they may fall.

Patients who suffer a minor head injury can often go on to develop persisting symptoms following what might appear to be a good recovery. Rimel et al in 1981 studied a large group of patients who had suffered minor head injuries which were defined as a history of unconsciousness of 20 minutes or less duration, a Glasgow Coma Score of 13–15 and a hospital stay of less than 48 hours; and assessed 424 patients 3 months following the injury. They found 79% of their patients had persisting headaches at evaluation and a total of 59% also described persisting problems with their memory; 34% of those patients who had been employed prior to their accident had still not returned to work at 3 months. Interestingly, they found that only 6 of the 424 patients were involved in any litigation at the time of re-assessment. Rutherford (1977) had similar results, with half of his group of 131 patients reporting at least one symptom of the post-concussional syndrome 6 weeks following the injury.

The post-concussional syndrome describes a variety of symptoms which comprise headaches, dizziness, poor memory, irritability and difficulty in concentration, very often associated with alcohol or noise intolerance. Miller (1966) felt that most patients who reported such symptoms were more likely to be malingering rather than suffering from any genuine mental illness. Others, such as Oppenheimer (1968), have described pathological evidence for neuronal damage following minor head injuries and Levins and his group (1987) provided further support with radiological studies. Taylor & Bell (1966) demonstrated some slowing of cerebral circulation in a number of patients with persisting symptoms following a head injury.

The most likely hypothesis to explain the persistence of symptoms following a minor head injury is a combination of the psychological response of the patient and ongoing organic symptoms which the patient had not anticipated or been advised about on discharge from hospital. Those who suggest that symptoms are resolved when litigation which is pending is settled are contradicted by the study of Fee & Rutherford (1988) which found that a significant proportion of patients continues to have symptoms following settlement of any legal case.

The natural history of these symptoms is one of spontaneous improvement over time with most symptoms improving by 3 months or so, but 15% of patients with minor concussion will still have symptoms a year following their head injury. Those factors which are associated with the persistence of symptoms include female sex, being over 40 years of age and being in a lower educational and socio-economic group. Previous head injury, alcohol abuse and multiple trauma are also associated with persistence of the symptoms.

Those patients who report a deterioration in their condition may well have some additional psychogenic factors which may be of additional importance in causing their deterioration.

Other than reassurance and symptomatic treatment, there is nothing that can be specifically offered to help patients who have post-concussional syndrome, but some have advised active forms of treatment in order to reduce the impact of the persisting symptoms (Bremner & Gillingham 1974, Relander et al 1972).

SPINAL CORD INJURY

Spinal cord injury is relatively rare compared to head injury with an incidence of approximately 20 per million per year in the United Kingdom. More than 20% of patients with spinal cord injury will have multiple injuries affecting the limbs or pelvis, with 19% suffering a significant head injury and 15% having associated chest injuries. Significant abdominal injuries are much less frequently associated with spinal cord injury, with approximately 2% of patients with spinal cord injury requiring a laparotomy. Patients aged between 15 and 35 are most often affected, with the cervical cord the most common site of injury.

Classification

Following severe spinal cord injury, spinal shock can occur which is accompanied by symmetrical weakness below the level of the lesion and loss of spinal reflexes. Thereafter, there can be recovery and return of spinal function depending on the extent of the injury. However, if the degree of bony disruption to the spinal column is severe enough, then spinal cord transection can occur where there is no likelihood of any return of neurological function.

In those patients who have incomplete spinal cord injuries, recognised patterns of spinal cord injury have been identified depending on the anatomical pattern of the damage to the spinal cord.

If the spine is subjected to lateral flexion and rotational force, or if there is an anterior dislocation or a compression fracture of a vertebral body with bony involvement of the spinal canal, then the anterior spinal artery can become compressed or damaged resulting in ischaemic injury to the corticospinal and spinothalamic tracts. There can also be an element of direct injury to this area of the spinal cord from the mechanical impact on the spine. The clinical effects of such an injury are loss of power, reduced temperature and pain sensation below the level of the injury.

The central cord syndrome is more usually seen in elderly patients who have underlying cervical spondylosis, and these patients tend to suffer a hyperextension injury to the cervical spine which can occur following a relatively insignificant injury. The spinal cord becomes compressed within the narrow spinal canal with the main site of injury being the central part of the spinal cord, which is clinically manifested by flaccid weakness of the arms, but relatively more strength in the legs although there is spasticity in the legs.

In patients who have a hyperextension injury associated with fractures to the posterior elements of the vertebrae, direct contusion to the posterior columns can result in posterior column syndrome, where patients have good power, pain and temperature sensation, but can be extremely unsteady due to loss of proprioceptor function in the legs.

The Brown-Séquard syndrome usually occurs following a penetrating injury to the spine and is characterised by weakness with normal pain and temperature sensation on the side of the injury, but contralateral loss of pain and temperature sensation in the presence of normal power.

Complications

Where the injury is to the cervical spine, respiratory insufficiency is common due to paralysis of the intercostal muscles and if the lesion is high enough, a partial phrenic nerve palsy might be present. In thoracic cord injuries, any associated rib fractures or contusion to the lungs can also lead to respiratory difficulties, which can be compounded by cardiovascular problems brought about by overinfusion of fluids in an attempt to correct spinal shock. In the later phases of management of the spinal cord injured patient, pulmonary embolism can be a particular problem in patients who cannot be mobilised.

Heterotopic ossification can occur around joints, particularly the hip and the knee, and as spinal shock wears off, spasticity can become established which may eventually result in contractures developing.

Other complications which can affect the paraplegic patient include pressure sores, recurrent urinary tract infections and the development of urinary calculi.

Management

It is important to define whether the spinal column is stable or unstable, especially so in those patients suffering an incomplete spinal cord injury.

In order to avoid any secondary injuries to the spinal cord, it is important to immobilise the spine and, if a fracture or subluxation is present, to consider reducing the fracture either by traction or open techniques. If an open technique is required to reduce the fracture, then usually some form of internal fixation is performed at the same time. Bracken and his group (1990) provided some evidence that high dose methylprednisolone can improve the outcome following spinal cord injury, if administered within 8 hours of the trauma, but the use of methylprednisolone in spinal cord injury is not universal.

Following the immediate stabilisation of the spine, further management is co-ordinated through the disciplines of physiotherapy and occupational therapy, in addition to medical management of various complications which can occur following spinal cord injury.

Outcome

Following injury to the cervical spine, approximately 15% of patients will die and neurological morbidity ranges between 45% and 60%. Of those patients who do have neurological symptoms, 44% will have a complete spinal cord lesion with the remainder having one of the varieties of incomplete spinal cord lesion. Patients with a complete spinal cord lesion which shows no evidence of recovery of spinal cord function within 24–48 hours are very unlikely to regain any useful function thereafter.

Following an initial period of stability or even improvement, patients can deteriorate due to a progressive cystic or non-cystic myelopathy, but this late development probably occurs in only 5–8% of patients with spinal cord injury (Edgar & Quail 1994). This condition can develop between 1 month and 45 years after spinal cord injury, with the average being approximately 20 months after injury. Clinical symptoms include dissociated sensory loss, progressive motor loss, increased spasticity, hyperhidrosis, pain, autonomic dysreflexia and an alternating Horner's syndrome. In those patients where a cyst can be identified, shunting the cyst can be successful with 80% resolution of symptoms of sensory and motor deficits if treatment occurs within 3 months of the onset of the symptoms. If surgery is performed between 6 and 12 months, then the improvement is only 44% and reduces further if surgery is deferred beyond a year following the onset of symptoms.

BRACHIAL PLEXUS AND PERIPHERAL NERVE INJURIES

Brachial plexus injuries are relatively rare, occurring most often as a consequence of motorbike accidents or following sports injuries and work-related accidents.

Open injuries are unusual in the UK, but in the USA approximately 25% of brachial plexus injuries are caused by gunshot. Brachial plexus injuries can also occur following surgery such as mastectomy, first rib resections or orthopaedic operations on the shoulder joint or upper humerus. Obstetrical brachial plexus injury can occur in up to 3 per 1000 live births. The risk factors for this kind of palsy include forceps delivery, breech presentation and other complicated deliveries.

Injuries to peripheral nerves most often occur in association with fractures or subluxations of the skeleton, but they can also occur as a consequence of direct injury following laceration through the soft tissues overlying peripheral nerves.

Classification

Seddon (1943) first described three forms of peripheral nerve injury based on clinical observation. Where the nerve is stretched in a closed injury and full recovery occurs in the first 3 months after the injury, then the lesion is described as a neurapraxia. Axonotmesis is used to describe the same mechanism of injury, but the rate of recovery is much slower at a rate of approximately 1 mm per day. Following axonotmesis, the axon itself is interrupted, but the surrounding Schwann's cells, perineurium and endoneurium remain intact. If the nerve is completely divided, then this is described as neurotmesis.

This classification was further expanded by Sunderland (1951) when he described a neurapraxia as compatible with first degree injury, second degree injury being equivalent with Seddon's description of axonotmesis and a fifth degree injury with a neurotmesis. He included a third degree injury, where there was scarring of the endoneurium resulting in axons needing to regenerate through scar tissue; and if the nerve fascicles compromising the perineurium, endoneurium and basal membranes were disrupted, he described this as a fourth degree injury. Mackinnon & Dellon (1988) recognised that Seddon and Sunderland's classification did not take account of the variety of nerve fibre injury which might be present in a single peripheral nerve, and they added a sixth degree injury where there would be normal function through some fascicles, but varying degrees of injury in other fascicles.

In general terms, those injuries which are described as first to third degree usually recover spontaneously, but fourth and fifth degree injuries require surgery in order to allow regeneration of the nerve. Greater difficulty is experienced in deciding on the need for operative intervention for sixth degree injuries.

Brachial plexus injuries can be further classified according to the location of the injury, using the clavicle to subdivide the brachial plexus anatomically. If the brachial plexus lesion is supraclavicular and preganglionic before the dorsal ganglion, then there is no prospect for spontaneous regeneration nor of repair allowing any regeneration of the nerves.

Management of brachial plexus injuries

The vast majority of brachial plexus injuries are closed resulting from stretching, compression or ischaemia of the brachial plexus. If the arm is depressed with the neck flexed to the opposite side, then the upper roots are susceptible to injury, whereas if the arm is pulled upwards, then the lower roots are susceptible. Following a nerve injury, atrophic changes can develop fairly quickly in the denervated muscles and if this continues for 2 years following the injury, then the denervated muscle can undergo atrophy with degeneration of the muscles. At this stage, these changes are irreversible.

In patients who have an open brachial plexus injury, early exploration is advocated and if a clean laceration of the brachial plexus is identified, then a primary repair can be performed. However, if the ends of the damaged brachial plexus are badly damaged and contused, it is advisable to secure the severed ends on surrounding tissues and plan a secondary repair approximately 4 weeks later to allow viable nerve ends to become more obvious.

In those patients who have a closed brachial plexus injury, initial assessment with MRI or myelography can be useful to determine if traumatic meningoceles are present since this would usually indicate that repair of the brachial plexus is not possible. If there is no recovery of proximal muscle function within 3–5 months following the injury, or if severe neuritic pain is present, then exploration of the brachial plexus is justified and either a neurolysis of scar tissue can be performed or, if the exploration reveals that there is an area of no conduction within the brachial plexus, then this segment can be excised and either directly sutured or grafted. Those patients with closed injuries who show spontaneous recovery of proximal muscle function can continue to be managed conservatively.

In neonates, the vast majority of children with obstetrical brachial plexus palsy will improve spontaneously within the first year of life, although Gilbert (1991) advocated early exploration of the brachial plexus in neonates if no recovery of biceps function occurred within the first 3 months of birth.

Management of peripheral nerve injuries

Since most peripheral nerve injuries occur in relationship to skeletal injuries, the initial treatment aims are directed towards stabilisation of the fracture and monitoring the improvement and return of function in the damaged nerve. If the nerve has been divided, then the technique of repair is dependent on the complexity of the peripheral nerve, with monofascicular and polyfascicular nerves amenable to epineural repair. Where the nerve is oligofascicular and contains mixed sensory and motor fascicles, it is better repaired using an interfascicular technique.

Given the fact that peripheral nerves need to accommodate excursion during the normal movement of a limb, any gap might need to be bridged with nerve grafts.

REFERENCES

Adams J H, Doyle D, Ford I, Genarelli T A, Graham D I, McLellan D R 1989 Diffuse axonal injury in head injury: definition, diagnosis and grading. Histopathology 15: 49–59
Anderson R L, Panje W R, Gross C E 1982 Optic nerve blindness following blunt forehead trauma. Ophthalmology 89: 445–455
Annegers J F, Grabow J D, Groover R V, Laws A R, Elveback L R, Kurland L T 1980 Seizure after head trauma: a population study. Neurology 30: 683–689
Brackman R 1971 Survey and follow up of 225 consecutive patients with a depressed skull fracture. Journal of Neurology, Neurosurgery and Psychiatry 34: 106
Bracken M B, Sheppard M J, Collins W F, Holford T R et al 1990 A randomised controlled trial of Methyl Prednisolone or Naloxone in the treatment of acute spinal cord injury. New England Journal of Medicine 322: 1405–1411
Bremner D N, Gillingham F J 1974 Patterns of convalescence after minor head injury. Journal of The Royal College of Surgeons of Edinburgh 19: 94–97
Calcaterra T C 1980 Extracranial surgical repair of cerebrospinal rhinorrhoea. Annals of Otology 89: 108–116
Cooper P R 1993 Post-traumatic intracranial mass lesions. In Cooper P R (ed) Head injury, 3rd edn. Williams & Wilkins, Baltimore
Edgar R, Quail P 1994 Progressive post-traumatic cystic and non cystic myelopathy. British Journal of Neurosurgery 8: 7–22
Eljamel M S, Foy P M 1990 Acute traumatic CSF fistulae, the risk of intracranial infection. British Journal of Neurosurgery 4: 381–385
Fee C R, Rutherford W H 1988 A study of the effect of legal settlement on post concussion symptoms. Archives of Emergency Medicine 5: 12–17
Feeney D M, Walker A E 1979 The prediction of post-traumatic epilepsy: a mathematical approach. Archives of Neurology 36: 8–12
Galbraith S C 1973 Age distribution of extradural haemorrhage without skull fracture. Lancet 1: 1217–1218
Genarelli T A, Spielman G M, Langfitt T W et al 1982 Influence of the type of intracranial lesion on outcome from severe head injury. Journal of Neurosurgery 56: 26–36
Gentleman D, Teasdale G, Murray L 1986 Cause of severe head injury and risk of complications. British Medical Journal 292: 449
Gilbert A, Brackman R, Carlioz H 1991 Surgical treatment of brachial plexus birth palsy. Clinical and Orthopaedic Related Research 264: 39–47
Guidice M A, Berchou R C 1987 Post-traumatic epilepsy following head injury. Brain Injury 1: 61–64
Hashimoto T, Watanabe O, Takase M 1988 Collet-Sicard syndrome after minor head trauma. Neurosurgery 23: 367–370
Hickey A M, O'Boyle C A, McGee H M 1992 Head injury: of looking beyond the patient. Irish Medical Journal 84: 109–110 .
Hooper R 1959 Observations on extradural haemorrhage. British Journal of Surgery 47: 71–87
Hughes B 1964 In: Rowbotham G F (ed) Acute injuries of the head: their diagnosis, treatment, complications and sequels, 3rd edn. Williams & Wilkins, Baltimore
Jacobs H E 1988 The Los Angeles head injury survey: procedure and initial findings. Archives of Physical Medicine and Rehabilitation 69: 425–431
Jamieson K G, Yelland J D N 1968 Extradural haematoma: report of 167 cases. Journal of Neurosurgery 29: 13–23
Jamieson K G, Yelland J D N 1972a Surgically treated traumatic subdural haematomas. Journal of Neurosurgery 37: 137–149
Jamieson K G, Yelland J D N 1972b Traumatic intracerebral haematoma: report of 63 surgically treated cases. Journal of Neurosurgery 37: 520–532
Jennett B 1975 Epilepsy after non missile head injuries. Heinemann Medical, London
Jennett B, Bond M 1975 Assessment of outcome after severe brain damage. Lancet 1: 480–484
Jennett B, MacMillan R 1981 Epidemiology of head injury. British Medical Journal 282: 101–104
Jennett B, Teasdale G 1981 Management of head injuries. Davis, Philadelphia
Kraus J F 1993 Epidemiology of head injuries. In: Cooper P R (ed) Head injury, 3rd edn. Williams and Wilkins, Baltimore.

Levins H S, Amporo E, Eisenberg H M et al 1987 MRI and CT in relation to the neurobehavioural sequelae of mild and moderate head injuries. Journal of Neurosurgery 66: 706–713

Lewin W 1954 CSF rhinorrhoea in closed head injury. British Journal of Surgery 42: 1–18

Luxon L M, Harrison M J G 1979 Chronic subdural haematoma. Quarterly Journal of Medicine 189: 43–53

Mackinnon S E, Dellon A L 1988 Surgery of the peripheral nerve. Thieme Verlag, New York

Mahapatra A K, Tandon D A 1994 Optic nerve injury: a prospective study of 250 patients. In Samii M (ed) Skull base surgery, Karger, Basel

Mendelow A D, Karmi M Z, Paul K S et al 1979 Extradural haematoma: effects of delayed treatment. British Medical Journal 1: 1240–1242

Miller H 1966 Mental after-effects of head injury. Proceedings of the Royal Society of Medicine 59: 257–261

Miller J D, Butterworth J F, Gudeman S K et al 1981 Further experience in the management of severe head injury. Journal of Neurosurgery 54: 289–299

Oppenheimer D R 1968 Microscopic lesions of the brain following head injury. Journal of Neurology, Neurosurgery and Psychiatry 31: 299–306

Pagni C A 1990 Post-traumatic epilepsy, incidence and prophylaxis. Acta Neurochirurgica (Suppl) 50: 38–47

Pilz P 1983 Axonal injury in head injury. Acta Neurochirurgica (Suppl) 32: 119–123

Raskind R, Glover M B, Weiss S R 1972 Chronic subdural haematoma in the elderly: a challenge in diagnosis and treatment. Journal of American Geriatric Society 20: 330–334

Relander M, Troupp H, Bjorkesten G 1972 Controlled trial of treatment for cerebral concussion. British Medical Journal 4: 777–779

Rimel R W, Giordani B, Barth J T, Boll T J, Jane J A 1981 Disability caused by minor head injury. Neurosurgery 9: 221–228

Rouah E, Rogers B B, Buffone G J 1987 Transferrin analysis by immunofixation as an aid in the diagnosis of cerebrospinal fluid otorrhoea. Archives of Pathological Laboratory Medicine 111: 756–757

Rovit R L, Murali R 1993 Injuries of the cranial nerves. In: Cooper P R (ed) Head injury, 3rd edn. Williams and Wilkins, Baltimore

Russell W R, Schiller F 1949 Crushing injuries to the skull: clinical and experimental observations. Journal of Neurology, Neurosurgery and Psychiatry 12: 52–60

Russell W R 1960 In: Brock S (ed) Injuries of the brain and spinal cord and their coverings, 4th edn. Springer Verlag, New York

Rutherford W H 1977 Sequelae of concussion caused by minor head injuries. Lancet 1: 1–4

Salazar A M, Jabbari B, Vance S C, Grafman J, Amin D, Dillon J D 1985 Epilepsy after head injury 1. Clinical correlates: a report of the Vietnam head injury study. Neurology 35: 1406–1414

Sandeman D R, Cummins B C 1986 The provenance of extradural haematomas. British Medical Journal 292: 522–523

Seelig J M, Becker D P, Miller J D 1981 Traumatic acute subdural haematoma: major mortality reduction in comatosed patients treated within 4 hours. New England Journal of Medicine 304: 1511–1518

Seelig J M, Marshall L F, Toutant S M et al 1984 Traumatic acute epidural haematoma: unrecognised high lethality in comatosed patients. Neurosurgery 15: 617–620

Seddon H J 1943 Three types of nerve injury. Brain 66: 238–288

Strich S J 1956 Diffuse degeneration of cerebral white matter in severe dementia following head injury. Journal of Neurology, Neurosurgery and Psychiatry 19: 163–185

Sumner D 1962 On testing the sense of smell. Lancet 2: 895–903

Sunderland S 1951 A classification of peripheral nerve injuries producing loss of function. Brain 74: 491–516

Taylor A R, Bell T K 1966 Slowing of cerebral circulation after a concussional head injury: a controlled trial. Lancet 2: 178–180

Teasdale G, Jennett B 1974 Assessment of coma and impaired consciousness: a practical scale. Lancet 2: 81–83

Teasdale G M, Murray G, Anderson E, Mendelow D A, MacMillan R, Jennett B, Brookes M 1990 Risks of acute traumatic intracranial haematoma in children and adults: implications for managing head injury. British Medical Journal 300: 363–367

Zimmerman R A, Bilaniuk L T, Genarelli T et al 1978 Cranial computed tomography in diagnosis and management of acute head trauma. American Journal of Roentgenology 131: 27–34

4. Maxillofacial injuries

John E. deB. Norman

What are the long-term effects of injuries? The answers to the question are not to be found in the surgeon's selective memory, nor in the hospital notes, however full and legible. The facts and a critical assessment of them rest in the solicitor's medical reports, but even here there remain open-ended questions of prognosis.

Sir Paul Bramley 1972

Fractures of the facial skeleton and mandible and injuries to the temporomandibular joint

Fractures of the facial skeleton are common, and occur in civilian and military practice. They may be the result of a fracas, assault or a vehicular accident, and may occur in the workplace or the sporting field. They may be trivial and require no treatment, or devastating, resulting in disfigurement, defacement or even death. In military and guerrilla action, they may result from low or high energy projectiles, fragments or bullets (Gillies 1920, Kazanjian 1920), flechette or blast injury (Owen-Smith 1981, Haywood & Skinner 1991, Cooper & Ryan 1990).

Applied anatomy

The mandible has the characteristics of a tubular bone, with a thicker anterior cortex becoming thinner posteriorly. Between the mandibular and mental foramina it is traversed by the neurovascular bundle which innervates bone, teeth and investing mucoperiosteum. Fractures in the region of the neurovascular conduit may result in injury to the mandibular nerve, and resultant anaesthesia within the dermatome. Although the neonate is edentulous, the deciduous teeth erupt rapidly and are progressively replaced by the permanent dentition from the age of 6 years. If the dentition is lost in early adulthood, atrophy of the jaw slowly progresses, and by middle age the edentulous mandible may be thin and atrophic, or even osteoporotic and subject to the risk of pathological fracture.

The mandible articulates with the skull base by means of a two-compartment synovial joint. The mandibular fossa is shallow, bounded posteriorly by the tympanic plate of the temporal bone, and anteriorly by the articular eminence. The joint is enclosed in a fibrous capsule, lined by synovial membrane and strengthened by the lateral temporomandibular ligament, which is supplemented by accessory ligaments maintaining the mandibular condyle in close functional apposition with the intervening and mobile meniscus (Hawthorn & Flatau 1990).

Middle third of face. This zone lies below the rhinobase and between the occlusal plane of the maxillary teeth and a line passing between the fronto-zygomatic synchondroses. It is made up of the following bones:

- Maxillae (right & left, containing the teeth)
- Zygoma or malar complex (plus zygomatic process of temporal bone)
- Ethmoidal complex and turbinates (conchae)
- Sphenoid bone (greater & lesser wings & pterygoid buttress)
- Palatine bones
- Lacrimal bones
- Nasal septum (vomer, perpendicular plate of ethmoid and septal cartilage)
- Nasal bones (alar & nasal cartilages).

The bulk of the middle third is composed of thin membrane bone with intervening buttresses of a dense cortical nature. The ethmoidal complex is of particular importance, forming the medial wall of the orbit, the lateral wall of the nasal cavity and a portion of the floor of the anterior cranial fossa, where its cribriform plate is perforated by filaments of the olfactory nerve. Frontobasal fractures may result in anosmia, and the risk of meningeal fistula, cerebrospinal fluid (CSF) rhinorrhoea, pyogenic meningitis and orbital deformity (Kup 1978).

General comments

Fractures may be caused by sudden injury, either direct or indirect violence (normal bone, abnormal force). Fractures occurring in association with local disease are termed pathological fractures (abnormal bone, 'normal' force). Such fractures more commonly involve the mandible, as in metastatic malignant disease or osteomyelitis, or in the edentulous, atrophic and osteoporotic mandible of the elderly patient. Some consider that spontaneous stress or fatigue fractures occur in these patients with heavy mastication.

Fractures may be classified according to aetiology, anatomical position and pattern, and in long bones descriptions such as transverse, oblique, spiral are used. Fractures may be displaced or undisplaced, in good or poor alignment, horizontally or vertically favourable or unfavourable. A precise classification of nasal fractures was proposed by Murray et al (1984, 1986), based on experimental study of the cadaveric nose. A simple classification which commends itself to medicolegal practice and reporting follows. The medicolegal referee should obtain pretreatment radiographs, confirm the anatomical position of the fractures and comment, in non-judgemental fashion, on the diagnostic value of the radiographs, bearing in

Table 4.1 Classification of fractures

Type	Injury
Simple (closed)	no communication between the fracture site and the exterior, periosteal envelope almost invariably intact
Compound fractures	a. compound from within b. compound from without
Complicated fractures	involving nerves, blood vessels or viscera
Comminuted fractures	multiple fragments

mind that an intoxicated, head injured or critically injured patient may be extremely difficult to image.

Those fractures involving erupted teeth, even when undisplaced, are compounded into the mouth via the tooth root and periodontal space, and prophylactic antibiotics are required. Prior to the advent of antibiotics, teeth in the line of a fracture were routinely removed, as the risk of serious infection and osteomyelitis was extremely high. Nowadays, teeth in the line of fracture are usually conserved, and if non-vital are endodontically treated, although obviously infected and grossly carious teeth are removed (Kamboozia & Punnia-Moorthy 1993). Fractures involving the paranasal sinuses are invariably of a compound nature, and antibiotic cover is mandatory.

Clinical

The history of injury is often of crucial importance in the preparation of the medicolegal report, although it may be difficult to obtain if the patient has suffered a head injury or multisystem trauma. Patients involved in a fracas are unlikely readily to admit to the use or abuse of alcohol or recreational drugs, and the writer remains cynical in regard to a patient's recalling his or her obligations to veracity under such circumstances. Women and children injured in the home may have suffered as a result of domestic violence, and such a history should be actively sought.

The clinician should perform a thorough examination of the head and neck and upper aerodigestive tract, including the cranial nerves; and accurate and legible contemporaneous records must be kept. Visual acuity is recorded, and in the case of a malarorbital fracture an ophthalmic opinion is obtained (Gossman et al 1992, al Qurainy et al 1991a & b).

MAXILLOFACIAL INJURIES

Maxillofacial injuries may occur in isolation or as part of multisystem trauma which results in the death of the critically ill patient at the scene of the accident or during transportation (Gilligan 1990) from hypovolaemia, asystolic cardiac arrest, tension pneumothoraces or respiratory obstruction. The patient with a severe maxillofacial injury undergoes assessment by an ambulance or recovery team whose first priority is to establish and maintain the airway. This may require endotracheal intubation, fitting of a MAST suit, the correct application of a hard collar to stabilise the neck and the arrest of obvious haemorrhage if possible. Oropharyngeal toilet includes the removal of blood clot, vomitus, tooth and denture fragments and other foreign matter. If there is swelling or bruising of the middle or lower third of the neck or the posterior pharyngeal wall, the greatest care is taken when examining the laryngopharynx and achieving suction clearance.

If there is any dubiety regarding a fracture of the cervical spine or larynx, and there is respiratory difficulty, bruising, oedema, tenderness, emphysema, or crepitus over the anterior or lateral neck, a flexible fibreoptic instrument is used in preference to a rigid laryngoscope. With the airway secured and the patient haemodynamically stable, a more detailed examination of the head, neck, maxillofacial skeleton and jaws is carried out.

Bleeding from the ear is a cause for concern, and may be indicative of a fracture of the skull base, temporal bone or tympanic plate. An haemotympanum indicates a fracture of the temporal bone or skull base, and may be associated with dislocation of the auditory ossicles. CSF otorrhoea is proof positive of a meningeal fistula. A laceration of the antero-inferior aspect of the cartilaginous meatus or the junction of the cartilaginous and bony meatus is generally indicative of a fracture of the tympanic plate associated with fracture or fracture dislocation of the mandibular condyle. Blood may be present in the ear canal as a result of laceration of the face or scalp. In all these cases, the ear should be covered with sterile gauze and the opinion of an ENT surgeon obtained. Battle's sign consists of bruising over the mastoid process, and may be the result of either direct trauma or a fracture of the middle cranial fossa. Anterior rhinoscopy will confirm whether a septal haematoma is present, and if so it is drained.

Physical signs associated with fractures include cervicofacial oedema and deformity, visible in the early stages but later obscured by soft-tissue swelling, nonetheless remaining palpable. Ecchymosis and haematoma formation are common, particularly in association with orbital injury. Submucosal bleeding in the mouth floor, labiobuccal sulci or junctional soft palate are generally indicative of an adjacent fracture. Function is impaired when either jaw is fractured, and if the patient is dentate and the fracture displaced there will be malocclusion of the teeth.[1] Trismus may be profound, and associated with profuse salivation, due to the patient's reluctance to swallow. Teeth may be fractured, loosened, luxated or lost, and it should be established that a lost tooth or fragment of radiolucent denture material has not been inhaled or ingested. Mobility of the fragments will cause both crepitus and pain. Disturbance of sensory nerve function is common and is discussed below.

Mandibular fractures

Single-site mandibular fractures are commonest, followed in descending order by double and triple fractures. Fractures involving more than three sites within the mandible are very uncommon.

Vincent-Townend & Shepherd 1994

Mandibular fractures are common: they may be unilateral, bilateral or multiple and there is a peak incidence amongst young men aged 20–29 years. Alcohol consumption is frequently a factor. Fractures may result from accidents involving vehicle occupants, cyclists or pedestrians, industrial or agricultural accidents, fights, falls or sport. It is customary to describe the fracture at the site of a blow as a coup injury, and if there is a contralateral fracture it is a contrecoup. A meticulous analysis of 2137 patients treated at Canniesburn Hospital 1974–83 was carried out by Ellis et al (1985). The list below indicates the anatomical site of the fracture in patients involved in motor vehicle accidents, and this distribution varies slightly with other causes:

- Mandibular condyle 34.1%
- Mandibular angle 12.9%
- Mandibular body 34.8%
- Parasymphyseal 11.7%
- Alveolar process 4.2%
- Coronoid process 2.3%.

Such fractures may occur in isolation or as part of multisystem trauma, and may be associated with the following physical signs:

- Deformity: physical or palpable and often obscured by oedema and haematoma.
- Oedema: over the fracture site and, generally, cervicofacial and intra-oral.
- Ecchymosis: intra-oral and particularly in the labiobuccal sulcus and in the mouth floor extending beneath the tongue, the latter sign being pathognomonic of an adjacent mandibular fracture.
- Local tenderness.
- Impaired function: malocclusion of the teeth, trismus or difficulty in opening the mouth fully, associated with excess salivation and drooling of blood-stained saliva. As a consequence of pain and muscle spasm, the patient is unable or reluctant to swallow. The stomach may also contain recently eaten food and alcohol, and the patient may have inhaled gastric contents.
- Abnormal mobility of the fragments.
- Crepitus: a physical sign not usually elicited.
- Mandibular neuropathy: hemianaesthesia or paraesthesia of the ipsilateral lower lip in those fractures involving the neurovascular conduit between the mandibular and mental foramina and, occasionally, with

fracture dislocation of the mandibular condyle. The latter may be accompanied by a delayed (12–36 hr) lower motor neurone facial (VII) palsy.

- Teeth: loose, fractured, luxated, lost or spat out, inhaled (chest radiograph) or ingested (plain film abdomen).
- Soft-tissue injury: laceration of skin, mucosa and mucoperiosteum.

In the interests of radiological hygiene and economy the radiographic survey, in two planes, includes an orthopantomograph (OPG) and antero-posterior (AP) film of the mandible. If the OPG is unavailable lateral oblique films of the mandible are supplemented by an AP and occlusal radiograph of the mandible. Intra-oral periapical radiographs of the teeth involved in the line of fracture may be required but not as a routine, although tangential and alveolar fractures may require this for assessment of damage to the roots of the teeth. Reliance should not be placed on the OPG alone, as fractures at the mandibular angle may be overlooked.

Management

Surgeons are sometimes unreasonably criticised for not fixating an undisplaced fracture. However, it should be pointed out that the surgeon treats the patient and not the radiograph, and if the fragments are neither mobile nor displaced and there is no malocclusion, an operation is not required, and the referee in a case of alleged negligence would examine the notes and X-rays and then confirm this. Illum (1991) emphasises the importance of the specialist opinion in regard to the undisplaced linear fracture of the nasal bones in good position and requiring no treatment.

The isolated undisplaced mandibular fracture may not require fixation, and a conservative regimen of management would include dietary rest, vigorous oral hygiene, and the use of an antiseptic mouthwash such as 0.1% chlorhexidine. In addition, antimicrobial cover would include oral penicillin and metronidazole.

If fragments are displaced or mobile, or the occlusion is deranged, the fracture requires reduction and fixation. In former times, this was accomplished by means of interdental wiring, arch bars or interdental buttons and intermaxillary fixation or cast German silver splints. Methods of internal rigid fixation have developed over the last 25 years, and it is the preference of the majority of maxillofacial surgeons to fixate fractures internally with miniplates (Heslop et al 1994). As a general rule, the fractures are reduced under general anaesthesia and interdental wiring is applied to maintain the teeth in anatomical occlusion. The fracture is exposed through a transoral incision, and fine tuning of the reduction is then carried out under direct vision. The plate, or plates, are contoured tridimensionally, drill holes are placed with copious irrigation to prevent bone necrosis, and self-tapping screws inserted.

Following completion of rigid fixation and meticulous haemostasis with diathermy, the surgeon closes the wound in layers, and it is the writer's preference to use a tiny suction drain passed through a small stab incision in the upper neck, which is removed after 24–48 hours. Such fractures are compounded into the mouth, and antibiotic prophylaxis is continued for a period of 72 hours, but preferably maintained for 5–7 days: failure so to do may result in infection and delayed union.

Extraskeletal pin fixation, first developed in the First World War, is of value in the management of gunshot wounds and infected fractures, and has particular application in the stabilisation of major fragments during bone grafting of the mandible and when facilities are limited.

Complications of open reduction of facial fractures

In the medicolegal report these should be enumerated after an examination of the medical records. As with any form of surgery, the complications of open reduction and internal fixation (ORIF) of a compound fracture of the mandible include the complications of surgery in general: the general anaesthetic, the drugs used, and blood or blood products transfused. A patient cannot be relied upon to recollect every aspect of management, and may not recall being told that he or she had pulmonary atelectasis or a thrombo-embolic complication during hospitalisation: hence the desirability of reviewing the contemporaneous notes.

In the patient whose jaws are immobilised by intermaxillary fixation, there is an immediate risk in the postoperative period of acute airways obstruction or the inhalation of blood and vomitus. For this reason, some surgeons prefer elastic bands as the form of intermaxillary fixation in preference to stainless steel wire. The recovery ward staff should be familiar with the technique of release of this fixation and functional angled wire scissors should accompany the patient from operating room to ward. The patient should be discharged with these wire scissors, and given appropriate instruction as to how to cut the wires. Some surgeons elect to pass a nasogastric tube during the course of the operation to ensure that the stomach is empty.

The pulmonary complications include atelectasis, bronchopneumonia and pulmonary embolus. Whilst thrombo-embolic disorders are not commonly seen in patients who have undergone reduction of mandibular fracture, they do occur and appropriate care of the legs during the course of the operation includes intermittent calf stimulation and the application of antithrombo-embolic stockings. As a general rule, these patients are not given low dose heparin (Hopkins & Wolfe 1991, Mackie 1986). In the older, debilitated or alcoholic patient, postoperative confusion and disorientation may occur and, in the alcoholic patient, delirium tremens. Urinary tract infections are more likely to occur in those who have been bedridden for some time, or who have been catheterised.

Local complications: haemorrhage and wound infection

Local complications include primary haemorrhage which may occur in those taking aspirin, non-steroidal anti-inflammatory drugs including anti-cancer chemotherapy, in patients with thrombocytopaenia from a variety of causes, or with myeloproliferative disorders etc, or in the alcoholic. Reactionary haemorrhage occurs in the first 24 hours and careful haemostasis, suction drainage and a pressure dressing minimise this risk. If a haematoma forms, it should be promptly evacuated. Secondary haemorrhage occurs between postoperative days 5 and 7 and is the result of infection. It is for this reason that prophylactic antibiotics are, to the writer's mind, mandatory.

Wound infection may be superficial or deep, simple or serious. It is uncommon for the non-immunocompromised patient with an isolated mandibular fracture who has undergone an open reduction to suffer significant sepsis if treatment has been prompt and effectively carried out under antibiotic cover. If there is an acute infection and an abscess forms it should be promptly drained and a specimen of pus submitted for bacteriological examination. Systemic sepsis, septicaemia and pyaemia are rare. Wound dehiscence is usually obviated by layered closure, haemostasis and suction drainage.

Other local complications include loosening, or loss, of bone screws, with failure of rigid fixation, mobility of the fragments and non-union requiring reoperation, with or without autogenous bone grafting. Overheating of the drill and failure adequately to irrigate the drill at the time of preparation of the holes may contribute in part to the failure of the self-tapping screw. Plates or screws which become the seat of infection should be removed and, in the event that there is an established osteomyelitis, it may be necessary to abandon any form of internal fixation and retreat to an external pin fixator.

Surgical scars within the oral cavity are not usually of significance, although they may result in tethering and band formation which interfere with the satisfactory wearing of a denture. Cervicofacial surgical scars are not commonly hypertrophic or keloidal, although there may be a personal or racial characteristic resulting in such scars, requiring fine revision with or without Z-plasty.

Malocclusion and non-union

In the immediate postoperative period, it may become apparent that there is a minor degree of malocclusion, the teeth not quite interdigitating. In some cases, this may be within acceptable limits or amenable to a minor occlusal equilibration. If there is gross post-traumatic malocclusion or open bite, the patient will probably require secondary or even, in rare cases, tertiary reduction and fixation. Long-standing malocclusion will require formal assessment with computerised analysis of lateral cephalometric radiographs, and orthodontic assessment. This course of action is strongly endorsed: the need for fixed appliance orthodontic treatment should be addressed in the treatment plan, and a quotation for the fees obtained from the orthodontist, with an estimate as to the duration of treatment.

Non-union is uncommon, and in the first instance the surgeon would look to the tooth in the fracture line or on either side of it and, notwithstanding the efficacy of endodontic treatment, may find it necessary to remove reluctantly a tooth. On occasion parasymphyseal fractures, particularly in the premolar region, may fail to unite, in which case it may be necessary to remove the tooth in the line of fracture, and carry out a bone graft with rigid internal fixation.

Complications of mandibular fractures

Infection. Low grade, often odontogenic. Endodontically treat or extract the tooth and ensure the fixation is rigid.

Non-union. Due to infection or inadequate fixation, requiring the fracture site to be revisited with freshening up of the bone margins until bleeding bone has been uncovered. The removal of any foreign material is a sine qua non, and a non-vital tooth should be extracted and rigid fixation reapplied. An autogenous iliac cancellous graft may be required.

Malunion with malocclusion or non-occlusion of the teeth. If within 3 weeks of injury, it should usually be possible to carry out a secondary reduction and correct the malocclusion. Fractures extant for 3–5 weeks in a patient with a previously anatomical occlusion require reopening of the fracture site with osteotomy, preservation of the neurovascular conduit and rigid internal fixation. If the fracture has been malunited for months or years and bony union established, an orthodontic/orthognathic assessment with cephalometric analysis is recommended, and a formal osteotomy planned. Bone grafting is almost routinely required in such cases.

Acute osteomyelitis. The patient is hospitalised and the infection treated vigorously with intravenous antibiotics. This regimen is revised once the results of the antibiogram become available. Any teeth in, or immediately adjacent to, the fracture site are removed and the medullary space is decompressed with several judiciously placed unicortical drill holes. It is important to avoid perforating the neurovascular conduit, and damaging the mandibular nerve or the roots of any related teeth. Plate fixation is not in accordance with general surgical principles, and formal fixation should be deferred for 7–10 days until the acute infection is controlled. A specimen of exudate or pus is submitted promptly for bacteriological examination.

Chronic osteomyelitis. The patient is hospitalised, and the radiographic examination is supplemented by nuclear imaging with single photon emission computed tomography (SPECT Tc^{99m}MDP). Intravenous antibiotics are administered, and if over a long period an intravenous line or Hickman catheter is inserted. The mandible is decompressed and any obvious sequestrum which has declared itself is removed. As a general surgical principle, foreign matter, whether organic or inorganic, merely contributes to persistence of the infection, so non-vital teeth, bone plates and screws are also removed. The fracture is stabilised with an external pin fixateur. Hyperbaric oxygen (HBO) should be considered and the matter discussed with the physician. Chronic osteomyelitis associated with osteo-radionecrosis may require resection of involved bone and placement of a vascularised bone graft. In the older patient and those with malignant disease whose prognosis is guarded, a generous sequestrectomy is appropriate under antibiotic cover.

Neural complications: assessment and management

Sensory and motor neuropathy may result from the original injury or the operative treatment and the referee may be invited to give an opinion on the possible cause, percentage loss of nerve function, and prognosis. An outstanding summary on iatrogenic injuries by Bonney (1986) enumerates the possible causes: pressure or traction on the nerve, ischaemic or tourniquet damage, or direct division, to which the writer would add desiccation as a result of prolonged exposure beneath the theatre light, and thermal damage from either the unipolar or, more rarely, the bipolar diathermy. Bad positioning of the surgical patient may cause a nerve palsy (Anderton et al 1988), and on occasion the injection of an inimical solution may cause permanent nerve damage, leading to a claim of negligence.

Incisions placed near the angle of the mandible may damage both the marginal mandibular and cervical branches of the facial (VII) nerve, with resulting wry lip deformity, and informed consent includes an appropriate warning by the surgeon. In addition, there is potential risk to branches of the greater auricular nerve. The nerve is located at Erb's point which is demonstrated with the head in an axial position and a line drawn between the tip of the mastoid process and the mandibular angle. The vertical bisector marks the main trunk of the greater auricular nerve (C2 & C3) as it crosses the sternocleidomastoid muscle. The referee should appreciate that the nerve is routinely divided during the operation of parotidectomy, but not necessarily during exposure of the body and ramus of the mandible.

The mandibular division of the trigeminal nerve and its mental branch are frequently damaged at the time of injury, but nonetheless it remains at some risk during the operation of a misplaced incision, excessive retraction by the assistant or misplacement of the bone screws, with the screw traversing the nerve canal and its contained neurovascular bundle. The maxillary nerve and its infra-orbital branch are frequently damaged in fractures of the zygoma and maxilla. The ophthalmic division of the trigeminal nerve may be damaged at the time of injury, but may also suffer neurapraxia or division during open operations on the frontal bone, frontal sinus and upper orbit. Irreparable damage to the optic nerve results in blindness, and this is an occasional complication of para- and retrobulbar (intraconal) haematoma following orbital fracture, orbitotomy or malar fracture elevation. The superior orbital fissure and orbital apex syndromes are described by Rowe & Williams (1994).

The calculation of percentage loss of function of a sensory or motor nerve is not an exact science, and whereas a patient with dense hemianaesthesia of the lower lip may accept the disability with equanimity, another patient with paraesthesia, hyperaesthesia or formication in the same dermatome may not. The chapter on cranial nerve impairment in the American Medical Association guides to the evaluation of permanent impairment (Engelberg 1988) is a thoughtful statement on a difficult subject.

Mandibular neuropathy. In the postoperative weeks or months, hemianaesthesia of the lower lip and the mandibular dermatome may give rise to paraesthesia or even progress to distressing formication or, in rare instances, causalgia. A decompression neurolysis may be required. The referee should obtain a careful history and clinical assessment and record the precise area of disturbed sensation on a dermatome map. Clinical tests include those for light touch, pin prick sensation and pin prick sensation threshold, and two-point discrimination (Robinson 1994, Robinson et al 1992). The patient's ability to distinguish between a sharp and a blunt stimulus using a sterile disposable needle provides a starting point. An excellent review of the methods available for the clinical evaluation of sensory function has been provided by Essick (1992).

The use of trigeminal somatosensory evoked potentials is endorsed although this means of assessment is not always reliable nor the results necessarily repeatable. The patient may complain of distressing paraesthesia or formication and the somatosensory evoked potential tracing shows no apparent abnormality on either side.

Post-traumatic lingual neuropathy. This is less commonly encountered following mandibular fracture although lingual nerve injury is reported to occur in upwards of 11% of patients who have undergone third molar surgery and the referee may be invited to give an opinion in a case of alleged dental or medical negligence. It is occasionally damaged in the course of mandibular osteotomy, submandibular sialadenectomy or operations on the posterior mouth floor and the reader is referred to seminal research carried out by Blackburn (1990, 1992) and by Blackburn & Bramley (1989). Patients with post-traumatic mandibular and lingual neuropathy are notoriously difficult to treat successfully but, nonetheless, exploration of the nerve may be indicated if the patient is very greatly distressed by neuropathy (anaesthesia, paraesthesia, causalgia) present over a period of 24 months. A decompression neurolysis may be sufficient but, if an obvious post-traumatic neuroma is palpable it should be resected with an adequate margin and if the resultant nerve gap precludes direct epineural suture a sural nerve graft is inserted using microsurgical techniques. If the symptoms of lingual neuropathy are longstanding (> 2 years) and causing minimal distress, operation would not be considered. Under some circumstances it might be considered advisable to resist operating on a patient with a sensory neuropathy until litigation is concluded, for the simple reason that persistence of the disability is equated with a higher quantum of damages and secondary gain.

Table 4.2 Fractures of the middle third of the facial skeleton

Injury	Symptoms
Deformity	Dish face, concave, markedly lengthened and grossly oedematous
Periorbital oedema	Plus ecchymosis with subconjunctival ecchymosis with no posterior limit
Submucosal ecchymosis	The labiobuccal sulcus extends beneath the upper lip and is associated with gross oedema of the lips and cheeks
Soft tissue lacerations	The scalp, face, lips, eyelids, nose and pinna with visceral damage; in addition trauma to the lacrimal conduits, parotid gland and duct, facial and trigeminal nerves
Epistaxis	Associated with oral haemorrhage; blood loss may be torrential and even exsanguinating[2]
CSF rhinorrhoea	Meningeal fistula and dural tear (Fig. 4.1). The patient with a high level le Fort III fracture may have avulsed the olfactory filaments on one or both sides at the level of the cribriform plate and be permanently anosmic
Orbital trauma	Direct damage to the ocular globe and blindness. There may be an intact globe with non-perception of light (NPL) secondary to optic nerve trauma. In addition, if palpebral oedema is not gross, it may be possible to demonstrate diplopia in the early stages, associated with orbital floor or medial orbital wall fractures and incarceration of periorbita, or isolated cranial nerve lesions (oculomotor, trochlear and abducens nerves)
Sensory neuropathy	Almost invariably, damage to one or both maxillary divisions of the trigeminal nerve with anaesthesia in the appropriate dermatome. In the early stages, the patient is unlikely to complain of anaesthesia: other symptoms tend to predominate and it is only several days later, when the oedema is settling and the patient's condition improved, that he or she will complain or admit to these symptoms
Malocclusion	The maxilla may be loose and 'floating' rather than impacted, although there may be compaction of the middle third with gagging of the molar teeth. The patient is unable to close the mouth, and an anterior open bite is extant
Dental injuries	As with mandibular fractures, teeth may be lost, fractured, loosened or luxated, with the risk of either inhalation or ingestion of dental fragments

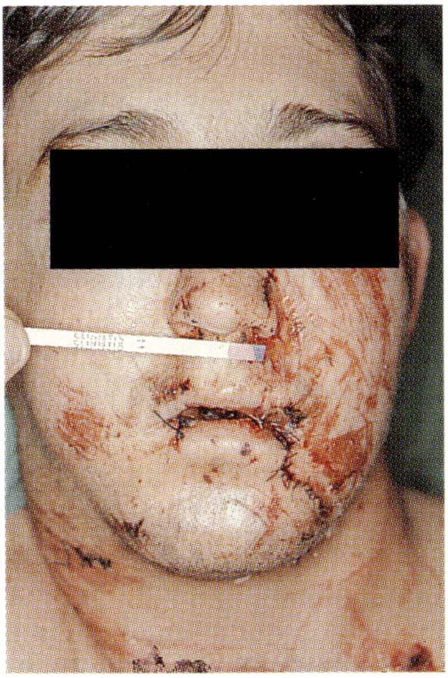

Fig. 4.1 Fracture of the middle third at Le Fort II and III levels. Meningeal fistula and CSF rhinorrhoea.

Fractures of the middle third of the facial skeleton

Fractures of the middle third of the facial skeleton were classified by the French surgeon, Rene le Fort (1901) into three levels, designated le Fort I–III. Those of the lateral middle third (malarorbital complex) constitute nearly 85% of this group, and fractures of the frontonasal, nasoethmoidal and le Fort levels the remainder. Whilst these fractures may occur in isolation, they may be one facet of multisystem trauma or craniofacial injury, and the following physical signs may be present:

The diagnosis is clinical and, while plain radiography may be helpful, the CT or MRI scan provides precise anatomical detail. Providing the patient is young and there is no damage to the cervical spine, it may be possible, when the patient's condition is stabilised, to carry out direct coronal CT scans of the middle third of the facial skeleton. In the early stages, however, it is more likely than not that the neurological surgeon will require a CT scan of the brain and skull base, and this axial scan should be extended to show the middle third. The referee should endeavour to examine these films at first hand and not rely on the radiologist's report.

Management

Military practice has established the importance of triage of the seriously injured. The general management of the patient includes establishing and maintaining the airway, fluid resuscitation and restoration of blood volume, and the prompt and systematic examination of head, spine, chest, abdomen, pelvis and extremities (Judson 1990).

If the patient has a combination of head injury, a reduced level of consciousness, a fracture of the middle third and an injury to the chest, he or she is safer with a tracheostomy, although many intensivists prefer an indwelling oral endotracheal tube.

Surgical management. Undisplaced fractures of the middle third of the facial skeleton may require no treatment, but the majority require either closed reduction and a short period of intermaxillary fixation or open reduction and internal fixation utilising miniplates. The plaster of Paris headcap and craniomaxillary fixation of yesteryear are now recognised to be less than satisfactory, and experienced surgeons prefer either craniomandibular fixation utilising a box frame, or craniomaxillary fixation utilising a Levant frame or similar apparatus. Alternatively, reliance is placed on rigid internal fixation. Access to the middle third may be via a combination of a bicoronal flap for le Fort III fractures or frontolateral orbitotomy incisions to gain access to the frontozygomatic synchondrosis. While a bicoronal flap gives excellent access to the frontonasal region, a seagull incision placed between the medial aspects of the brow and with an inclination to the glabella heals well and is greatly appreciated by young men with a family history of male pattern baldness. (The referee should include this in the report.) A scar which is covered by natural hair in a young man may become conspicuous as the hairline recedes. More extensive fractures involving the frontonasal complex are better approached via a bicoronal flap. Such reductions are usually stable if plated or wired, but the referee should carry out a very careful anterior rhinoscopy, and assess the need for a septorhinoplasty. There is a risk of fronto-ethmoidal mucocoele developing in these fractures some years after the accident: a CT or MRI scan is required, and reliance should not be placed on the clinical examination alone. The technical minutiae of reduction of various forms of middle third fractures are described by Bowerman et al (1994).

Complications of fractures of the middle third of the facial skeleton

Meningitis and cerebral abscess. These are life-threatening, and high level fractures of the middle third of the face are seen in consultation with the neurosurgeon.

Meningeal fistula, aerocoele and CSF leak. Prophylactic antibiotics are mandatory in the presence of a CSF leak.

Anosmia. This is invariably permanent, but may be unilateral.

Nasal obstruction and septal deviation. These may require septoplasty or septorhinoplasty, with or without autogenous bone or cartilage grafting. Septal perforations are encountered not infrequently and, while it is possible to close these with a septal button or labiobuccal mucoperiosteal flap, the technique is tedious and most patients accept a small septal perforation in the absence of unpleasant crusting.

Non-union. Non-union is rare. The membrane bones of the middle third of the facial skeleton tend to unite, albeit in some cases with stable fibrous or fibro-osseous union.

Deformity. As a consequence of inadequate reduction or relapse, dish face deformity and anterior open bite are encountered in medicolegal clinics, and may be associated with nasal deformity and malar flattening.

Anaesthesia, paraesthesia. Infra-orbital nerve distribution (maxillary division of trigeminus). If associated with pain, marked hyperaesthesia or causalgia, the patient is offered tripartite decompression neurolysis at the foraminal, canalicular and orbital floor levels, using the operating microscope (Norman et al 1982).

Malocclusion with molar gagging and anterior open bite. These may require revision osteotomy and bone grafting. As a general rule, it is preferable to treat the anterior open bite with a maxillary down fracture osteotomy at the le Fort I level. If the open bite is the result of bilateral condylar fractures it may require a condylar osteotomy with rigid internal fixation (cf. condylar fractures).

Limited movement of mandible (impingement or fusion of coronoid processes and zygoma).

Blindness.

Enophthalmos, diplopia. Depression of malar orbital complex may require orbital osteotomy and elevation, and in some cases orbital volume enhancement with iliac or calvarial bone graft. Extra-ocular muscle surgery may be required.

Epiphora. This results from damage to the nasolacrimal duct and requires a dacryocystorhinostomy (DCR) or appropriate reconstruction of the conduits. A Lester-Jones indwelling tube may rescue the patient from the tyranny of persistent epiphora.

FRACTURES OF THE ZYGOMATIC (MALAR) COMPLEX

Fractures of the zygoma or malar complex are extremely common. In the period 1983–93, 1200 zygomatico-orbital fractures were treated at Canniesburn Hospital, and a detailed review was carried out by Ayoub et al (1994). 56% of the malar fractures were the result of an assault, 26% of the patients were unemployed, and the majority of incidents were alcohol-related. 90% of the patients had flattening of the cheek prominence, and infra-orbital anaesthesia was present in 75% of cases, excluding those with isolated fractures of the zygomatic arch. Three patients operated on had a retro- or parabulbar haemorrhage at the time of operation. The writer has had experience of a total of 8 perioperative haemorrhages of this nature in the period 1972–95, and one patient with a silent intraconal bleed and no proptosis suffered permanent non-perception of light.

The majority of these fractures were of a tripod nature (Types III and IV, 70%), with inferomedial depression of the zygomatic body and resultant fracture of the anterolateral wall of the maxillary sinus and zygomatic arch (see Table 4.3). The zygoma was hinged on the frontozygomatic synchondrosis (Type III, 44%), which may be distracted (Type IV, 26%). The distinction is important, as 80% of the Type IV fractures are unstable and require rigid fixation (Ayoub et al 1994) (courtesy of Professor K.F. Moos OBE).

Imaging

- Plain radiography
  a. occipitomental (OM) + 15°, 30°, 45°
  b. submentovertical (SMV), zygomatic arch fracture
  Reverse Towne's projection
- CT scan
  a. axial
  b. axial with coronal reconstruction (not very satisfactory)
  c. direct coronal (not possible if badly injured, elderly, nervous or claustrophobic patient, or patient with osteo- or rheumatoid arthritis of the cervical spine)
- Magnetic resonance imaging (MRI)

Principal findings on imaging

- Fractured zygomatic arch: may be single or multiple fractures, depressed or grossly displaced
- Frontozygomatic synchondrosis: distracted or undistracted

Table 4.3 Henderson's classification

Type	%	Injury
I	2%	Fractured malar bone
II	9.5%	Fracture the malar arch
III	44%	Tripod fracture with an undistracted frontozygomatic suture
IV	26%	Tripod fracture with a distracted frontozygomatic suture
V	2%	Blowout fracture of the orbital floor
VI	3%	Fracture of the orbital rim: • superior rim/orbital roof, medial third involving the frontal sinus • inferior rim, medial and median • medial rim, lacrimal sac and medial canthal tendon • lateral rim (uncommon), lateral canthal tendon and suspensory ligament
VII	13.5%	Comminuted fracture of the malar bone

Table 4.4 Fractures of the zygomatic complex

Injury	Symptoms
Black eye	Periorbital ecchymosis and oedema may be gross, occluding the palpebral fissure and making examination of the eye difficult. It is essential to establish that visual acuity is present and not deteriorating, and an ophthalmic opinion should be obtained if there is any doubt
Subconjunctival haemorrhage	There may be no posterior limit to this haemorrhage: the conjunctiva is permeable and the extravasated blood remains oxygenated and bright red. The appearance is dramatic and a careful explanation should be given to the patient
Flattening of the cheek prominence	This may be masked by oedema for 3–4 days, but with detumescence of the swelling, the depression and facial asymmetry become marked. The clinician may therefore defer a decision on the need for operation at the first visit, and recall the patient for re-examination
Infra-orbital rim	While this may be relatively smooth, there may be palpable tenderness, and an irregularity and dehiscence of the rim
Infra-orbital neuropathy	Anaesthesia or paraesthesia involving the infra-orbital dermatome and mucosa of the upper lip and adjacent cheek and mucoperiosteum is common, as is anaesthesia of the incisor, canine and premolar teeth
Epistaxis	This will be unilateral with blood visible in the nares and in the oronasopharynx
Intra-oral tenderness or ecchymosis	The zygomatic buttress or key ridge lies immediately above and lateral to the maxillary first molar, and the examining finger may detect a tender step defect
Trismus	As a consequence of impingement of the zygoma on the coronoid process, mandibular movement is restricted. Elevation of the zygoma corrects this. In the case of gross trauma, there may be a haematoma in the belly of the temporalis muscle, and on occasion there may be an undisplaced avulsion fracture of the coronoid process
Diplopia	Double vision may be present in some malar fractures and is due to: • intra-orbital oedema or haematoma • depression of the suspensory ligament of the globe, corrected when the zygoma is elevated • a concurrent orbital floor fracture with incarceration of the periorbita • superior orbital fissure syndrome
Globe retraction	In patients with an orbital blow-out fracture and incarceration of the periorbita, there may be a complaint of nausea associated with upgaze, due to entrapment and vagal stimulation
Enophthalmos and pseudoptosis	As a result of enophthalmos there will be a degree of pseudoptosis

Surgical air emphysema	This is invariably the result of the patient's blowing the nose shortly after the accident, when air is forced from the nose into the maxillary sinus and thence into the pretarsal tissues and orbit (Hunts et al 1994)

- Infra-orbital dehiscence: overriding, step defect, fragmentation
- Fractured lateral wall maxillary sinus
- Opaque maxillary sinus, with or without air/fluid interface
- Fractured orbital floor with hanging drop (incarcerated periorbita).

Indications for operation

Some fractures require no operative reduction, some require elevation and no rigid internal fixation, others require rigid internal fixation. The indications for surgery include deformity or depression of cheek prominence, infra-orbital neuropathy – anaesthesia, diplopia and trismus.

ORBITAL FRACTURES

Surgical anatomy of the orbit

The orbit is a rigid bony box, with medial and lateral walls, and slightly more roof than floor. The orbital pyramid is 40 mm in diameter and depth, and 35 mm in height. The interorbital distance is approximately 25 mm. The orbital walls and floor are weakened by foramina and fissures with neurovascular structures making an entrance or exodus.

The orbital roof is thin, fragile, concave and triangular, and separates the orbital contents from the anterior cranial fossa and the frontal sinus. The medial wall or lamina papyracea is of surgical importance, and varies from 0.2–0.4 mm in thickness. It extends posteriorly to the body of the sphenoid and the optic foramen, and is perforated by the anterior and posterior ethmoidal foramina. The greater wing of the sphenoid and the zygoma form the lateral wall, and between this wall and the roof the superior orbital fissure leads into the middle cranial fossa. Between the lateral wall and the floor the inferior orbital fissure leads into the pterygopalatine and infratemporal fossae. The floor is not as thin as the roof, and is traversed by the infra-orbital neurovascular canal. The lid to this Pandora's box is formed by the orbital septum, the eyelids and the superior and inferior tarsal plates. It contains the ocular globe, which is not a globe but a sphere, and 3 cm of optic nerve with its covering of dura, arachnoid and pia mater. The almond-shaped lacrimal gland is contained in the fossa of the same name.

There are six extra-ocular muscles, four recti and two obliques, in addition to the levator palpebrae superioris. The orbital periosteum is the surgeon's friend, and it lines the bony cavity with a tough outer layer composed of oblique fibres, and a weaker inner layer. The periosteum is

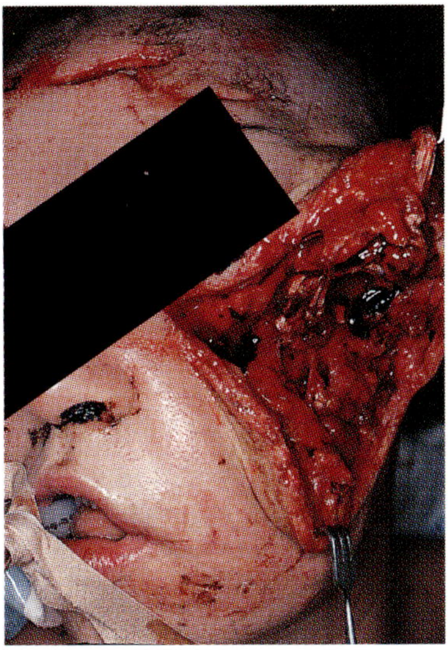

Fig. 4.2a Compound, complex and comminuted fracture of left orbital floor and rim, with transection of facial nerve (immediate greater auricular nerve graft) and parotid duct (reanastomosed using microsurgical techniques).

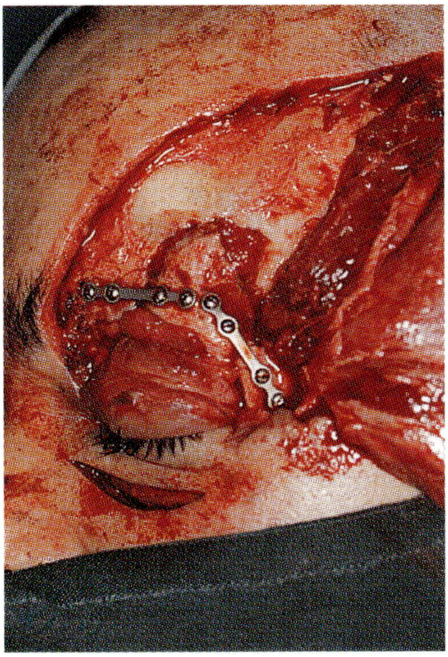

Fig. 4.2b Compound, comminuted and complex fronto-orbital fracture with involvement of frontal sinus, requiring dural repair and delayed orbital bone graft (Mr W. Stening MS, FRACS/J E deB Norman).

loosely attached to the bone, but firmly attached to the orbital rim, forming the arcus marginale. It is also attached to the fissures, sutures, foramina and the lacrimal fossa, and is continuous with the endosteal dura mater. The lacrimal sac lies in the lacrimal groove at the inferomedial angle of the orbit, and helps form a conduit for the circulation of the tears. A small fovea for the superior oblique pulley (trochlea) lies 4 mm posterior to the superomedial angle of the orbital rim. The supra-orbital notch, or foramen if the ligament ossifies, is 25 mm from the midline, and marks the position at which the supra-orbital nerve leaves the orbit. A secondary supra-orbital notch of Arnold is an occasional finding and lies medial to this. Of necessity, this description is limited by space, and readers are referred to Wolff (1968), Koornneef (1981) and Hotte (1970).

Classification of orbital fractures

- Zygomatico-maxillary or malar/orbital complex (cf. Henderson I–VII)
- Orbital blowout fractures

- a. Pure: orbital floor
  medial wall
- b. Impure: floor and orbital rim (Fig. 4.2a)
- Middle third facial skeleton le Fort II or III levels
- Orbito-ethmoid (Jackson 1989); frontonaso-ethmoidal crush (Markowitz et al 1991)
- Orbital roof/rim with or without involvement of frontal sinus (Rowe & Williams 1994) (Fig. 4.2b).

Orbital fractures: physical findings

Periorbital oedema and ecchymosis.

Subconjunctival haemorrhage. Often with no posterior limit.

Proptosis. This may be the result of postoperative oedema or of retro or parabulbar haemorrhage. An intraconal haemorrhage is silent and rare and may be productive of axial proptosis and early visual loss (NPL).

Visual acuity. Visual acuity should be assessed clinically at the initial examination. If visual acuity is deteriorating, an urgent ophthalmic opinion is obtained. The visual acuity and reflexes (direct, consensual and accommodation) should be recorded.

Mydriasis. This may be the consequence of direct trauma to the globe.

Enophthalmos. This may be masked by periorbital oedema and only become obvious with resolution of the oedema. It is the result of the displacement of periorbita through an orbital floor blowout fracture, an enlarged inferior orbital fissure or, uncommonly, a medial wall fracture. With posterior displacement of the globe, pseudoptosis becomes apparent.

Surgical (air) emphysema.

Sensory neuropathy. Supra-orbital and supratrochlear branches of the ophthalmic division of trigeminus, infra-orbital, zygomatico-facial and zygomatico-temporal branches of the maxillary division of trigeminus.

Lower motor neurone facial paresis. Paresis may result from lacerations lateral to the lids and affecting elements of the temporofacial branch of the facial nerve (VII).

Eyelids. Laceration of the lid may be superficial, involving the margins, or deep, involving the tarsal plates. There may be ptosis or pseudoptosis, and detachment of the medial canthal tendon may result in decreased width of the palpebral fissure.

Canthal tendons. There may be alteration in the level of the medial or lateral canthal tendon.

Medicolegal assessment

The referee determines if there is any orbital or ocular dystopia, flattening of the cheek prominence or other quadrants of the orbit. Scars are carefully assessed as described previously, and as to whether they constitute an aesthetic or functional deficit. Mensuration of the palpebral fissures and the intercanthal distance are noted, and enophthalmos or proptosis measured with an exophthalmometer. Function or malfunction of the lids is noted: is there a degree of ptosis or epiphora; does the patient complain of a dry eye? Visual acuity is assessed for distant and near vision, utilising charts of the Snellen type. Visual fields are assessed by the ophthalmic surgeon. Abnormal ocular motility and binocular diplopia are common following orbital fracture, and the function of the oculomotor, trochlear and abducens nerves is assessed. The patient's diplopia may be due to incarceration of periorbita in a floor or, less commonly, a medial wall blowout fracture, and a forced duction test and direct coronal orbito-antral CT scan may provide an immediate diagnosis. Visual impairment and percentage loss of function of the whole person are calculated by the ophthalmic surgeon after careful examination. If further surgery is required, the referee makes the appropriate recommendation and provides an estimate of costs.

HIGH AND LOW ENERGY GUNSHOT WOUNDS

> The shot carried away the greater part of the face, including three-fourths of the lower jaw, and part of the tongue, and the man was thought to be dead. Under the solicitous care of Baron Larrey he re-covered, however, and lived for more than twenty years. It can be seen at a glance that speech and mastication were impossible.
>
> Heath 1884

With the increasing use of firearms in the community it is necessary for the medicolegal referee to be familiar with the mechanics of projectile wounds in order to make an informed evaluation of a surviving patient in the medicolegal clinic, or to assist the forensic pathologist, coroner or medical examiner.

Table 4.5 Wound ballistics and weight of bullet

Weight	Calibre		Speed
11.7 g	.303	2540 fps LE	780 mps
9.4 g	7.62 mm	2790 fps FN/SLR	860 mps
3.6 g	5.56 mm	3185 fps (Armalite)	980 mps

Table 4.6 Wound ballistics and effect of velocity of projectile

Velocity		Speed
LVM (low energy transfer)	<1100 fps	350 mps
HVM (high energy transfer)	>1100 fps	military calibres
Fragments (energy transfer varies)		100 – >1000 mps

The study of wound ballistics is the study of penetrating missiles (fragments > bullets) in flight and the tissues and their wounding capacity and is predicated on the following factors: size, shape, weight (Table 4.5), velocity (Table 4.6), design and composition of the bullet, stability, and the structures involved.

Size and shape. While arrows and darts are aerodynamically stable, other projectiles are subject to oscillation or yaw (tumble), precession or circular yaw about the centre of gravity and nutation (Owen-Smith 1981, Cooper & Ryan 1990).

Structures:

- **dense** bone, brain, liver, kidney, spleen
- **elastic** lung, skin and mucosa.

Design and composition. The design has a profound effect on the resulting wound. Most rifle projectiles are cylindro-conoidal with a cupro-nickel or gilding metal jacket and basal cannelures. The hollow base originated with Delvigne in 1841 and Minnie in 1847. The bullet expands to fit the rifling of the weapon and the rifling imparts a spin which enhances accuracy and stability and increases the range of the projectile.

The wounding power of a projectile depends on the transfer of energy from the projectile to the body and the retardation is proportional to the area of the bullet and the velocity cubed. The kinetic energy of a missile in motion is given by the following formula:

$$KE = \frac{M(kg) \times V^2 \ (m/sec)}{2}$$

KE = kinetic energy in joules
M = mass in kilograms
V = velocity in metres per second

If the tissues arrest the bullet, the energy liberated would equal the total KE of the missile. If the bullet passes through the tissues there is residual velocity (V1 strike velocity; V2 residual velocity) according to this formula:

$$KE = \frac{M\ (V1^2 - V2^2)}{2}$$

- Low energy transfer, most handguns 300–500 joules
- High energy transfer, rifle bullet 500–3000 joules
- Fragments 10–150 joules

Increasing the velocity increases the KE dramatically, and the wounding power. The projectile produces injury in three ways:

Laceration and crushing: generally characteristic of a low energy transfer. Little energy is given up to the wound track, nothing is hidden and the damage seen is the damage done. The analogy of a knife wound is apposite.

Stress waves: originally described in the 19th century as shock waves. The bullet compresses the tissues in its passage and this zone of compression moves away as a wave lasting a millionth of a second and at an extremely high pressure of one hundred atmospheres (10 350 KPa) and a velocity of 1500 mps. It causes damage at a distance and especially along fluid filled tubes such as arteries and veins. Solid tissues are particularly susceptible: indirect injury of adjacent tissues (e.g. spinal cord) is recognised and the projectile does not need to strike bone to cause a fracture.

Cavitation is temporary and pulsatile, many times the diameter of the projectile and highly destructive. It has a subatmospheric pressure and debris is sucked into the cavity from the entrance and exit wound and dispersed radially. Hence bacteria, skin, clothing and dirt may be found within the wound tract and adjacent fascial planes, with the obvious risk of sepsis, tetanus and gas gangrene, particularly in wounds of the buttock and lower limbs. The cavity may be the size of a fist and, in a limb wound, contain up to 500 ml of dead muscle which does not bleed, does not contract when stimulated and is of an abnormal colour. The entrance wound is generally small and the exit wound is variegated and may be large or small. In wounds of the head and neck (Fig. 4.3), and particularly the mouth and jaws, secondary missiles are common and include fragments of bone, teeth, fillings and radiolucent denture acrylic. The bullet may fragment and produce additional wound tracts. Large arteries, veins and nerves may be pushed to one side, but in the case of high energy transfer wounds, there will be damage to the tunica intima of the vessel and this may lead to thrombosis and stasis, and plasma leak with tense oedema and compressive ischaemia. While it may be thought that this is of less importance in

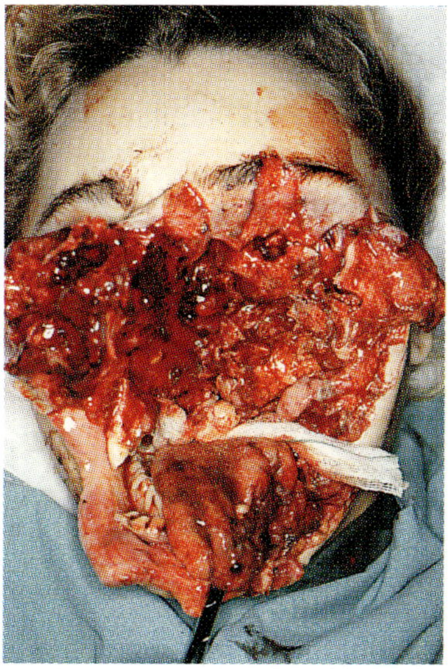

Fig. 4.3 Accidental high energy wound – face and jaws, 0.303 Lee Enfield. Patient died on postoperative day 6.

the head and neck than it is in the limbs, massive cervicofacial oedema may occur with or without air emphysema, requiring prompt tracheostomy.

Principles of management of gunshot wounds

Missile wounds of the face, neck and jaws are particularly serious as the airway may be rapidly compromised. The principles of management are those of any other patient and include maintenance of **A**irway, **B**reathing, the **C**irculation and assessment of neurological **D**eficit (Haywood & Skinner 1991, Westaby 1989). The techniques of wound management may vary somewhat between civilian (Broome et al 1988) and military practice, the facilities available, and the skill of the surgeon (Banks et al 1994). Cervicofacial wounds must be carefully explored and débrided. Wounds of the pharynx are explored, drained and carefully closed in layers. Suction drains should be multiple, generous and dependant. The major vessels are often injured, and the wound may rapidly be fatal. Spinal cord injury and quadriplegia may occur as the result of a high energy projectile passing close to the cervical vertebrae. In wounds of the upper neck, face, oropharynx and mandible, even low energy projectiles may give rise to cranial nerve damage. If there is no bone loss, the recent wound and compound fracture are explored and débrided, and the fracture fixated with miniplates, providing the wound is adequately drained and tensionless skin and mucosal cover are achieved. Exposed bone should be covered by skin or mucosa, and if there is any doubt mucosa may be safely sutured directly to skin for a temporary repair. Intravenous antibiotic therapy is mandatory. If there is a large bony gap, there may be a place for an immediate bone graft or the space may be maintained with either a Kirschner wire or an external pin fixator. A delayed definitive reconstruction is carried out with either a vascularised or non-vascularised bone graft. The extensive excision of muscle indicated in wounds of buttock and lower limbs is clearly not practical in wounds of the face, neck and jaws.

Shotgun wounds

Shotgun wounds are classified (Sherman & Parrish 1963, Owen-Smith 1981) into three types depending on the range, the pattern of shot distribu-

Table 4.7 Shotgun wound classification

Type	Injury
I	Wounds with penetration of subcutaneous tissue or deep fascia (clean and dress). Range: long – over 7 yards
II	Wounds perforating structures beneath the deep fascia (explore). Range: close – 3–7 yards
III	Wounds with extensive (massive) tissue destruction (organ injury and treat for high energy wound). Range: point blank – under 3 yards

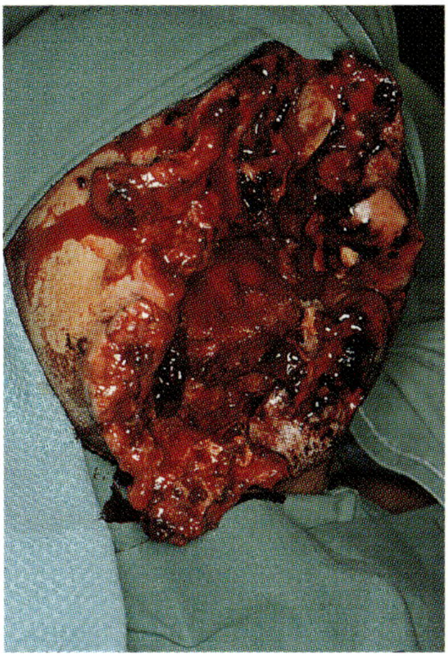

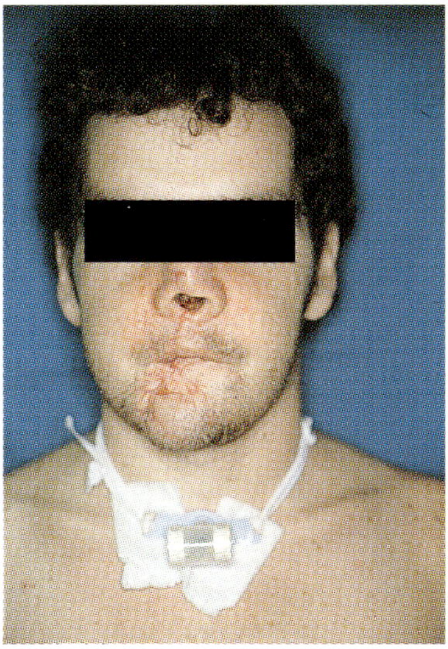

Fig. 4.4a and b Accidental shotgun wound at close range, 12 guage, No. 5 shot. Pre- and postoperative photographs.

tion (Breitenecker 1969) and the depth of penetration. Shotgun wound patterns are of some importance for the forensic pathologist who may be invited to speculate or opine on the possible distance of wounding (Table 4.7).

While wounds to the neck are almost invariably fatal at point blank range, those to the face and jaws are not necessarily so, and with modern methods of reconstruction may produce an acceptable aesthetic and functional result (Fig. 4.4a and b).

Disability assessment

The medical referee obtains a history of the wounding where possible and, if available, the calibre of the weapon. Banks et al (1994) provide a classification of tissue damage and loss which has been expanded to accommodate medicolegal assessment:

- Loss of specialised organs which cannot be replaced:
  - — sense of smell
  - — sight (optic pathway and globe)
  - — middle and inner ear
  - — larynx
- Loss of specialised tissue whose function cannot be fully restored:
  - — facial and trigeminal nerves
  - — lips, eyelids and nose
  - — muscle bulk and teeth

- Loss of less specialised soft tissue, skin and mucosa
- Loss of bone and cartilage, bony deformity and malunion of facial and jaw fractures.

The referee will include in the report a detailed list of both the injuries and disabilities, including facial deformity involving the upper, middle and lower thirds of the face, extent of loss of bone and cartilage, mensuration and description of skin, mucosal defects and scars, sensory and motor neuropathy, and dental disability. An indication should be given to the solicitor, insurer or tribunal requesting the report whether opinions should be obtained from other specialists, including an ophthalmologist, otolaryngologist, plastic, vascular or neurological surgeon; or dental specialist. An estimate of future treatment costs should be prepared based on current professional fees, and with a disclaimer that the fees have a currency of 6–12 months from the date of the report, and are not an estimate of what the fees might be in 5–10 years. This is a matter for the court to decide.[3]

Fine scar revision may be carried out with Z-plasty, or if there is tissue loss replacement may require free flap transfer using microsurgical techniques. Mucosal scars and tethering of lip and mucosal cheek may require inlay grafting of skin or mucosa before the dentist can prescribe a satisfactory denture. Nasal deformity and dysfunction may require complex rhinoseptoplasty and autogenous bone and cartilage grafts, and this is also included. The facial and trigeminal nerves may be reconstructed (Batchelor et al 1995) with microneurosurgical and other techniques. Loss of bone will require a vascularised or non-vascularised bone graft. After the graft is consolidated osseous integrated implants may be placed as a prelude to dental rehabilitation. Prosthetic rehabilitation extends not only to the teeth, and a missing ear may be reconstructed (Firmin 1994), or a prosthetic ear attached with an osseous integrated technique. These prosthetic appliances will require a maintenance fee and replacement at intervals, and the referee should indicate the intervals, but not speculate on the possible future fee. When calculating the cost of a prosthetic eye it is necessary to advise that there may be further alterations to the socket, which may necessitate further surgery to the socket and regular replacements of the shell.

An estimate of surgical, hospital and other costings might be given along the following lines:

Operation: Reconstruction of left mandible utilising vascularised autogenous iliac bone graft and microsurgical techniques

Hospital: days @ $ per day depending on whether shared ward, single or double room or luxury suite $...

Operating theatre fee (dependent on time)

Category	Fee	Approximate time	$...

Surgeons' fee (with aftercare) Co-surgeons: A B Smith & C D Jones	Surgeon 1 Surgeon 2	\$... \$...
Specialist assistant surgeon's fee		\$...
Anaesthetist's fee		\$...
***Pathology fees:** haemoglobin, FBC, MBA equivalent, group and cross match 2 units, serology – hepatitis B & C & HIV		\$...
Autologous blood, 2 units, + tests associated with these donations		\$...
***Postoperative biochemistry/haematology/microbiology**		\$...
***Radiology fees** (including CXR & 3D CT scan of mandible)		\$...
***Physiotherapy fees**		\$...
***Drugs and dressings**		\$...
***Intensive Care Unit** (per day)		\$...
Pre-operative consultation with physician		\$...
Convalescence: 28 days		\$...

* in normal circumstances of the operation and assuming no untoward postoperative complications, unlikely to be greater than the estimate.

Costings in relation to hospital charges and operating theatre fees are an approximation based on reasonable assessment of operating theatre time.

Medicolegal assessment

> Facial disfigurement can be considered total if it is severe and grossly deforming of face and features; also, it must involve at least the entire area between the brow line and the upper lip on both sides. Severe disfigurement above the brow line should be deemed, at a maximum, 1% impairment of the whole person. If it is severe below the upper lip, it may be deemed 8% impairment of the whole person.
>
> Engelberg 1988

It is interesting to note that this author and his colleagues assign 25% of the whole person for loss of the entire nose, but only 8% for bilateral total facial paresis, and 5% for a unilateral paresis. Elsewhere, in their table containing the values for impairment of cranial nerves, they indicate 30–45% impairment for the former and 10–15% for the latter. It is emphasised that these are guidelines, and that 'reasonable impairment values can be placed on other facial disfigurements'. There is no doubt that there will always be room for spirited debate between clinicians as to the percentage loss of function with a particular deformity. A small scar on the eyelid or cheek may be regarded as a significant handicap by one patient, and of no consequence by another.

As with any facial injury, disfigurement (shape, colour and structure) is assessed in addition to function. Disfigurement may result entirely from the original trauma, or be compounded by surgery or wound infection. In the case of an uncomplicated tripod fracture of the zygoma, surgical elevation may restore the cheekbone to its anatomical position, with no facial asymmetry or loss of cheek prominence. In such a case, there would be no percentage loss of function. Where there is a subtle degree of flattening of the cheek prominence, osteotomy of the zygoma may not be warranted, and loss of function is estimated at 2%, or a slightly higher value if there is an overlying scar, with an additional increment to cover any associated infra-orbital neuropathy. Gross depression of the zygoma is unsightly (5–10%), and the unilateral anti–Mongoloid slant of the palpebral fissure associated with diplopia is worthy of correction by zygomatic osteotomy.

In addition to disfigurement secondary to underlying bony or cartilaginous deformity, there may be soft-tissue loss or scarring of the periorbital tissues and eyelids. These scars should be described according to anatomical site, length, width and if relevant, height (hypertrophic or keloidal), together with colour, texture and attachment to underlying structures, and finally whether fine surgical revision or other treatment is recommended. It is also appropriate to indicate if the scar is associated with alopecia, solar sensitivity, loss of pigmentation, or sweat gland dysfunction. Damage to the facial (VII) and trigeminal (V) nerves is assessed independently (Engelberg 1988).

The assessment of percentage loss of visual acuity due to abnormal ocular motility and binocular diplopia is complex, and should be carried out by an ophthalmic surgeon. Displacement of the ocular globe is relatively common in the case of an orbital fracture, and may be unsightly. Enophthalmos is assessed clinically with the exophthalmometer, and volume enhancement of the orbit with an autogenous bone graft (calvarial or iliac) may only partly correct the deformity. Enophthalmos is accentuated by depression of the ocular globe, and should also be recorded in relation

Table 4.8 Facial disfigurement (After Engelberg 1988)

Class	Disfigurement	%
1	Impairment of the whole person Disfigurement limited to skin, visible scars and abnormal pigmentation	0–5
2	Loss of bone or cartilage, with or without cutaneous disorder, depressed zygoma, nose or frontal bone	5–10
3	Loss of an eye or part of nose, or absence of a normal anatomical area of face	10–15
4	Facial disfigurement so severe that it precludes social acceptance	15–35

to the contralateral globe. The width and height of the palpebral fissures are recorded in addition to the intercanthal distance.

The AMA's assessment of facial disfigurement is seen in Table 4.8 (Engelberg 1988).

CONDYLAR FRACTURES

Fractures of the mandibular condyle are common (Silvennoinen et al 1992) and may occur in isolation or in association with other fractures of the mandible. Just as the elderly patient who falls on the outstretched hand develops a Colles fracture, the patient, falling on the point of the chin may develop the typical 'parade ground' injury with a fracture of the parasymphyseal region in conjunction with anteromedial fracture dislocations of the mandibular condyles. A blow to one side of the face results in fracture of the left body of the mandible and a fracture, with or without dislocation of the contralateral mandibular condyle. As with any synovial joint, trauma may be associated with either an effusion of synovial fluid or an haemarthrosis. Despite the fact that some condylar fractures are compounded into the ear canal through a laceration of the cartilaginous meatus, few become infected, giving rise to pyarthrosis.

The temporomandibular meniscus is a relatively resilient structure and acts as a shock absorber between the mandibular condyle and the glenoid fossa. Meniscal injury is not uncommon, although there have been no large long-term series demonstrating precisely how common.

Mandibular dislocation may occur in the absence of fracture and is almost invariably anterior. The Hippocratic method of reduction is still employed. Posterior, lateral and superior dislocations are uncommon (Norman & Bramley 1990).

Fractures of the mandibular condyle are either intra- or extracapsular. The former may not be diagnosed at the time of the injury and a high index of suspicion is required. In the child and young adult, the slipped epiphysis is encountered rarely. There is a greenstick-type fracture encountered in the growing child and radiographs confirm angulation of the condyle and its surgical neck. Over a period of 3–5 years, the writer notes that there may be a gradual uprighting of the angulated condyle in the younger patient (Altmann & Gundlach 1992).

Intracapsular fractures

- Microfracture of the articular dome.
- Compression fracture with collapse of the articular plateau. This almost invariably leads to accelerated post-traumatic osteoarthritis.
- Comminuted fracture.
- Vertical fracture with sagittal splitting of the condyle on the anteroposterior plane. This may be subdivided into either medial or lateral sagittal splitting.

Table 4.9 Intra- and extracapsular fracture classification

Grade	
I	No displacement
II	Greenstick fracture (fracture deviation)
III	Fracture displacement with overlap of the condylar process and mandibular fragment
IV	Fracture dislocation of the mandibular condyle

Extracapsular fractures

- Undisplaced hairline fracture of the condylar neck.
- Displaced or deviated angulation of the condyle and its anatomical neck.
- Displaced fracture with medial or lateral overlap or rarely, anteroposterior overlap.
- Anteromedial fracture dislocation.
- Avulsion of the mandibular condyle.

Maclennan (1952) proposed a quadripartite classification of commendable simplicity (Kamitani et al 1989) (Table 4.9).

Physical signs

An accurate history is supplemented by appropriate imaging including orthopantomography, right and left lateral oblique films and posteroanterior film of the mandible. If there is bleeding from the ear canal, a CT scan of the mandibular condyle, tympanic plate and temporal bone is advisable, the opinion of an ENT surgeon is sought and auditory acuity assessed in order that ossicular dislocation or disruption is not overlooked. Patients with involvement of the tympanic plate and temporal bone are at greater risk of developing a lower motor neurone facial paresis.

Clinical findings include:

- Pre-auricular swelling with an effusion or haemarthrosis
- Marked tenderness overlying the joint, with trismus and pain on opening or closing the mouth
- Occlusal derangement
- If there is a unilateral fracture dislocation there will be telescoping of that side, with a posterior open bite on the contralateral side and a premature contact on the side of the fracture
- If there are bilateral fracture dislocations with foreshortening of the mandibular rami, the anterior open bite will be of an anterior nature with gagging of the posterior occlusion.

Management

- For undisplaced isolated condylar fracture, there is a conservative regimen of management, including dietary rest, ice packs and a short course of a non-steroidal anti-inflammatory drug. The effusion/haemarthrosis may result in transitory derangement of the occlusion with a posterior open bite on the side of the fracture. This will settle as the effusion resorbs. It is usually unnecessary to aspirate such an effusion or haemarthrosis.
- For anteromedial fracture dislocation, a short period of intermaxillary fixation may be required, achieved with interdental eyelet wires and intermaxillary wires or elastics. Alternatively, the application of orthodontic bands to the premolar and molar teeth on both sides and intermaxillary elastics for 3–5 weeks can be used.
- Some condylar fractures require open reduction and internal fixation, but in the British Commonwealth, as a general rule, it has been customary to treat the fracture dislocation either conservatively or with a period of intermaxillary fixation. In continental Europe a more aggressive approach is adopted, involving open reduction and internal fixation using miniplates (Bradley et al 1994).
- Some prefer the use of external pin fixators, and the Kirschner wire enjoyed a period of popularity (Brown & Obeid 1984).

Paediatric condylar fractures

The child who has sustained a comminuted fracture of the mandibular condyle is at considerable risk of developing mandibular ankylosis. Damage to the condylar growth centre may result in lack of development of the ipsilateral mandible and asymmetric micrognathia (James 1990, 1994, Hall 1972, Thoren et al 1992, Stylogianni et al 1991). The writer and others believe that an intact temporomandibular meniscus generally gives some protection against development of ankylosis, but trauma sufficient to fragment the articular plateau almost invariably tears or splits the meniscus, and permits bone to bone contact.

It is useful to compare the condylar fracture in the child with fractures of the upper radial epiphysis. The older the child the less acceptable is the deformity, and avascular necrosis may occur at either site, jaw or radius, however well the injury is treated (Wadsworth 1990).

Post-traumatic temporomandibular joint disorders

There is good evidence that mandibular trauma may either precipitate or exacerbate dysfunction of the temporomandibular joints in the absence of mandibular fracture or even a direct blow to the lower jaw. It may unleash the myofascial pain dysfunction syndrome, affecting the cervicofacial and masticatory musculature, and is seen in conjunction with Arnold's greater occipital neuralgia. Trauma may initiate internal derangement, with pain, crepitus and locking. Direct trauma may result in microfractures of the articular dome and subsequent osteoarthritis. Severe trauma may result in a slipped condylar epiphysis in the growing child, or a crushed capitulum or fracture of the condylar neck. The latter may be associated with anteromedial dislocation. Medial and lateral dislocation are almost invariably accompanied by mandibular fracture, and posterior and superior dislocation are extremely rare. Patients may develop subluxation or chronic recurrent dislocation following trauma. Mandibular ankylosis results from both trauma and suppurative arthritis, and is relatively uncommon (Norman 1978, 1982). An effusion may be seen following trauma, and as a general rule resolves without need for aspiration. Suppurative arthritis is an uncommon complication (Norman & Bramley 1990). There is no convincing evidence that trauma causes active condylar hyperplasia (Norman & Painter 1980), but it may play a part in the genesis of chondropathy, surface articular dome fractures and the formation of osteocartilaginous loose bodies (Norman et al 1988). Irrespective of the method of reduction and fixation, the patient may develop long-term dysfunction associated with the damaged joint, and Brooke & Stenn (1978) note that the response to therapy of myofascial pain dysfunction syndrome is much less favourable when the patient has been involved in a motor vehicle or other accident.

The categories of post-traumatic temporomandibular joint disorders are as follows:

- Myofascial pain dysfunction syndrome and temporalis insertion tendonopathy
- Emergence of an internal derangement requiring exploration and meniscectomy/meniscoplasty
- Post-traumatic osteoarthrosis of either a slowly developing or accelerated nature
- Mandibular ankylosis (fibrous, fibro-osseous or osseous).

Myofascial pain dysfunction syndrome. This requires conservative management with an explanation as to its genesis. The patient should prosecute a regimen of vocal and dietary rest, local heat and simple analgesics. The dentist may wish to arrange an occlusal analysis and minor occlusal equilibration in an effort to restore anatomical occlusion. The patient may benefit from the provision of a delicate and aesthetic full arch occlusal splint. If the symptoms persist, further investigation should be by temporomandibular arthrography or magnetic resonance imaging (Pressman et al 1992, Palacios et al 1990) with video recording. The medical referee should provide the costings of such treatment in the report, and decline to provide a prognosis until there has been a reasonable trial of conservative treatment.

Internal derangement. This may occur in the absence of a condylar fracture and may be seen in association with other mandibular fractures.

Injuries to the temporomandibular meniscus include detachment, splitting, perforation and displacement, and are accompanied by an effusion or haemarthrosis with temporary malocclusion. The patient complains of pain and crepitus, associated with otalgia, in the absence of aural disease. There is often limitation of mouth opening, and the referee should record the gape and lateral excursive movements of the mandible and initiate a dental referral. Conservative treatment is offered, but in the event that there is no satisfactory respite within 2 months, further imaging is carried out. Meniscoplasty per arthroscope or via arthrotomy or meniscectomy with vascularised temporalis muscle flap repair is usually curative, although some patients require total meniscectomy and meniscal reconstruction. The vascularised fasciomuscular temporalis flap is an excellent replacement for meniscus perforans or the markedly degenerate disc (Bradley et al 1994).

Osteoarthritis. The true incidence of post-traumatic temporomandibular osteoarthritis is unknown, and the degree of osteoarthritis and the rapidity of its onset do not appear to be related to the degree of displacement. It is the intracapsular crush fracture of the condyle which is prone to osteoarthritis with comminution of the weightbearing articular dome, in common with a similar injury to the hip joint. Fractures of the articular fossa are relatively uncommon and if displaced may be associated with a lower motor neurone facial paresis. The majority of intracapsular

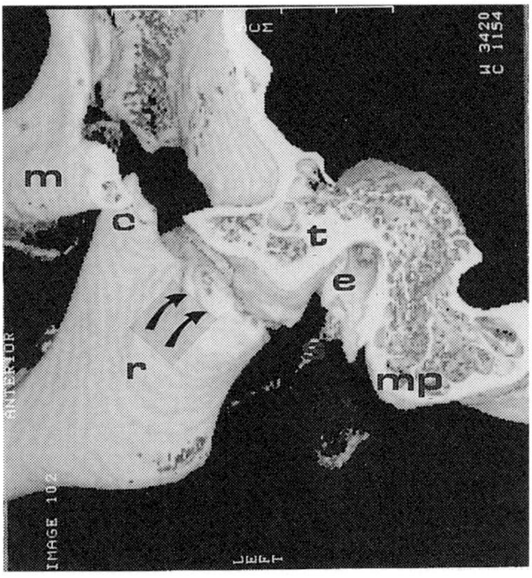

Fig. 4.5 Three-dimensional reconstruction of a CT scan of mandibular ankylosis showing the lateral aspect of fusion of mandible and temporal bone. Key: r – ramus mandible; m – malar; t – temporal bone; e – external auditory meatus; mp – mastoid process; s – styloid process; c – coronoid process mandible.

fractures probably go undiagnosed at all ages and in the elderly osteoporotic patient accelerated osteoarthritis or avascular necrosis may follow and the edentulous elderly patient may be reassured and sent on her way.

Post-traumatic degenerative joint disease (OA) may be of a slowly developing or accelerated nature and the patient presents with joint pain of a persistent and severe aching character, present at rest and with function, and accompanied by a deep-seated otalgia in the absence of aural disease. Irrespective of its aetiology, advanced osteoarthritis is accompanied by coarse grating and chronic, aching pain and limitation of mouth opening. The diagnosis is established on the history and radiographs of good quality, including direct sagittal tomograms or a CT scan. Again, conservative treatment may be productive of some symptomatic respite but, in the long term, patients with advanced degenerative joint disease and chronic pain require an arthroplasty.

Ankylosis. Mandibular ankylosis may be of a fibrous, fibro-osseous, osteocartilaginous or osseous nature, and this complication is managed by osteo-arthrectomy and costochondral grafting in the child and young adult (James 1990). Ankylosis may also be classified as short or long fibrous ankylosis, or intra or extracapsular bony ankylosis (Fig. 4.5).

Post-traumatic jaw strain secondary to neck injury

> Most victims of whiplash injury have, however, sustained no more than a minor sprain to the soft tissues and unusually severe or protracted complaints may demand explanations which lie outside the fields of organic and psychiatric illness.
>
> Pearce 1989

> Whiplash injuries can also traumatise the temporomandibular joint, resulting in internal derangement or a myofascial injury with associated jaw pain and headaches.
>
> Evans 1992

Neck strain: soft tissue injuries of the neck

It is suggested that the referee approach the subject with an open mind, and in the first instance obtain an accurate and detailed medical history. It should become apparent during the history taking whether the patient is prone to exaggeration or embellishment.

Neck strain is not infrequently a major cause of protracted disability following a vehicular accident (Maimaris et al 1988, Deans et al 1987, Newman 1990). Approximately 77% of patients complain of the onset of pain in less than 12 hours, 13% within 12–23 hours and the remainder in less than 48 hours (Deans et al 1987). Approximately 25% of patients experience pain in the neck 12 months after the accident and the majority of these describe an intermittent rather than a continuous pain. The complaint is more common in women (Evans 1992) who have a slender neck than in men, and this has been borne out in the writer's own clinic. Acute

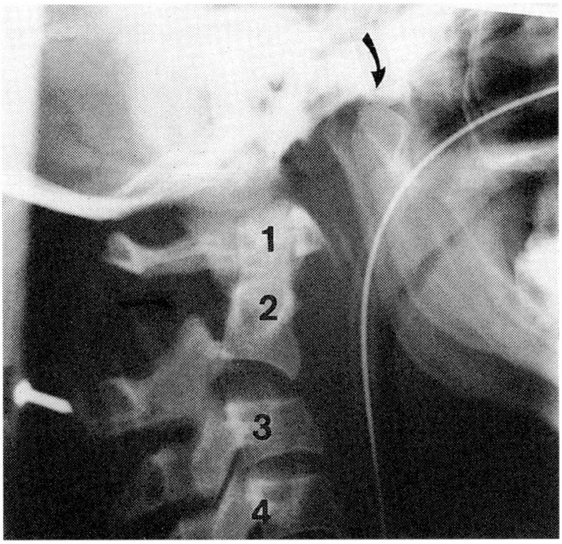

Fig. 4.6 Lateral radiograph of upper cervical spine and mandible, with fracture of the axis (C2) and mandibular condyles. No neurological deficit.

neck strain gives rise to pain which may continue for many years and in some it is grossly disruptive of the patient's life, although a minority undoubtedly perpetuate their symptoms (Hohl 1974) for emotional or for secondary gain in legal proceedings.

Mechanism of jaw and neck strain

A violent flexion and hyperextension of the neck might damage the vertebra or the soft parts including cervical nerve roots, muscles, ligaments, the intervertebral disc or even the spinal cord. The precise mechanism of nerve injury is unclear, but there may be transient dislocation or momentary posterior movement of the intervertebral disc into the spinal canal, and the presence of pre-existing spondylosis adds to this risk. On occasion the patient with a tripartite 'parade ground' fracture sustained in a high energy vehicular accident will be found to have a fracture of the cervical spine (McSwain et al 1989) (Fig. 4.6).

The writer strives not to use the term 'whiplash', although it has currency, and there is hesitancy to employ 'jawlash' or 'mandibular whiplash' which has entered our vocabulary (Levandoski 1990). There is reason to believe that in the patient with a slender neck who has sustained an acute extension and flexion injury (Howard et al 1991, Goldberg 1990, Weinberg & Lapointe 1987) to the lower jaw, the sudden contraction of the pterygo-masseteric sling and the temporalis muscles may result in sudden closure of the mouth and, in extreme cases, cusps of antagonist teeth may be fractured, or avulsion fracture of the mandibular coronoid process may occur. The articular dome may be damaged by the impact, and there may be a crushing injury to the meniscus. Whereas the symptoms of the majority settle with either the lotion of time or conservative treatment, a minority develop protracted and sometimes incapacitating symptoms of jaw joint dysfunction and headache. In some patients, these symptoms are perpetuated by stress-related bruxism and diurnal jaw clenching. Symptoms of a depressive illness are superimposed and exacerbated by chronic pain and an ever-increasing regimen of analgesic and anxiolytic drugs. Notwithstanding the severity of the pain, the writer and his colleagues urge conservative management and the temptation to operate or even reoperate on the temporomandibular joint 'for pain' should be resisted unless there is crystal clear evidence of joint pathology.

The dynamics of the injury are considered by Schneider et al (1989) in a computer simulation, and Bedrune et al (1992) and Torfs & Lenssen (1989) consider the medicolegal aspects of whiplash and TM joint dysfunction in French and Belgian law respectively.

Clinical presentation

The patient, frequently a woman, complains of neck pain radiating into the trapezii, posterior triangles and sometimes the shoulder and even radicular symptoms. Suboccipital neuralgia of Arnold involves not only the dermatomes subserved by the posterior rami of C2, C3 (C1 does not reach the surface) but may extend to become bitemporal, bifrontal or circumorbital (Bogduk 1980). The patient complains of deep seated neck pain and headache (Wolff 1963) but usually in the absence of the visual phenomena of a vascular headache. Migrainous-type headaches may be precipitated or exacerbated in a known migraineur.

Severe neck pain may precipitate nausea in a minority, and neck stiffness, tenderness and guarding are noted. In addition, the patient may complain of temporomandibular joint pain which involves the pre-auricular region and the parotideal margin down to the angle of the mandible and the mandibulomastoid sulcus. The writer believes that this pain at the mandibular angle and between the mandible and the mastoid process is referred pain along the greater auricular distribution, and tenderness may be demonstrated at Erb's point, and over the adjacent paracervical muscles. It is neck rather than jaw joint pain. Tenderness may be present over the mandibular condyle and the insertion of the temporalis muscle which embraces the coronoid process in a tendinous and tenacious fashion. It is best demonstrated transorally with the finger palpating the anteromedial and lateral aspect of the tendon with the mouth half open. This is perhaps a variety of the insertion tendonopathy recognised in orthopaedic practice (Jackson 1990). Early morning jaw stiffness may be a feature (Kronn 1993) with upwards of 50% reduction in the gape (Range 40–45 mm). On

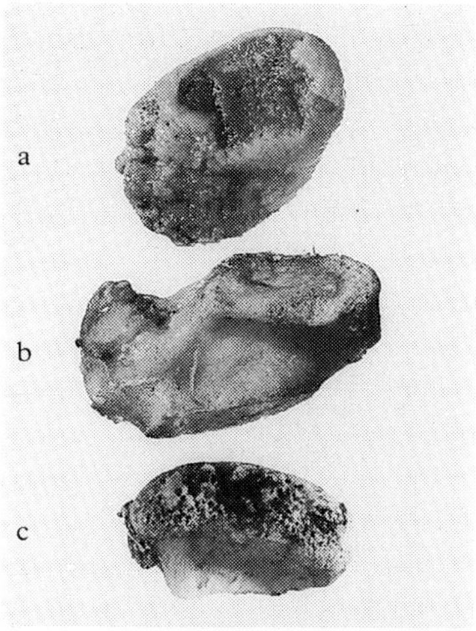

Fig. 4.7 Post-traumatic osteoarthritis of the mandibular condyle (Stage III): (a) male, 26 years; (b) male, 19 years; (c) female, 21 years.

rare occasions the patient may complain of anaesthesia in the ipsilateral anterior two-thirds of the tongue (Lance & Anthony 1980) and the writer has noted, on three occasions, flitting anaesthesia in the dermatome subserved by the mandibular division of the trigeminal nerve. In patients with protracted symptoms it is common to encounter impaired memory and concentration, irritability, insomnia, fatigue, personality change and depression.

Post-traumatic osteoarthritis

Microfractures of the articular dome may proceed in an unknown percentage of cases to post-traumatic osteoarthritis (Fig. 4.7). Pre-auricular pain with and without temporocervical radiation was the early and predominant symptom of temporomandibular osteoarthritis whatever the cause. The pain was generally of a persistent, deep, aching character, sometimes extremely severe and associated with a deep, aching otalgia in the absence of aural disease. Joint noise varied from fine crepitus to a coarse staccato crunch and was almost invariably associated with pain and sometimes locking. Cramp-like pain may be described, and it has been shown with EMG that local areas of muscle spasm may give rise to diffuse pain (Wolff 1963).

Irrespective of the aetiology, Grade III/IV (Toller 1974) osteoarthritis is accompanied by coarse grating and constant aching. Some patients complain of early morning trismus and restriction of mandibular movement, but describe some increased flexion and extension of the jaw as the day progresses. Intermittent locking occurs, but is usually cleared by a trick lateral movement of the jaw. Osteoarthritis may follow both intra- and extracapsular condylar fractures, microfractures of the articular dome may go unrecognised. Meniscal injuries include perforation with force majeure or, more commonly, anteromedial displacement, posterior or posterolateral tearing.

Assessment

The referee should record the description and anatomical distribution of the pain, the precipitating factors, the character of any headache, and analgesic use, and assess the masticatory apparatus, dentition and cervicofacial musculature, including the range of neck movements. The dental examination should include the extent of mouth opening and whether there has been any actual or perceived change in the occlusion. The gape, protrusion and right and left lateral excursions of the mandible are measured in millimetres, and it is recorded if these movements are associated with pain, crepitus or locking. Radiographic assessment should include orthopantomography or plain films of the TM joints and, if there is an internal derangement, an arthrogram or MRI scan with video record. The patient's response and compliance, or lack of it, with previous treatment should be noted.

Management

Conservative measures are recommended in the management of an acute jaw strain secondary to the whiplash. It is self-evident that both neck and jaw will require treatment, although in those with entrenched symptoms an entirely mechanistic approach is unlikely to be occasioned by success. If the pain is particularly severe and there are no medical contraindications, a non-steroidal anti-inflammatory drug is prescribed. Cervical traction, with a halter beneath the chin, may exacerbate the temporomandibular pain. If traction is required, an occlusal splint should be worn (Shore et al 1979), or it should be achieved by means of a mechanical device such as the Saunder's traction apparatus. Passive joint movements are contraindicated, but short wave diathermy or ultrasound may be beneficial, as are other forms of local heat or even an ice pack. The patient is referred for occlusal splint therapy.

In the case of the patient who complains of incapacitating cervicofacial and jaw pain, and headache, and has either not sought treatment, or failed to comply with the measures advised, the medicolegal referee may conclude that perhaps the pain is not as incapacitating as claimed, and there may be a motive of secondary gain behind the exaggeration. The patient with established and chronic symptoms of cervicofacial pain persisting

Table 4.10 Percentage impairment of joint function (Engelberg 1988, by kind permission of the author)

Persistent joint subluxation or dislocation		% joint impairment
Mild:	can be completely reduced manually	20
Moderate:	cannot be completely reduced manually	40
Severe:	cannot be reduced manually	60

longer than 2 years will be markedly resistant of treatment and the writer believes it is important not to over-treat this patient. Under many circumstances it would be appropriate to obtain a psychiatric opinion.

Medical evaluation of the jaw joint

It is important to delay the medicolegal report for at least 12 months. The 1 year rule in relation to the hip (Lowell 1979) is not sufficient for assessment of the growing child and young adult, and the writer prefers at least 18 months to 2 years in the case of the latter. In the former, the referee should resist overtures by the insurer or solicitor to press for an early opinion, and should emphasise the necessity of waiting until skeletal growth has ceased in the late teens.

If the meniscus is torn or disrupted the resulting bone on bone contact may hasten the onset of osteoarthritis, or in extreme cases, of ankylosis. Opening and closing is only one of a number of jaw movements, and dental practitioners would in addition assess the occlusion, and measure protrusion and right and left lateral excursions of the mandible. As with other joints, the clinician endeavours to compare the damaged side with the uninvolved contralateral joint. The principles of evaluating normal motion used in the extremities are not directly applicable to the temporomandibular joints, and as a general rule flexion and extension are not terms in common currency. There may be loss of extension and in the extreme case total loss of mobility is encountered in bony ankylosis. Hence, A = E + F (where A = ankylosis [total loss of joint motion], E = loss of extension, F = loss of flexion).

Hyperextension may be associated with subluxation or dislocation, and the following percentage impairment of joint function is suggested by Engelberg (1988) (Table 4.10).

Clinicians assessing derangements in other joints recognise that a multitude of other factors should be taken into account, such as joint crepitus, deformity, associated muscles and tendons, overlying scars and sensory neuropathy. Little attempt has been made to include these factors in the evaluation of temporomandibular joint dysfunction, and the bulk of the literature associated with this subject relates to the dentition. Joint adhesions, meniscal degeneration, anteromedial subluxation and perforation may only be diagnosed with certainty with arthrography, MRI or arthroscopy.

Complications of surgical treatment of condylar fractures

The complications are those enumerated earlier in this chapter, but in addition there are the complications of arthrotomy in a complex joint lying immediately anterior to the auditory canal, caudal to the middle cranial fossa and deep to the facial, greater auricular and auriculotemporal nerves.

Facial palsy and condylar fracture

A lower motor neurone paresis may be temporary or permanent, partial, or global, affecting all branches (Batchelor et al 1995). While some may consider this remote, the writer has had two such cases in the last 30 years, where bilateral lower motor neurone facial paresis occurred in association with fracture of the mandibular condyle. In one case the palsy developed slowly within 12–24 hours of a closed reduction.

No calculation for sensory loss is made as the sensory dermatome is small (Engelberg 1988). Unilateral loss of taste to the anterior two-thirds of the tongue is rare in association with fractures of the mandibular condyle. Bilateral loss of taste to the anterior two-thirds must be of singular rarity, but is assessed at 3% impairment of the whole person. As a rule conservative management is advised, as the palsy is the result of oedema and a full recovery should be anticipated in most cases. An examination by an ENT surgeon is advised, and this clinical assessment would be supplemented by special tests of vestibulo-cochlear function and a CT scan of the temporal bones.

Greater auricular nerve

If an incision placed at the angle of the mandible crosses Erb's point the greater auricular nerve may be damaged. If all three branches are involved there will be anaesthesia which in time may give rise to paraesthesia, but is sometimes associated with causalgia and formication. The percentage impairment of the whole person is 0–3%.

Auriculotemporal nerve

This nerve may be divided unavoidably during operations on the temporomandibular joint, and the patient should be advised pre-operatively of this. There will be anaesthesia in the dermatome and it is uncommon for the patient to complain since the area is small. The auriculotemporal syndrome of Frey may develop and if severe can be an embarrassment associated with pain, flushing and gustatory sweating. The AMA tables do not consider this syndrome, but from a personal study (Norman 1995) of 50 patients with post-parotidectomy greater auricular neuropathy and Frey's syndrome, the writer believes that the auriculotemporal syndrome is as debilitating, and suggests 0–3% impairment of the whole person. Transmeatal tympanic neurectomy generally relieves up to 80% of the symptoms of flushing and gustatory sweating. The use of dilute Botulinum toxin appears promising.

Assessment of nerve dysfunction

> In order to evaluate impairment resulting from the effects of peripheral spinal nerve lesions, it is necessary to determine the extent of loss of function due to: 1) sensory deficit, pain, or discomfort; and 2) loss of muscle strength and motor control of muscles. Although atrophy, vasomotor and trophic changes, reflex changes, and certain characteristic deformities are also effects of peripheral nerve lesions, it is not necessary to evaluate all of these separately, because they would be reflected in the sensory disturbance, and loss of muscle strength or control.
>
> Engelberg 1988

It is the purpose of this chapter to draw the clinician's attention to the fact that both cranial and peripheral spinal nerves of the head and neck may be involved as a result of the operative management of fractures of the facial skeleton and mandible. The grading scheme (Engelberg 1988) is valuable and since some patients involved in litigation may be prone to exaggerate or embellish the anatomical extent of an area of anaesthesia, they should be requested to mark out the area slowly and accurately with one finger of one hand. If the patient with a unilateral mandibular body fracture marks out the mental dermatome, one tests this area, comparing the ipsi- and contralateral sides. If he or she marks out both mental dermatomes and much of the infra-orbital dermatome, an effort is made to exclude a zygomatico-maxillary fracture prior to carrying out sensory testing. Exaggeration and embellishment are not uncommon, and for reasons of secondary gain both financial and emotional.

The grading scheme and procedure for determining impairment of affected body part due to pain, discomfort or loss of sensation described by Engelberg (1988) are strongly recommended. Specific unilateral cranial and spinal nerve impairment is also well described, and the tables are easy to apply.

NOTES

1. The medicolegal referee should enquire if there was a pre-existing malocclusion, and may wish to ask the patient's regular dental officer for an opinion.
2. Profuse haemorrhage from a fracture of the middle third may be controlled, in part, by en bloc forward traction by the index and middle fingers of the dominant hand hooked behind the soft palate. Torrential nasal haemorrhage is best controlled with both posterior and anterior nasal packing or balloon tamponade. 1–2 inch nasal packs should be steeped in acriflavine emulsion (BPC). Alternatively, large expansile nasal tampons are lightly

lubricated with chloromycetin ointment and inserted after suction clearance of each nasal airway, and Povidone iodine is dripped onto the tampon, which expands to fill the space. On occasion it may be necessary to ligate the ethmoidal arteries via a medial wall orbitotomy. The maxillary artery may be ligated in the pterygopalatine fossa by a transantral approach. The writer and his colleagues favour this method for epistaxis uncontrolled by efficient packing under general anaesthesia. Direct embolisation of the maxillary artery is occasionally required.

3. The Australian Medical Association, the Australian Dental Association, the Association of Surgeons, and workers' compensation insurance companies have prepared fee schedules on which these calculations of the fees for surgical and dental procedures may be based. Costings in regard to hospitalisation should be obtained by the referee from the hospital, and clearly laid out in the manner shown (vide supra).

REFERENCES

al Qurainy I A, Dutton G N, Ilankovan V, Titterington D M, Moos K F, el Attar A 1991a Midfacial fractures and the eye: the development of a system for detecting patients at risk of eye injury: a prospective evaluation. British Journal of Oral and Maxillofacial Surgery 29: 368–369

al Qurainy I A, Stassen L F, Dutton G N, Moos K F, el Attar A 1991b The characteristics of midfacial fractures and the association with ocular injury: a prospective study. British Journal of Oral and Maxillofacial Surgery 29: 291–301

Altmann I S, Gundlach K K 1992 Mandibular condyle fractures in childhood: the clinico-roentgenological follow-up. Deutsche Zahn Mund und Kieferheilkunde mit Zentralblatt 80: 269–273

Anderton J M, Keen R I, Neave R 1988 Positioning the surgical patient. Butterworths, London, p 19

Ayoub A, Philiben T, Hislop W, Cope M 1994 An analysis of 1200 cases of malar fractures (a retrospective study). Journal of Craniomaxillofacial Surgery 22 (Suppl 1): 37

Banks P, Mellor S, Haywood I R, Wilson J S P, Sanders R 1994 Gunshot wounds. In: Williams J Ll (ed) Rowe & Williams' maxillofacial injuries, 2nd edn. Churchill Livingstone, Edinburgh, p 665–748

Banks P, Terry W, Whitlock R I H, Kendrick R W, Chapman C W, Maynard R L 1994 Treatment of maxillofacial injuries in various theatres of war. In: Williams J Ll (ed) Rowe & Williams' maxillofacial injuries, 2nd edn. Churchill Livingstone, Edinburgh, p 749–810

Batchelor A G, Atlas M D, Vaughan E D 1995 The facial nerve. In: Norman J E deB, McGurk M (eds) Colour atlas and textbook of the salivary glands: diseases, disorders and surgery. Mosby Wolfe, London, pp 301–307

Bedrune B, Jammet P, Chossegros C, Cianfarani F, Souyris F, Lachard J 1992 Temporomandibular joint pain-dysfunction syndrome after whiplash injury: medicolegal problems in common law. Revue de Stomatologie et de Chirurgie Maxillo-Faciale 93: 408–413

Blackburn C W 1990 A method of assessment in cases of lingual nerve injury. British Journal of Oral and Maxillofacial Surgery 28: 238–245

Blackburn C W 1992 Experiences in lingual nerve repair. British Journal of Oral and Maxillofacial Surgery 30: 72–77

Blackburn C W, Bramley P A 1989 Lingual nerve damage associated with the removal of lower third molars. British Dental Journal 167: 103–107

Bogduk N 1980 The anatomy of occipital neuralgia. Clinical and Experimental Neurology 17: 167–184

Bonney G 1986 Iatrogenic injuries of nerves. Journal of Bone and Joint Surgery 68B: 9–13

Bowerman J E, Neil-Dwyer G, Bailey B M W 1994 Fractures of the middle third of the facial skeleton. In: Williams J Ll (ed) Rowe and Williams' maxillofacial injuries, 2nd edn. Churchill Livingstone, Edinburgh: 591–663.

Bradley P, James D, Norman J E deB Injuries of the condylar and coronoid process. In: Williams J Ll (ed) Rowe & Williams' maxillofacial injuries, 2nd edn. Churchill Livingstone, Edinburgh, p 405–474

Bramley P 1972 Long-term effects of facial injuries. Proceedings of the Royal Society of Medicine 65: 916–918

Breitenecker R 1969 Shotgun wound patterns. American Journal of Clinical Pathology 52: 258–269

Brooke R J, Stenn P G 1978 Postinjury myofascial pain dysfunction syndrome: its etiology and prognosis. Oral Surgery 45: 846–850

Broome G, Butler-Manuel A, Budd J, Carter P G, Warlow T A 1988 The Hungerford shooting incident. Injury 19: 313–317

Brown A E, Obeid G 1984 A simplified method for the internal fixation of fractures of the mandibular condyle. British Journal of Oral and Maxillofacial Surgery 22: 145

Cooper G J, Ryan J M 1990 Interaction of penetrating missiles with tissues: some common misapprehensions and implications for wound management. British Journal of Surgery 77: 606–610

Deans G T, Magalliard J N, Kerr M, Rutherford W H 1987 Neck sprain: a major cause of disability following car accidents. Injury 18: 10–12

Ellis E II, Moos K F, El-Attar A 1985 Ten years of mandibular fractures: an analysis of 2137 cases. Oral Surgery 59: 120–129

Engelberg A L (ed) 1988 Guides to the evaluation of permanent impairment, 3rd edn. American Medical Association, Chicago, p 100–103

Essick G K 1992 Comprehensive clinical evaluation of perioral sensory function. Oral and Maxillofacial Surgery Clinics of North America 4: 503–526

Evans R W 1992 Some observations on whiplash injuries. Neurologic Clinics 10: 975–997

Firmin F 1994 Total ear reconstruction. Journal of Craniomaxillofacial Surgery 22 (Suppl 1): 8–9

Gillies H D 1920 Plastic surgery of the face based on selected cases of war injuries of the face including burns. Henry Frowde, London

Gilligan J E 1990 Transport of the critically ill. In: Oh T E (ed) Intensive care manual, 3rd edn. Butterworths, Sydney, p 13–21

Goldberg H L 1990 Trauma and the improbable anterior displacement. Journal of Craniomandibular Disorders 4: 131–134

Gossman M D, Roberts D M, Barr C C 1992 Ophthalmic aspects of orbital injury. A comprehensive diagnostic and management approach. Clinics in Plastic Surgery 19: 71–85

Hall R K 1972 Injuries of the face and jaws in children. International Journal of Oral Surgery 1: 65

Hawthorn R, Flatau A 1990 Temporomandibular joint anatomy. In: Norman J E deB, Bramley P (eds) A textbook and colour atlas of the temporomandibular joint: diseases, disorders, surgery. Wolfe Medical, London, p 1–25

Haywood I, Skinner D 1991 Blast and gunshot injuries. In: Skinner D, Driscoll P, Earlin R (eds) ABC of major trauma. British Medical Journal, London

Heath C 1884 Injuries and diseases of the jaws: the Jacksonian Prize Essay of the Royal College of Surgeons of England, 1867, 3rd edn. J & A Churchill, London

Heslop I H, Cawood J I, Stoelinga R, Becker R, Blenkinsop P, Boyne P, Williams J Ll 1994 Mandibular fractures: treatment by closed reduction and direct skeletal fixation. In: Williams J Ll (ed) Rowe & Williams' maxillofacial injuries, 2nd edn. Churchill Livingstone, Edinburgh, p 341–385

Hohl M 1974 Soft-tissue injuries of the neck in automobile accidents: factors influencing prognosis. Journal of Bone and Joint Surgery 56A: 1675–1682

Hopkins N F G, Wolfe J H N 1991 Thrombosis and pulmonary embolism. British Medical Journal 303: 1260–1262

Hotte H H A 1970 Orbital fractures. William Heinemann, London

Howard R P, Benedict J V, Raddin J H Jr, Smith H L 1991 Assessing neck extension-flexion as a basis for temporomandibular joint dysfunction. Journal of Oral and Maxillofacial Surgery 49: 1210–1213

Hunts J H, Patrinely J R, Holds J B, Anderson R L 1994 Orbital emphysema: staging and acute management. Ophthalmology 101: 960–966

Illum P 1991 Legal aspects in nasal fractures. Rhinology 29: 263–266

Jackson I T 1989 Classification and treatment of orbitozygomatic and orbitoethmoid fractures: the place of bone grafting and plate fixation. Clinics in Plastic Surgery 16: 77–91

Jackson J P 1990 Repetitive stress injury. In: Foy M A, Fagg P S (eds) Medicolegal reporting in orthopaedic trauma. Churchill Livingstone, Edinburgh, p 447–456

James D 1990 Growth problems. In: Norman J E deB, Bramley P (eds) A textbook and colour atlas of the temporomandibular joint: diseases, disorders, surgery. Wolfe Medical, London, p 187–224

James D 1994 Maxillofacial injuries in children. In: Williams J Ll (ed) Rowe & Williams' maxillofacial injuries, 2nd edn. Churchill Livingstone, Edinburgh, p 387–403

Judson J A 1990 Management of severe and multiple trauma. In: Oh T E (ed) Intensive care manual, 3rd edn. Butterworths, Sydney, p 422–426

Kamboozia A H, Punnia-Moorthy A 1993. The fate of teeth in mandibular fracture lines: a clinical and radiographic follow-up study. International Journal of Oral and Maxillofacial Surgery 22: 97–101

Kamitani K, Murakamik, Chen W H, Nose M, Matsuki M, Hyo Y, Iizuka T 1989 Clinical study on mandibular condyle fracture. 2: Long-term follow-up study in 48 patients with 66 joints. Nihon Ago Kansetsu Gakkai Zasshi 1: 63–72

Kazanjian V H 1920 Observations on war surgery of the face and jaws. Dental Cosmos 62: 283–294

Koornneef L 1981 Sectional anatomy of the orbit. Aeolus Press, Buren, The Netherlands

Kronn E 1993 The incidence of TMJ dysfunction in patients who have suffered a cervical whiplash injury following a traffic accident. Journal of Orofacial Pain 7: 209–213

Kup W 1978 Permanent damage after frontobasal fractures of the skull: its evaluation according to medical reports. Zentralblatt für Chirurgie 17: 1149–1154

Lance J W, Anthony M 1980 Neck-tongue syndrome on sudden turning of the head. Journal of Neurology, Neurosurgery and Psychiatry 43: 97–101

Le Fort R 1901 Etude expérimentale sur les fractures de la mâchoire supérieure. Revue de Chirurgie 1: 208–227, 361–379, 479–507

Levandoski R R 1993 Mandibular whiplash. Part I: An extension flexion injury of the temporomandibular joint. Functional Orthodontics 10: 26–29, 32–33

Lowell D 1979 External fixation: the current state of the art. Williams & Wilkins, Baltimore

Mackie M J 1986 Deep venous thrombosis and pulmonary embolus. Prescribers' Journal 26: 153–159

Maclennan W D 1952 Consideration of 180 cases of typical fractures of the mandibular condylar process. British Journal of Plastic Surgery 5: 122–126

McSwain N E, Martinez J A, Timberlake G A 1989 Cervical spine trauma: evaluation and acute management. Thieme Medical Publishers, New York

Maimaris C, Barnes M R, Allen M J 1988 Whiplash injury of the neck: a retrospective study. Injury 19: 393–396

Markowitz B L, Manson P N, Sargent L, Van der Kolk C A, Yaremchuk M, Glasman D, Crawley W A 1991 Management of the medial canthal tendon in nasoethmoid orbital fractures: the importance of the central fragment in classification and treatment. Plastic and Reconstructive Surgery 87: 843–853

Murray J A, Maran A G, Mackenzie I J, Raab G 1984 Open v closed reduction of the fractured nose. Archives of Otolaryngology 110: 797–802

Murray J A, Maran A G, Busuttil A, Vaughan G 1986 A pathological classification of nasal fractures. Injury 17: 338–344

Newman P K 1990 Whiplash injury. British Medical Journal 301: 395–396

Norman J E deB 1978 Ankylosis of the temporomandibular joint. Australian Dental Journal 23: 56–66

Norman J E deB 1982 Post-traumatic disorders of the jaw joint. Annals of the Royal College of Surgery in England 64: 29–36

Norman J E deB, Bramley P (eds) 1990 A textbook and colour atlas of the temporomandibular joint: diseases, disorders, surgery. Wolfe Medical, London

Norman J E deB, Painter D M 1980 Hyperplasia of the mandibular condyle: a historical review of important early cases with a presentation and analysis of twelve patients. Journal of Maxillofacial Surgery 8: 161–175

Norman J E deB, Dan N G, Rogers P A 1982 Post-traumatic infra-orbital neuropathy: another entrapment syndrome. Orbit 1: 259–266

Norman J E deB, Stevenson A R L, Painter D M, Sykes D G, Feain L A 1988 Synovial osteochondromatosis of the temporomandibular joint: a historical review with presentation of three cases. Journal of Craniomaxillofacial Surgery 16: 212–220

Norman J E deB, McGurk M 1995 Colour atlas and text of the salivary glands: diseases, disorders and surgery. Mosby Wolfe, London, pp 154–156

Owen-Smith M S 1981 High velocity missile wounds. Edward Arnold, London

Palacios E, Valvassori G E, Shannon M, Reed C F 1990 Magnetic resonance of the temporomandibular joint: clinical considerations, radiography, management. Thieme, New York

Pearce J M S 1989 Whiplash injury – a re-appraisal. Journal of Neurology, Neurosurgery and Psychiatry 52: 1329–1331

Pressman B D, Shellcock F G, Schames J, Schames M 1992 MR imaging of temporomandibular joint abnormalities associated with cervical hyperextension/hyperflexion (whiplash) injuries. Journal of Magnetic Resonance Imaging 2: 569–574

Robinson P 1994 Raw nerves. British Journal of Oral and Maxillofacial Surgery 32: 69–70

Robinson P P, Smith K G, Johnson F P, Coppins D A 1992 Equipment and methods for simple sensory testing. British Journal of Oral and Maxillofacial Surgery 30: 387–389

Rowe N L, Williams J Ll 1994 Fractures of the zygomatic complex and orbit. In: Williams J Ll (ed) Rowe & Williams' maxillofacial injuries, 2nd edn. Churchill Livingstone, Edinburgh, p 581–584

Schneider K, Zernicke R F, Clark G 1989 Modeling of jaw-head-neck dynamics during whiplash. Journal of Dental Research 68: 1360–1365

Sherman R T, Parrish R A 1963 Management of shotgun injuries: a review of 152 cases. Journal of Trauma 3: 76–86

Shore N A, Schaefer M G, Hoppenfeld S 1979 Iatrogenic TMJ difficulty: cervical traction may be the etiology. Journal of Prosthetic Dentistry 41: 541–542

Silvennoinen U, Iizuka T, Lindqvist C, Oikarinen K 1992 Different patterns of condylar fractures: an analysis of 382 patients in a 3-year period. Journal of Oral and Maxillofacial Surgery 50: 1032–1037

Stylogianni L, Arsenopoulos A, Patrikiou A 1991 Fractures of the facial skeleton in children. British Journal of Oral and Maxillofacial Surgery 29: 9–11

Thoren H, Iizuka T, Hallikainen D, Lindqvist C 1992 Different patterns of mandibular fractures in children: an analysis of 220 fractures in 157 patients. Journal of Craniomaxillofacial Surgery 20: 292–296

Toller P A 1974 Temporomandibular arthropathy. Proceedings of the Royal Society of Medicine 67: 153–159

Torfs P, Lenssen H 1989 Temporomandibular joint injuries: disability evaluation according to quantitative and qualitative aspects. Acta Stomatologica Belgica 86: 37–47

Vincent-Townend J R L, Shepherd J P 1994 Appendix: the epidemiology of maxillofacial trauma. In: Williams J Ll (ed) Rowe & Williams' maxillofacial injuries, 2nd edn. Churchill Livingstone, Edinburgh, p 1063

Wadsworth T G 1990 The elbow. In: Foy M A, Fagg P S (eds) Medicolegal reporting in orthopaedic trauma. Churchill Livingstone, Edinburgh, p 107–136

Weinberg S, Lapointe H 1987 Cervical extension-flexion injury (whiplash) and internal derangement of the temporomandibular joint. Journal of Oral and Maxillofacial Surgery 45: 653–656

Westaby S 1989 Trauma: pathogenesis and treatment. Heinemann Medical Books, London

Wolff E 1968 Eugene Wolff's anatomy of the eye and orbit, including the central connections, development, and comparative anatomy of the visual apparatus, 6th edn. H K Lewis, London

Wolff H G 1963 Headache and other head pains. Oxford University Press, New York, p 618–621

5. Dental traumatic injuries

Alastair R. L. Stevenson

Damage to the teeth and their supporting structures can range from the trivial requiring minimal treatment, to the devastating which commands a large financial, biological and psychological cost. The prognosis for rehabilitation is dependent on many factors, most particularly the nature of the injury, its severity and the patient's age. It is therefore appropriate initially to classify the type of injuries which can be sustained and then relate them to rehabilitation and prognosis.

It is also important when formulating an injury classification to be clear on the anatomical structure of the dento-alveolar complex. The clinical crown of an erupted tooth is completely covered by enamel while the root surface is covered with cementum. The body of the tooth is composed of dentine and contains a central chamber containing neurovascular tissue known as the pulp. The teeth are housed in sockets within the alveolar bone of both the maxilla and the mandible and attached by a complicated soft tissue structure collectively known as the periodontal tissues. The alveolar bone is covered and protected by oral mucosa which the tooth penetrates at the gingival margin.

CLASSIFICATION

The first successful attempt to classify dental injuries was made by Ellis & Daury (1970). This classification was expanded by the World Health Organisation (1978) and again more recently by Andreasen & Andreasen (1994).

Currently, dental injuries classification is divided into four categories: injuries to the hard dental tissues and the pulp; injuries to the periodontal tissues; injuries to the supporting bone; and injuries to the gingiva and oral mucosa.

INJURIES TO HARD DENTAL TISSUES AND PULP (FIG. 5.1)

A. Enamel infraction: an enamel crack without loss of tooth structure
B. Enamel fracture: an enamel fracture with loss of tooth structure confined to the enamel

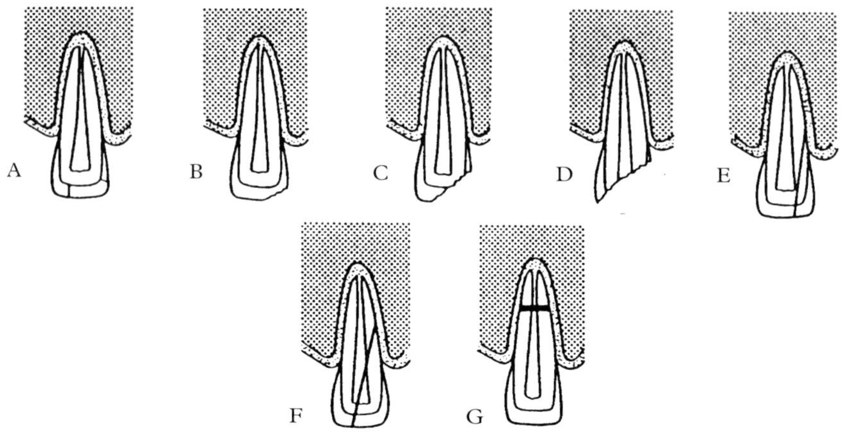

Fig. 5.1 Injuries to hard dental tissues and pulp (Sowray 1994).

C. Enamel-dentine fracture: a fracture involving the loss of both enamel and dentine structure without pulpal involvement
D. Complicated crown fracture: a fracture involving enamel, dentine and pulp tissue
E. Uncomplicated crown-root fracture: a fracture involving enamel, dentine and cementum without pulpal involvement
F. Complicated crown-root fracture: a fracture involving enamel, dentine and cementum with pulpal involvement
G. Root fracture: a fracture involving dentine, cementum and the pulp.

INJURIES TO PERIODONTAL TISSUES (FIG. 5.2)

A. Concussion: an injury to the periodontal tissues which elicits pain on percussion but without tooth displacement or loosening
B. Subluxation: an injury to the periodontal tissues with loosening of the tooth but without displacement
C. Extrusive luxation: a partial dislocation of the tooth out of its socket
D. Lateral luxation: a partial lateral dislocation of the tooth, usually associated with an alveolar bone fracture

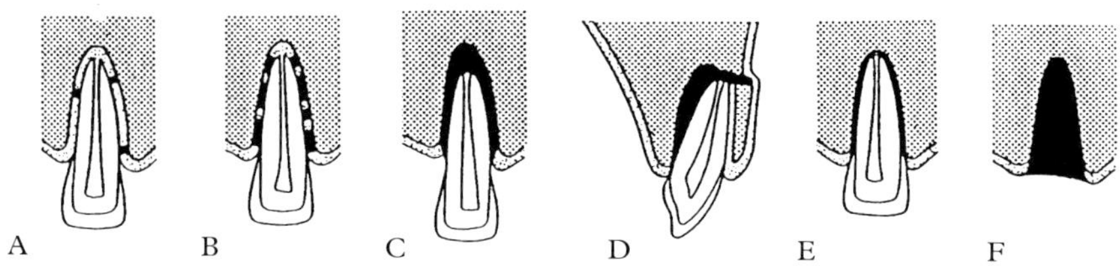

Fig. 5.2 Injuries to periodontal tissues (Sowray 1994).

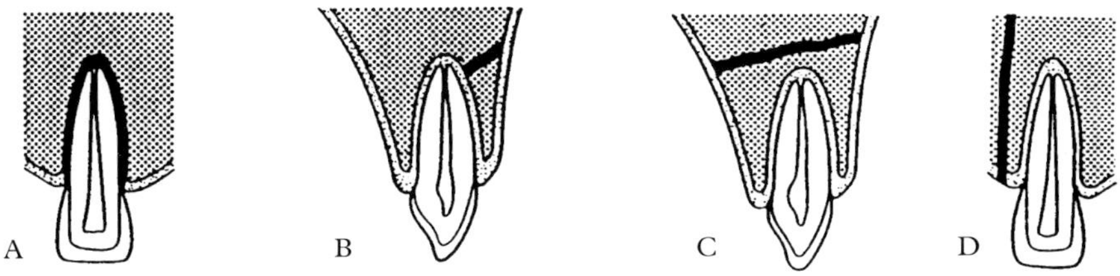

Fig. 5.3 Injuries to supporting bone (Sowray 1994).

E. Intrusive luxation: an impaction of the tooth into the alveolar bone
F. Avulsion: a total dislocation of the tooth from its socket.

INJURIES TO SUPPORTING BONE (FIG. 5.3)

A. Comminution of the socket wall: a crushing or compression of the alveolar bone, usually in association with an intrusive or lateral luxation injury
B. Fracture of the socket wall: a fracture confined to the bone surrounding the socket
C. Fracture of the alveolar process: a fracture involving the tooth-bearing portion of the jaw
D. Fracture of the mandible or maxilla: a fracture involving the full thickness of the jaw.

INJURIES TO GINGIVA AND ORAL MUCOSA

A. Laceration: a wound resulting from a tear or penetration with a sharp object
B. Contusion: a wound from a blunt object which does not create a mucosal breach
C. Abrasion: a raw bleeding surface produced by a rubbing or scraping of the mucosa.

Incidence and aetiology

For children the most common causes of injury are falls, particularly between the ages of 2 and 4 and 8 and 10, and especially while using items such as bicycles, skateboards or roller blades. Contact sports continue to account for many injuries but the promotion and acceptance of mouthguards has ameliorated this hazard to some degree.

Males are twice as prone to traumatic dental injuries as females, with up to 33% of all males sustaining some damage to their permanent teeth, compared to 19% of females (Andreasen & Andreasen 1994). This is most particularly due to their greater involvement in contact sports, motor vehicle accidents and physical assaults. The most commonly traumatised region is the anterior maxilla, particularly the central incisors.

Table 5.1 Injured tissue and associated treatment options

	DENTAL							PERIODONTAL						BONE				MUCOSA		
	A	B	C	D	E	F	G	A	B	C	D	E	F	A	B	C	D	A	B	C
INITIAL TREATMENT																				
Conservative measures	1	1						1	1			1							1	1
Suturing																		1		
Re-implantation										1	1		1							
Splinting							1		(2)	2	2		2	1	1	1	1			
Adhesive restorations		2	1	2	2															
Pulp capping				(1)	1															
Endodontics	(2)	(4)	(3)	3	(5)	1	(2)			(3)	(3)	(3)	3							
Crowns+/– post and core		(3)	(2)	(4)	(4)	3														
Orthodontics					(3)	2						(2)								
POTENTIAL SEQUELAE																				
Pulp necrosis	L	L	M	–	M	–	H	L	M	H	H	H	–	H*	H*	M*	M*	–	–	–
Pulp obliteration	L	L	L	–	M	–	H	L	M	H	H	H	–	M*	M*	M*	M*	–	–	–
Root resorption	L	L	L	L	L	H	H	L	M	M	M	H	H	M*	M*	M*	L*	–	–	–
Extraction	L	L	L	L	L	H	M	L	L	M	M	H	H	M*	M*	M*	M*	–	–	–

( ) Indicates treatment which may be required in the future
* Refers to tooth in fracture line
Numbers indicate treatment sequence

L Low (<5%)
M Medium (5–20%)
H High (>20%)

Appendix to Table 5.1

Definitions of treatment options

- **Conservative measures**
  These include smoothing sharp edges, mouthguards, soft diet, observation and review.
- **Suturing**
  Closing a wound with either resorbable (intra-oral) or non-resorbable (extra-oral) sutures.
- **Re-implantation**
  Relocation or replacement into the original socket of a displaced or avulsed tooth within 3 hours, assuming the periodontal tissues on the tooth surface have been protected from trauma and dehydration.
- **Splinting**
  The support of mobile teeth with either a rigid or semi-rigid appliance, or the immobilisation of bone fragments either indirectly using intra-maxillary fixation or directly via bone plates.
- **Adhesive restorations**
  The bonding of tooth-coloured filling materials to enamel or dentine with minimal tooth preparation.
- **Pulp capping**
  The placement of a sedative dressing over an exposed pulp to protect it from contamination and allow formation of a calcific barrier of secondary dentine.
- **Endodontics**
  The placement of a root canal filling to obliterate the pulp chamber following the death or irreversible contamination of the pulp tissue.
- **Crowns +/− post and core**
  The reduction of the clinical crown to allow the fitting of a porcelain or porcelain/metal crown over the residual tooth substance. The post placed in the prepared root canal adds retention to the restoration.
- **Orthodontics**
  In traumatic injuries this involves the movement of neighbouring teeth into the space created by the loss of a tooth. Alternately, it can refer to the extrusion of a root fragment from which the crown has been lost (Fig. 5.1 G) or of a whole tooth which has been intruded into the bone (Fig. 5.2 E).

Definitions of treatment sequelae

- **Pulp necrosis**
  The death of the pulp tissue, requiring its removal and the completion of endodontic therapy.
- **Pulp obliteration**
  The slow occlusion of the pulp chamber with secondary dentine laid down by the damaged pulp tissue, which often subsequently dies.
- **Root resorption**
  The loss of tooth tissue either from within the pulp (internal resorption) or of the root surface (external resorption). It is most often first identified on radiograph as it is symptomless. It can be due either to the action of toxins from the necrotic pulp (inflammatory resorption), or to the action of osteoclasts from the socket wall acting on the root surface where it has been denuded of its periodontal tissues (replacement resorption). It is a common sequela of avulsed or luxated teeth when the periodontal tissues have been grossly disrupted. Inevitably it leads to the loss of the tooth within about 5 years.
- **Extraction**
  The removal of a tooth or tooth remnant.

Table 5.2 Treatment options following the loss of a tooth

Treatment	Service	Cost	Restrictions
Auto-transplant	Lifelong	Low	Only applicable in developing dentitions
Removable denture	5–10 years	Low	Poor patient acceptance
Adhesive bridge	5 years?	Medium	Requires sound neighbouring teeth without large restorations
Conventional bridge	15 years+	High	Mutilation of neighbouring teeth
Implant supported crown	Lifelong? (crown 15 years+)	High	Not suitable until completion of skeletal growth

Appendix to Table 5.2

Definitions of treatment options following the loss of a tooth

Auto-transplant
The surgical transfer of a partially developed tooth into the socket or a prepared space within the edentulous ridge. The vitality of the pulp tissue is maintained and the root and periodontal tissues develop normally. The crown usually requires some aesthetic contouring to mimic the missing tooth.

Removable denture
A missing tooth or teeth can be replaced using an acrylic or porcelain tooth attached to a plastic or metal base. It is retained by clips around the remaining teeth and can be removed to clean.

Adhesive bridge
The bonding to neighbouring teeth of a cast-metal framework which supports a replacement tooth. It cannot be removed.

Conventional bridge
The reduction of the crowns of teeth on either side of an edentulous space to allow the attachment of a metal and porcelain framework which replaces the missing tooth. It is cemented to the teeth and cannot be removed.

Implant supported crown
The surgical placement of a metal (usually titanium) implant which is subsequently exposed into the mouth after a healing period of between 3 and 6 months. The integrated implant can then be used to support a crown (or bridge) directly, without attachment to or preparation of the neighbouring teeth.

Table 5.3 Costs of treatment

	DENTAL							PERIODONTAL						BONE				MUCOSA		
	A	B	C	D	E	F	G	A	B	C	D	E	F	A	B	C	D	A	B	C
COSTS: Initial Treatment																				
Financial	L	L	L	M	H	H	M	L	L	M	M	H	H	L	L	L	L	L	L	L
Biological	L	L	L	M	M	H	M	L	L	M	M	H	H	L	L	M	M	L	L	L
Psychological	L	L	L	M	H	H	M	L	L	M	M	H	H	L	L	M	M	L	L	L
POTENTIAL COSTS: Long-term																				
Financial	L	M	M	H	H	H	M	L	M	H	H	H	H	M	M	M	L	L	L	L
Biological	L	L	L	M	M	M	M	L	L	M	M	M	M	L	L	M	M	L	L	L
Psychological	L	L	L	M	M	M	M	L	L	M	M	M	M	L	L	M	M	L	L	L

L Low; M Medium ; H High

Appendix to Table 5.3

Treatment options following the traumatic loss of a tooth

Issues considered when arriving at an estimate of:

Financial cost
— Cumulative cost of total treatment plan
— Ongoing maintenance costs of definitive treatment.

Biological cost
— Patient's age
— Prognosis of definitive treatment
— Intensity of maintenance required
— Potential complications
— Degree of residual disability.

Psychological cost
— Time spent under treatment in dental environment
— Length of time taken to complete definitive treatment
— Distress caused by the initial trauma
— Any compromise in functional and/or aesthetic rehabilitation.

The incidence and severity of particular injuries seem to vary greatly between different population groups and countries (Andreasen & Andreasen 1994). However, damage to the crowns of permanent teeth (Fig. 5.1 Injuries A,B,C and D) and associated periodontal injuries (Fig. 5.2 Injuries A,B,C,D and E) are the most common. In contrast root fractures (Fig. 5.1 Injuries E,F and G) and avulsions (Fig. 5.2 Injury F) are rare (Andreasen & Andreasen 1994).

Treatment options

It is evident from the aetiology and incidence of traumatic dental injuries that damage is often sustained by the permanent dentition soon after its establishment in the dental arch between the ages of 6 and 14. Uncompromised, this dentition would be functional and aesthetic for the remainder of the patient's life and therefore any discussion of treatment must encompass the full 60 to 70 years of life expectancy as well as the immediate control of symptoms and the provision of initial restorations. Experience also indicates that more severe injuries require a greater range and sophistication of procedures to re-establish a functional and aesthetic dentition and to maintain rehabilitation in the long-term. This allows correlation of treatment options with the injury classification and ultimately prognosis.

Table 5.1 tabulates treatment options, the injuries to which they apply and the potential sequence of treatment which may be required over time. This is supplemented by a list of potential long-term complications and an assessment of the potential for the occurrence of these complications.

Table 5.2 details treatment options available following the loss of a tooth, either immediately following trauma or at a later stage if treatment fails. Potential long-term service of each option, its financial cost and any restrictions to its application are also compared.

Table 5.3 considers the financial, biological and psychological costs arising from the original injuries and any long-term sequelae. Various factors relevant to this assessment of costs are detailed in the adjoining list.

Prognosis

Table 5.4 quantifies the range of success rates relevant to each treatment option outlined in the previous text and tables. It is immediately evident that more minor injuries require less treatment and have a far more favourable long-term prognosis. As treatment becomes more extensive and complex the possibility that further treatment and maintenance will be required long-term increases, with a correspondingly greater incidence of complications. Consideration must also be given to those who are exposed to repeated trauma concentrated at the same site, such as occurs

Table 5.4 Treatment options success rates

Damaged tooth and associated structures	
Conservative measures	Resolution of symptoms should be complete within 2 weeks, with no long-term consequences
Suturing	Intra-oral healing is complete within 2 weeks, usually without scarring
Re-implantation	51–89% of teeth survive, endodontics is mandatory for all but teeth with unformed roots, and resorption rates are high*, as is the possibility of ankylosis (fusion of the tooth to the bone)
Splinting	Applied for between 2 weeks (subluxation injury) and 12 weeks (root fractures), pulp necrosis requiring endodontics is common
Adhesive restorations	92% successful at 3 years* 65% successful at 5 years* 40% successful at 10 years*
Pulp capping	71%–88% successful*
Endodontics	79%–95% successful*
Following loss of a damaged tooth	
Auto-transplant	98% successful at 5 years* 87% successful at 10 years*
Removable dentures	48% successful at 5 years† 35% successful at 10 years†
Adhesive bridges	74% successful at 4 years*
Conventional crowns and bridges	97% successful at 5 years* 90% successful at 10 years* 74% successful at 15 years*
Implant supported crowns and bridges	95% successful at 5 years*

* Andreasen & Andreasen 1994; †Wetherell and Smales 1980

in contact sport or in such conditions as uncontrolled epilepsy. In such cases it is prudent to delay definitive treatment until the threat is past. This is because further damage to a fully restored and therefore compromised dentition inevitably creates a substantially more complex rehabilitation problem.

It is difficult on a cost/benefit analysis to compare directly different treatments, as the nature of the injury dictates what is appropriate or contra-indicated. However, as new information becomes available, there is a constant reappraisal of treatment outcomes. For example, extensive research has been directed into the process of root resorption following re-implantation of an avulsed tooth (Bakland 1992). Attempts to counter this phenomenon, extending from patient education on the immediate care of an avulsed tooth to the benefits of physiological splinting and earlier endodontics have not improved the disappointing long-term prognosis for such a tooth. Conversely, the use of dental implants to rehabilitate an edentulous space has become accepted as a reliable method of achieving a good functional and aesthetic result without many of the disadvantages inherent in the more traditional treatments. The future should see less reluctance of the clinician to sacrifice a tooth which requires extensive and costly restorative work with poor long-term prognosis, as it is now apparent that judiciously placed dental implants allow definitive dental rehabilitation to be completed in a shorter time with predictable results, thus providing a long-term saving in costs.

REFERENCES

Andreasen J O, Andreasen F M 1994 Textbook and colour atlas of traumatic injuries to the teeth, 3rd edn. Munksgaard, Copenhagen

Bakland L F 1992 Root resorption. Dental Clinics of North America 36: 491–507

Ellis R G, Daury K W 1970 The classification and treatment of injuries to the teeth of children, 5th edn. Year Book Medical Publishers, Chicago

Sowray J H 1994 Localised injuries of the teeth and alveolar process. In: Williams J Ll (ed) Rowe and Williams' maxillofacial injuries, 2nd edn. Volumes I and II. Churchill Livingstone, Edinburgh, pp 217–219

Wetherell J D, Smales R J 1980 Partial denture failures: a long-term clinical survey. Journal of Dentistry 8: 333–340

World Health Organisation 1978 Application of the international classification of diseases and stomatology, IDC-DA 2nd edn. WHO, Geneva

6. Head and neck injuries

A. J. Curran C. V. I. Timon

Twenty years ago the commonest causes of injury to the head and neck region were road traffic accidents, occupational and sports injuries. Over the past two decades domestic and interpersonal violence have assumed a much greater role as a cause of these types of injuries according to Holt (1992). The severity and type of injury to the head and neck depends on the mechanism and momentum of the trauma. The aim of treatment is to restore form and function and to avoid and minimise morbidity of surgical intervention. Due to the important sensory, neural, and vascular structures in this region trauma to the head and neck can produce a range of symptoms which interfere with the individual's daily activities, compromising their quality of life and ability to communicate.

EXTERNAL EAR

Injuries to the external ear are common, and early and appropriate intervention is critical to avoid disfigurement. The skin of the lateral surface of the pinna is tightly adherent to the underlying elastic fibrocartilage that moulds the ear. Due to its complex surface anatomy, injuries usually cause most problems from a cosmetic viewpoint rather than a functional one. Typically, injuries to the external ear occur in active people or those involved in sports such as rugby, boxing and cycling.

Haematoma

Blunt trauma to the ear may result in a haematoma. The force of the injury separates the perichondrium from the cartilage and blood fills the space between the two interfaces. The immediate importance of this results from the fact that the cartilage depends on the perichondrium for blood supply. Cartilage necrosis and infection are likely sequelae if the ear is left untreated. Eventually the untreated haematoma is replaced by fibrosis and possibly new cartilage, resulting in significant cosmetic deformity – 'cauliflower ear'.

Treatment options

The aim of treatment is speedy evacuation of the blood and maintenance of opposition between the cartilage and skin. The usual initial management is aspiration and pressure dressing in an out-patient setting. Liston (1987) has proposed treating the haematoma by repeated aspiration and pressure dressings. This may be tried as a simple out-patient procedure initially but commonly, although effective, it may be difficult to keep the dressings in place in active individuals (Templer & Renner 1990). A more definite treatment is open evacuation under aseptic technique via an incision between the helix and the antihelix, or at the base of the antihelix as described by Schuller et al (1989). This can be performed under local or general anaesthesia. The haematoma is then evacuated and a dental roll is placed over the soft tissue of the pinna and held in place using through and through sutures. Occasionally two rolls are necessary and a topical antibiotic is then applied to the wound. A light bulky dressing consisting of cotton wool soaked in acroflavin may then be applied to the crevices of the pinna. This form of treatment (Schuller et al 1989) is advantageous as it allows the patient to remain active. Occasionally the patient is seen several days after the injury when the clot has organised. Using a similiar incision to that described above the underlying material is removed by curettage. Patients should also be advised prior to drainage that the pinna will not return completely to its previous shape and that some alteration in its appearance will occur despite speedy treatment. People involved in high risk activities and sports should be advised to wear protective head gear to prevent re-occurrence.

Complications

Complications of surgical treatment include re-accumulation of the haematoma, infection, cartilage proliferation or necrosis and the 'cauliflower deformity'. The prognosis for a successful outcome is dependent on early and appropriate treatment.

Lacerations

Lacerations of the pinna vary from those of minor significance to complete amputation. Those with exposed cartilage introduce the possibility of infection. Areas where perichondrium is separated from cartilage may result in scarring and minor asymmetry with the opposite ear, resulting in noticeable cosmetic deformity.

Treatment options

Where possible, photographs should be taken of the initial injury. Simple lacerations are treated as any other facial laceration by careful cleansing and accurate approximation. It is important to remove all dirt from the wounds to prevent later engraining and an unacceptable cosmetic appearance. Some of those lacerations with cartilage disruption may be sutured by skin to skin approximation. Lacerations with more complex disruption of cartilage and skin are difficult to repair and the landmarks of the ear serve as a guide for proper re-approximation of structures. Mladick (1978) believes that cartilage sutures should be avoided, or if necessary, should be as fine as possible. The skin on the anterior and posterior surfaces of the helix can be closed with fine interrupted absorbable sutures. Meticulous care is required to match all fragments and prevent loss of tissue.

Due to the pinna's excellent blood supply a near total avulsion may be viable on a small pedicle. The separated tissues should be accurately approximated and sutures placed loosely. The ear must then be carefully assessed for venous congestion. Stasis may be relieved by stab incisions through the skin. Medical leeches have been employed to restore venous flow and to relieve congested tissue through release of vasodilatators and anti-coagulants, but are not routinely used.

The treatment of total amputation is controversial. Some authors (Bernstein & Nelson, 1982, Clemens & Connelly 1973) advocate re-attachment as a composite graft using heparin and low molecular weight dextrans to reduce congestion. Mladick (1978) describes dermabrading the amputated pinna, suturing it to the remaining ear stump and then burying it in a post-auricular pocket for 2 weeks. Juri et al (1987) have described successful repair using microvascular anastomosis. The end result of re-attachment is often a scarred and deformed pinna despite a number of case reports giving the impression that the procedure is simple and usually successful. When large losses of the helix have occurred the underlying cartilage may be salvaged by coverage with a local flap.

Complications

Due to the good blood supply, infection is uncommon. Increasing pain, redness and tenderness are the typical features of chondritis. The end result of delayed treatment will be a loss of cartilage and a deformed pinna. *Pseudomonas aeruginosa* and *Staphylococcus aureus* are the usual responsible pathogens. To avoid serious deformity treatment must be prompt with removal of pus and necrotic cartilage and treatment with intravenous antibiotics.

External auditory canal

Injuries to the external auditory meatus may result in long term stenosis and associated hearing loss particularly where the laceration traverses the cartilage or bony cartilaginous junction. The resulting stenosis causes wax impaction and occasionally keratosis obturans. In this latter condition a keratin plug accumulates, causing a conductive hearing loss and with time the epithelial mass may cause bony erosion and tympanic membrane perforation. Prolonged stenting may be required to prevent stenosis. Surgical removal of adhesions or fibrous bands is necessary if the ear develops this tendency to accumulate keratin.

MIDDLE/INNER EAR

The short- and long-term sequelae of significant injury to the middle and inner ear are hearing loss, vertigo, imbalance, tinnitus and, less likely, facial nerve paralysis. Injury to the middle ear that occurs through the external auditory meatus usually results in tympanic membrane perforation and disruption of the ossicles. Commonly domestic violence such as a blow from an open hand to the side of the head causes a compression effect sufficient to rupture the tympanic membrane. Trauma to the temporal bone may impair the individual's ability to perform daily functions or limit the ability to communicate. This may then result in loss of employment and have an effect on the person's socio-economic status.

Hearing loss

An audiogram should be performed to assess injury to the ossicles and inner ear. This should be performed as soon as possible. A conductive hearing loss is usually due to a tear in the tympanic membrane and blood in the middle ear. A hearing loss of >40 dB suggests an ossicular chain dissociation. Sensorineural loss indicates cochlear or retrocochlear damage.

Treatment options

Considerable diversity exists as to the best form of treatment of tympanic membrane perforations. Some authors (Mawson & Ludman 1979, Kerr & Smyth 1987) advocate expectant observation exclusively, while others (Merwin & Bolies 1980, Camnitz & Bost 1985) recommend immediate surgical repair. In a comprehensive review of more than 500 texts covering over a century's literature, Kristensen (1992) found the spontaneous healing rate was 78.7% in 760 cases of traumatic tympanic membrane perforations diagnosed within 14 days of injury. As most traumatic tympanic membrane perforations heal spontaneously, authors adopt a conservative approach to their management. The healing process may take 3–6 months to complete and during this period the patient must keep the ear completely waterproofed as well as free from infection.

Many different techniques have been suggested to improve healing of the damaged tympanic membrane. Bellucci (1983) describes removal of blood clot around the perforation and supporting the torn edge of the drum with gelfoam. He also describes cautery to the damaged edges of the perforation to activate the healing process. In any case the drum may be repaired at a later stage by myringoplasty. This is usually delayed until at least 6 months following the injury. Kinney (1992) advocates examination of the ear and the removal of all blood clots. He suggests teasing folded portions of the ruptured drum back into position. Generally it is advisable not to treat dry perforations with antibiotic drops as they may delay the healing process. It is best to withhold these agents for cases with definite infection.

Injury to the ossicles is suggested by a large air/bone gap on audiometry which is not in keeping with a simple tympanic membrane perforation. The injuries vary in degree and type and there is a corresponding range of treatment options depending on the severity of damage. The most frequently injured ossicle is the incus, typically dislocated at the incudostapedial joint (Hough 1970). Less commonly, stapes footplate dislocation, total dislocation of the incus, dislocation of the malleus, fixation of the malleus head and total dislocation of the ossicular chain may occur. Surgery to correct an ossicular disruption is best delayed until the mucosa of the middle ear has healed. When the stapes has been preserved the chances of re-establishing the ossicular chain are much greater. Remodelling the ossicular chain may be performed using the patient's own ossicle or by a form of biocompatible prosthesis. Hough describes successful surgical treatment of most cases of persistent conductive hearing loss, restoring speech reception threshold to 90% in his patients. In many cases hearing may be subsequently improved by ossiculoplasty.

Prognosis

Conductive hearing loss due to haemotympanum resolves without any specific treatment, usually over a 6-week period. The persistence of a conductive hearing loss suggests a persistent tympanic membrane perforation or an ossicular disruption. Partial sensorineural hearing loss, especially in the high tones, may improve over a period of months. Complete sensorineural hearing loss is usually due to cochlear nerve disruption or injury to the cochlea or membranous labyrinth, and is permanent.

Complications

Attempts at surgical repair of the tympanic membrane may fail and often, despite initial success, the grafted drum may break down at a later date. Whenever synthetic material such as those used to make ossicular prostheses, e.g. porous polyethylene sponge, are introduced into the middle ear there is a tendency for erosion of the tympanic membrane as well as extrusion of the prosthesis from the middle ear. Following myringoplasty and ossiculoplasty the principal risks are loss of hearing, balance, facial nerve function and the development of tinnitus. While these are rare, ideally the operating surgeon should indicate the percentage risks and success in their hands. Realistically the chances of improving hearing following ossicular disruption are approximately 50%. For patients who are not keen on surgery a hearing aid may be of benefit.

FACIAL NERVE PARALYSIS

A facial nerve paralysis is a serious and debilitating deformity. While causing severe psychological sequelae it also interferes with eye function, mastication and emotional response. Although the general principles of management of facial nerve paralysis remain similar, the details of treatment differ depending on the location of the injury. Despite advances in surgical technique the optimal method of treatment of this injury remains controversial. A severely damaged nerve rarely regains full function. Injuries may be classified as immediate or delayed onset and treatment is best discussed by separating extracranial from intratemporal injury. The mechanism of injury may be penetrating or blunt.

Intratemporal injury

Treatment options

Sunderland (1978) proposed a classification system of the degree of injury which is useful when considering treatment. First degree or conduction block occurs when the axons and endoneurial tubes are compressed and intact. The Schwann sheath, myelin layer and cell bodies are not damaged in this type of injury. Increasing levels of injury up to Grade V corresponding to total nerve disruption may occur. In patients with Grades I and II spontaneous recovery is to be expected and therefore no surgical intervention is usually necessary. Increasing levels of neural injury following blunt trauma to the temporal bone are often treated expectantly. Electroneurography is useful when uncertainty exists as to whether the paralysis is delayed or immediate in onset. It is only valid after 4 days of an acute injury. When degeneration exceeds 90% and there is an absence of voluntary motor potentials on electromyography, exploration may be required. Penetrating injuries typically result from gunshot or stab wounds and require exploration. The nerve may be completely severed, contused or crushed. In a series by Duncan et al (1986), facial paralysis occurred in 60% of gunshot injuries to the temporal bone and in most the paralysis was of immediate onset. Primary re-anastomosis is rarely possible and frequently interpositional grafts are necessary and give the best results. The fallopian canal may be used as a stent to lay the grafted nerve in. A contused nerve should be decompressed and any penetrating bony spicules removed. A transmastoid approach is the treatment of choice if the patient has residual hearing (Coker 1991). The translabyrinthine approach is an alternative if no serviceable hearing exists. The aim of these procedures is to decompress the nerve in its bony canal.

Extracranial injury

Treatment options

The optimum time of repair when the nerve is known to be transected is the subject of much debate. Some authors (Crumley & Scott 1993, Kreutzberg & Tetzlaff 1984) advocate early repair within 72 hours, claiming that there is less likelihood that the nerve ends will need resection and identification during this time will be easier. Ducker (1969) and McQuarrie & Graftstein (1973) prefer delayed repair (3–5 weeks). At this stage axonal sprouting is at its maximum and perineurium thicker and capable of holding sutures. In general most surgeons presently advocate early repair.

Injury as a result of facial lacerations may be repaired through a parotid approach once the patient's general condition permits. Injuries to the main trunk of the facial nerve or to the cervicofacial or temporozygomatic branches should be repaired by primary end-to-end anastomosis. In the event of a contaminated field the severed ends of the nerve should be identified and tagged. The wound can then be dressed with a bacteriocidal agent and delayed repair performed once the area is clean. Even injury to the smaller distal branches of the nerve may respond better to a neural microscopic repair rather than if a spontaneous recovery is allowed to run its course. It is critical that the anastomosis is not under any tension as this will impair healing. Monofilament 9/0 or 10/0 nylon or prolene to repair the epineurium using microscopic or loupe magnification remains the gold standard with which other techniques must be compared.

In a recent review by Terris & Fee (1993), the literature proposing other forms of nerve repair such as tissue adhesives, laser neurorrhaphy and tubulization were critically assessed. At present fibrin glue must be considered an inferior method for suturing especially considering the risk of acquired immunodeficiency syndrome and hepatitis from this material. Laser repair results in a thermal burn and avoids the disadvantages of a foreign body reaction. However, the high risk of dehiscence outweighs the benefit of the procedure. Trophic factors administered exogenously have not been demonstrated to improve repair and tubulization with non-absorbable conduits have no role clinically.

It is important that all patients with facial paralysis have appropriate eye care and an early ophthalmological consultation. Virtually all patients with a facial paralysis can be managed with eye moisturisers, lubricants or eye patches during the first 4–8 weeks of the injury. The aim of treatment is to preserve vision and relieve corneal discomfort initially and later to improve cosmesis. Management of the affected eye in patients who have persistent paralysis has been dramatically improved in the past decade. Previously, partial or complete tarsorrhaphy was the primary treatment to prevent corneal ulceration or exposure keratitis. In the late 1960s gold was introduced as an eyelid loading device and over the past decade gold weight implantation in the upper eyelid and surgery to tighten the lower lid have become routine procedures for restoration of function and cosmesis of the paralysed eyelids.

When the penetrating injury occurs near to the anterior margin of the masseter muscle a concomitant injury to the parotid duct should be suspected. Ductal lacerations are commonly associated with injuries to the buccal branch of the facial nerve as the two travel adjacent to each other. Ductal injuries can be managed by repair with fine sutures over a stent tube which is left in place for 2 weeks. Adkins & Osguthorpe (1991) recommend repair with 6/0 nylon suture over a polyethylene tube secured to the buccal mucosa. Relocating the duct into the oral cavity has been described although is rarely necessary.

An interposition graft should be considered in cases where nerve loss is more extensive. The sural, greater auricular and lateral cutaneous nerves of the thigh may be used. In cases such as gunshot wounds, end-to-end anastomosis and interposition grafts may be precluded due to extensive soft tissue loss. Static (facial suspension) and dynamic (muscle slings) may then be required for rehabilitation.

Prognosis

In general, patients with delayed onset paralysis or incomplete paralysis have a better prognosis. Once the facial nerve has been completely severed it is rare for complete recovery to occur. O'Connell & Robin (1991) have emphasised that once the nerve axon sheath has been disrupted recovery cannot be complete and some degree of synkinesis or altered facial function can be expected. The most important prognostic factors for injury to the intratemporal portion of the facial nerve are the degree of paralysis and the speed of onset. Patients with total paralysis of immediate onset have a poorer prognosis. Approximately 25% of patients suffering a temporal bone fracture have facial paralysis and the majority recover completely or partially without any treatment. In general a partial facial palsy requires no surgical treatment and is treated expectantly (Kinney 1992). As the incidence of longitudinal fractures is much greater than transverse fractures, the former is more frequently associated with paralysis.

When considering extratemporal injury it is generally agreed that primary repair will always yield a superior result compared to other substitution techniques. According to Terris & Fee (1993) it appears the earlier the nerve is repaired the greater the chance of regeneration. There is no advantage to waiting 3 weeks to perform neurorrhaphy as McCabe (1973) suggested.

A classification system proposed by House & Brackmann (1985) is widely used for reporting results of recovery from facial paralysis. This is an internationally accepted system which correlates well with the pathological injury to the nerve. Patients who are undergoing facial nerve exploration must be advised pre-operatively that the length of time before any expected return of facial function may vary a great deal. An uninterrupted nerve will regenerate at approximately 1 mm per day or 1 inch per month. Kinney (1986), has shown that the rate of regeneration following primary re-anastomosis or grafting cannot be predicted. It may take 12–18 months before any return of facial function occurs following primary repair.

Vertigo

Vertigo and imbalance are very common after head injury. In the majority of cases the cause of the imbalance is postconcussional. If the injury is severe the round or oval windows and occasionally the intralabyrinthine membranes may rupture resulting in sudden loss of hearing, vertigo and tinnitus. Postconcussional syndrome is typically associated with unsteadiness related to posture, and concomitant headaches. Disturbance of balance may be caused by benign positional paroxysmal vertigo (BPPV) which is characterised by alteration in balance associated with fatigable rotatory nystagmus which is always precipitated by head movement. Injury to the vestibular aqueduct may result in a secondary endolymphatic hydrops and a Menières syndrome.

Treatment options

Severe vertigo following trauma is initially treated conservatively with bedrest. Labyrinthine sedatives are beneficial in the immediate period after a head injury when severe vertigo is incapacitating. The patient must limit physical activity and avoid coughing or manoeuvres that will raise intracranial pressure.

Persisting vertigo associated with a fluctuating sensorineural hearing loss raises the possibility of a perilymph leak most frequently as a result of oval window damage. Surgical intervention via an exploratory tympanotomy is warranted if symptoms fail to resolve after 6 months following the trauma. The damaged area may be grafted with fascia or perichondrium once the middle ear has been exposed via a tympanomeatal flap. Gacek (1974) has described relieving persistent symptoms of benign positional vertigo by sectioning the singular nerve through the middle ear although this is rarely necessary. The technique is technically demanding and carries an associated risk of failure and sensorineural hearing loss.

Prognosis

The unsteadiness that is associated with postconcussional syndrome typically resolves within 6 months. Young people tend to recover more quickly than elderly. A complete loss of vestibular function can be expected with transverse temporal bone fractures. Typically vertigo is severe for a number of days and then gradually improves. Occasionally the vertigo may last for up to 4 weeks making normal life impossible and confining the patient to bed. Elderly patients may take months to fully recover balance and up to 50% may be left with BPPV. This generally resolves within 6 months according to Bellucci (1983). Head repositioning manoeuvres have been described for BPPV and recently Harvey et al (1994) have modified these with encouraging results. The head repositioning is designed to redisperse endolymphatic debris within the posterior semicircular canals into the vestibule. Of 25 patients with the condition, 11 (44%) had complete resolution of symptoms, 6 (24%) noted a partial response and in 8 (32%) there was no improvement. The authors stated that the overall response to treatment was no better than the rate of spontaneous recovery, although the manoeuvre did hasten the resolution of symptoms. Surgical intervention for perilymph leaks according to Kerr & Smyth (1987) will relieve imbalance and has usually no effect on hearing.

TEMPORAL BONE FRACTURES

Trauma to the temporal bone is usually seen following road traffic accidents or less commonly following gunshot wounds. Treatment of immediate life-threatening emergencies takes precedence over the treatment of the ear and frequently airway obstruction, shock and the acute neurological status of the patient are the priorities. The traumatised ear should be kept waterproofed until an assessment can be made. Fractures that involve the temporal bone may be classified into longitudinal, transverse or mixed. A gunshot wound to the temporal bone often results in sudden death. Due to the density characteristics of the temporal bone and the ballistic properties of the bullet the patient may survive and be left with considerable injury to the adjacent structures. High velocity copper-coated bullets tend to shatter the temporal bone (Holt 1992). Low velocity lead bullets may only imbed in the skull base. Cranial nerve deficit (typically the 9th, 10th and 11th nerves) following such trauma rarely recovers although the facial nerve can be repaired with some return of function. Repair of a major vascular injury will be the most frequently performed surgical procedure following a gunshot wound.

Longitudinal fractures

This accounts for 80% of temporal bone fractures resulting typically from a blow to the temporal or parietal region of the skull. The fracture line usually traverses the external auditory canal lacerating the tympanic membrane. Bleeding from the ear or blood in the middle ear is clinical evidence that a fracture has occurred. At the initial examination facial nerve function should be assessed. A conductive hearing loss is due to haemotympanum, tympanic membrane rupture or ossicular damage. Occasionally mild sensorineural hearing loss occurs although this is due to cochlear concussion and the fracture does not involve the inner ear. Facial nerve paralysis occurs in 20% of cases and is usually temporary.

Transverse fractures

This type of fracture occurs typically with an occipital blow to the head. Although less common (20% of temporal bone fractures) than longitudinal the facial nerve is damaged in 50% of cases. Usually the nerve is more severely damaged with an associated worse prognosis than longitudinal fractures. Sensorineural hearing loss and vertigo are a result of cochlear and labyrinthine damage. The treatment of the injuries associated with temporal bone fractures are dealt with in other sections.

NASAL FRACTURE

Fracture of the nasal bones is the commonest fracture in humans. Failure to detect and correct such an injury results in nasal deformity and possibly nasal obstruction. Nasal bone X-rays are unreliable and treatment is directed at correction of external deformity, restoring nasal alignment and nasal function. It is important in the initial assessment to rule out associated mid-facial fractures and cervical spine injury.

Maran (1987) has simply classified nasal fractures into three types. A Class 1 fracture breaks the quadrilateral cartilage between its two fixed points or takes a portion of the distal nasal bones with it. A Class 2 fracture breaks the nasal bone, including the frontal process of the maxilla and a Class 3 break means the fracture has extended to include the ethmoid labyrinth. The immediate significance of the injury and the resulting nasal deformity depends on the severity of the trauma. Initially soft tissue swelling may make interpretation difficult and it may be necessary to re-examine the nose after 48 hours, when this has subsided. Frequently there is an associated deviation of the nasal septum which will result in nasal obstruction.

Treatment options

If there is no significant nasal deviation and no cartilaginous obstruction surgical reduction is not required. Generally reduction of a nasal fracture is delayed until soft tissue swelling has subsided. The bones can then be manipulated under local or general anaesthesia. Closed reduction with or without splinting gives a satisfactory outcome in most cases. After 2 or 3 weeks manipulation may not be possible as the fracture unites, and so closed reduction should usually be performed within 5–10 days from the onset of the injury. In children nasal trauma frequently results in a 'green-stick' fracture and earlier manipulation may be required. At the time of manipulation a deviated septum may be repositioned using an Asch's forceps.

Open methods of reduction may provide more accurate and cosmetic results as the deviated bones can be re-aligned more precisely. In general most avoid the open approach in favour of a closed reduction. Residual nasal/septal deformity may require more definitive surgery and septorhinoplasty should be considered only after 6 months.

Complications

Bleeding may be profuse following nasal trauma and failure to arrest the bleed with pressure may necessitate packing. Location of bleeding in the anterior part of the nose is usually controlled by anterior packing with bismuth iodoform paraffin-paste (BIPP). Occasionally bleeding from a torn anterior ethmoidal artery or sphenopalatine artery may require packing under general anaesthesia or vessel ligation.

Complications of treatment are generally residual deformity and nasal obstruction. The nasal obstruction may be due to residual septal deviation or adhesions. Following reduction patients should be advised to restrict activity as there is a risk of bleeding and re-fracture. As most nasal fractures are compound with associated lacerations of the skin or mucosa, prophylactic antibiotics are often necessary.

Patients should avoid nose-blowing, contact sports and situations which may lead to damage to the nose for 6 weeks following the reduction, until the fracture heals.

Haematomas

Although infections are uncommon in the nose they are likely to occur with haematomas. A collection of blood under the mucoperichondrial flaps lining the septal cartilage will result in irreversible damage to the cartilage if untreated. Loss of the supporting cartilage causes a saddle deformity and columellar retraction which is a serious cosmetic deformity of the nose. Typically patients complain of bilateral nasal obstruction and examination reveals a boggy swelling occluding both nares. The most serious complication of a haematoma is the development of an abscess. Infection of the haematoma is characterised by pain and swelling and will rapidly lead to cartilage necrosis if not treated. When identified the haematoma can be drained by aspiration with a needle and syringe initially. Large collections should be evacuated by incision as soon as possible and a small drain left under the mucoperichondrium to ensure re-accumulation does not occur. This can be kept in place with splints or an anterior pack for 48 hours and the patient must be started on an antibiotic. Septal haematoma is more frequently seen in children.

CEREBROSPINAL FLUID LEAKS

Cerebrospinal fluid (CSF) leaks occur in approximately 3% of closed head injuries, 9% of penetrating head injuries and 10–30% of skull base fractures (Marentette & Valentino 1991). They may be classified as high pressure or low pressure depending on whether intracranial pressure is elevated or not. The leaks may also be classified according to their location, as CSF otorrhoea, otorhinorrhoea or rhinorrhoea. The importance of early recognition and treatment of CSF fistulae stems from the fact that untreated, death complicates most unrecognised cerebrospinal fluid leaks as a result of meningitis. Traumatic CSF rhinorrhoea also occurs with temporal bone fractures. The fluid escapes down the eustachian tube and presents as rhinorrhoea. If the tympanic membrane ruptures, CSF otorrhea results. Hicks et al (1980) have classified CSF otorrhoea into an open or closed type depending on the state of the tympanic membrane.

Treatment options

The decision as to whether to adopt a nonoperative or an operative approach will depend on the neurological status of the patient, the surrounding facial and cranial fractures and the site of the leak. Initially the leak may be managed by bedrest for 2 weeks if indicated. Straining, coughing and nose-blowing must be avoided as these activities will raise intracranial pressure. According to MacGee et al (1970) reduction of associated skull fractures has an indirect effect of sealing the leak in patients with anterior skull base and facial fractures. Of 54 patients with anterior skull base leaks reported by Mincy (1966) 35% ceased within 24 hours, 68% within 48 hours and 85% by the end of 1 week. Patients with pneumocephalus and a severely comminuted anterior fossa fracture are likely to need surgical intervention.

Klastersky et al (1976) reported the incidence of meningitis in patients with CSF leakage to be 5–20%. Applebaum (1960), in a review of 91 patients, found the incidence of meningitis to be greatest in the first 2 weeks following the injury. Prophylactic antibiotics have therefore been advocated by a number of authors. Calcaterra (1980) and Klastersky et al (1976) suggested in double blind studies that prophylactic antibiotics are not effective. Eljamel (1993) also states that it is justifiable to withhold antibiotics. In practice most surgeons would recommend antibiotic prophylaxis given the consequences of meningitis.

Recurrent or delayed onset fistulae require more active management. A leakage which persists for more than 2–3 weeks is less likely to repair spontaneously and should be considered for surgery. An immediate surgical approach is recommended except in the situation where meningitis is present. Raised intracranial pressure may require shunt procedures prior to surgery. A leakage which is localised to the frontal sinus may be approached extra- or intracranially. Small fistulae can be managed by an extracranial approach through a brow or coronal incision. Direct dural repair can then be undertaken. Larger fistulae are best managed intracranially. Leaks in the ethmoidal region may be approached through an external ethmoidectomy incision. Using fascia or mucosal flaps the defect may then be sealed. Sphenoid sinus fistulae can often be treated utilising the trans-septal approach (Chandler 1983).

Fistulae in the petrous temporal bone may also be treated by an intra- or extracranial surgical repair. If hearing is present then this should be preserved. Small defects in the tegmen can be repaired via a mastoidectomy approach using temporalis fascia or muscle flaps to seal the leak.

Complications

The main complications are associated with intracranial repair where infection may have serious sequelae. Anosmia will occur following retraction on the frontal lobes. The risk of developing seizures is also increased following intracranial exploration.

TRAUMA TO THE NECK

The management of trauma to the neck has changed over the past 20 years from one of mandatory exploration of all wounds that penetrate the platysma to a selective approach based on a variety of less invasive investigations. The incidence of violence has increased with a large proportion of injuries caused by stab wounds and firearms. The organ systems that may be injured include the larynx and trachea, the great vessels, the oesophagus, the spinal cord and the brachial plexus. Vascular and combined airway and oesophageal injuries are by far the commonest, occurring in 40% sustaining penetrating neck trauma (Miller & Duplechain 1991).

Vascular injuries

Treatment options

40% of all penetrating neck injuries will be associated with a vascular injury (Miller & Duplechain 1991). Brisk haemorrhage should be controlled by direct pressure and if this is unsuccessful surgical exploration is necessary. Blind clamping of bleeding wounds is not recommended. The neck can be divided into three zones based on the anatomical site of injury. This serves as a guide to the need for angiography, surgical intervention and prognosis. Zone 1 lies below the sternal notch, Zone 2 lies between the sternal notch and the angle of the mandible and Zone 3 is the area above the angle of the mandible. Injuries to Zones 1 and 3 are best assessed by angiography. In a series of patients described by Flint (1973) 32% of patients with vascular injuries in Zone 1 had no signs on pre-operative examination. Injuries in this region are the most dangerous due to the large number of major vessels and the possibility of major haemorrhage.

Repair of injuries in this area may require a thoracotomy. Flint et al (1973) recommend mandatory exploration for Zone 1 injuries or any injury where a missile traverses close to a vessel. May et al (1974) reported that of 210 patients requiring exploration, 88% had significant injuries. The mortality rate was 3%. Injuries to Zone 2 are the most easily observed and generally exposed when necessary. Exploration of Zone 3 wounds are the most difficult. Although there is considerable disagreement as to which patients should undergo exploration it is generally agreed that all patients with obvious injury or unstable injuries should be explored, and any patient with a wound that penetrates the platysma should be admitted to hospital. Current literature advocates the utilisation of selective angiography and selective surgical exploration (Stiernberg et al 1992).

The operative approach depends on the site of injury and its extent. An apron flap approach may be required if there is concomitant laryngeal injury. An incision along the sternocleidomastoid muscle may be more appropriate if only oesophageal and vascular injuries are present. All oesophageal and pharyngeal injuries are closed in layers and drained, and all vascular injuries should be repaired once proximal and distal control has been achieved. The alternatives to direct vessel repair are ligation or selective embolisation.

Prognosis

As no precise data exist correlating site of injury and outcome it is difficult to predict results of intervention. Miller & Duplechain (1991) point out that proponents in favour of mandatory exploration of all neck wounds argue that delays in treatment result in increased mortality rates. Delays in investigation have resulted in exsanguination and complications such as false aneurysms and mediastinitis. Reported rates of negative neck exploration are approximately 45% and mortality rates range from 2% to 9%.

Recent literature supports selective surgical exploration and selective angiography. The greatest morbidity is associated with Zone 1 injuries, and although techniques are available to expose the skull base in Zone 2 there is significant risk of cranial nerve injury in this region. This type of approach has gained popularity because of the lower negative exploration rates coupled with comparable mortality rates. May et al (1974) reported a negative exploration rate of 12% and a mortality of 3%. Noyes et al (1986) reported the hospital stay for patients with selective nonoperative intervention to be 2.8 days, compared with 4.2 days for those who underwent negative exploration. The approach taken is largely dependent on the institution involved as well as the experience of the surgeon and nursing personnel.

The larynx and trachea

External laryngeal trauma may be penetrating or blunt. Since these types of injury are uncommon few centres have extensive experience in their management. Trauma to the larynx is often life-threatening and if not, usually affects the quality of the patient's life. There is no standard treatment protocol for external laryngeal trauma and much controversy exists as to how best to manage these injuries. The immediate importance is that sudden airway obstruction and death may occur if a significant injury is missed or a minor injury inappropriately managed. Often minor direct trauma to the larynx or trachea may result in significant injury such as laryngo-tracheal disruption.

Classification

Miller & Duplechain (1991) classified laryngeal injuries into supraglottic tears and fractures, transglottic injuries, cricoid fractures, avulsions of the trachea from the cricoid, and lacerations of the trachea. In addition, fractures may occur to the hyoid bone and the thyroid cartilage. Fractures of the thyroid cartilage occur in approximately 25% of patients with acute laryngeal trauma. Bent & Porubsky (1994) described three types of fractures:

1. non-displaced with minimal associated injuries
2. moderately displaced with intralaryngeal defects
3. severely displaced with intralaryngeal avulsion injury.

These classifications serve as a guide to management and follow-up. Fractures of the cricoid are divided into supraglottic, glottic and infraglottic.

Treatment options

All symptomatic patients presenting with a history of laryngeal trauma must be assessed with the goal of securing the airway. In patients who present with a compromised airway, a tracheostomy or endotracheal intubation must be performed. Fibre-optic laryngoscopy is valuable in assessing the nature of the laryngeal injury and in predicting the need for either intubation or tracheostomy. Endotracheal intubation may aggravate the situation by further traumatising a partially compromised airway. Direct laryngoscopy, bronchoscopy, and oesophagoscopy should be performed in symptomatic patients to assess the extent of the injury and depending on the findings will dictate the need for operative intervention. Hypopharyngeal, subglottic and tracheobronchial injuries not evident on fibre-optic examination may be detected by this assessment.

There are two schools of thought as to when it is best to repair laryngeal injuries. Nahum (1969) suggested that the best time to explore the injury was less than 5 days after the trauma. His rationale was based on the belief that at this stage oedema and swelling would have subsided and repair would be technically easier. Fitz-Hugh et al (1962) and Pennington (1972) concurred with this belief. Schaefer (1992) suggested the ideal time for repair was within 24 hours of the injury. He reported 53 patients who underwent primary repair within 24 hours of trauma and argued that infection was less likely from a contaminated wound and that scarring and voice quality were better than if the procedure was delayed. Leopold (1983) reported that 87% of patients treated within 24 hours of injury had a good airway compared with 68% treated 2–7 days post injury and 27% treated after 8 days.

Schaefer (1992) found that a full recovery without operative intervention was likely when laryngeal oedema, haematomas, and small lacerations of the endolarynx not involving the anterior commisure or the vocal fold were present. Also small lacerations of the supraglottis could be managed conservatively. Conservative management consists of ICU observation, humidified oxygen, and voice rest. Antibiotic and steroids should be used depending on individual needs.

The decision to explore the larynx is dictated by the extent of the trauma and the endoscopic findings. Exposed cartilage, extensive mucosal lacerations, and penetrating laryngeal injuries are indications for exploration. The larynx may be exposed through a midline laryngofissure. Mucosal lacerations should be repaired with absorbable sutures, cartilage fractures reduced and internally fixed using wire or nonabsorbable sutures. For all non-displaced fractures, non-surgical management is recommended by Schaefer (1991). When a fracture is displaced open surgical stabilisation should be performed immediately and stainless steel, absorbable suture or mini-plates used to correct the displacement.

The use of stents is also controversial since, although they improve stabilisation and maintenance of the shape of the airway, they may also cause mucosal damage and increased scarring. They are best left for no longer than 2 weeks.

Oesophageal and pharyngeal injuries should be repaired as soon as possible. Results are best if repair is performed within 24 hours of injury. An inverting technique with absorbable suture is the preferred method of closure. All wounds must be drained and if possible covered with a local muscle flap.

Prognosis

The overall results of laryngeal trauma are largely dependent on the extent of the original injury and whether or not extensive surgical repair is needed. In a report by Ford et al (1995) children sustaining blunt injury had a poorer prognosis than those with penetrating injury. Patients with blunt injury had a significantly longer stay in the intensive care unit and a more prolonged hospitalisation. In addition the injury severity score (ISS) was nearly 10 times higher in those with blunt trauma. The time of presentation and the timing of surgery had a direct effect on the quality of voice and the subsequent airway in a series of patients reviewed by Leopold

(1983). Those undergoing exploration within 24 hours had a better outcome in terms of phonation and airway function. In a retrospective analysis of 30 patients by Cherian et al (1993) 11 patients with minor injury, such as superficial lacerations and oedema, had a good outcome as defined by an absence of hoarseness and a normal patient airway. Thirteen of the 15 patients with major injury, such as large mucosal lacerations and fracture displacement of laryngeal cartilages, had a significantly better outcome as a result of early surgical intervention.

Complications

Neurological injury from penetrating injury to the spinal cord is associated with the most morbidity and mortality. Complications such as aspiration pneumonia are common in those that survive.

The important complications which have an adverse effect on voice and airway function are granulation tissue and stenosis. These are best avoided by meticulous care at the time of surgery and coverage of all exposed cartilage. Decannulation should be possible once the stent has been removed and all wounds have healed. The development of subglottic stenosis or a vocal cord paralysis may prevent safe decannulation. No surgical intervention is recommended if subglottic stenosis is present until at least 6 months has elapsed to allow for scar maturation.

Complications following oesophageal and pharyngeal injury include development of abscess, fistula formation and, rarely, carotid blowout.

Palatal injuries

Impalement injuries of the soft palate and oropharynx are common injuries especially in children. Devastating neurologic sequelae secondary to thrombus propagation in the internal carotid are rare but well documented complications from these injuries. Most injuries heal spontaneously and if the patient is being discharged parents should be counselled and given instructions similar to those in cases of head injury with a view to possible neurological symptoms. Many surgeons observe patients with these injuries for a number of days in hospital as neurological sequelae may occur up to 60 hours after injury. However, of 131 children with palate injuries over a 17-year period Hellmann (1993) reported no complications during hospitalisation or during follow-up, demonstrating that the majority of these injuries can be managed on an out-patient basis.

REFERENCES

Adkins W Y, Osguthorpe J D 1991 Management of facial trauma. Otolaryngologic Clinics of North America 24: 587–611

Applebaum E 1960 Meningitis following trauma to the head and face. Journal of the American Medical Association 173: 1818–1822

Baker D C, Conley J 1979 Regional muscle transposition for rehabilitation of the paralyzed face. Clinics in Plastic Surgery 6: 317–331

Bent J P, Porubsky E S 1994 The management of blunt fractures of the thyroid cartilage. Otolaryngology – Head and Neck Surgery 110: 195–202

Bernstein L, Nelson R H 1982 Reimplanting the severed auricle: an update. Archives of Otolaryngology 108: 587

Bellucci R J 1983 Traumatic injuries of the middle ear. Otolaryngologic Clinics of North America 16: 633–642

Calcaterra T C 1980 Extracranial surgical repair of cerebrospinal rhinorrhoea. Annals of Otolaryngology 89: 108–116

Camnitz P S, Bost W S 1985 Traumatic perforations of the tympanic membrane: early closure with paper tape patching. Otolaryngology – Head and Neck Surgery 93: 220–223

Chandler J R 1983 Traumatic cerebrospinal fluid leakage. Otolaryngologic Clinics of North America 16: 623–630

Cherian T A, Rupa V, Raman R 1993 External laryngeal trauma: analysis of thirty cases. Journal of Laryngology and Otology 107: 920–923

Clemens J, Connolly M 1973 Re-attachment of a totally amputated auricle. Archives of Otolaryngology 97: 269

Coker N J 1991 Management of traumatic injuries of the facial nerve. Otolaryngologic Clinics of North America 24(1): 215–226

Crumley R L, Scott T A 1993 Rehabilitation of facial paralysis. In: Cummings C W (ed) Otolaryngology: head and neck surgery, 2nd edn. Mosby – Year Book, St Louis

Ducker T B 1969 Metabolic factors in surgery of peripheral nerves. Surgical Clinics of North America 53: 1109

Duncan N O, Coker N J, Jenkins H A 1986 Gunshot injuries of the temporal bone. Otolaryngology – Head and Neck Surgery 94: 47–55

Eljamel M S 1993 Antibiotic prophylaxis in unrepaired CSF fistulae. British Journal of Neurosurgery 7: 501–506

Fitz-Hugh L W, Wallenborn W M, McGovern F 1962 Injuries of the larynx and cervical trauma. Annals of Otolaryngology, Rhinology and Laryngology 71: 419

Flint L W, Snyder W H, Perry M O 1973 Management of major vascular injuries in the base of the neck. Archives of Surgery 106: 407

Ford H R, Gardner M J, Lynch J M 1995 Laryngotracheal disruption from blunt pediatric neck injuries: impact of early recognition and intervention on outcome. Journal of Pediatric Surgery 30(2): 331–335

Gacek R 1974 Transection of the posterior ampullary nerve for relief of benign paroxysmal positional vertigo. Annals of Otolaryngology, Rhinology and Laryngology 83: 596

Harvey S A, Hain T C, Adamiec L C 1994 Modified liberatory maneuver: effective treatment for benign paroxysmal positional vertigo. Laryngoscope 104: 1206–1212

Hellmann J R, Shott S R, Gootee M J 1993 Impalement injuries of the palate in children. International Journal of Paediatric Otorhinolaryngology 26(2): 157–163

Hicks G W et al 1980 Cerebrospinal fluid otorrhoea. Laryngoscope Suppl 25: 90

Holt G R 1992 A commentary on violence. Archives of Otolaryngology Head and Neck Surgery 118: 580

Hough J V D 1970 Fractures of the temporal bone and associated middle and inner ear trauma. Proceedings of the Royal Society of Medicine 63: 245

House J W, Brackman D E 1985 Facial nerve grading system. Otolaryngology – Head and Neck Surgery 93: 146–147

Juri J, Irigaray A, Juri C et al 1987 Ear implantation. Plastic and Reconstructive Surgery 80: 431

Kerr A G, Smyth G D L 1987 Ear trauma. In: Booth J B (ed) Scott Brown's otolaryngology Butterworths, London, vol 3: 172–184

Kinney S 1986 Middle ear and temporal bone. In: Trauma, vol 4. Mosby, St Louis

Kinney S 1992 Violence and the ear and temporal bone. Archives of Otolaryngology Head and Neck Surgery 118: 581–583

Klastersky J, Sadeghi M, Brihaye J 1976 Antibiotic prophylaxis in patients with rhinorrhoea or otorrhoea: a double blind study. Surgical Neurology 6: 111–114

Kreutzberg G W, Tetzlaff W 1984 Response of facial motoneurons to conditioning lesions. In: Portmann J (ed) The facial nerve. Masson, New York

Kristensen S 1992 Spontaneous healing of traumatic membrane perforations in man: a century of experience. Journal of Laryngology and Otology 106: 1037–1050

Leopold D A 1983 Laryngeal trauma. Archives of Otolaryngology 109: 106
Liston S L 1987 Injury to the external ear. In: Current therapy in otolaryngology – head and neck surgery, 3rd edn. B C Decker, Philadelphia
MacGee B F, Cauthen J C, Brackett C E 1970 Meningitis following acute traumatic cerebrospinal fluid fistulae. Journal of Neurosurgery 39: 312–316
Maran A G D 1987 The fractured nose. In: Kerr A G (ed) Scott Brown's otolaryngology, 5th edn. Rhinology. Butterworths, London, pp 212–221
Marentette L J, Valentino J 1991 Traumatic anterior fossa cerebrospinal fluid fistulae and craniofacial considerations. Otolaryngologic Clinics of North America 24: 151–162
May M, Chadartana P, West J W 1974 Penetrating neck wounds: selective exploration. Laryngoscope 85: 57
Mawson S R, Ludman H 1979 Diseases of the ear: a textbook of otology. Edward Arnold, London
McCabe B F 1973 Injuries to the facial nerve. Laryngoscope 82: 1891–1896
McQuarrie I, Graftstein B 1973 Axon outgrowth enhanced by a previous nerve injury. Archives of Neurology 29: 53–55
Merwin G E, Boies L R 1980 Paper patch repair of blast rupture of the tympanic membrane. Laryngoscope 90: 853–860
Miller R H, Duplechain J K 1991 Penetrating neck wounds. Otolaryngologic Clinics of North America 24 (1): 15–29
Mincy J E 1966 Post-traumatic cerebrospinal fluid fistulae of the frontal sinuses. Journal of Trauma 6: 618–622
Mladick R A 1978 Salvage of the ear in acute trauma. Clinics in Plastic Surgery 5: 427
Nahum A M 1969 Immediate care of acute blunt laryngeal trauma. Journal of Trauma 9: 112
Noyes L D, McSwain N E, Markowitz I 1986 Panendoscopy and arteriography versus mandatory exploration of penetrating wounds of the neck. Annals of Surgery 192: 21
O'Connell J E, Robin P E 1991 Rehabilitation of facial nerve palsy. Clinical Otolaryngology 16: 470–475
Pennington C R 1972 External trauma of the larynx and trachea. Annals of Otolaryngology, Rhinology and Laryngology 81: 546
Schaefer S 1992 The acute management of external laryngeal trauma: a 27-year experience. Archives of Otolaryngology Head and Neck Surgery 118: 598–605
Schuller D E, Dankle S D, Strauss R H 1989 A technique to treat wrestler's auricular hematoma without interrupting training or competition. 115: 202
Stiernberg C M, Jahrsdoerfer R A, Gillenwater A, Joe S A, Alcalen S V 1992 Gunshot wound to the head and neck. Archives of Otolaryngology Head and Neck Surgery 118: 592–597
Sunderland S 1978 Nerve and nerve injuries, 2nd edn. Churchill Livingstone, Edinburgh, pp 88–9, 96–7, 103
Templer J, Renner G J 1990 Injuries of the external ear. Otolaryngologic Clinics of North America 23(5):1003–1018
Terris J T, Fee W E 1993 Current issues in nerve repair. Archives of Otolaryngology Head and Neck Surgery 119: 725–731

7. Plastic surgery

Patricia A. Eadie

The speciality of plastic surgery encompasses many aspects of trauma care and in particular deals with the soft tissue closure of facial, hand and lower limb injuries. In addition plastic surgeons are responsible for the acute and long-term care of the burned patient where their skills are concerned with skin cover initially and with functional and aesthetic reconstruction subsequently.

The initial patient contact is of paramount importance in establishing rapport and empathy. Many of these patients, especially with mutilating injuries of the hand or severe burns, face an upheaval in their livelihood and lifestyle. Considerable input on the part of the patient for their long-term rehabilitation is required and this is aided by confidence in their treatment from the outset. As with any injury it is mandatory that a complete history and physical examination be performed. It is important not to be side-tracked from life-threatening injuries by an amputated finger, and the treatment of multiple injuries must be prioritised. However, a multidisciplinary approach to major injuries is required allowing the simultaneous treatment of different parts by different teams of surgeons and as such, plastic surgeons have a major role to play in the trauma setting.

Because of space constraints it is not possible to deal with all aspects of trauma management where plastic surgeons have an input in this chapter, but those areas in which there is little overlap with different specialities have been singled out. In addition description of different treatment protocols are brief, but the reader is referred to other texts for elaboration of these.

NAILBED INJURIES

Traumatic lacerations of the nailbed should always be repaired to prevent subsequent nail deformity (McCarthy 1990). Large subungual haematomas can cause severe pain and should be drained by means of puncture of the nail by a hot needle or paper-clip under aseptic conditions (Foucher 1991). A laceration of the nailbed should be suspected when greater than 25% of the nail is undermined by haematoma which should be repaired, following nail removal and debridement, under magnification with fine absorbable sutures (Zook et al 1984). Once repair of the matrix is completed the nail plate is replaced as a stent as recommended by Iselin et al (1963).

More complex injuries may involve fractures of the distal phalanx or loss of substance of the nailbed. 51% of 299 nailbed injuries reviewed had an associated distal phalangeal fracture (Zook et al 1984). While these injuries have a worse prognosis, careful and appropriate treatment can yield good results. Non-displaced fractures will be adequately splinted by nailbed repair and replacement of the nail, or a stent dressing if the nail is not available. Unstable fractures will require fixation with a longitudinal wire (Zook et al 1984) or suturing of the fragments (Foucher 1991). Loss of nailbed results in scarring, abnormal nail regeneration and lack of adherence of the nail. Partial avulsion of nailbeds should be accurately replaced and sutured appropriately. Complete avulsions can be replaced without separation from the nail plate as a free graft (Schiller 1957). When the nail has not been recovered some form of graft is required. Split thickness and full thickness grafts have been described for this (Flatt 1955, Hanrahan 1946, Swanker 1947), but the best results have been obtained with a split thickness nailbed graft from the toe (Shepard 1983).

Deformities following nailbed injuries include change in shape, loss of adherence, splitting and rough texture of the nail and notching of the eponychial fold. In a review of 184 nailbed repairs with a follow-up of at least 6 months, 55% had an excellent result (i.e. identical to the opposite nail), 35% were graded good or very good and 10% fair or poor (Zook et al 1984). Crush and avulsion injuries had significantly worse results and two nailbeds that became infected had poor results. Similarly combinations of nailbed and fold injuries had poorer results.

FINGERTIP INJURIES

As in the initial assessment of any hand injury, an adequate history must be obtained including the cause and time of injury, the occupation, age and hand dominance of the patient and any underlying medical condition. Local examination of the part should include the angle of amputation, the status of the nailbed and distal phalanx, whether there is exposed bone and the adequacy of any remaining soft tissue. The circulation, sensation and tendon function of the finger must be assessed. A plain radiograph should be performed to delineate any fractures. On the basis of this assessment the injury can be evaluated in the light of the patient as a whole and treatment selected accordingly. Treatment policy can be broadly divided into two groups: conservative or operative.

Conservative treatment

Skin and soft tissue losses with only a small amount of exposed bone can be treated by regular dressings following an adequate debridement. This technique is particularly applicable to children where it is postulated that lost tissues can partially regenerate (Douglas 1972). However, several studies have shown this to be an acceptable form of treatment for fingertip injuries without bone exposure in adults (Louis et al 1980, Holm & Zachariae 1974, Fox et al 1977, Mennen & Wiese 1993). However, in a study comparing conservative versus surgical treatment for tip amputations with bone exposure, the conservative group had satisfactory healing, with less stiffness and grasping difficulty and, while the surgically treated group healed in a shorter time, the loss of working days was equal in both groups (Soderberg et al 1983). A semi-occlusive dressing is recommended if the conservative line of treatment is being adopted (Mennen & Wiese 1993). Healing times vary, depending on the extent of soft tissue loss, between 3 and 10 weeks, but in the experience of Louis et al (1980), 21 out of 38 patients returned to work the day after injury. Time to healing, return to work, incidence of hypaesthesia and two point discrimination (2PD) as reported in different studies is shown in Table 7.1. In a prospective study of patients treated conservatively, Chow & Ho (1982) demonstrated that complications such as amputation neuroma and stiffness were extremely rare, but there was a 27% incidence of nail deformity.

Operative treatment

Many fingertip injuries can be treated by the primary closure of adjacent soft tissue. The bone must be shortened to allow a tension free closure with ample soft tissue over the bone end (McCarthy 1990). There are few studies analysing the results of primary closure and those that there are give contradictory results. Sturman & Duran (1963) had poorer results in those treated by primary closure than by cross finger flaps, however other authorities found equivalent results between primary suture and conservative treatment (Holm & Zachariae 1974, Conolly & Goulston 1973).

Skin grafts

Skin grafts have a limited role to play in fingertip injuries. They have been used for temporary cover allowing time and facilities to be organised for definitive reconstruction (Foucher 1991). Skin grafts used as definitive treatment are best situated away from areas where good sensitivity and pinch are required. Both split thickness and full thickness grafts have been used, however a split thickness graft is more likely to 'take' and will contract to a greater extent, a desirable property when considering a fingertip. Full thickness skin grafts have been shown to have similar results in terms of tenderness and cold sensitivity. However, the return of 2PD was worse in the full thickness grafts, an average of 9 mm in comparison to 5 mm for split thickness grafts (Sturman & Duran 1963).

Comparison studies between conservative treatment and skin grafts have shown varying results, with one group having the most problems in the skin grafted group (Holm & Zachariae 1974), and another group

Table 7.1 Time to healing, return to work, hypaesthesia and 2PD following different treatments of fingertip injuries

Authors	Treatment	No.	Healing time	Return to work	Hypaesthesia	Abnormal 2PD
Bojsen-Moller et al 1961	Conservative	34	N/A	94% in 8 weeks	47%	26%
	Skin graft	36	N/A	89% in 8 weeks	19%	55%
	Amputation	45	N/A	84% in 8 weeks	20%	47%
Holm & Zachariae 1974	Conservative	38	81% in 4 weeks	N/A	26%	8%
	Primary suture	32	61% in 4 weeks	N/A	38%	28%
	Skin graft	18	57% in 4 weeks	N/A	67%	67%
	Amputation	19	33% in 4 weeks	N/A	26%	26%
Louis et al 1980	Conservative	38	Up to 10 weeks	55% in 1 day	0%	0% (Av = 3.5 mm)
Chow & Ho 1982	Conservative	90	27.3 days (Av)	41 days (Av)	N/A	13% > 6 mm
	Surgery	100	25 days (Av)	46 days (Av)	N/A	N/A
Soderberg et al 1983	Conservative	19	4.5 weeks	33 days	N/A	< 50%
	Surgery	36	3.6 weeks	34 days	N/A	> 66%
Mennen & Wiese 1993	Conservative	200	20–30 days	N/A	N/A	N/A Av = 2.5 mm

N/A = information not available

showing similar results to conservative treatment (Bojsen-Moller et al 1961). A study between skin grafting and flap closure showed a similar sensory recovery between the two groups (Porter 1968). Another group found that the skin grafted group fared worse with regard to both subjective complaints and objective testing in comparison to local hand flaps (Sturman & Duran 1963). Overall the literature points to a limited role for skin grafting in the treatment of fingertip injuries, and in addition has the risk of an unsightly donor site scar.

Local flaps

Flap coverage of a fingertip injury is indicated when bone is exposed and maintenance of length of the digit is desirable. Many different flaps have been described, either from the injured finger (homodigital), an adjacent finger (heterodigital) or the palm. V–Y advancement flaps, described first by Tranquilli-Leali (1935) and Kutler (1947) and later popularised by Atasoy et al (1970), are neurovascular island flaps (Evans 1992) and require a meticulous technique in order to advance them up to 1 cm. These flaps suffer from a number of problems including hypersensitivity at the suture line (Foucher 1991). Long-term follow-up of the technique by authors other than their originator, have recorded different disadvantages. Tupper & Miller (1985) noted diminished sensation in all of their 16 patients and in another study up to 70% of patients complained of hypaesthesia (Fransden 1978).

More recently other homodigital neurovascular flaps have been described such as the oblique triangular flap (Venkataswami & Subramanian 1980), the monopedicled volar flap (Mouchet & Gilbert 1982), the retrograde vascularised island (Glicenstein 1988), and the step advancement flap (Evans & Martin 1988). These flaps can advance a greater distance, up to 22 mm (Foucher 1991), but from their descriptions are of most use for transverse or oblique amputations with more dorsal loss. Residual problems cited are of an extension deficit of the proximal interphalangeal (PIP) joint (Foucher et al 1989, Evans & Martin 1988) and there is a risk of devascularisation of the finger. The attraction of these flaps is the provision of sensate adjacent skin to the injured tip. Sensory testing has shown normal sensation in all 78 Venkataswami flaps, with a static 2PD less than or equal to 5 mm in 59% of homodigital neurovascular island flaps (Foucher et al 1989), and 10 out of 14 step advancement flaps had normal sensation (Evans & Martin 1988). Further long-term studies on these flaps are required by workers other than their originators.

The cross-finger flap, first described by Gurdin & Pangman (1950), has proved to be a simple and reliable flap. It provides dorsal, insensate skin and as such is not ideal for tip reconstruction. Long-term studies on this flap have shown that while moving 2PD does recover, an average of 7 mm in 53 flaps with a follow-up greater than 19 months (Vidal et al 1994), the recovery of tactile gnosis is poor and there are significant deficits in overall hand function (Nishikawa & Smith 1992). The inclusion of the dorsal branch of the sensory nerve has been shown to improve sensory recovery in the flap (Cohen & Cronin 1983), but this technique is frequently not applicable due to anatomical variations. The other disadvantages of this flap are that it is a two-staged procedure and, due to the required immobilisation of the digits for a period of 2 weeks, stiffness of the PIP joints of both the donor and injured finger is a risk. In a review of 26 cases, Hoskins (1960) found diminished joint mobility in five recipient fingers and six donor fingers, while in the series of Vidal et al (1994) all donor fingers regained good or excellent range of movement (ROM) on Strickland's scale. This flap is not recommended in the over-40 age group due to the higher risk of donor site stiffness.

The indications for a thenar flap are similar to those for a cross-finger flap. However, it is only suitable for the index and long fingers, as the ulnar two digits will not comfortably flex to the thenar eminence. The two main criticisms of the thenar flap are of joint stiffness and of donor site tenderness. In a review of 150 cases, Melone & Carstens (1982) found an incidence of 4% of joint contractures, all of which were felt to be due to the original trauma, and 3% of patients developed sensitive hypertrophic donor scars. The quality of sensory recovery in the thenar flap is no better than the cross-finger flap.

While local flaps are the first choice for fingertip injuries, distant flaps are occasionally used. Abdominal or groin flaps give very poor results, functionally and aesthetically, for tip cover (Foucher 1991).

Free neurovascular flaps from the toes, of pulp, bone and part or all of the nail complex can give very elegant results, especially in the younger patient with good potential for sensory recovery (Morrison et al 1978).

FLEXOR TENDON INJURIES

Injuries to the flexor tendons of the hand are a common occurrence and though usually caused by a laceration, closed injuries can occur. Diagnosis, with an adequate knowledge of the anatomy of the flexor tendons, should be straightforward, though in an uncooperative child or unconscious patient it may be difficult. The fingers may lie in an abnormal resting position, there will be inability to actively flex the distal interphalangeal (DIP) joint with injury to the flexor digitorum profundus (FDP), inability to independently flex the PIP joint with the other digits held in extension with injury to the flexor digitorum superficialis (FDS), and inability to flex the IP joint of the thumb actively may indicate injury to the flexor pollicis longus (FPL). However, the only completely accurate method of diagnosing these injuries is by surgical exploration in the appropriate setting by an experienced hand surgeon.

Primary repair of flexor tendons is indicated in all acute injuries with a few exceptions. The exceptions are severe soft tissue crushing, overlying skin loss, very dirty wounds or extensive damage to the pulley system (Steinberg 1992). Underlying fractures or associated neurovascular injuries are not contraindications (Strickland 1985). It is possible to perform a successful primary repair up to 1 month after injury (Kleinert & Verdan 1983), however in general earlier repair will allow earlier return of function. It is now well established that primary repair of flexor tendon lacerations in all zones of the hand is the treatment of choice (Kleinert et al 1973, Verdan 1960), and that it is better to repair both FDS and FDP rather than FDP alone (Verdan 1960, Kleinert & Verdan 1983, Jupiter 1991).

Flexor tenorrhaphy is a demanding procedure and should be performed in an operating theatre with proper lighting, instrumentation, magnification and assistance. The actual technique of repair is beyond the scope of this chapter but general principles include adequate exposure, Bunnell's 'atraumatic' technique (Bunnell 1918), a central core suture (Bunnell 1918, Kessler & Nissimu 1969, Strickland 1985, Tsuge et al 1977) and a running epitendinous suture. In addition to the variety of suture techniques, many different suture materials have been utilised including nylon, Ethibond, stainless steel, prolene, Mersilene and PDS (Adamson et al 1971, Bunnell 1940, Ketchum 1985). All repairs regardless of material used or suture technique, require some form of protective splinting in the postoperative period.

The method by which tendons heal has relevance to the postoperative management of tendon repairs. Prior to the 1970s, it was believed that the tendons within the flexor sheath healed by the fibroblastic response of the sheath and the surrounding tissues, and that nutrition of the healing tendon was dependent on adhesion formation (Potenza 1962, Lindsay & Birch 1964). However, Lundborg (1976, Lundborg & Rank 1978) has shown that flexor tendons deprived of their blood supply can heal without adhesion formation, and this has been substantiated in other animal models by Manske et al (1984), Gelberman et al (1991) Mass & Tuel 1991, and others. This has resulted in the postoperative management changing from one of immobilisation to some form of controlled protective mobilisation.

A number of techniques of early motions have been developed in an attempt to prevent the effects of adhesion formation (Young & Harmon 1960, Kleinert et al 1967, Duran & Houser 1975, Small et al 1989) ranging from controlled passive mobilisation, through controlled mobilisation using rubber band traction, to controlled active mobilisation. Strickland & Glogovac (1980) have shown that early passive motion can improve substantially the results of flexor tendon repairs in Zone 2. Published reports of the results of the different postoperative mobilisation regimes show a return of excellent or good function between 56% and 83% of fingers (Table 7.2).

Complications

Complications of tendon repair include adhesion, rupture, triggering and bowstringing. Adhesions unresponsive to a period of hand therapy of 3 to 6 months, and in fingers in which the passive range of joint motion exceeds that of the active joint motion are best managed by surgical tenolysis which in Whitaker et al's (1977) series of 77 digits gave an improvement in 80% of fingers.

Early rupture following flexor tenorrhaphy is best managed by prompt re-exploration and repair (Green 1993). Late rupture or those secondary to crush injuries will require secondary reconstruction either as a one or two stage procedure utilising a tendon graft (Green 1993).

Table 7.2 Results of different methods of postoperative controlled mobilisation regimes following flexor tendon repair

Authors	Regime	Percentage (Excellent/Good)
Lister et al (1977)	Kleinert's Dynamic splint (KDS)	57
Strickland & Glogovac (1980)	Immobilisation Passive mobilisation	12 56
Earley & Milward (1982)	Kleinert's Dynamic splint	55
Gault (1987)	Kleinert's Dynamic splint	72
May et al (1992)	• Kleinert's Dynamic splint • KDS + Passive • KDS with short splints	72 62 83
Small et al (1989)	Controlled active mobilisation	77
Cullen et al (1989)	Controlled active mobilisation	77

Triggering following flexor tendon repair may require re-exploration if conservative management such as ultrasound and scar massage is unsuccessful (Steinberg 1992). Bowstringing of the tendon is secondary to damage to the pulley system at the time of initial injury. This requires reconstruction of the pulley system, which is often done in conjunction with two stage tendon grafting (Green 1993).

NERVE INJURIES

Nerve injuries have been classified by Seddon (1943) and Sunderland (1978) into five different groups depending on the severity of injury, ranging from minimal derangement to complete division (Table 7.3).

Injury to a peripheral nerve resulting in a loss of continuity and a distal deficiency is a common problem. While the results of nerve repair have improved with the advent of microsurgery, advances in this area are probably going to be by influencing the ability of the nerve to regenerate and of the target organs to recover function (McCarthy 1990). In addition, assessment of the results is subjective and, especially of sensory recovery, difficult to quantify. There is recent speculation that cognitive capacity factors may play a role in the functional outcome following nerve repair and that variations in these factors may explain the variability of outcome of nerve repair (Rosen et al 1994).

The current procedure of choice for repairing a nerve injury is by suturing with the aid of magnification, although other methods of coapting the

Table 7.3 Classification systems of nerve injuries

Seddon (1943)	Sunderland (1978)	Damage	Prognosis
Neurapraxia	Grade I	Axonal continuity interrupted	Totally reversible
Axonotmesis	Grade II	Severed axon	Full recovery
Neurotmesis	Grade III	Severed axon & endoneurium	Slow, incomplete recovery
Neurotmesis	Grade IV	Severed axon, endoneurium & perineurium	Rarely proceeds to useful recovery. Surgical repair indicated
Neurotmesis	Grade V	Loss of continuity of nerve trunk	Surgical repair is essential for any recovery

nerve are currently under investigation (McCarthy 1990). Ideally a nerve repair should be performed as a primary procedure, without tension across the repair and with perfect alignment. The nerve ends should be viable and lying in a well vascularised bed, and the wound should be stable.

Nerve repairs are of three general types: epineural, perineural and group fascicular (Daniel & Terzis 1977). Opinion is divided as to which type of repair is superior, with some authors favouring perineural repair (Yamamoto 1974, Brushart et al 1983), some epineural (Orgel 1984), and many investigators finding no difference between techniques (Young et al 1981, Cabaud et al 1976). Group fascicular repair is possible when branches are well formed and identifiable within the nerve trunk, (Orenstein 1992) and Jabaley et al (1980) have cited specific areas in the upper extremity where this is possible.

Factors other than the type of suturing performed that influence the outcome of nerve recovery include the timing of repair, the age of the patient, the type and level of injury, gap size and the presence of tension. Primary repair is the treatment of choice for a sharp nerve transection in a minimally contaminated wound in a healthy patient, and when the appropriate surgical magnification and operating staff are available (Green 1993, Birch & Raji 1991). Otherwise a delayed repair is a better option. Children achieve a better result following nerve repair than adults. Berger and Mailander (1991) found that all children except one achieved a good result in comparison to 69% in the 11–40-year-old patients and 41% in the older patient group. Young et al (1981) found useful 2PD in 80% of patients under 20 years old but none in those over 40 years old.

The type of injury and the condition of the wound have an influence on the results of nerve repair. Traction injuries, high-velocity missile wounds and other types of extreme trauma result in a poorer result following nerve repair (Orenstein 1992). The presence of infection, scarring, tissue loss and contusion all have an adverse affect on nerve recovery and as alluded to already are best managed by a delayed primary or secondary repair (Millesi 1981a, Green 1993). Proximal nerve injuries have a worse prognosis than those more distally (Sunderland 1978), however muscle groups that are proximally innervated recover faster.

A nerve gap results from one of or a combination of elastic retraction, fibrotic retraction or a defect of the nerve (Millesi 1986). The nerve gap can be managed by mobilisation of the nerve, transposition of the nerve, flexing the joints, shortening the extremity or bridging the gap with a graft or conduit (Green 1993). Extensive mobilisation of the nerve has been shown to be detrimental to recovery (Nicholson & Seddon 1957), and Millesi (1981b) has stated that elongation of a human nerve by more than 20% impairs its conductivity. When a nerve repair is not possible without tension then a nerve graft is necessary (Mackinnon 1989). The anastomoses must be performed without tension using careful microsurgical techniques. Donor nerves that have been used include the sural nerve, the medial cutaneous nerve of the forearm and the terminal sensory branch of the posterior interosseous nerve. Various conduits have been utilised in the experimental and clinical situation in order to allow a nerve to regenerate across a gap. These include bio-absorbable synthetic conduits, venous conduits and muscle grafts (Dellon & Mackinnon 1988, Chiu & Strauch 1990, Norris et al 1988). Results from these series are encouraging for nerve gaps of up to 3 cm but poor for larger gaps.

REPLANTATION

Thirty years ago the era of clinical replantation was ushered in by Malt and McKhann's (1964) successful replantation of an arm in a 12-year-old boy at the proximal humeral level. Komatsu and Tamai (1968) performed the first digital replantation for a complete amputation of a thumb, and this report was followed shortly by the successful replantation of many amputated extremities worldwide. Initially the emphasis was on survival of the part but this changed with increasing experience and expertise to its functional recovery.

Indications

While today replantation of all amputated parts is indicated, the goal of the surgery must be remembered; the reattachment of an optimally functioning hand or limb that will be preferable to amputation with or without a prosthesis (McCarthy 1990). In addition there are certain factors which prevent replantation including other life-threatening injuries or poor general health of the patient. Parts that have been totally destroyed or improperly preserved cannot be reattached (Feller et al 1991).

The patient's age, sex, occupation and wishes must be taken into account when making a decision about replantation, and the surgeon must not only be microsurgically trained, but also have a knowledge of the long-term prospects for the limb or digits. Guillotine amputations and moderate crush injuries are the most favourable for replantation whereas avulsion injuries can present many problems and have a lower success rate.

The demands on the lower limb are of support and locomotion. Lower extremity replantation survival rates are worse than for upper extremity (Kleinert et al 1980), and their long-term functional results must be compared with the excellent prostheses that are available for the lower limb. In contrast, any upper limb replantation that restores sensation and some motor function will be better than any of the presently available prostheses.

Because of the large muscle mass involved in a limb the ischaemic period is critical, and revascularisation must be achieved within 6 hours of injury if the part has not been cooled. Even with proper cooling and storage a proximal limb amputation may only be replantable after 12 hours (Leung 1981). In contrast more distal amputations can withstand cold ischaemia for longer periods of time and successful replantation has been reported following up to 24 hours ischaemia (Van Giesen et al 1983).

When considering microreplants most authors would consider amputations of the thumb, multiple digits, hemi-hand, bilateral, and proximal forearms to be absolute indications for replantation (Zhong-Wei et al 1981, Feller et al 1991, May & Gallico 1980, Morrison et al 1977). Amputation of parts in children is considered by some authors to be an absolute indication for replantation because of their unique capacity for regeneration and adaption (Morrison et al 1977). However, Feller et al (1991) feel that this may not always be the case as replanted parts do show growth retardation and develop deformities if epiphyses are involved, and children can compensate for missing digits.

In general single finger amputations should not be replanted, as unless it has excellent sensibility and function it will interfere with the function of the rest of the hand (McCarthy 1990). However, amputations distal to the insertion of FDS have been shown to have good functional recovery (Foucher et al 1981, Urbaniak et al 1985), and consideration should be given to replanting these, depending on the patient's needs.

Single fingers may be replanted in women for cosmetic, social and psychological motives, especially in the younger age group (Morrison et al 1977). In certain cultures, e.g. Japanese and Indian, the loss of a digit carries certain social stigmata, so that there is a strong desire on the part of the patient for replantation (Tamai 1982).

Results

Survival

The survival rates following replantation vary from 74% to greater than

Table 7.4 Survival rates following digital replantation

Authors	No. of parts	Survival rate (%)
Weiland et al (1977)	86	>90
Yoshizu et al (1978)	99	92.6
Tamai (1978)	163	89
Chow et al (1979)	17 (thumbs only)	82.4
Berger & Millesi (1980)	N/A	82
Biemer & Duspiva (1982)	450	87.3
Morrison & O'Brien (1987)	160	74

N/A = information not available

90% (Table 7.4). Guillotine type amputations have a better survival rate, with 85% surviving in comparison to 51% of avulsion and diffuse crush injury in a series of 160 digits (Morrison & O'Brien 1987). Tamai (1982) analysed 33 failed digital replants; ten digits had more than 8 hours' ischaemia, 11 were amputations distal to the DIP joint or with severe tissue damage and 12 were deemed to be technical failures.

The number of veins anastomosed has also been shown to increase the chances of digit survival, with a 50% success rate when one venous anastomosis was performed in comparison to 100% success rate when three veins were repaired (Urbaniak et al 1985). Replantation of digits can be successfully accomplished in very small children with the survival rate being significantly influenced by the number of venous repairs, bone shortening and the use of intra-osseous wires to achieve bony fixation (Baker & Kleinert 1994).

Function

As with the survival rates, the mechanism of injury has a strong influence on long-term functional results, with avulsion injuries having the least satisfactory results (Morrison et al 1977).

Secondary reconstructive procedures are frequently required post-replantation in order to maximise functional recovery. In Tamai's (1982) series of 293 replants, 73% required some form of reconstructive surgery. In a review of 274 replanted parts from Vienna, 22% underwent some form of secondary surgery (Berger & Millesi 1980). The most common procedures needed are tenolyses and joint releases (Wilson et al 1983), with secondary nerve surgery and the provision of better skin cover frequently necessary as well (Tamai 1982).

Reviewing the literature for long-term functional results post-replantation is difficult as there is no universal grading system. Most authors assess some aspects of the ability to return to work, the joint range of motion, sensory recovery, cold intolerance or muscle power. Zhong-Wei describes a system based on these five criteria, graded 1–4, with 1 being excellent and 4 being tissue survival with no useful function (Zhong-Wei et al 1981), and reviewed the experience in Shanghai, China, Zurich, Switzerland and Louisville, USA. 69% of the Shanghai patients, 72% of the Zurich patients and 41% of the Louisville patients achieved Grade 1 or 2 functional recovery. Tamai (1982) assessed his replants on the same grading system and had 72% with Grade 1 or 2 recovery. The American Replantation Mission (1973) visited China and found an impressive figure of 80% of patients returned to work following replantation, 60% to their original job. In a series of 347 replanted parts, two-thirds of the patients had returned to work 2½ years after injury, with patient motivation being a key factor (Kleinert et al 1980). In a comparison of amputation versus replantation no difference was found in the time taken to return to work between the two groups (Jones et al 1982).

The recovery of useful sensation is vital in order for the patient to use the digit effectively. Every effort should be made at the primary operation to achieve precise coaptation of the nerve repair, using nerve grafts if necessary. Nerve recovery should be comparable to that of repair of an isolated peripheral nerve injury (Green 1993). The return of 2PD is used by many authors as a means of assessing sensory recovery and varies between 2 mm and greater than 20 mm (Table 7.5). Younger patients have a better prognosis with regard to sensory recovery. Cold intolerance is frequently a problem post-replantation, but is generally not disabling and the symptoms improve with time (Chow et al 1979, Kleinert et al 1980, Morrison & O'Brien 1987). One patient in a series of 59 consecutive replantations

Table 7.5 Sensory recovery as measured by 2PD following replantation

Authors	No. of replants	2PD (mm)
Chow et al (1979)	10	3–14: av = 5
Hamilton et al (1980)	Adults Children	2–>20: av = 9 2–10: av = 4
Berger & Millesi (1980)	37	2–Protective
Kleinert et al (1980)	243	60% < 15
Foucher et al (1981)	12	9–13
Tamai (1982)	258	70% < 15
Urbaniak et al (1985)	51	Adult av = 11.7 Child av = 9.2

requested an amputation for severe cold intolerance (Urbaniak et al 1985).

The range of motion of the PIP joint post finger replantation is an important factor for the long-term function of the finger. Fingers amputated proximal to the insertion of FDS had an average range of motion of 35° in comparison to 82° for those amputated distal to FDS insertion (Urbaniak et al 1985, Foucher et al 1981). The poor recovery of mobility of the PIP joint is a strong argument for not replanting single fingers amputated at a level proximal to FDS insertion. For other joints, stiffness is largely related to the level and type of injury, motivation and co-operation of the patient (BMJ editorial 1983). For multiple digit amputations, replantation of all possible digits should be performed as the functional results are better than any available prostheses. For upper extremity replantations the return of intrinsic muscle function is poor and has a strong influence on the long-term functional recovery (Tamai 1982, Russell et al 1984).

SOFT-TISSUE INJURIES OF THE LOWER LIMB

Traumatic injuries of the lower limb frequently involve both bone and soft tissue and there is increasing awareness of the need to involve both the Orthopaedic and Plastic Surgery specialities.

Compound fractures of the lower limb were classified as Types I, II or III depending on soft-tissue injury (Gustilo et al 1969), with further subclassification of Type III into A, B or C (Gustilo et al 1984). This classification system has prognostic value with regard to rates of infection, delayed union and need for amputation. Types IIIB and IIIC fractures are of the most concern to the plastic surgeon, with Type IIIB consisting of extensive soft-tissue loss with periosteal stripping and bone exposure and Type IIIC having an associated arterial injury.

Management

The wound should be serially debrided until all non-viable tissue has been excised. This may need to be done at two or three operating sessions as marginal tissue may not declare its viability until 24–72 hours after injury (Yaremchuk 1986). Once the wound is stable, a decision can be taken on the best method of obtaining soft tissue coverage. The ultimate decision depends on the size of the defect, its location and the state of the surrounding skin and muscle. It may be possible to close defects of the upper and middle one-third of the lower limb with local flaps, but in general those of the lower one-third will require a free microvascular transfer.

There is a wide body of evidence supporting the use of muscle flaps to cover these wounds. Vascularised muscle can effectively cover a wound contaminated with up to 10^6 bacteria per gram of tissue without developing infection (Feng & Eaton 1986). They have the theoretical advantage of increasing the delivery of antibiotics to the area by their increased vascular density (Chang & Mathes 1982), but their ability to conform to the wound and to obliterate any dead space is felt to be their major advantage (Ecker & Sherman 1993, Yaremchuk 1986). The decision of which particular flap to choose for a certain area is beyond the scope of this chapter.

Bacterial contamination has been shown to be present in up to 70% of compound fractures (Gustilo & Anderson 1976, Lawrence et al 1978). Analyses of the contaminating organisms have shown that while aerobic Gram-positive cocci and aerobic Gram-positive rods are the commonest present (Wilkins & Patzakis 1991), aerobic Gram-negative cocci and rods are also found and the antibiotic choice must take these into account as they are major disease producing organisms.

Timing of coverage varies in different reports. Some reports recommend that free flaps be either performed within 6 days of injury or after 6 weeks (Byrd et al 1985, Godina 1986, Tan et al 1988), however others have shown performing flaps between 1 and 6 weeks of injury, the 'sub-acute' phase, has not led to an increased incidence of flap loss, osteomyelitis or non-union (Yaremchuk 1986, Ecker & Sherman 1993). Table 7.6 illustrates the results of different series with regard to flap failure, bony union time and infection rates.

Table 7.6 Flap failure rates, bony healing time, infection rates following muscle flap repair of severe compound fractures of the lower leg

Authors	Timing	No. (%)	Flap failure (%)	Bone healing (mths)	Infection (Acute) (%)	Infection (Chronic)
Godina (1986)	Early	134 (25)	1 (0.75)	6.8	2 (1.5)	N/A
	Delayed	167 (31)	20 (12)	12.3	29 (17.5)	N/A
	Late	231 (43)	22 (9.5)	29	14 (6)	N/A
Yaremchuk (1986)	Most closed in 7–14 days	46 (Free)	4 (9)	N/A	1 (2)	0
		36 (Local)	1 (3)		4 (11)	0
Fischer et al (1991)	Early	11		13.5	2 (18)	1
	Sub-acute	6		22.5	5 (83)	2
	Late	7		16.25	4 (57)	2
	Open Rx	19		11.25	10 (53)	1
Ecker (1993)	2–6 weeks	>30	0	N/A	0	N/A
Byrd et al (1985)	1–5 days	27	3 (11)	6	N/A	2 (7)
	1–6 weeks	20	7 (35)	8–9 (3 non-union)	N/A	8 (40)
	> 6 weeks	7	2 (28)	> 6 (2 non-union, 2 early bone graft)	N/A	2 (33)

N/A = information not available

SOFT-TISSUE INJURIES OF THE FACE

Soft-tissue trauma to the face can result from automobile accidents, assaults, industrial and domestic accidents, dog or human bites and war injuries. Associated injuries are common, either elsewhere on the body or locally including the intracranial contents, the eye and the underlying facial skeleton. Initial assessment and resuscitation should be undertaken according to standard Advanced Trauma and Life Support guidelines. Facial injuries are not usually life-threatening apart from uncontrollable haemorrhage, but their management should be co-ordinated with the treatment of other injuries, in order to avoid unnecessary anaesthetics. Underlying facial fractures should be treated first, as otherwise management of the fracture may disrupt the soft-tissue closure. Early skilful management of the soft tissue in the facial area decreases the possibility of permanent facial disfigurement (McCarthy 1990).

All facial wounds are potentially contaminated and active measures should be taken against the development of tetanus (Rowe & Williams 1985). Contaminated wounds must be converted to clean wounds by irrigation and surgical debridement. All foreign material must be removed at the initial treatment, in particular abrasion-type injuries which have come into contact with dirt or the road surface, by means of careful scrubbing or surgical excision. Failure to remove all imbedded particles at this time results in traumatic tattooing in the long-term with a significant cosmetic deformity which it is difficult to resolve satisfactorily. A debridement of any dead or severely contused tissue should be performed, but due to the excellent blood supply in the head and neck region tissue will survive that in other situations would not, so radical debridement is not indicated.

Traditional teaching on facial lacerations sustained from either human or animal bites has contra-indicated primary repair and reconstruction (Curtin & Greeley 1961, Schwartz et al 1979). Recently reports have contradicted this concept, and primary repair and immediate reconstruction in these types of injuries have been successfully carried out with good results and without significant levels of infection (Lackmann et al 1992, Agrawal et al 1992).

Facial lacerations can be divided into simple or complex depending on the degree of soft-tissue injury and the involvement of underlying structures. Simple lacerations can be repaired under local anaesthetic, following haemostasis, with fine sutures. Involvement of other structures such as branches of the fifth and seventh cranial nerves, salivary glands and ducts requires more specialised treatment. The lacerations can extend into adjacent structures such as the orbit, the nose, the sinuses or intracranially. Many of these injuries can be diagnosed pre-operatively by clinical examination (Greco 1991). The proximal trunks and named branches of the facial nerve should be repaired as a primary procedure. Some authors recommend that small divisions should also be repaired as well (McCarthy 1990), but in practice the majority of motor function will recover from injury to these within 6–12 months (Rowe & Williams 1985).

Unrepaired lacerations of the parotid duct may result in fistula formation and it is recommended that primary repair over a stent be carried out (Greco 1991). Inability to locate the distal end or loss of a portion of the duct can be managed by ligation of the proximal duct or diversion of it into the mouth. Ligation of the proximal duct can result in swelling and chronic infection of the gland. Complex injuries extending into surrounding structures require identification of all injured tissue and repair as appropriate.

Scars

The inevitable outcome of any laceration or skin loss is a scar. On the face this can result in significant disfigurement and lead to psychosocial problems. The aim of the plastic surgeon is to minimise scarring by the use of atraumatic techniques, fine sutures, the avoidance of tension on the wound and the early removal of sutures. Because many patients believe that a plastic surgeon can eliminate scars completely, it is important that prior to any scar revision that the patient be counselled so that the limitations of this procedure are understood. A 'good' scar can be defined as one which is a fine line which falls within or parallel to a skin wrinkle or relaxed skin tension line, is of regular contour, is of normal colour for that particular area and does not produce distortion of the surrounding area (Georgiade et al 1987). A clinical distinction must be made between a keloid, a hypertrophic and a normal but unsightly scar (Nicoletis et al 1977). These distinctions have treatment and prognostic implications.

Scar revision aims to change the scar's direction as necessary, to decrease the width, improve contour irregularities, correct pigment abnormalities and to release any contractures. Factors which should be taken into account when attempting to predict the outcome of a scar revision include the time since injury, the location of the scar, the age of the patient, the nature of the injury and the patient's race. In general scar revision should be delayed until the scar has matured, which can be from 6 to 24 months post injury (Parsons 1977). A better result can be obtained in the older patient. The outcome in the sternal and deltoid area is often less than ideal. Poor results seen after scar revision include recurrence of hypertrophy and width in the scar, hyperpigmentation and milia or small inclusion cysts, and all patients should be counselled concerning these.

Non-surgical adjuncts to scar management include the use of pressure, irradiation, and certain pharmacological substances. These are often used in combination therapies and some have been discussed in the section on postburn reconstruction.

BURNS

Burns are a major cause of injury in all age groups. There is a variety of aetiological causes of burns, including hot liquids, flame, chemicals, electricity, radiation and even extreme cold. Regardless of the cause of the injury the basic principles in the care of the burn patient and their wounds are similar.

Immediate care

The first priority in caring for a patient with a burn is to remove the source of burning and any clothes that may be smouldering or soaked in chemicals or hot liquids, which will act to prolong the burning process. Very viscous liquids may need to be mechanically removed. The immediate application of cold water will also help in limiting the burning process, but continuous cooling of the thermal burn is controversial (Martyn 1990). There is a danger of hypothermia with the injudicious use of cooling solutions in burns of greater than 20% total body surface area (TBSA). However, immediate copious irrigation of chemical burns is very important. Prior to transport to hospital an adequate airway must be secured and if possible an intravenous infusion commenced. Transfer should be effected as rapidly as possible, without the application of elaborate dressings. On arrival at hospital a brief history of the accident should be obtained from both the patient and any accompanying personnel, and in particular the time and cause of the burn should be ascertained. The ensuing treatment involves managing the airway, fluid resuscitation, burn wound assessment and obtaining skin cover, the treatment of any underlying medical conditions, the prevention and treatment of any infections and the rehabilitation of the patient.

Airway management

On the patient's arrival at hospital the first priority is to check the patency of the airway. Endotracheal intubation may be necessary for severe burns of the head and neck or for smoke inhalation injury. Upper airway obstruction secondary to laryngeal oedema is a real risk with severe facial burns and can occur with little warning (Settle 1986a). Early intubation in a controlled manner by an experienced anaesthetist is always preferable to an emergency intubation at a stage when the laryngeal oedema is so severe that complete obstruction has occurred. If the situation has progressed to this stage, then an immediate tracheotomy may be necessary, but it is safer and wiser to intubate early rather than to adopt an expectant policy.

Smoke inhalation

Smoke inhalation injury is a major cause of mortality in burn patients (Herndon et al 1988). Clinical signs that point to this injury include upper body burns, in particular head and neck, a history of loss of consciousness, singeing of the nasal hair, soot in the oropharynx and carbonaceous sputum. Inhalation of steam is a rare injury and while the clinical signs of smoke inhalation are absent, burns can be produced as far distally as the alveoli, in contrast to smoke which will usually only burn as far as the terminal bronchi.

Smoke inhalation causes its effects in two ways: (1) carbon monoxide poisoning and (2) smoke toxicity. Carbon monoxide poisoning results in tissue hypoxia which affects all end organs, and is also believed to interfere with the cytochrome system (Chance et al 1970). High levels of carboxyhaemaglobin on admission may give an indication of the severity of carbon monoxide poisoning but these may well have returned to normal if oxygen was administered during transportation.

The products of combustion including hydrochloric acids, hydrogen cyanide, nitrogen dioxide and acrolein cause airway irritation and bronchoconstriction (Crapo 1981). Microvascular permeability is increased with the release of inflammatory mediators leading to pulmonary oedema and atelectasis 2–3 days after injury and pneumonia 7–14 days postburn (Muller & Herndon 1994).

While survival from smoke inhalation is to a large extent dependent on the severity of injury, the prevention of aspiration, pulmonary oedema, pneumonia and hypoxia will forestall additional complications. High frequency, flow-interrupted mechanical ventilation has been shown to decrease the incidence of pneumonia and deaths in adults (Cioffi et al 1991).

Fluid resuscitation

Adequate initial volume resuscitation is critical to the survival of a major burn. As a general rule, children with a burn greater than 10% and adults with a burn greater than 15% require intravenous resuscitation. The best way of administering intravenous fluids is via a peripheral vein. There is a very high rate of septic and embolic complications with central venous lines in burn patients, and they should be used only when absolutely necessary for monitoring purposes (Martyn 1990).

Multiple fluid resuscitation formulae have been developed with the aim of preventing hypovolaemia and renal failure (Table 7.7). The formulae differ with regard to the amount of fluid delivered, the ratio of colloid to crystalloid and the tonicity of the crystalloid. The literature is scanty with regard to controlled trials comparing different formulae, and the fact that these different formulae have all been used with success is a testament to the physiological reserves of the average burn patient. The total fluid requirement of the burn patient is between 2 and 4 ml/kg/% burn (Settle 1986b), and the aim is to deliver half of the total requirement within the first 12 hours. Because of the large loss of sodium with a burn injury, the resuscitation fluid should contain 130–150 mmol/l sodium. It is important to remember that any formula is only a guide to resuscitation. The vital

Table 7.7 Fluid resuscitation formulae for burns patients

	Evans et al (1952)	Modified Brooke/Kenney et al (1977)	Muir & Barclay (1962)	Baxter (1974)	Monafo et al (1984)
1st 24 hours					
Crystalloid	1 ml/kg/% burn	Lactated Ringer's, 2 ml/kg/% burn (adult), 3 ml/kg/% burn (child)	None	Lactated Ringer's, 4 ml/kg/% burn	Hypertonic saline (250 mEq/1) Na, 100 mEq/1 Cl, 150 mEq/1 lactate Titrate to urine flow
Colloid	1 ml/kg/% burn	None	3 ml/kg/% burn	None	None
5% Dextrose	2000 ml/m^2	None	2500 ml	None	Up to 3500 ml (including oral)
Rate	50% volume in first 8 hrs, 25% in next 8 hrs, 25% in next 8 hrs	As Evans	50% volume in first 12 hrs, 33% in next 12 hrs	As Evans	Constant infusion
2nd 24 hrs					
Crystalloid	50% of requirements of 1st 24 hrs	None	None	None	
Colloid	50% of requirements of 1st 24 hrs	0.3–0.5 ml/kg/% burn	17% of volume	0.3 ml/kg/5% burn	
5% Dextrose	2000 ml	Sufficient to maintain urine	2500 ml	Sufficient to maintain urine	

signs of the patient must be monitored closely, with the single most important parameter being the urinary output. This should be maintained between 0.5–1 ml/kg/hr. The resuscitation fluids should be altered according to the clinical condition of the patient.

The burn wound

The primary concern of the burn surgeon is to achieve wound closure as rapidly as possible. Conventional therapy consists of allowing the burn eschar to separate spontaneously with the application of split thickness skin grafts onto granulation tissue. Early excision and grafting has been acceptable treatment of small burns since first described by Lustgarten in 1891 (Artz & Moncrief 1969), but the last 25 years has seen a change in the management policy for large burns. The technique of tangential excision and grafting developed and reported by Janzekovic (1975) showed a significant decrease in hospital stay and pain in 2615 patients. While early excision and grafting have been shown to decrease the number of septic episodes in major burns (Heimbach & Engrav 1984) and to decrease total blood transfusion requirements in paediatric burns greater than 30% (Desai et al 1990), it has not been shown to decrease mortality to the degree that had been postulated. Herndon et al (1989) have shown a significant improvement in survival in patients less than 30 years old, but there was no difference in the older age group. Other authors have shown a trend towards improved survival following early excision and grafting, but without statistical significance (Pietsch et al 1985, Chicarilli et al 1986), and it is difficult to separate other changes in treatment such as meticulous attention to the patient's physiologic, metabolic and immunological status which may also account for improvements in mortality (Tompkins et al 1986). However, the benefits accrued from fewer septic episodes, decreased transfusion requirements and shorter hospital stay make early excision and grafting a very advantageous treatment.

Scar management and postburn reconstruction

During the healing and scar maturation phase attention must be paid to minimising hypertrophic scar formation and to the prevention of joint contractures, two of the long-term sequelae of burn injuries. Distortion of a part by scar contraction leads to deformity, requiring reconstruction particularly on the face.

Hypertrophic scars are a common sequela of thermal injury. Children and coloured people are particularly susceptible to them. The time required for healing is also thought to influence their development, with a shorter time having a decreased incidence of hypertrophic scar formation (Deitch et al 1983). The theory that early burn wound excision and grafting would control the development of hypertrophic scars has not been borne out clinically. Larson et al (1971) advocated the use of pressure to prevent hypertrophic scars. The mechanism by which this works is unknown, but it has been shown to decrease the rate of collagen synthesis and to accelerate its remodelling (Naismith 1980). Whatever its mode of action, it is effective and while the optimum pressure or duration of treatment is not known, it should be continued until permanent remodelling of the scar has occurred (Larson et al 1974). This is on average 6–12 months, though in practice pressure garments are left on for longer periods.

Corticosteroids have been shown to influence scar remodelling (Baker & Whitaker 1950, Maguire 1965, Ketchum et al 1966). The intralesional injection of Triamcinolone appears to promote scar regression with minimal side-effects. The dosage schedule has been determined by Ketchum et al (1974). The use of steroids to help prevent further scarring, when used in combination with surgery, is also beneficial.

Following a report from Perkins et al (1983), Quinn (1987) reported her results of the use of silicone gel as a topical treatment for hypertrophic scars in 125 burn patients. 81% of those followed showed an improvement in their scars and these results were borne out by the work of Ahn et al (1989).

The management of contractures of individual areas of the body is beyond the scope of this text. General principles that would apply to each area include splinting in the acute and maturation phase, early physiotherapy and occupational therapy, release of established contractures from proximal to distal in the extremities (Levine & Buchanan 1986), and the introduction of new skin into the contracture in the form of split thickness skin grafts, local or distal flaps as required (Stallings et al 1982).

The expansion of local unburned skin has been of considerable benefit for certain scarred areas and currently has supplanted other methods of scalp reconstruction for burn alopecia (Hunt et al 1991, Cohen et al 1989, Neligan & Peters 1989).

REFERENCES

Adamson J E, Srouji S, Mladick R, Horton C 1971 Tissue reaction to contemporary tendon suture. Journal of Bone and Joint Surgery 53A: 815

Agrawal K, Mishra S, Panad K N 1992 Primary reconstruction of major human bite wounds of the face. Plastic and Reconstructive Surgery 90: 394–398

Ahn S T, Monafo W W, Mustoe T A 1989 Topical silicone gel: a new treatment for hypertrophic scars. Surgery 106: 781–786

American Replantation Mission to China 1973 Replantation surgery in China. Plastic and Reconstructive Surgery 52: 476–489

Artz C P, Moncrief J A 1969 The treatment of burns. W B Saunders, Philadelphia

Atasoy E, Ioakimidis E, Kasdan M L, Kutz J E, Kleinert H E 1970 Reconstruction of the amputated fingertip with a triangular volar flap. Journal of Bone and Joint Surgery 52B: 921–926

Baker B L, Whitaker W L 1950 Interference with wound healing by local action of adrenocortical steroids. Endocrinology 46: 544–551

Baker G L, Kleinert J M 1994 Digit replantation in infants and young children: determinants of survival. Plastic and Reconstructive Surgery 94: 139–145

Baxter C R 1974 Fluid volume and electrolyte changes in the early postburn period. Clinics in Plastic Surgery 1: 693–703

Berger A, Mailander P 1991 Advances in peripheral nerve repair in emergency surgery of the hand. World Journal of Surgery 15: 493–500

Berger A, Millesi H 1980 Functional results from replantation surgery: a five-year report from the Viennese replantation team. Australian and New Zealand Journal of Surgery 50: 244–247

Biemer E, Duspiva W 1982 Reconstructive microvascular surgery. Springer-Verlag, Berlin

Birch R, Raji A R 1991 Repair of median and ulnar nerves: primary suture is best. Journal of Bone and Joint Surgery 73B: 154–157

Bojsen-Moller J, Pers M, Schmidt A 1961 Fingertip injuries: late results. Acta Chirurgica Scandinavica 122: 177–183

British Medical Journal Editorial 1983 Replantation. 287: 1–2

Brushart T M, Tarlov E C, Mesulam M M 1983 Specificity of muscle re-innervation after epineurial and individual fascicular suture of the rat sciatic nerve. Journal of Hand Surgery 8: 248–253

Bunnell S 1918 Repair of tendons in the fingers and description of two new instruments. Surgery, Gynecology and Obstetrics 26: 103–110

Bunnell S 1940 Primary repair of severed tendons. The use of stainless steel wire. American Journal of Surgery 47: 502–516

Byrd H S, Spicer T E Cierney G III 1985 The management of open tibial fractures. Plastic and Reconstructive Surgery 76: 719–730

Cabaud H E, Rodkey W G, McCarroll H R Jr et al 1976 Epineurial and perineurial fascicular nerve repairs: a critical comparison. Journal of Hand Surgery 1: 131–137

Chance B, Erecinska M, Wagner M 1970 Mitochondrial response to carbon monoxide poisoning. Annals of New York Academy of Sciences 174: 193–204

Chang N, Mathes S J 1982 Comparison of the effect of bacterial inoculation in musculocutaneous and random pattern flaps. Plastic and Reconstructive Surgery 70: 1–10

Chicarilli Z N, Cuono C B, Heinrich J J, Fichandler B C, Barese S 1986 Selective aggressive burn excision for high mortality subgroups. Journal of Trauma 26: 18–25

Chiu D T W, Strauch B 1990 A prospective clinical evaluation of autogenous vein grafts used as a nerve conduit for distal sensory nerve defects of 3 cm or less. Plastic and Reconstructive Surgery 86: 928–934

Chow J A, Bilos Z J, Chunprapaph B 1979 30 thumb replantations: indications and results. Plastic and Reconstructive Surgery 64: 626–630

Chow S P, Ho E 1982 Open treatment of fingertip injuries in adults. Journal of Hand Surgery 7: 470–476

Cioffi W G Jr, Rue L W III, Graves T A, McManus W F, Mason A D Jr 1991 Prophylactic use of high-frequency percussive ventilation in patients with inhalation injury. Annals of Surgery 213: 573–582

Cohen B E, Cronin E D 1983 An innervated cross-finger flap for fingertip reconstruction. Plastic and Reconstructive Surgery 72: 688–697

Cohen M, Marschall M A, Dolezal R F, Hanumadass M M 1989 The role of tissue expansion in the reconstruction of secondary burn defects. Journal of Burn Care and Rehabilitation 10: 220–225

Conolly W B, Goulston E 1973 Problems of digital amputations: a clinical review of 260 patients and 301 amputations. Australian and New Zealand Journal of Surgery 43: 118–123

Crapo R O 1981 Smoke inhalation injuries. Journal of the American Medical Association 246: 1694–1696

Cullen K W, Tolhurst P, Lang D, Page R E 1989 Flexor tendon repair in Zone 2 followed by controlled active mobilisation. Journal of Hand Surgery 14B: 392–395

Curtin J W, Greeley P W 1961 Human bites of the face. Plastic and Reconstructive Surgery 28: 394–397

Daniel R K, Terzis J K 1977 Reconstructive microsurgery. Little & Brown, Boston

Deitch E A, Wheelahan T M, Rose M P, Clothier J, Cotter J 1983 Hypertrophic burn scars: analysis of variables. Journal of Trauma 23: 895–898

Dellon A L, Mackinnon S E 1988 An alternative to the classical nerve graft for the management of the short nerve gap. Plastic and Reconstructive Surgery 82: 849–856

Desai M H, Herndon D N, Broemeling L, Barrow R E, Nichols R J Jr, Rutan R L 1990 Early burn wound excision significantly reduces blood loss. Annals of Surgery 211: 753–759

Douglas B S 1972 Conservative management of guillotine amputation of the finger in children. Australian Pediatric Journal 8: 86–89

Duran R J, Houser G 1975 Controlled passive motion following flexor tendon repair in Zones 2 and 3. In AAOS symposium on tendon surgery in the hand. C V, Mosby, St Louis

Earley M J, Milward T M 1982 The primary repair of digital flexor tendons. British Journal of Plastic Surgery 35: 133–139

Ecker J, Sherman R 1993 Soft-tissue coverage of the distal third of the leg and ankle. Orthopedic Clinics of North America 24: 481–488

Evans D M 1992 Skin cover in the injured hand. Churchill Livingstone, Edinburgh

Evans D M, Martin D L 1988 Step advancement island flap for fingertip reconstruction. British Journal of Plastic Surgery 41: 105–111

Evans E I, Purnell O J, Robinett R W, Batchelor A, Martin M 1952 Fluid and electrolyte requirements in severe burns. Annals of Surgery 135: 804–815
Feller A, Graf P, Biemer E 1991 Replantation surgery. World Journal of Surgery 15: 477–485
Feng L, Eaton C 1986 Soft-tissue infection in lower extremity trauma. Clinics in Plastic Surgery 13: 735–745
Fischer M D, Gustilo R B, Varecka T F 1991 The timing of flap coverage, bone grafting and intramedullary nailing in patients who have a fracture of the tibial shaft with extensive soft-tissue injury. Journal of Bone and Joint Surgery 73A: 1316–1322
Flatt A E 1955 Nailbed injuries. British Journal of Plastic Surgery 8: 34–37
Flynn J E 1966 Hand surgery. Williams & Wilkins, Baltimore
Foucher G 1991 Finger and nailbed injuries. Churchill Livingstone, Edinburgh
Foucher G, Henderson H R, Maneau M, Merle M, Braun F M 1981 Distal digital replantation: one of the best indications for microsurgery. International Journal of Microsurgery 3: 263–270
Foucher G, Smith D, Pempinello C, Braun F M, Citron N 1989 Homodigital neurovascular island flaps for digital pulp loss. Journal of Hand Surgery 14B: 204–208
Fox J W IV, Golden G T, Rodeneaver G et al 1977 Nonoperative management of fingertip pulp amputation by occlusive dressings. American Journal of Surgery 133: 255–256
Fransden P A 1978 V–Y plasty as treatment of fingertip amputations. Acta Orthopedica Scandinavica 49: 255–259
Gault D T 1987 A review of repaired flexor tendons. Journal of Hand Surgery 12B: 321–325
Gelberman R H, Steiberg D, Amiel D, Akeson W 1991 Fibroblast chemotaxis after tendon repair. Journal of Hand Surgery 16A: 686–693
Georgiade N G, Georgiade G S, Riefkohl R, Barwick W J 1987 Essentials of plastic, maxillofacial and reconstructive surgery. Williams & Wilkins, Baltimore
Glicenstein J 1988 Table ronde: les lambeaux en ilots en chirurgie de la main. Annales de Chirurgie de la Main 7: 120–121
Godina M 1986 Early microsurgical reconstruction of complex trauma of the extremities. Plastic and Reconstructive Surgery 78: 285–292
Greco R J 1991 Emergency plastic surgery. Little, Brown, Boston
Green D P 1993 Operative hand surgery, 3rd edn. Churchill Livingstone, New York
Gurdin M, Pangman W J 1950 The repair of surface defects of fingers by transdigital flaps. Plastic and Reconstructive Surgery 5: 368–371
Gustilo R B, Anderson J T 1976 Prevention of infection in the treatment of 1025 open fractures of long bones: retrospective and prospective analyses. Journal of Bone and Joint Surgery 58A: 453–458
Gustilo R B, Mendoza R M, Williams D N 1984 Problems in the management of Type 3 (severe) open fractures: a new classification of Type 3 open fractures. Journal of Trauma 24: 742–746
Gustilo R B, Simpson L, Nixon R et al 1969 Analysis of 511 open fractures. Clinics in Orthopedics 66: 148–154
Hamiliton R B, O'Brien B McC, Morrison W A, MacLeod A M 1980 Replantation and revascularisation of digits. Surgery, Gynaecology and Obstetrics 151: 508–512
Hanrahan E M 1946 The split thickness skin graft as covering following removal of a finger nail. Surgery 20: 399–400
Heimbach D M, Engrav L H 1984 Surgical management of the burn wound. Raven Press, New York
Herndon D N, Barrow R E, Linares H A et al 1988 Inhalation injury in burned patients: effects and treatment. Burns Including Thermal Injury 14: 349–356
Herndon D N, Barrow R E, Rutan R L, Rutan T C, Desai M H, Abston S 1989 A comparison of conservative versus early excision therapies in severely burned patients. Annals of Surgery 209: 547–553
Holm A, Zachariae L 1974 Fingertip lesions: an evaluation of conservative treatment versus free skin grafting. Acta Orthopedica Scandinavica 45: 382–392
Hoskins H D 1960 The versatile cross-finger pedicle flap. Journal of Bone and Joint Surgery 42A: 261–277
Hunt J L, Purdue G F, Rodrich R J 1991 Acute burns, burn surgery and postburn reconstruction. Selected Readings in Plastic Surgery 6 (12): 1–33
Iselin M, Recht R, Bazin C 1963 La primante de la conservation de l'ongle dans les écrasements de la pulpe. Memoires de l'Academie de Chirurgie 89: 717–723

Jabaley M E, Wallace W H, Heckler F R 1980 Internal topography of major nerves of the forearm and hand: a current view. Journal of Hand Surgery 5: 1–18
Janzekovic Z 1975 The burn wound from the surgical point of view. Journal of Trauma 15: 42–62
Jones J M, Schenck R R, Chesney R B 1982 Digital replantation and amputation: comparison of function. Journal of Hand Surgery 7: 183–189
Jupiter J B 1991 Flynn's hand surgery, 4th edn. Williams & Wilkins, Baltimore
Kenney M J, Bendixen H H, Powers S R 1977 Manual of surgical intensive care. W B Saunders, Philadelphia
Kessler I, Nissimu F 1969 Primary repair without immobilization of flexor tendon division within the digital sheath. Acta Orthopedica Scandinavica 40: 587–601
Ketchum L D, Cohen I K, Masters F W 1974 Hypertrophic scars and keloids: a collective review. Plastic and Reconstructive Surgery 53: 140–154
Ketchum L D, Smith J, Robinson D W 1966 Treatment of hypertrophic scars, keloids and scar contractures by triamcinolone acetonide. Plastic and Reconstructive Surgery 38: 209–218
Ketchum L D 1985 Suture materials and suture techniques used in tendon repair. Hand Clinics 1: 43–53
Kleinert H E, Verdan C 1983 Report on the committee on tendon injuries. Federation of Societies of Surgery of the Hand. Journal of Hand Surgery 8: 794–798
Kleinert H E, Jablon M, Tsai T M 1980 An overview of replantation and results of 347 replants in 245 patients. Journal of Trauma 20: 390–398
Kleinert H E, Kutz J E, Ashbell T S, Martinez E 1967 Primary repair of lacerated flexor tendon in no man's land (abstract). Journal of Bone and Joint Surgery 49A: 577
Kleinert H E, Kutz J E, Atasory E et al 1973 Primary repair of flexor tendons. Orthopedic Clinics of North America 4: 865–876
Komatsu S, Tamai S 1968 Successful replantation of a completely cut-off thumb: case report. Plastic and Reconstructive Surgery 42: 374–378
Kutler W 1947 A new method for fingertip amputations. Journal of the American Medical Association 133: 29–30
Lackmann G M, Draf W, Isselstein G, Tollner U 1992 Surgical treatment of facial dog-bite injuries in children. Journal of Cranio-Maxillofacial Surgery 20: 81–86
Larson D L, Abston S, Evans E B et al 1971 Techniques for decreasing scar formation and contractures in the burned patient. Journal of Trauma 11: 807–823
Larson D L, Abston S, Willis B et al 1974 Contracture and scar formation in the burn patient. Clinics in Plastic Surgery 1: 653–656
Lawrence R M, Hoeprich P D, Huston A C, Benson D R, Riggins R S 1978 Quantitative microbiology of traumatic orthopedic wounds. Journal of Clinical Microbiology 8: 673–675
Leung P C 1981 Prolonged refrigeration in toe-to-hand transfer: case report. Journal of Hand Surgery 6: 152
Levine N S, Buchanan R T 1986 The care of the burned upper extremities. Clinics in Plastic Surgery 13: 107–118
Lindsay W K, Birch J R 1964 The fibroblast in flexor tendon healing. Plastic and Reconstructive Surgery 34: 223–232
Lister G D, Kleinert H E, Kutz J E, Atasoy E 1977 Primary flexor tendon repair followed by immediate controlled mobilisation. Journal of Hand Surgery 2: 441–451
Louis D S, Palmer A K, Burney R E 1980 Open treatment of digital tip injuries. Journal of the American Medical Association 244: 697–698
Lundborg G 1976 Experimental flexor tendon healing without adhesion formation – a new concept of tendon nutrition and intrinsic healing mechanisms: a preliminary report. Hand 8: 235–238
Lundborg G, Rank F 1978 Experimental intrinsic healing of flexor tendons based upon synovial fluid nutrition. Journal of Hand Surgery 3: 21–31
McCarthy J G 1990 Plastics surgery. W B Saunders, Philadelphia
Mackinnon S E 1989 Surgical management of the peripheral nerve gap. Clinics in Plastic Surgery 16 (3): 587–603
Maguire H C 1965 Treatment of keloids with triamcinolone acetonide injected intralesionally. Journal of the American Medical Association 192: 325–326
Malt R A, McKhann C F 1964 Replantation of several arms. Journal of the American Medical Association 189: 716–722

Manske P R, Gelberman R H, Vande Berg J S, Lesker P A 1984 Intrinsic flexor tendon repair: a morphological study in vitro. Journal of Bone and Joint Surgery 66A: 385–396
Martyn J A 1990 Acute management of the burned patient. W B Saunders, Philadelphia
Mass D P, Tuel R J 1991 Intrinsic healing of the laceration site in human superficialis flexor tendons in vitro. Journal of Hand Surgery 16A: 24–30
May E J, Silfverskiold K L, Sollermann C J 1992 Controlled mobilisation after flexor tendon repair in Zone 2: a prospective comparison of three methods. Journal of Hand Surgery 17A: 942–952
May J W Jr, Gallico G 1980 Upper extremity replantation. Current Problems in Surgery 17: 633–717
Melone C P, Carstens J H 1982 The thenar flap – an analysis of its use in 150 cases. Journal of Hand Surgery 7: 291–297
Mennen U, Wiese A 1993 Fingertip injuries management with semi-occlusive dressing. Journal of Hand Surgery 18B: 416–422
Millesi H 1981a Reappraisal of nerve repair. Surgical Clinics of North America 61 (2): 321–340
Millesi H 1981b Interfascicular nerve grafting. Orthopedic Clinics of North America 12: 287–301
Millesi H 1986 The nerve gap: theory and clinical practice. Hand Clinics 2 (4): 651–663
Monafo W W, Halverson J D, Schechtman K 1984 The role of concentrated sodium solutions in the resuscitation of patients with severe burns. Surgery 95: 129–135
Morrison W A, O'Brien B McC 1987 Reconstructive Microsurgery. Churchill Livingstone, Edinburgh
Morrison W A, O'Brien B McC, Hamilton R B 1978 Neurovascular free foot flaps in reconstruction of the mutilated hand. Clinics in Plastic Surgery 5: 265–272
Morrison W A, O'Brien B McC, MacLeod A M 1977 A long-term review of digital replantation. Australian and New Zealand Journal of Surgery 47: 767–773
Mouchet A, Gilbert A 1982 Couverture des amputations distales des digits par lambeau neurovasculaire homodigital en îlot. Annales de Chirurgie de la Main 1: 180–182
Muir I F K, Barclay T L 1962 Burns and their treatment. Lloyd-Luke, London
Muller M J, Herndon D N 1994 The challenge of burns. Lancet 343: 216–220
Naismith R S 1980 Hypertrophic scar therapy: pressure induced remodelling and the determinates (PhD thesis). University of Strathclyde, Glasgow
Neligan P C, Peters W J 1989 Advances in burn scar reconstruction: the use of tissue expansion. Annals of Plastic Surgery 22: 203–210
Nicholson O R, Seddon H J 1957 Nerve repair in civil practice: results of treatment of median and ulnar nerve lesions. British Medical Journal 2: 1065–1071
Nicoletis C, Bazin S, LeLous M L 1977 Clinical and biochemical features of normal, defective and pathologic scars. Clinics in Plastic Surgery 4: 347–359
Nishikawa H, Smith P J 1992 The recovery of sensation and function after cross-finger flaps for fingertip injury. Journal of Hand Surgery 17B: 102–107
Norris R W, Glasby M A, Gattuso J M, Bowden R E 1988 Peripheral nerve repairs in humans using muscle autografts: a new technique. Journal of Bone and Joint Surgery 70B: 530–533
Orenstein H H 1992 Hand II: peripheral nerve and tendon transfers. Selected Readings in Plastic Surgery 6 (23): 1–40
Orgel M G 1984 Epineurial versus perineurial repair of peripheral nerves. Clinics in Plastic Surgery 2: 101–104
Parsons R W 1977 Scar prognosis. Clinics in Plastic Surgery 4: 181–186
Perkins K, Davey R B, Wallis K A 1983 Silicone gel: a new treatment for burn scars and contractures. Burns Including Thermal Injury 9: 201–204
Pietsch J B, Netscher D T, Nagaraj H S, Groff D B 1985 Early excision of major burns in children: effect on morbidity and mortality. Journal of Pediatric Surgery 20: 754–757
Porter R W 1968 Functional assessment of transplanted skin in volar defects of digits: a comparison of free grafts and flaps. Journal of Bone and Joint Surgery 53A: 955–963
Potenza A D 1962 Tendon healing within the flexor digital sheath in the dog. Journal of Bone and Joint Surgery 44A: 49
Quinn K J 1987 Silicone gel in scar treatment. Burns 13: S33–S40
Rosen B, Lundborg G, Danlin L B, Holmberg J, Karlson B 1994 Nerve repair: correlation of restitution of functional sensibility with specific cognitive capacities. Journal of Hand Surgery 19B: 452–458

Rowe N L, Williams J Ll 1985 Maxillofacial injuries. Churchill Livingstone, Edinburgh
Russell R C, O'Brien B McC, Morrison W A, Pamamull G, MacLeod A 1984 The late functional results of upper limb revascularisation and replantation. Journal of Hand Surgery 9A: 623–633
Schiller C 1957 Nail replacement in fingertip injuries. Plastic and Reconstructive Surgery 19: 521–530
Schwartz S I, Shires G T, Spencer F C, Storer F H 1979 Principles of surgery. McGraw-Hill, New York
Seddon H J 1943 Three types of nerve injury. Brain 66: 237–288
Settle J A D 1986a Burns – the first five days. Smith & Nephew, England
Settle J A D 1986b Fluid therapy in burns. Part 1: the basic principles. Care Critical Illness 2: 185
Shepard G H 1983 Treatment of nailbed avulsions with split-thickness nailbed grafts. Journal of Hand Surgery 8: 49–54
Small J O, Brennan M D, Colville J 1989 Early active mobilisation following flexor tendon repair in Zone 2. Journal of Hand Surgery 14B: 383–391
Soderberg T, Nystrom A, Hallsman G, Hulten J 1983 Treatment of fingertip amputations with bone exposure. Scandinavian Journal of Plastic and Reconstructive Surgery 17: 147–152
Stallings J O, Ban J L, Pandeya N K, Abramsohn L, Bergman R S 1982 Secondary burn reconstruction: recent advances with microvascular free flaps, regional flaps and specialised grafts. American Surgery 48: 505–513
Steinberg D R 1992 Acute flexor tendon injuries. Orthopaedic Clinics of North America 23: 125–140
Strickland J W 1985 Flexor tendon repair. Hand Clinics 1: 55–68
Strickland J W, Glogovac S V 1980 Digital function following flexor tendon repair in Zone 2: a comparison of immobilisation and controlled passive motion techniques. Journal of Hand Surgery 5: 537–543
Sturman M J, Duran R J 1963 Late results of fingertip injuries. Journal of Bone and Joint Surgery 45A: 289–298
Sunderland S 1978 Nerves and nerve injuries, 2nd edn. Churchill Livingstone, Edinburgh
Swanker W A 1947 Reconstructive surgery of the injured nail. American Journal of Surgery 74: 341–345
Tamai S 1978 Digit replantation: analysis of 163 replantations in an 11-year period. Clinics in Plastic Surgery 5: 195–209
Tamai S 1982 20 years experience of limb replantation: review of 293 upper extremity replants. Journal of Hand Surgery 7: 549–556
Tan E, Katsaros J, Zoltie N 1988 Free tissue transfer to the lower extremity. Australian and New Zealand Journal of Surgery 58: 369–372
Tompkins R G, Burke J F, Schoenfeld D A, Bondoc C C, Quinby W C, Behringer G C, Ackroyd F W 1986 Prompt eschar excision: a treatment system contributing to reduced burn mortality. Annals of Surgery 204: 272–281
Tranquilli-Leali E 1935 Riconstruxione dell'apice delle falangi ungueali mediante autoplastica volare peduncolate per scorrimento. Infort Trauma Lavoro 1: 186–193
Tsuge K, Yoshikazu I, Matsuishi Y 1977 Repair of flexor tendons by intertendinous suture. Journal of Hand Surgery 2: 436–440
Tupper J, Miller G 1985 Sensitivity following volar V–Y plasty for fingertip amputations. Journal of Hand Surgery 10B: 183–184
Urbaniak J R, Roth J H, Nunley J A, Goldner R D, Koman L A 1985 The results of replantation after amputation of a single finger. Journal of Bone and Joint Surgery 67A: 611–619
Van Giesen P J, Seaber A V, Urbaniak J R 1983 Storage of amputated parts prior to replantation: an experimental study with rabbit ears. Journal of Hand Surgery 8A: 60–65
Venkataswami R, Subramanian N 1980 Oblique triangular flap: a new method of repair for oblique amputations of the fingertip and thumb. Plastic and Reconstructive Surgery 66: 296–300
Verdan C E 1960 Primary repair of flexor tendons. Journal of Bone and Joint Surgery 42A: 647–657
Vidal P, Eadie P A, Sykes P J 1994 A long-term assessment of cross-finger flaps. British Association of Plastic Surgeons Meeting, Swansea

Weiland A J, Villarreal-Rios A, Kleinert H E, Kutz J, Atasoy E, Lister G 1977 Replantation of digits and hands: analysis of surgical techniques and functional results in 71 patients with 86 replantations. Journal of Hand Surgery 2: 1–12
Whitaker J H, Strickland J W, Ellis R K 1977 The role of flexor tenolysis in the palm and digits. Journal of Hand Surgery 2: 462–470
Wilkins J, Patzakis M 1991 Choice and duration of antibiotics in open fractures. Orthopedic Clinics of North America 22: 433–437
Wilson C S, Alpert B S, Buncke H J, Gordon L 1983 Replantation of the upper extremity. Clinics in Plastic Surgery 10: 85–101
Yamamoto K 1974 A comparative analysis of the process of nerve regeneration following funicular and epineurial suture for peripheral nerve repair. Archives of Japanese Surgery 43: 276–301
Yaremchuk M J 1986 Acute management of severe soft-tissue damage accompanying open fractures of the lower extremity. Clinics in Plastic Surgery 13: 621–632
Yoshizu T, Katsumi M, Tajima T 1978 Replantation of untidily amputated finger, hand, and arm: experience of 99 replantations in 66 cases. Journal of Trauma 18: 194–200
Young L, Wray R C, Weeks P M 1981 A randomised prospective comparison of fascicular and epineurial digital nerve repairs. Plastic and Reconstructive Surgery 68: 89–93
Young R E, Harmon J M 1960 Repair of tendon injuries of the hand. Annals of Surgery 151: 562–566
Zhong-Wei C, Meyer V E, Kleinert H E, Beasley R W 1981 Present indications and contraindications for replantation as reflected by long-term functional results. Orthopedic Clinics of North America 12: 849–870
Zook E G, Guy R J, Russell R C 1984 A study of nailbed injuries: causes, treatment and prognosis. Journal of Hand Surgery 9A: 247–252

8. Thoracic injuries

Stephen Westaby

Considering the minefield of potential clinical problems in thoracic trauma, litigation remains an unusual event. The vast majority of chest injuries are managed by junior hospital doctors in the accident and emergency department or by trainees in orthopaedics or general surgery. For 90% of the patients a well-positioned chest drain and appropriate pain relief provide the keystone to a successful outcome (Westaby 1994a). Less than 10% of patients require surgical intervention for life-threatening problems such as aortic transection, intrapleural haemorrhage, ruptured bronchus or diaphragm (Westaby 1994b). These patients are of necessity managed by experienced cardiothoracic surgeons and unfavourable outcomes are usually deemed inevitable whatever the course of events. In practice the frequent cause of poor outcome in thoracic trauma is failure to recognise an important injury or act on clinical evidence. Despite increasing awareness of the Advanced Trauma Life Support (ATLS) guidelines, it is almost routine to overlook a ruptured bronchus or lacerated diaphragm. Even the ATLS guidelines for fluid replacement in thoracic trauma are questionable (Westaby 1994c).

THE SETTING FOR LITIGATION IN THORACIC TRAUMA

Until 5 years ago Crown immunity protected National Health Services (NHS) hospitals from legal action and two mutual societies, the Medical Defence Union and the Medical Protection Society, insured doctors. Then after a series of problems concerning fire hazards and unhygienic kitchens, hospitals were made accountable for their mistakes. This has proved to be very expensive for the NHS, since insurance companies will not touch the hospital trusts. Consequently, in April 1995 the Government set up the Clinical Negligence Scheme for Trusts as a mutual insurer. Meanwhile the premiums for general practitioners and specialists with private practice rose by 60% in the next year. Personal injury claims will inevitably increase following the pattern in the USA unless physicians in Europe actively work against this legal initiative. In August 1995, the *Daily Telegraph*'s leading story was entitled 'Solicitors in Ambulance Chasing Row'. Hugh Muir's article revealed that the names and addresses of accident victims throughout the UK are being sold to solicitors. This allows them to generate business by pursuing personal injury claims. Although in the previous 3 years net legal aid costs to the taxpayer for personal injury and medical negligence claims increased from £22 million to £44 million, the English Law Society failed to censor this approach. The cost to the NHS in malpractice suits has risen from £53 million in 1990–91 to a projected £150 million in 1995, equivalent to the budgets of three district general hospitals. An estimated rise of 20% annually is expected unless something is done and about £1 billion worth of claims are said to be in the pipeline. Under these circumstances the best deterrent from the medical profession is consistently to decline to undertake legal work as an expert witness. This approach is preferable to pursuing dubious claims against one's colleagues for financial rewards. The response of hospital trusts has been to hire risk managers and private investigators (at an average cost of £1000 per day) to collect evidence against claimants (*Sunday Telegraph* leading article 3 September 1995).

Claims are rising because the British public and legal profession alike have been influenced by the huge awards in the USA. Also changes in both the law and rules on legal aid have made it easier to sue doctors. Children are now eligible for legal aid which is one reason that the number of personal injury legal aid cases rose from around 5000 10 years ago to 15 700 in 1994–95. From July 1995 lawyers have been able to take on personal injury cases on a 'no win, no fee' basis making it easier still for people to go to court. Until recently medical experts in trials were not required to share their evidence before proceedings began in court. 'Trial by ambush' meant that although the defence usually knew the outline of the plaintiff's case, the plaintiff did not know the defence's counter evidence until presented. Now that both sides must provide their outline before the trial, the plaintiff is prepared for the defendant's arguments.

The rock upon which medical defence still stands, albeit precariously, is the Bolam principle established in 1957. John Bolam, a manic depressive, sued his doctor for injuries inflicted during electroconvulsive therapy. Bolam lost the case because the doctor was able to prove that other doctors would have acted in a similar way. Currently a doctor can defend himself against a negligence claim by producing one colleague from anywhere in the world who says he would have done the same. However, the Bolam principle was overturned in an Australian court in 1995 and the same may soon happen in the UK.

As in any other surgical speciality, the safest way to avoid litigation after thoracic injuries is through careful documentation, use of appropriate investigations carried out in an acceptable time frame, accurate diagnosis, then early and skilled intervention by adequately trained personnel. Experience has shown that designated trauma centres with immediate access to thoracic and neurosurgeons provide the optimum setting for a satisfactory outcome. The worse case is to identify an immediately life-threatening thoracic injury in a district general hospital with remote access to a consultant cardiothoracic surgeon (Westaby 1989a). In this case, a fatality may result from failure to intervene.

There are five situations where the outcome may lead to litigation:

- fatality
- chronic disability
- missed diagnosis
- inappropriate treatment
- iatrogenic injury.

In an increasingly litigious society the patient, if alive, or his relatives have certain basic expectations. In the event of an unsatisfactory outcome, lack of communication is often the source of an aggressive response.

There are many inherent difficulties in the management of thoracic trauma from a legal standpoint. The majority of patients seen by a cardiothoracic surgeon have serious injuries, are often unconscious and have usually received narcotic or amnesic drugs. Many patients have an associated head injury and a proportion will be recovering from surgery for an abdominal injury. Informed consent is frequently impossible and for many patients there will be no pre-operative information. Documentation of the extent of the injuries may well come retrospectively from junior hospital doctors with little appreciation of the surgical risk or prognosis. In the case of a penetrating cardiovascular injury or blunt transection of the thoracic aorta, the patient may be rushed to the operating room with no discussion of the projected morbidity or mortality with the relatives. In these circumstances, mortality is seldom challenged but morbidity, particularly paraplegia after descending aortic cross clamping, is of great concern (Von Oppell et al 1994).

Leaving aside major thoracic surgery, pleural drainage by intercostal tube insertion should be a safe and effective therapeutic manoeuvre, within the scope of any physician or emergency medical technician. In practice, no other simple procedure generates more anxiety, technical failure or iatrogenic morbidity. Obviously chest drain insertion requires knowledge of the relationship between surface landmarks and the intrathoracic and abdominal viscera. Fatalities occur through laceration of the heart or aorta and morbidity through penetration of the lung particularly in the 10–15% of patients with pleural adhesions after pneumonia. As for any other practical procedure, an unsatisfactory outcome usually follows inadequate experience or misunderstanding of the basic principles of thoracic drainage.

LITIGATION AFTER A FATALITY

This is surprisingly rare but may occur after delay in diagnosis, delay in treatment or when there is a question about the appropriateness of an intervention or the degree of seniority of the surgeon. Many deaths follow-

Table 8.1 Criteria for thoracotomy in open or closed chest injury

- When the initial chest drain insertion yields more than 1250 ml of blood immediately or more than 1000 ml plus 250 ml in the first hour, or if 500 ml is drained in 3 consecutive hours with no decreasing trend.
- When cardiac tamponade is present even if pericardiocentesis is negative or relieves symptoms.
- For massive air leak where pneumothorax persists despite adequate drainage, suggesting major bronchial or tracheal injury. Bronchoscopy is performed first to confirm the diagnosis and to clear blood and secretions.
- In all transmediastinal wounds.
- For chest wall defects and diaphragmatic lacerations.
- For removal of clotted haemothorax in order to expand the underlying lung and prevent empyema or fibrothorax. This should be considered after 48–72 hours of drainage. Enzymic clot lysis is seldom successful.
- For combined thoracic and abdominal wounds before laparotomy except where entry and exit wounds preclude heart or great vessel injury, or when the source of major haemorrhage is abdominal.

ing road traffic accidents or penetrating injuries to the chest are accepted as inevitable whether this is the case or not. Also the other motorist or assailant is the subject of litigation as opposed to the medical staff. Nevertheless, there are clear guidelines as to how and when to intervene for intrathoracic haemorrhage, and failure to perform a thoracotomy when indicated can be criticised by the well-informed (Table 8.1) (Westaby 1989b). The relatives may ask, 'Should this patient have died?' 'Was appropriate treatment available in a reasonable time?'

Actual cases from teaching hospital experience are as follows:

Patient 1 A 22-year-old motorcyclist was involved in a deceleration injury and presented at the accident department with a right-sided pneumothorax. The junior hospital doctor had never inserted a chest drain and no senior cover was available. The doctor failed to enter the pleural cavity with the drain but took serial chest X-rays as the patient's condition deteriorated. The last X-ray immediately before the patient suffered cardiorespiratory arrest showed a massive tension pneumothorax from his ruptured bronchus (Fig. 8.1). The time course of this death was 2 hours and could have been easily prevented.

Patient 2 A 25-year-old motorcyclist sustained left-sided rib fractures with an underlying haemothorax (Fig. 8.2). An intercostal drain of appropriate size was inserted into the left chest and drained 1.5 l of blood. The drain was not placed on suction and a central venous pressure line was not inserted. There was no further drainage into the underwater seal but despite regular observation the patient suffered a hypovolaemic cardiac

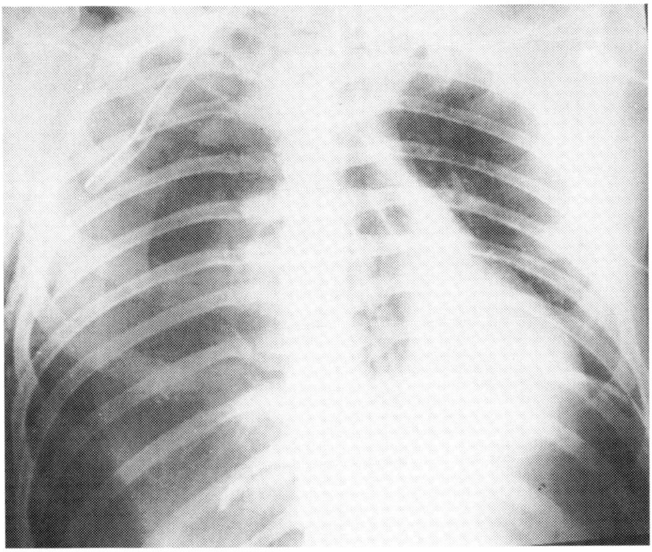

Fig. 8.1 Tension pneumothorax after blunt chest injury. The intercostal drain did not enter the pleural cavity.

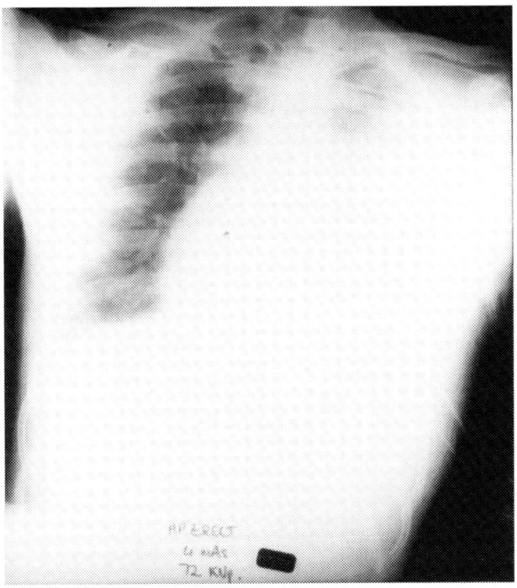

Fig. 8.2 Blunt chest injury with left haemothorax.

arrest 2 hours later without further treatment. The chest drain had blocked with blood clot and at post mortem there were 2 l of blood in the pleural cavity. Young patients initially compensate well for bleeding but deteriorate rapidly at the point of exsanguination. This was an easily preventable death due to poor management.

Patient 3 A 30-year-old male was stabbed in the left chest and admitted to a hospital with a thoracic surgical department. An intercostal drain was inserted and placed on suction. The measured blood loss was 1 l and continued at the rate of 500 ml/hr. The consultant was called after midnight and suggested continued observation. The drain blocked, the patient died 5 hours after admission from concealed exsanguination into the pleural cavity. The assailant's legal counsel successfully argued that the victim should not have died. The victim's relatives sued the hospital for negligence whilst the assailant was given a short prison sentence for assault.

These fatalities were preventable, given appropriate treatment by an experienced physician. In contrast, over-zealous resuscitation may also cause death in patients with serious cardiovascular injuries. ATLS guidelines suggest immediate infusion of 2 l of clear fluid for patients with a major injury (Westaby 1994c). Does the patient with a cardiac stab wound or lacerated aorta benefit from this policy? Clearly, when existing guidelines for resuscitation are deemed inappropriate by surgical specialists, there is great potential for legal conflict.

Patient 4 A 36-year-old motorist was admitted following a deceleration road traffic accident. He was fully conscious with a blood pressure of 95/60 mmHg, a heart rate of 110/min, a fractured sternum and bilateral fractured femurs. Aggressive ATLS resuscitation was instigated despite the fact that he was cardiovascularly stable. Chest X-ray then showed a widened mediastinum with appearances characteristic of traumatic aortic transection (Fig. 8.3) but the patient had received in excess of 3 l of fluid,

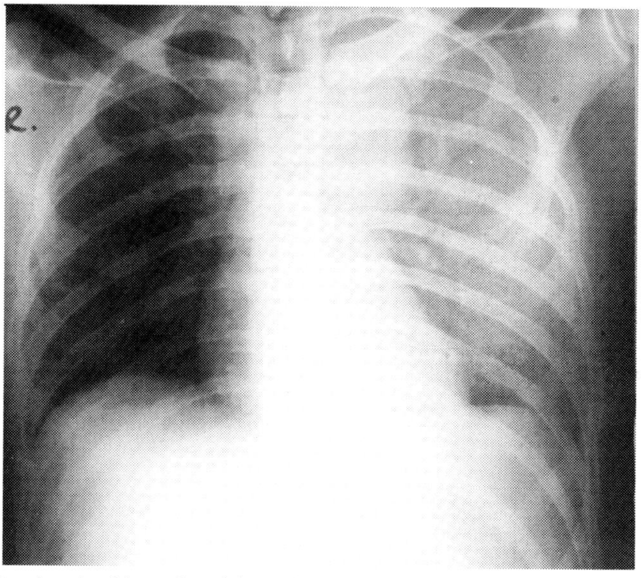

Fig. 8.3 Deceleration blunt chest injury with wide mediastinum. The appearances are characteristic of traumatic aortic laceration and there is a left-sided haemothorax.

causing the blood pressure to rise to 150/100 mmHg. Before the patient could be transferred for aortography and surgical repair, the aorta ruptured into the left hemithorax and he exsanguinated.

Was this appropriate care? The death was deemed inevitable but occurred in a cardiothoracic hospital and should have been prevented. Infusion of cold fluids without oxygen-carrying capacity may exacerbate peripheral vasoconstriction and increase cardiac afterload. Blood pressure increase in a hypotensive but stable patient may precipitate fatal aortic haemorrhage or cardiac tamponade in a situation where surgical access is impossible. In major vascular or cardiac injury it is possible to accelerate the rate of blood loss or provoke fatal secondary haemorrhage by raising blood pressure from hypotensive levels before the opportunity for surgical repair. The patient with tamponade following a cardiac stab wound (Fig. 8.4) is generally transfused with more than four times the volume that can be accommodated within the pericardial sac (about 500 ml). Those who reach hospital alive with a blunt aortic laceration are a self-selected group (less than 15% with this injury) in whom the mediastinal haematoma prevents exsanguination when the blood pressure falls. These patients also have inappropriate baroreceptor responses and artificially raised blood pressure. The fine pathophysiological balance can easily be disturbed with fatal consequences during inappropriate resuscitation. There are now both experimental and clinical data reinforcing the overwhelming clinical impression that early aggressive volume replacement is harmful for some

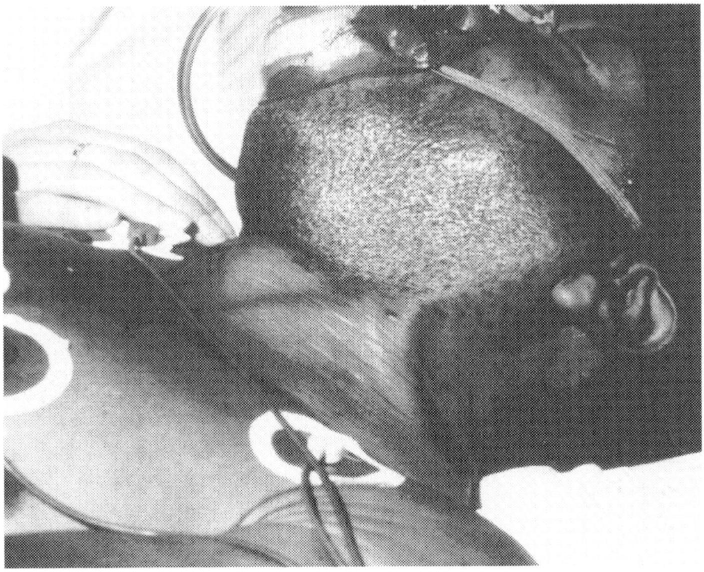

Fig. 8.4 Patient with a precordial stab wound and cardiac tamponade. The distended neck veins despite blood loss are characteristic of a cardiac wound.

patients with chest injury (Martin et al 1992). Vascular injury should be predicted or diagnosed from the history, physical signs and plain chest radiograph (Fig. 8.5). On the basis of this information obtainable within 10 minutes of admission, full intravenous fluid resuscitation can either proceed or be restricted pending further investigational surgery. After high-speed deceleration trauma or penetrating chest injury, often a considerable time before hospital admission, those who arrive conscious with perceptible blood pressure are unlikely to suffer further by waiting 10 minutes for the result of the chest radiograph (Glinz 1986).

MISSED DIAGNOSIS

In the setting of multiple injuries, it is not unusual to fail to recognise a potentially serious chest injury. Failure to recognise a transected thoracic aorta usually results in death from delayed rupture. On rare occasions the peri-aortic haematoma organises and becomes a calcified false aneurysm. Inappropriate baroreceptor responses lead to chronic hypertension which may be very difficult to control on drug therapy. This chronic problem also occurs in those who undergo successful repair of traumatic aortic transection. Hypertension in a young injured patient has the potential to shorten life and is frequently the object for legal claims.

Other injuries which are most often overlooked are ruptured diaphragm and ruptured bronchus (Westaby 1994b). Both occur in

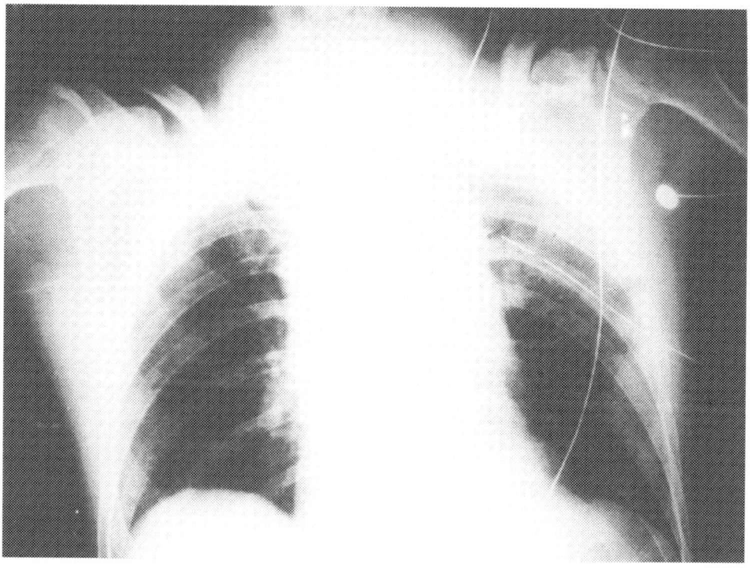

Fig. 8.5 The characteristic radiological appearance of transected thoracic aorta after blunt chest injury. The mediastinum is widened with haematoma capping the pleural cavities. A haemothorax has been drained on the left.

deceleration-type road traffic accidents which cause anteroposterior compression of the chest, though ruptured hemidiaphragm also occurs with unilateral impact from the side.

In practice it is usually a functionally unimportant problem such as an undiagnosed rib fracture or costochondral dislocation which leads to chronic pain and litigation. Claims along the lines of 'the hospital missed my broken rib and I have been in pain ever since and cannot work' should be actively discouraged by the medical and legal professions alike.

Ruptured diaphragm

This is seldom recognised during the initial assessment. On the left side the stomach usually herniates through the diaphragmatic rupture, producing a characteristic chest X-ray appearance (Fig. 8.6). This may be masked by a haemopneumothorax. A chest drain may then penetrate the stomach, spilling gastric contents into the chest. On the right side the liver may herniate through the diaphragm but the radiological appearance is indistinguishable from a raised right hemidiaphragm (Fig. 8.7). When the patient presents with respiratory distress and is intubated and ventilated, the positive intrathoracic pressure usually reduces the abdominal contents back through the diaphragm and obscures the diagnosis. Rupture diaphragm may or may not be recognised when attempts are made to wean the patient from ventilation. Late presentation occurs when respiratory function is clearly impaired weeks or months after the accident. The patient is then

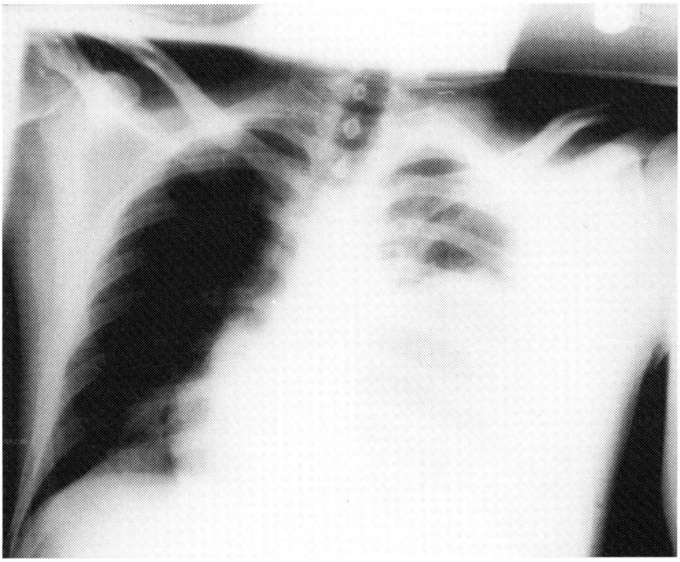

Fig. 8.6 The characteristic appearance of ruptured left hemidiaphragm with the fundus of the stomach distended in the chest. The mediastinum is displaced towards the right.

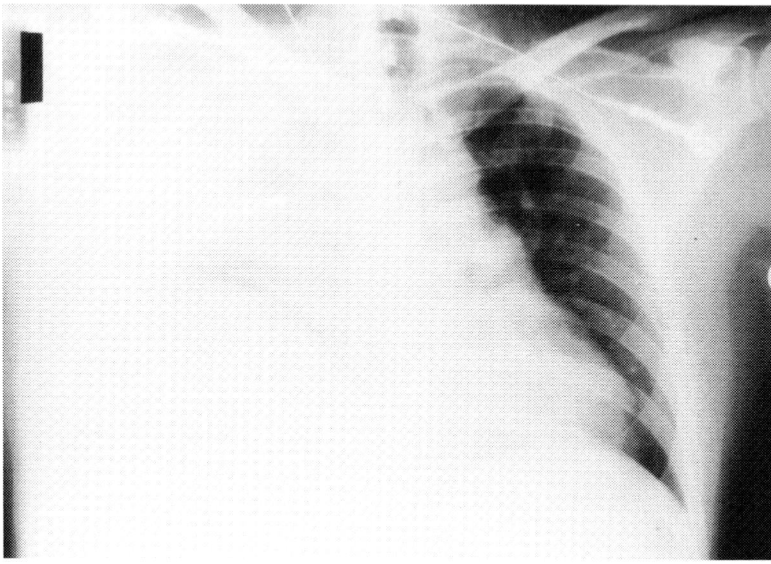

Fig. 8.7 Rupture of the right hemidiaphragm with herniation of the liver into the right pleural cavity. There is a right haemothorax and the mediastinum is displaced towards the left.

referred back to the same or a different hospital for investigation of breathlessness. On this occasion the cause of the residual disability is recognised and late surgical repair is recommended.

Ruptured bronchus

This injury usually causes a tension pneumothorax with a brisk and continuous air leak after thoracic drainage. A proportion of patients occlude the right or left main bronchus with blood clot so that the lung collapses and the injury remains unrecognised. If the airless lung is not re-expanded then chronic infection occurs. The lung may eventually re-expand but the site of injury narrows to form a bronchial stenosis. This situation leads to considerable chronic disability. In the presence of persistent post-traumatic airleak through a chest drain or persistent collapse of a lobe or lung, bronchoscopy must be performed to rule out this diagnosis (Figs 8.8 a & b). Failure to do so can be regarded as negligent.

Patient 5 A 10-year-old boy was playing on a climbing frame in the playground at school when he slipped and received a blow to the front of the neck. He was distressed by his injury and his mother was called to take him to hospital for a check-up. He attended the Accident and Emergency department of a famous teaching hospital, where some bruising of the neck was noticed, but he was sent home. Soon afterwards he developed stridor (airway obstruction) and was brought back. On this occasion the junior

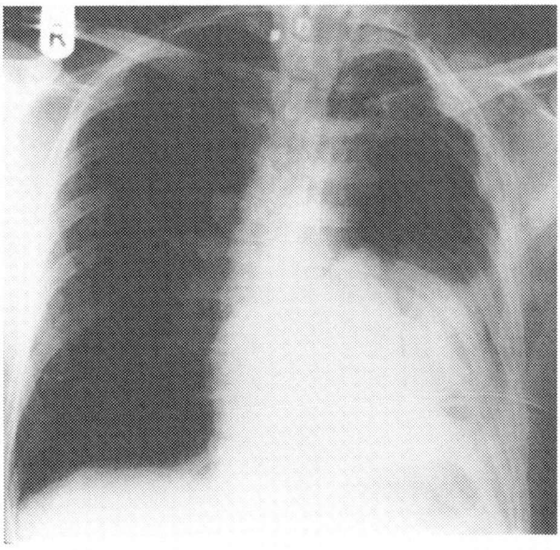

Fig. 8.8a Blunt chest injury with complete rupture of the left main bronchus. There is a large pneumothorax with a chest drain in situ. The lung is completely collapsed and resting on the diaphragm.

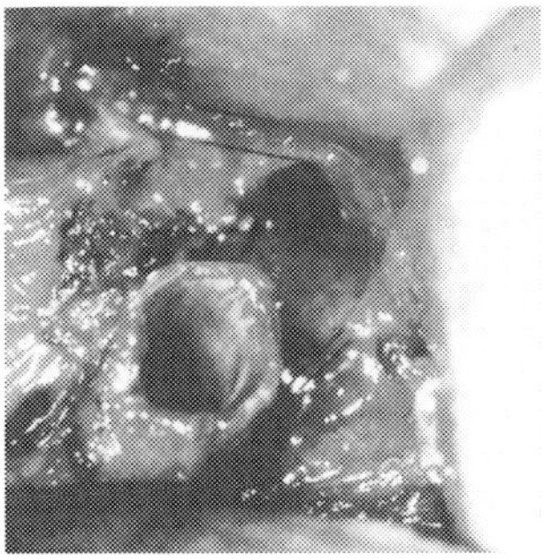

Fig. 8.8b At thoracotomy the ends of the ruptured bronchus were completely separate.

doctor called a general surgical registrar but despite the stridor, he was again discharged. The nurse in charge of the A.&E. department was unhappy with this and called the cardiothoracic senior registrar, who recommended bronchoscopy. Whilst waiting for this procedure, the airway obstruction worsened and lateral X-rays of the neck showed air and swelling in the tissues. The correct diagnosis of ruptured larynx was made and a tracheostomy performed before endoscopy, then surgical exposure of the larynx. At operation the larynx itself was found to be completely transected (Fig. 8.9). The injury was repaired and the boy recovered. This is a typical history for laryngeal injury with gradually increasing airways obstruction due to bruising and progressive oedema. The boy's parents were distressed and hostile about the first two medical opinions but in the face of a satisfactory result did not proceed with legal action.

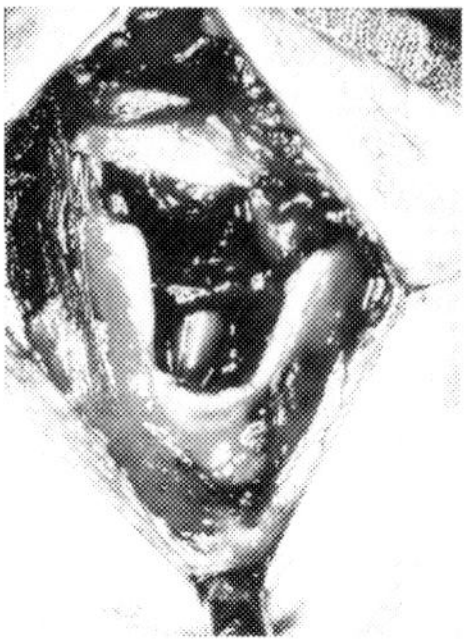

Fig. 8.9 Transverse neck incision to reveal complete transection of the larynx.

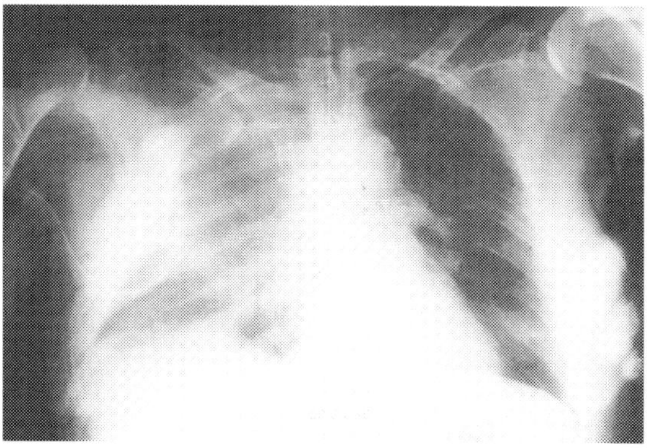

Fig. 8.10 Plain chest X-ray after a run-over injury in an elderly patient. The patient is intubated and on a ventilator. There is a poorly positioned intercostal drain in the right pleural cavity. There are multiple rib fractures on the right with a haemothorax. What was not apparent was the spinal fracture obscured by the mediastinal shadow. The patient was paraplegic with a fractured 7th thoracic vertebra.

Fractured thoracic spine

An unconscious patient cannot complain of pain from a spinal fracture and it is extremely difficult to recognise this problem on a plain chest X-ray (Fig. 8.10). This is a particularly good reason to perform a thorough neurological examination and elicit peripheral reflexes in patients with thoracic trauma. A proportion of patients who undergo surgical repair of traumatic aortic transection will be paraplegic on admission. If this is not recognised, the paraplegia will be blamed on aortic cross clamping during the surgical repair. Again the emphasis must be on careful pre-operative examination and documentation of findings.

Cardiac injuries

Blunt cardiac injury seldom causes left or right ventricular failure in the absence of a valve lesion or coronary thrombosis (Westaby 1990). Such events are particularly rare. Myocardial contusion usually resolves without treatment or residual disability. Occasionally myocardial contusion causes fatal ventricular dysrhythmia or sudden complete heart block. Rarely, acute thrombotic occlusion of a coronary artery causes actual myocardial infarction with residual disability. These events are sufficiently rare to be overlooked without risk of litigation.

CHRONIC POSTOPERATIVE DISABILITY

There are two postoperative problems which cause chronic disability despite an otherwise successful procedure.

Post-thoracotomy pain

Persistent severe pain can occur after emergency surgery for thoracic trauma to the same degree as for elective thoracotomy for lung cancer. This can be related to transection of intercostal nerves or to malunion of rib fractures. The pain may be persistent or exacerbated by movement and frequently interferes with sleep or the capacity to work. Persistent pain causes depression and anger which in turn may lead to attempted, though groundless, litigation. Patients with post-thoracotomy pain move from general practitioner to surgeon to pain clinic to acupuncturist. To be told that pain is an inevitable consequence of surgery often exacerbates hostility. Occasionally the surgical wound is re-explored to remove any knots, scar or suture material which may impinge on an intercostal nerve. Chronic pain syndromes are addressed in Chapter 12.

Paraplegia after traumatic aortic rupture

Paraplegia is a well-documented (10–15% of cases) but devastating complication of surgery on the descending thoracic aorta (Westaby 1994d). Although the aetiology of paraplegia is multifactorial, the final common pathway is neuronal ischaemic injury. The anterior (motor) and posterior (sensory) columns are supplied by their corresponding descending spinal arteries. Perfusion of the distal spinal cord is usually dependent on a few major radicular arteries which anastomose with the anterior spinal artery. The most important of these is the great radicular artery of Adamkiewicz that arises from an intercostal artery between T9 and T12 in 60% of individuals. Whilst patients with chronic problems such as coarctation of the aorta or atherosclerotic aneurysms develop collateral circulation, fit young adults with normal spinal anatomy are more susceptible to interruption of the intercostal or lumbar arterial radicular supply. Paraplegia therefore develops more frequently after aortic surgery for traumatic injury of the descending thoracic aorta than for chronic lesions. Much useful information on this condition was supplied by the Meta analysis of mortality and risk of paraplegia by Von Oppell and colleagues, who summarised the English language literature on this subject between 1972 and 1992 (Von Oppell et al 1994). The overall mortality in 1742 patients who arrived at hospital alive was 32% with one-third of deaths occurring before surgical repair. Paraplegia was diagnosed pre-operatively in 2.6% of patients and occurred subsequent to surgical repair in 10% of those who reached the operating room in stable condition. There was no information about the delay between hospital admission and definitive operation but the conduct of the surgical procedure was found to influence outcome. Patients were analysed according to the surgical methods used. Simple aortic cross clamping was associated with a hospital mortality of 16% and a 19.2% incidence of paraplegia despite lower average aortic cross clamp times (32 min; $p < 0.01$ versus passive or active methods of providing distal perfusion). Cumulative risk of paraplegia increased substantially if the duration of aortic cross clamping exceeded 30 minutes but only when distal perfusion was not augmented by an active or passive bypass procedure. Passive perfusion shunts were associated with a mortality of 12.3% and an incidence of paraplegia of 11.1%. Pump augmented distal perfusion had the lowest incidence of paraplegia at 2.3% but subdivision of this group showed the use of cardiopulmonary bypass (with full systemic heparinisation) to be associated with an 18.2% mortality in contrast to heparinless methods of providing distal perfusion (11.9%; $p < 0.01$). The cross clamp time required to repair the aortic rupture exceeded 30 minutes in the majority of reported cases with an international average of 41 minutes. Heparinisation complicates other injuries, hence the recommendation of heparinless centrifugal pump partial bypass for aortic repair in stable patients. This is useful information from the medicolegal standpoint though the majority of operations are still performed without pump bypass.

INAPPROPRIATE TREATMENT

Because cardiothoracic surgical expertise is restricted to regional centres, there may be very little expertise within the district general hospital when faced with a potentially life-threatening chest injury. Inappropriate treatment or complete lack of care may occur through inexperience. This is the principal argument for transport of injured patients to a trauma centre but after 10 years of deliberation, there is no sign that such a policy will be implemented. Failure to instigate proper treatment through lack of expertise is a potential source of criticism and litigation.

When a patient presents with a cardiac stab wound and tamponade but stable haemodynamics, there may be no surgeon prepared to drain the pericardium and suture the cardiac wound (Figs 8.11a–c). There is then a tendency to put the patient in another ambulance for transport to the regional centre. If the patient then dies 1 hour later in transit, where does the responsibility lie? Currently the assailant is responsible for the death, though increasingly defence counsel realise that this sequence of events constitutes lack of care. Similarly, if a patient presents with cardiac tamponade following a blunt chest injury (where no assailant is involved) and dies without treatment during secondary transfer, this amounts to failure to intervene in a life-threatening situation. This causes a dilemma, since ineffective surgical intervention by an inexperienced operator may also leave the surgeon open to criticism. In the case of homicide, defence counsel could argue that death was caused by unskilled surgical treatment.

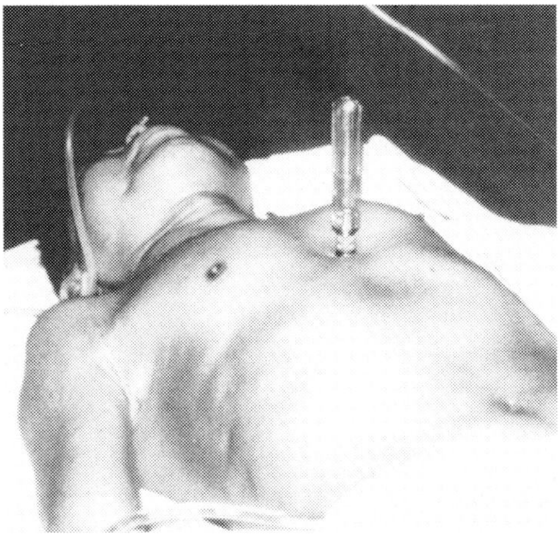

Fig. 8.11a Screwdriver transfixing the chest wall and heart. The implement should not be removed before adequate surgical exposure.

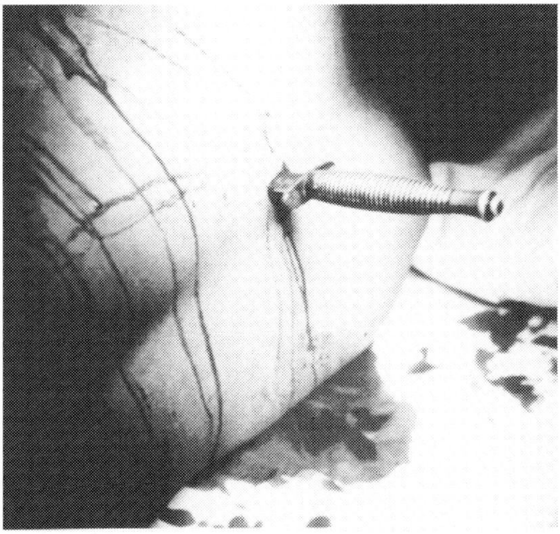

Figure 8.11b Stiletto knife in the left paravertebral region. This passed through the descending thoracic aorta but the patient was saved by prompt surgery.

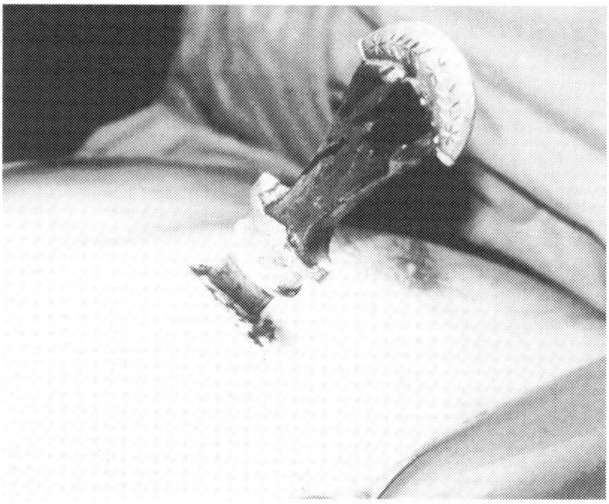

Fig. 8.11c A near miss. This knife passed through the pericardium, skirting the acute margin of the heart and entering the right lobe of the liver. Attempted homicide should be carefully documented. Forensic evidence must be carefully preserved.

In a national health service which encourages complaints and an environment where lawyers seek to expand their practice, these organisational aspects of treatment should be addressed. Medical staff who find themselves forced to intervene in a situation where their training and experience proves inadequate should document the incident carefully, and explain the limitations of the system to the patient's relatives. If the patient dies through lack of skilled intervention within a reasonable time frame the medical staff involved should record clearly the constraints which led to failure to intervene.

Patient 6 An 18-year-old motorcyclist was admitted to the Accident and Emergency department of a district general hospital following collision with a tree. He was conscious with extensive bruising over the left chest. Examination showed multiple rib fractures and absence of air entry on this side. Chest X-ray showed an opaque left hemithorax. There was some abdominal tenderness but this was attributed to referred pain from intercostal nerves. A peripheral venous line was inserted and 1 l of crystalloid fluid infused. The surgical registrar was called and, on scrutinising the chest X-ray, the registrar recommended transfer to the regional cardiothoracic centre. He argued that intercostal drainage might promote further bleeding from the chest and abrogated responsibility. The arrangements to transfer the patient took 1 hour, during which the patient received a second litre of clear fluid. His blood pressure remained around 110/60 mmHg with a tachycardia of 110/min.

Transfer to the cardiothoracic unit took another hour. By this time it was 4 hours after the accident. Before the patient could be assessed he suffered cardiorespiratory arrest and could not be resuscitated. Post mortem examination showed an extensive left haemothorax but from superficial pulmonary lacerations only. There were at least 1.5 l of blood in the abdominal cavity from a ruptured spleen. Early treatment with intercostal drainage, blood transfusion and careful assessment of the abdomen would have resulted in splenectomy (or repair) followed by uneventful recovery. No-one was prepared to take responsibility for this death and the relatives accepted that everything possible had been done to save their son's life. Had the outcome been questioned, the inappropriateness of his treatment would have been apparent.

IATROGENIC INJURY

Both intercostal drainage and pericardiocentesis lend themselves to iatrogenic injury. Most proprietary intercostal drains are supplied with a sharp, rigid metal introducer. Inexperienced operators regard this as a penetrating instrument with which to traverse the muscular layers of the chest. Consequently it is not unusual to witness chest drain insertion with the doctor pushing hard and the patient in considerable pain. When the device penetrates the pleural cavity the drain will overshoot and may penetrate a vital structure. The author is aware of a number of deaths during drainage of simple pneumothorax through penetration of the left ventricle, aorta or pulmonary artery. With one exception these deaths occurred through inexperience of the operator and the outcome is indefensible.

Another potentially dangerous manoeuvre is the prophylactic insertion of intercostal drains into patients with broken ribs before intermittent positive pressure ventilation. If the lung is fully expanded without air or blood between the lung and the chest wall, chest drain insertion is potentially hazardous. Between 10 and 15% of patients will have an obliterated pleural cavity through previous pneumonic adhesions. Under these circumstances the drain is likely to penetrate the pulmonary parenchyma and cause haemorrhage.

Needle pericardiocentesis used to be advocated for relief of cardiac tamponade but may lacerate the myocardium. In penetrating injuries fresh blood usually clots within the pericardium so that needle aspiration is ineffective (Fig. 8.12). Pericardiocentesis has been replaced with surgical subxiphoid pericardial window. An example of the dangers of chest drain insertion and pericardiocentesis is as follows:

Patient 7 A 19-year-old female passenger in a deceleration road traffic accident sustained blunt injuries to the head and chest. She was assessed in the accident department of a district general hospital and found to be hypotensive. Resuscitation was supervised by the orthopaedic team and an anaesthetist. Because of her deteriorating level of consciousness, she was intubated and ventilated. Chest drains were inserted into left and right pleural cavities in case of pneumothorax during transfer to a regional neurosurgical unit. Positive pressure ventilation caused a fall in blood pressure and a

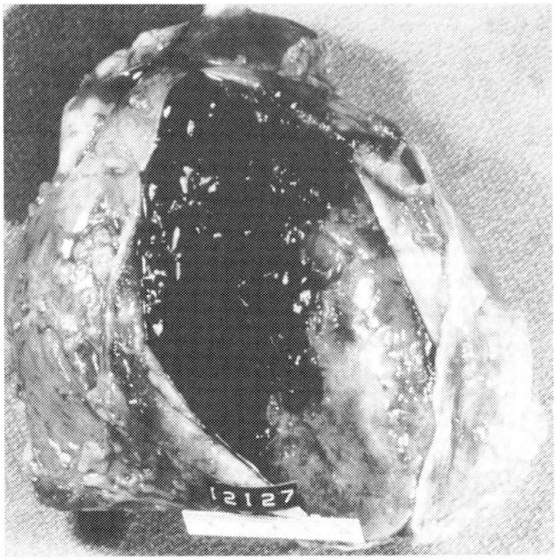

Fig. 8.12 Death from cardiac tamponade. The blood within the pericardium is clotted and not amenable to needle aspiration.

spurious diagnosis of possible cardiac tamponade. Needle pericardiocentesis was attempted but produced fresh blood from the right ventricle. She was then placed in an ambulance for a journey which lasted 50 minutes.

The neurosurgeons performed a brain scan which showed some oedema but was otherwise unremarkable. However, her overall condition had deteriorated substantially with profound hypotension. The cardiothoracic surgeons were called to assess the situation. A mediansternotomy was performed and carried down the midline into the distended abdomen. The pericardium was full of blood caused by laceration of the right ventricle by the pericardiocentesis. There was a left-sided haemothorax from a pulmonary laceration caused by the chest drain. The spleen was ruptured and there was 1500 ml of blood in the abdomen.

Prior to this iatrogenic debâcle, the girl's injury consisted of a minor head injury which would have resolved spontaneously, some bruising of the chest wall and a ruptured spleen. She died during the thoracolaparotomy from the metabolic effects of prolonged low cardiac output and infusion of cold clear fluid. Injuries sustained in the accident itself could have been easily treated. Again the bereaved parents were persuaded that this was an inevitable death from a road traffic accident and there was no question of litigation. Had aggressive relatives asked appropriate questions the course of events could not be defended.

Should ambulance chasing persist and increase to the extent that our system resembles that in the USA, the NHS will not be in a position to sustain increasing rates of compensation to bereaved relatives. Perhaps then the arguments for trauma centres will be more persuasive.

CLAIMS FOR MEDICAL NEGLIGENCE

A medical negligence case revolves around acceptable standards of care. The onus is on the claimant's legal team to demonstrate that the treatment received by the patient in question fell short of that which one might reasonably expect. Currently claims for medical negligence in patients who sustain thoracic trauma are rare. This is because those who undertake a legal challenge usually do so against the assailant or other party involved in the road accident. Treatment of the seriously injured patient is rarely placed under the microscope. The types of case described in this chapter are not remarkable but occur with monotonous regularity. This is because standards of care are enormously variable, depending on the expertise available in an individual hospital. The appropriateness of resuscitation and definitive surgery depends entirely on the degree of experience of available medical personnel, access to appropriate investigations, and the availability of specialist surgeons should the need arise. It is reasonable to argue that the standard of care should be that of a trauma centre, otherwise lives will be lost unnecessarily. Given this situation a persuasive barrister with an experienced expert witness can criticise care in practically any case with unsatisfactory outcome. How does this affect the junior hospital doctor or consultant faced with a serious chest injury in a district general hospital? As long as appropriate steps are made to reach a diagnosis and instigate treatment compatible with the scope of the surroundings and within a reasonable time frame, it is possible to deflect criticism. Failure to initiate resuscitation, perform a chest X-ray or reach a diagnosis within 15–30 minutes of arrival of the patient leaves the medical staff open to criticism.

Any doctor must be able to read a chest X-ray and be in a position to insert an appropriately sized chest drain without risk to the patient (Westaby & Trotman-Dickenson 1994, Mattox & Allen 1986). Intercostal drainage must be accompanied by suction on the drain and an appropriate response to the results. Drainage of more than 1 l of blood with continued bleeding dictates that the patient should undergo thoracotomy (see table 8.1). If this cannot be performed quickly, an appropriate standard of care will not be achieved. Recognition of a transected thoracic aorta through the chest X-ray appearance does not abrogate further responsibility. If the patient is to be transferred to a cardiac centre then appropriate blood pressure control must be carried out during the transfer. Failure to instigate this type of treatment again constitutes a less than acceptable standard of care.

Clearly an increased interest in litigation after injury will place many hospitals at a disadvantage. Increasing litigation may force more hospitals to insist on 24-hour consultant cover in their A.&E. departments. Trainees in orthopaedic and general surgery will become progressively more unwilling to intervene in thoracic trauma in an increasingly hostile environment.

How do standards of care relate to the experience and seniority of available medical staff? On the whole the NHS provides immediate senior medical cover only between the hours of 9.00 a.m. and 5.00 p.m. Trauma is not restricted to daylight hours and consequently levels of care vary considerably. In life-threatening thoracic trauma, thoracic surgeons are seldom called until a major injury has been identified or by such time that an adverse outcome is unavoidable. Does the legal profession accept variable levels of care and will patients' relatives accept adverse outcomes when senior medical cover is unavailable? This organisational problem is part of the British medical system but would not be acceptable in the USA.

REPORTING IN PERSONAL INJURY CLAIMS

The medical report for a personal injury claim requires a clear statement of the patients' current state of health, the disability relating to the incident in question and the prognosis. It is important to determine how the patient's state of health differs from before the accident and how residual disabilities will influence longevity and quality of life. Clear outcome measures such as New York Heart Association functional class, respiratory function tests, or levels of hypertension after aortic injury are important.

In order to determine the true impact of traumatic event on long-term outlook, it is also important to have a clear picture of the patient's health profile before the accident. Middle-aged or elderly patients may have debilitating smoking-related lung disease or ischaemic heart disease before the event. This may magnify the impact of a chest injury or account for the symptoms for which compensation is claimed.

It is often difficult to ascertain a clear picture of the patient's medical history unless there are records from the general practitioner. Functional capacity after a serious chest injury may be limited by cardiac or pulmonary problems. Blunt cardiac injury which is relatively common after deceleration road traffic accidents usually resolves completely without disability. Injuries to the heart valves or coronary arteries are extremely rare but do occur and may require surgery.

Patient 8 An 18-year-old car driver sustained a deceleration-type injury with direct impact of his chest against the steering wheel. After recovery of consciousness several days later he complained of breathlessness. Two-dimensional echocardiography was performed which showed impaired left ventricular function with anteroapical akinesia. The appearances were those of a recent myocardial infarction and were accompanied by mild to moderate mitral regurgitation. Coronary arteriograms were performed and showed an occluded left anterior descending coronary artery with a false aneurysm at the origin. He underwent repair of the coronary false aneurysm with a bypass graft to the left anterior descending coronary artery and recovered uneventfully. Assessment by exercise tolerance test using the standardised Bruce protocol, together with echocardiography 3 months after the operation showed no apparent disability. Left ventricular function was normal and there was no mitral regurgitation.

This patient suffered a particularly serious cardiac injury from which he made a complete recovery. It is difficult to speculate as to the influence of this injury on life span. There was a fine dividing line between death and complete recovery in this patient, who was the innocent party in the accident. In view of his complete recovery and excellent long-term outlook, what degree of compensation should be offered?

Patient 9 A 24-year-old driver was involved in a very similar accident but without unconsciousness. On admission to the accident department a widened mediastinum was recognised on the plain chest X-ray. An aortogram was performed urgently and showed a transected thoracic aorta. The patient was conveyed directly to the operating theatre for surgical repair. Despite aortic cross clamp times of only 20 minutes, he suffered permanent paraplegia. His residual disabilities consisted of post-thoracotomy pain which resolved within 6 months, hypertension which was difficult to control with medical therapy and permanent paraplegia restricting him to a wheelchair.

Hypertension results from inappropriate baroreceptor responses and is an inevitable consequence of the thoracic aortic repair. The aortic replacement was a life-saving operation and paraplegia is an accepted complication related more to the patient's spinal cord blood supply than to the surgeon's performance as long as cross clamp times are less than 30 minutes.

Clearly, the outlook for this patient is poor with considerable long-term disability and the likelihood of a shortened life span. A paraplegic requires considerable physical effort in order to mobilise. The physical effort will exacerbate the hypertension which is a potent source of early mortality. In turn an aggressive antihypertensive regime will impair the paraplegic's physical efforts and cause fatigue.

Though the nature of the accident was similar in both patients and both suffered life-threatening injuries requiring cardiovascular surgery, the outcome for the second patient was considerably worse than for the first and the amount of compensation should reflect these differences.

Many patients with blunt chest injuries suffer pulmonary contusion with haemothorax. About 5% of these patients suffer intrapleural infection following chest drain insertion in the accident department and may require surgery for empyema. In addition, patients with multiple trauma may suffer Adult Respiratory Distress Syndrome requiring days, weeks or months of intermittent positive pressure ventilation in an intensive care unit. This may severely impair lung function long-term.

When assessing lung function objectively, respiratory function tests are useful but baseline levels are seldom available from before the accident. For smokers it is easy to argue that respiratory function was impaired beforehand. Predicted values for respiratory function tests based on the patient's height and weight should not be used for comparison unless the patient has been a non-smoker. Diaphragmatic injuries also affect respiratory function tests and a ruptured diaphragm frequently separates a large proportion of the muscle from its nerve supply. Given that diaphragmatic injuries are often overlooked, assessment of diaphragmatic movement is a useful adjunct to the use of respiratory function tests when assessing residual disability. When a patient complains of breathlessness after a chest injury the initial management should be scrutinised. Failure to drain a haemothorax results in a fibrothorax which impairs chest wall movement and ventilatory capacity. On examination there is crowding of the ribs and decreased inspiratory movement on the affected side. Chronic pleural sepsis causes the same problem and residual disability should not occur if appropriate treatment is given at the time.

There are two common outcomes for which it is difficult to provide a measure of disability or prognosis. These are chronic chest wall pain and the psychological problems which follow prolonged intensive care. These problems co-exist in patients who require prolonged ventilation for multiple rib fractures. The degree of disability is influenced by the patient's age and psychological outlook. Persistent chest wall pain, either from the rib fractures themselves or post-thoracotomy pain can be attributed to specific lesions such as costochondral separation, malunion of rib fractures or development of an intercostal neuroma. When chest wall compliance is decreased the chest wall discomfort can be exacerbated by the sensation of breathlessness. These symptoms often resolve with time and sometimes with psychiatric treatment. Specific sources of pain may be treated surgically or in the pain clinic. Because of this it is difficult to make a reasonable statement of prognosis through an interview at one particular time, even if this is 12 months after the accident.

For this type of patient the legal system usually obtains multiple opinions from different types of specialist and chooses those which best suit the case. In general medicolegal reporting in this area is low key. For the surgical specialist it is a tedious exercise which proves time-consuming and may lead to further inconvenience if the case reaches the law courts. Financial rewards are inconsequential compared with those for private surgical practice. An increase in the volume of claims will further discourage specialists from participating in the legal process to the detriment of those with justifiable grievances.

REFERENCES

Glinz W 1986 Priorities in diagnosis and treatment of blunt chest injuries. Injury 17: 318–321

Martin R R, Bickell W H, Pepe P E, Burch J M, Mattox K L 1992 Prospective evaluation of pre-operative fluid resuscitation in hypotensive patients with penetrating truncal injury. Journal of Trauma 33: 354–362
Mattox K L, Allen M K 1986 Systematic approach to pneumothorax, haemothorax, pneumomediastinum and subcutaneous emphysema. Injury 17: 309–312
Westaby S 1994a Principles and practice of thoracic drainage. In: Morris P J, Malt R A (eds) Oxford textbook of surgery. Oxford Medical Publications, Oxford, pp 1942–1958
Westaby S 1994b Thoracic trauma. In: Morris P J, Malt R A (eds) Oxford textbook of surgery. Oxford Medical Publications, Oxford, pp 1958–1981
Westaby S 1994c Resuscitation in thoracic trauma. British Journal of Surgery 81: 929–931
Westaby S 1989a Trauma: the problem and some solutions. In: Westaby S (ed) Trauma, pathogenesis and treatment. Heinemann Medical, London, pp 1–19
Westaby S 1989b Penetrating injuries to the chest and abdomen. In: Westaby S (ed) Trauma, pathogenesis and treatment. Heinemann Medical Books, London, pp 159–180
Westaby S 1990 The injured heart. Clinics in Intensive Care 1: 210–219
Westaby S 1994d Surgery of the thoracic aorta. In: Morris P J, Malt R A (eds) Oxford textbook of surgery. Oxford Medical Publications, Oxford, pp 1806–1832
Westaby S, Trotman-Dickenson B 1994 Surgical anatomy and radiology of the chest. In: Morris P J, Malt R A (eds) Oxford textbook of surgery. Oxford Medical Publications, Oxford, pp 1857–1876
Von Oppell U O, Dunne T T, De Groot M K, Zilla P 1994 Traumatic aortic rupture: 20-year meta-analysis of mortality and risk of paraplegia. Annals of Thoracic Surgery 58: 585–593

9. Vascular injuries

Orla M.B. Austin H. Paul Redmond Pierce A. Grace

Injuries to the vascular tree are being seen more frequently. Approximately 3% of all major civilian injuries are now exclusively vascular or have a vascular component. There has recently been a dramatic improvement in outcome following vascular trauma; this has resulted from experience gained in military conflict over the last 50 years, improvements in the general management of multiple and vascular trauma and increased understanding of the pathophysiology of vascular injury, notably ischaemia-reperfusion injury.

In 1761 Lambert first reported an arterial repair of a traumatic aneurysm sustained following an injury to an arm. Makins (1919) reviewed the British experience with vascular trauma during the First World War while DeBakey & Simeone (1946) published a similar review of the American experience with vascular injuries during the Second World War. Prior to that time vascular injury was universally managed by vessel ligation. DeBakey & Simeone observed a 40% amputation rate with this form of treatment. The adoption of a policy of arterial reconstruction during the Korean and Vietnam Wars reduced the amputation rate to 12.7% (Whelan et al 1968, Rich & Hughes 1969), while more recently the development of trauma centres together with better pre-hospital care, has significantly improved the prognosis for patients sustaining vascular injuries (D'Sa Barros 1994).

PATHOGENESIS OF VASCULAR TRAUMA

Analysis of the data gathered following the two world wars suggests that the nature of the wounding agent is more important in determining the outcome after vascular trauma than the anatomical site of the injury (Adai et al 1980, Elkin & DeBakey 1955). The spectrum of military vascular trauma is different from the civilian experience and geographical differences have also been noted (Bergentz et al 1983). In Scandinavia (Risberg 1976, Bergquist et al 1987) and the United Kingdom (D'Sa Barros 1994, Robbs & Baker 1978a, Thomas & Baird 1983), stabbings account for most vascular injuries, except in Northern Ireland where blast injuries and 'knee cappings' account for a significant amount of vascular trauma (D'Sa Barros 1994). Gunshot wounds are a major cause of vascular trauma in the USA (Feliciano et al 1984, Sharma et al 1985, Drapanas et al 1970). Motor vehicle and industrial accidents also account for vascular injury (Hardin et al 1985, Creagh et al 1991, Cikrit et al 1990) and more recently a significant number of injuries have occurred following arterial puncture for diagnostic or therapeutic purposes; these may account for as many as 30–60% of vascular injuries seen at major medical centres (Orcutt et al 1985, Golledge et al 1995). Both acute and chronic arterial injury may also occur following parenteral drug abuse (Yu et al 1987, Yu et al 1983).

TYPE OF INJURY

Penetrating trauma causes the most common type of vascular injury and is usually secondary to gunshot or stab wounds. The degree of injury following a stab wound ranges from a small puncture with minimal vascular damage to complete vessel transection. Firearms are more destructive than knives but the amount of tissue damage depends on the type of weapon used (smooth bore vs rifled) and the velocity of the bullet (Mendelson 1991, Hollerman et al 1990). Low velocity bullets (<200 m/sec) damage only the structures penetrated by the bullet whereas high velocity rounds (>200 m/sec) produce extensive damage to adjacent structures (Hollerman et al 1990).

Blunt trauma may rupture an artery but more often it ruptures the intima without any effect on the outer layers of the vessel wall. Such an injury produces an intimal flap with thrombus formation and occlusion of the lumen of the vessel. Blunt arterial trauma is often associated with orthopaedic injuries, e.g. popliteal artery injury in association with femur fractures, knee dislocations and tibiofibular or plateau fractures (McCabe et al 1983). Blunt vascular trauma has a much poorer prognosis than penetrating vascular injury (Hardin et al 1985, Creagh et al 1991, Cikrit et al 1990).

The concept that arterial spasm may be the cause of reduced perfusion following arterial injury has been discredited. However, a minority still consider it to be an important clinical entity (Rich & Spencer 1978). The phenomenon was first documented by Montgomery & Ireland (1935) and has been reported with an incidence varying from 0.6% to 7.0% since then (Robbs & Baker 1984). Connell rightly claimed that it was a dangerous diagnosis often resulting in delayed treatment and prolonged ischaemia (1962). Samson & Pasternak re-emphasised the existence of arterial spasm as a distinct pathophysiological entity (1980), but all are agreed that the diagnosis of arterial spasm should only be considered on the basis of exclusion, i.e arteriography or surgical exploration.

Pathologically three types of vessel injury are recognised:

1. *Non-severed injury* results from stretching of the vessel, usually secondary to blunt trauma. As a result there is reduced blood flow through the damaged portion of vessel without external bleeding. In addition, damage to the intima may result in platelet aggregation and

subsequent thrombosis. The tissues distal to the site of injury may initially appear healthy but may later develop signs of ischaemia. Thus, the need for repeated evaluation of the arterial circulation in the traumatised patient cannot be over-emphasised.

2. *Partially severed injury*, which is characterised by incomplete disruption of the arterial wall secondary to penetrating trauma, is the commonest type of vascular injury encountered. This type of injury may be associated with significant bleeding as the normal physiological responses of vessel retraction and spasm are unable to arrest the haemorrhage. Partially severed arterial injuries are also associated with a higher incidence of false aneurysm and arteriovenous fistula formation.
3. *Completely severed injury* is characterised by vessel transection, usually as a result of penetrating trauma. The ends of the transected vessel constrict and retract into the surrounding tissues and the combination of local tissue pressure and clot formation results in cessation of bleeding.

Ischaemia/reperfusion

Vascular trauma may result in ischaemia distal to the site of injury depending upon the size of the traumatised vessel, the degree of collateral circulation and the type of the tissue supplied by that vessel. Ischaemia is a condition of inadequate blood supply resulting in tissue hypoxia, depletion of cellular energy stores, accumulation of toxic metabolites and ultimately cell death (Grace 1994, Cambria et al 1991). While the consequences of ischaemia have been well understood for years, it has only recently been recognised that, paradoxically, restoration of blood flow to ischaemic tissues may cause further injury. This phenomenon has been called 'reperfusion injury' and it may lead to limb loss despite technically satisfactory surgery for correction of the primary cause of ischaemia (Grace 1994).

Reversal of prolonged ischaemia will result either in restoration of the circulation and reoxygenation of the injured tissues or failure of the microcirculation and prolonged hypoxia. Ischaemia causes tissue damage by hypoxia-induced depletion of cellular energy stores. Reperfusion induced injury is multifactorial being caused by the formation of oxygen free radicals, depletion of free radical scavengers, release of chemotactic agents (TNF, IL-1), and the activation of circulating polymorphonuclear leucocytes (Grace 1994). Other agents, including derivatives of arachidonic acid and xanthine oxide, have also been shown to play a role in ischaemia-reperfusion injury (Grace 1994, Cambria et al 1991).

Revascularisation of a limb following acute ischaemia may result in significant muscle damage. Adiseshiah et al prospectively studied reperfusion injury in skeletal muscle in patients with acute ischaemia treated by revascularisation (1992). They observed that revascularisation of an acutely ischaemic limb after several hours leads to rhabdomyolysis and high levels of circulating creatine kinase (CK) and myoglobin. The mechanism of muscle damage is unclear, but release of oxygen free radicals is thought to be an important causative factor (Grace 1994, McCutchan et al 1990). Biopsy has shown that histologically discernible muscle damage does not occur during the period of ischaemia, but develops at some stage after revascularisation.

Ischaemia reperfusion injury may also have serious and potentially fatal systemic consequences characterised by metabolic acidosis, hyperkalaemia, myoglobulinaemia, renal failure and non-cardiogenic pulmonary oedema; the myonephropathic-metabolic syndrome (Haimovici 1979). Acute renal failure following successful revascularisation of the ischaemic limb was first reported by Haimovici (1960). Precipitation of myoglobulin in the collecting tubules causes renal failure but reperfusion of a limb also results in a medullary renal perfusion defect possibly caused by oxygen free radicals. This defect may be prevented by a pre- or per-operative sodium bicarbonate infusion (Lennon et al 1993). Mannitol, which may ameliorate the degree of renal injury by promoting an osmotic diuresis may also have beneficial effects by its action as a free radical scavenger (Grace 1994).

Respiratory failure, characterised by non-cardiogenic pulmonary oedema, has long been recognised as a complication of reperfusion (Blaisdell et al 1966, Border 1992). Such pulmonary injury is caused by inflammatory mediators released during ischaemia reperfusion of a remote tissue, e.g. the lower limb. Reperfusion results in the production of free radicals and activated neutrophils. The latter produce proteases which, with the very destructive superoxide anion, are capable of inflicting considerable endothelial injury (Welbourne & Young 1992, Weiss 1989). Lung histology shows that ischaemia reperfusion injury results in marked interstitial oedema and neutrophil sequestration, accompanied by alveolar oedema, haemorrhage and fibrinous exudate (Weiss 1989).

MANAGEMENT OF VASCULAR TRAUMA

Assessment of the patient

The classical signs of limb ischaemia are often absent in patients with vascular trauma. It has been reported that up to 50% of patients with significant vascular injuries of the extremities do not have diminished or absent pulses (Reiche & Golsorkhi 1980). A high index of suspicion for vascular injury is essential when assessing the trauma patient (Bergentz et al 1983, Blacklay et al 1987, Ransom et al 1981). Signs of vascular trauma include arterial bleeding, an expanding haematoma, a bruit or a neurological deficit. The site of injury should make one suspicious of an underlying vascular injury, e.g. a stab wound in the femoral triangle.

The interval between the time of injury and the time of arrival to the emergency department plays a major part in determining the final outcome (Howe et al 1987). Rapid resuscitation should take place in tandem with a thorough clinical examination to locate the site of injury. Patients with obvious vascular injury should be transferred promptly to the operating theatre for exploration preferably after on-table angiography. In those patients in whom limb viability is not in doubt but where pulses are reduced or absent for reasons which are unclear, angiography should be performed either in theatre or in the radiology department. Patients who have strong and equal peripheral pulses and are clinically stable with a viable limb may be observed and undergo elective arteriography if this is deemed necessary (Smith et al 1981). Systemic anticoagulation should be avoided in the injured patient with vascular trauma.

Investigations

Doppler ultrasonography

This is a simple non-invasive modality which uses sound waves to detect the presence of flowing blood. It can be used to detect either arterial or venous blood flow in an extremity. It is particularly useful to confirm the absence of a pulse in a swollen extremity where palpation may be difficult (Mozersky et al 1973). The presence of a Doppler ultrasound signal in the absence of a palpable pulse should not be taken as evidence of an adequate circulation as Doppler signals may well be detected distal to a significant arterial injury (Ashworth et al 1988). Measurement of ankle brachial pressure index will give a useful assessment of the state of the circulation but this is often impractical in a painful injured limb.

Controversy exists regarding the role of arteriography in the diagnosis of vascular trauma. Cikrit et al recommended the liberal use of arteriography pre-operatively to detect proximal injuries and to localise clinically suspicious injuries (1990). MacFarlane et al argued that angiography could be performed in the emergency room without interrupting resuscitation (1989). However, a consensus opinion appears to be that arteriography should be reserved for specific indications: (1) to differentiate between arterial spasm or compression and intimal damage; (2) to confirm the presence of a suspected injury and to plan surgery accordingly and; (3) to avoid unnecessary exploration of normal uninjured vessels (Enge et al 1975, McDonald et al 1975, Gomez et al 1986).

Biplanar arteriography is not infallible in the diagnosis of arterial injury. In an analysis of 183 patients with penetrating injuries of the extremities, Snyder and colleagues reported 28 false-positive examinations (15%) and one false-negative examination (0.5%) (1978). Arteriography is of undoubted value in the diagnosis of the long-term complications of vascular trauma, such as arteriovenous fistula and pseudo-aneurysm.

Intra-arterial Digital Subtraction Arteriography (IADSA) is as reliable and as accurate as conventional arteriography in identifying significant vascular injury (Sibbitt et al 1986). It has a number of advantages over conventional arteriography: a shorter examination time, decreased radiation exposure, reduced cost and less patient discomfort (Sibbitt et al 1986, Norman et al 1985).

Transcutaneous oxygen monitoring

This is theoretically a useful non-invasive adjunctive method in the assessment of peripheral circulation in patients with major arterial trauma. Kram & Shoemaker showed that a bilateral transcutaneous oxygen ratio less than 0.90 was 80% sensitive and 91% specific in diagnosing major peripheral arterial injury (1984). In normal atmospheric conditions, this test is not sufficiently discriminative and it is too slow and cumbersome to use routinely in the clinical setting. However, Mathieu et al suggest that transcutaneous oxygen measurements in hyperbaric oxygen are valuable in predicting the outcome of major vascular limb trauma (1990).

Definitive treatment

Arterial injury

Since the Second World War, arterial reconstruction including primary suturing, end-to-end anastomosis and interposition grafting has been the treatment of choice for arterial injuries. The traumatised vessel should be exposed and the edges debrided to healthy vessel wall. It is essential to excise enough damaged vessel wall at the time of primary treatment to reduce local thrombosis (Wilson et al 1986). End-to-end anastomosis should be reserved for isolated lesions in which tissue trauma is minimal and in which the vessel ends can be brought together easily and without tension. In practice this is often not feasible; in this case an interposition vein graft should be used to provide optimum repair without tension. Cephalic vein or other suitable arm veins are preferred for reconstruction of arteries of the upper extremity while saphenous vein grafts are used in the legs, provided they have not been damaged by the injury (Drapanas et al 1970). Where possible, the vein should be harvested from a limb other than the injured limb. When the arterial repair has been completed, an on-table completion arteriogram should be obtained to ensure that the repair is technically satisfactory.

The use of prosthetic grafts in the management of vascular trauma is controversial. Lau and colleagues compared the use of vein and prosthetic grafts in a potentially contaminated operative field (1977). Sepsis in an autogenous graft invariably resulted in total disintegration with exsanguinating haemorrhage, whereas infection in prosthetic graft material gave rise to sentinel haemorrhages which were easier to manage. However, in potentially contaminated operative fields, autogenous vein grafts may be used, but the graft must be covered with viable muscle if delayed haemorrhage is to be avoided. If the wound remains clean and healthy, the skin may be closed or grafted after 5–7 days (Meek & Robbs 1984). Prosthetic grafts are reserved for use where vein grafts are too small to use as a conduit (Drapanas et al 1970).

Venous injury

Reports of the first repair of a vein date back to the late 1800s (Blumhoff et al 1982, Barkun et al 1988). As with arterial injury, venous repair has become standard policy only in the last 50 years. In contrast with the success seen following elective operations on veins (Raju 1983), many venous repairs following trauma thrombose, especially in the early postoperative period. This is true even when interposition vein grafts are used (Meyer et al 1987). Barkun et al (1988) showed that shock and trauma predispose venous repairs to failure and that altered platelet–endothelium interactions may be implicated. Failure of a venous repair in the lower limb results in marked postoperative oedema. In contrast veins of the upper extremity can be safely ligated without increasing morbidity (Ross et al 1985).

Associated injuries

Injuries responsible for significant vascular trauma also cause significant soft tissue injury. Whereas treatment of the vascular injury in a timely manner may be life- and limb-saving, care of the associated soft tissue injuries is of the utmost importance in preserving the function of a limb (Rodgers & Ketch 1988).

Orthopaedic injuries

The force required to disrupt an artery by means of blunt trauma is considerable and the energy is dissipated in the production of tissue trauma, including fractures and dislocations. Internal skeletal fixation undoubtedly provides the optimum method of fracture immobilisation, as it facilitates nursing and rehabilitation (Meek & Robbs 1984) but it may not be appropriate in the management of open wounds. External fixation is indicated if there is extensive soft-tissue damage, wound contamination or if the fracture is very comminuted. Re-establishing a circulation to the injured limb should take priority over other injuries. This may be achieved by formal repair of the vascular injury or placement of a temporary shunt while fracture fixation is undertaken. If formal vascular repair is performed first, great care must be exercised subsequently to avoid disruption of the vascular repair. Careful re-assessment of the peripheral circulatory status must be made after fracture fixation (Meek & Robbs 1984). Management of these complex injuries is best undertaken by teams of orthopaedic and vascular surgeons working together.

Nerve injuries

Functional recovery from neurovascular injuries depends on early revascularisation and restoration of nerve function. Nerve injury has become the primary cause of long-term disability which is related to failure of return of both sensory and motor nerve function (Creagh et al 1991, Nichols & Lillehei 1988). Neural injuries account for a permanent disability rate of between 27% and 44%. There is a higher incidence of nerve injury with upper limb vascular trauma (75%) compared with lower limb vascular trama (25%) (Visser et al 1980). Williams et al (1986) recommended urgent reconstruction of any vascular injuries followed by early investigation of the neurological injury, including exploration, to identify potentially salvageable limbs. At the time of initial operation, nerves must be explored in all patients who present with a sensory or motor deficit. However, the complex nature of these injuries in addition to the frequent association with other potentially lethal conditions caution against immediate repair except where this involves a single nerve.

Soft-tissue injuries

Extensive skin and muscle damage are frequently associated with vascular trauma. The extent of soft-tissue destruction may not be apparent initially, as the viability of crushed or avulsed tissue is difficult to determine in the acute phase (Rodgers & Ketch 1988). Debridement of any non-viable or heavily contaminated tissue should be carried out at the time of initial operation to prevent development of infection and to ensure a clean base for any subsequent procedure to obtain skin cover, i.e. grafting or flap formation.

Fasciotomy is frequently required in the management of extremity vascular trauma. The indications for fasciotomy are: extensive soft-tissue injury, massive pre-operative swelling, prolonged shock, combined arterial and venous injury, and actual or potential compartment syndrome (Marsen et al 1980). The compartment syndrome, in which the pressure within the osseofibrous compartments of a limb rises precipitously, due to late ischaemic muscle swelling is well recognised following delayed revascularisation of a limb, and may lead not only to limb loss but myoglobinuria and renal failure (Perry 1988). Mannitol may be helpful in the prevention of compartment syndrome but it may not work adequately in patients with direct crush injury to the muscle.

Compartment syndrome may be difficult to diagnose but pain, swelling and tenseness over the involved compartment may lead to a clinical diagnosis. However, measurement of compartment pressure is invaluable (Perry 1988). A solid state transducer intracompartmental pressure measuring device is commercially available and easy to use. It consists of a hand held microprocessor to which is attached a syringe, diaphragm chamber and a 16-gauge needle. The system is filled with sterile saline and purged of air. The needle is inserted into the desired compartment and the intracompartmental pressure may be read off after 2 minutes. Other more laborious methods have also been described (Marsen et al 1980, Mubarak & Hargens 1983). Measurement of tissue pressure can be misleading and the results difficult to interpret. While there is no consensus regarding the pressure at which fasciotomy should be performed, compartment pressures greater than 20 mmHg are abnormal (Jones et al 1989).

Immediate fasciotomy is mandatory for compartment syndrome as delay allows progression of the injury. Most patients who undergo fasciotomy within 12 hours of the onset of symptoms recover without permanent deficit, while a delay of longer than 12 hours almost always results in permanent loss of function or amputation (Perry 1988). Fasciotomy should always include division of the skin as well as the subcutaneous tissues, and surgeons should have a low threshold for performing this frequently limb-saving procedure.

PREDICTING OUTCOME

In an attempt to predict the outcome of extremity vascular trauma, a number of scoring systems have evolved. The Mangled Extremity Severity Score (MESS) (Johansen et al 1990) and the Mangled Extremity Syndrome Index (MESI) (Gregory et al 1985) are two such scoring systems. However, McNutt et al (1989b) showed that problems arose with the MESS system in the assessment of soft-tissue injury based on mechanism and not objective examination criteria, and the fact that shock and age are relatively non-specific indicators of physiology in individual patients.

COMPLICATIONS

Two long-term complications of vascular injury are arteriovenous fistula (AVF) and traumatic false aneurysm (TFA). TFA is almost twice as common in the upper extremity, whereas in the lower extremity AVF is seen more often (Adar et al 1980). Fistulae are usually created by simultaneous penetrating of the artery and vein. They carry the potential risks inherent in any AVF but may also be a source of haemorrhage. An aggressive therapeutic approach is therefore required. This may be achieved by surgical repair, or therapeutic arterial embolisation. Recently a number of traumatic AVFs have been treated successfully by an endovascular approach and placement of a covered stent (Marin et al 1993). False aneurysms usually present early as a pulsating swelling and require urgent surgical repair.

Graft failure secondary to infection is one of the most serious complications of vascular trauma, and is usually the result of inadequate tissue cover of the vascular anastomosis or a vein graft. Shotgun wounds are particularly notorious with respect to the development of subsequent infection and have been associated with an amputation rate three times that of other types of arterial injury (Peacock & Proctor 1977). In addition, infection in the damaged tissues may lead to failure of the vascular anastomosis with resultant rupture leading to limb loss or even death.

SPECIFIC VASCULAR INJURIES

Upper limb injury

Vascular injuries of the upper extremity are defined as those distal to the lateral border of the first rib, and include the axillary, brachial, radial and ulnar arteries as well as adjacent veins (Adar et al 1980, Orcutt et al 1986). Upper extremity vascular trauma constitutes nearly half of all vascular trauma injuries to the extremities in both civilian and military series (Adar et al 1980, Elkin et al 1955, Creagh et al 1991, Cikrit et al 1990, Orcutt et al 1986).

Penetrating injuries are by far the most common form of upper limb vascular trauma and account for 94% of such injuries (Hardin et al 1985, Cikrit et al 1990). These are due to lacerations, stab wounds, shotgun blasts and iatrogenic injury. Blunt trauma comprises the remainder, and is most commonly due to road traffic accidents and crush injuries (Creagh et al 1991).

Clinical features include pulse deficit, pulsatile bleeding, pallor of the extremity, paraesthesia, distal ischaemia and a bruit. The presence of a pulse is, however, a very unreliable sign. Studies have shown that up to 50% of patients with significant vascular injuries to the upper (and lower) extremity do not have diminished or absent pulsations (Cikrit et al 1990, Reiche & Gorsorkhi 1980). An abnormal Allen test is equally unreliable. A high index of suspicion is therefore required to prevent a delay in the diagnosis of vascular injury and arteriography should be performed if there is any doubt about the diagnosis. Many patients with vascular trauma have associated injuries. The commonest is neurological trauma occurring in approximately 50% of patients (Creagh et al 1991, Cikrit et al 1990, Visser et al 1980). Other associated injuries include tendon, bone and venous injuries.

The prognosis for upper limb vascular trauma has significantly improved with the introduction of arterial reconstruction. Over the past 50 years the amputation rate following upper limb trauma has decreased dramatically and recently Cikrit et al have reported an amputation rate of only 1% for vascular injuries to the upper limb (1990). These results are mainly due to improved management, but also due to the fact that civilian injuries are probably less destructive than combat trauma (Adar et al 1980, Feliciano et al 1984). The prognosis for vascular trauma to the upper limb is now dependent upon functional outcome. The degree of functional impairment is directly proportional to the extent of anatomic injury with concomitant nerve and tendon injury being particularly relevant in determining functional outcome (Creagh et al 1991).

Shotgun injuries have been shown to produce the most extensive tissue destruction and thus are more likely to result in functional disability (Hardin et al 1985). Lee et al noted that of the patients with an isolated arterial injury, 94.1% had normal extremity function; with associated tendon injury, 80% of such patients had an acceptable functional result. Only 20% of the patients with nerve injury and 15.8% of the patients with combined tendon and nerve injuries had normal extremity function at follow-up (1985). Thus neurological deficit associated with upper limb vascular injury is an important negative prognostic indicator (Creagh et al 1991). A particularly high incidence of neurological damage is found with axillary artery injuries (Adar et al 1980, Graham et al 1982). This is due to intimate proximity of the vessel with the brachial plexus.

When considering peripheral arterial damage in the upper limb, it is generally accepted that ligation of either the radial or ulnar artery following trauma is not associated with any significant long-term ischaemic sequelae, provided that clinical examination at the time of injury confirms the adequacy of circulation via the other wrist vessel (O'Shaughnessy et al 1991, Gelberman et al 1979).

Other important complications of upper limb arterial injury include compartment syndrome and Volkmann's ischaemic contracture. Therefore, the need for fasciotomy should be critically assessed before wound closure following arterial injury repair in this region (Lee et al 1985). Upper extremity vascular trauma can have major social and economic ramifications since it generally occurs in the young (Cikrit et al 1990).

Lower limb injury

Progress in the management of lower limb vascular trauma has also advanced rapidly in the last 50 years with a reduction in amputation rates from 50% to 13% (DeBakey & Simeone 1946, Ashworth et al 1988, Bishara et al 1986). Most series reporting civilian trauma over the past 15 years have identified penetrating wounds (57%–86%) as the main cause of injury to the lower extremity (Ashworth et al 1988, Bishara et al 1986, Keeley et al 1983, Snyder 1982, Weaver et al 1983). However, recent reports show an increased incidence of popliteal artery injury secondary to blunt trauma (Peck et al 1990, Reed et al 1990).

As in the upper limb physical examination may be unreliable in the diagnosis of lower limb vascular injuries (Ashworth et al 1988). A false negative diagnostic rate of 10%–30%, based on clinical assessment, has been reported (Bishara et al 1986, Keeley et al 1983, Snyder 1982, Weaver et al 1983, McCormick & Burch 1979). Initial physical examination can be used to categorise the severity of vascular injury to the lower limb as follows: (1) *minimal* – abnormal pedal pulse examination without evidence of ischaemia (warm foot, normal colour, normal capillary fill); (2) *moderate* –

abnormal pedal pulse examination with evidence of tissue ischaemia (cool foot, pale colour, delayed capillary refill); (3) *severe* – cadaveric limb with no pedal pulse, cold foot, pale colour, no capillary refill, and loss of motor and sensory function (McNutt et al 1989).

Although perigenicular vascular injury accounts for only 10% of vascular trauma, it is responsible for 65% of amputations (Peck et al 1990). Popliteal and trifurcation injuries are more commonly caused by blunt trauma, and such injury has an amputation rate of about 60% compared to 20% for penetrating injury (McNutt et al 1989b).

Arterial injuries occur in 30–50% of knee dislocations, 2% of tibial fractures and 0.5% of femoral fractures (Snyder 1982, Weaver et al 1983, Peck et al 1990). Peck et al identified significant morbidity associated with fracture-dislocations of the knee (1990). Anterior dislocation is caused by acute hyperextension of the knee joint which tears the posterior capsule and stretches the popliteal artery resulting in an intimal tear and secondary thrombosis (Snyder 1988). Considerable force (650–800 psi) is necessary to produce a posterior dislocation of the knee joint and rupture of the popliteal artery. The presence of an arterial injury should be considered in all patients that have sustained a blunt injury to the knee joint (Snyder 1988). The well-recognised relationship between knee dislocation and popliteal arterial disruption has led to vigorous evaluation and improved management of patients with this injury (Kjellstrom & Risberg 1980). A similar high index of suspicion with other knee injuries may also result in a reduced amputation rate (Fabian et al 1982).

Limb survival is related to the interval from injury to arrival in the operating room, the level of arterial injury and the quantitative degree of muscle, bone and skin injury (Howe et al 1987). By combining these variables, a limb salvage index can be calculated to identify lower extremities likely to require amputation after combined orthopaedic and vascular trauma. Peck and colleagues have suggested the following indications for primary amputation: (1) primary tibial nerve transection with an anaesthetic, paralysed leg; (2) crush injury with prolonged warm ischaemia, and; (3) other life-threatening injuries that make immediate amputation prudent (1990).

The advent of microvascular free tissue transfer has had a significant impact on the management of severe lower extremity trauma (Khouri & Shaw 1989). Early definitive reconstruction of soft-tissue defects has dramatically improved the limb salvage rate (Khouri & Shaw 1989, Godina 1986, Harris et al 1987). The ability to add healthy well-vascularised tissue to the traumatised limb appears critical to wound healing and restoration of function.

Fasciotomy has also become recognised as a vital adjunct to repair of arteries proximal to closed osseofascial compartments such as in the leg (Perry 1988). A tense compartment necessitates immediate and complete decompression by fasciotomy. Fasciotomy is required for one-third to one-half of lower limb vascular injuries (Perry 1988). Missed compartment syndromes are associated with significant morbidity which may result in limb loss; fasciotomy should be considered routinely following revascularisation of the traumatised limb (Perry 1988, Robbs & Baker 1978b).

Neck injury

Injury to the neck vessels accounts for approximately 5–12% of all vascular trauma (Bergentz et al 1983, Robbs & Baker 1978b, Mattox et al 1989). Neck injuries are considered in three anatomical zones: Zone 1 is located below the sternal notch; Zone 2, between the sternal notch and the angle of the mandible; and Zone 3, above the angle of the mandible (Saletta et al 1976). The most commonly injured vascular structures in the neck are the common carotid artery and internal jugular vein in Zone 2 (Davis & Zimmerman 1983). 90% of these injuries result from penetrating trauma, i.e., gunshot wounds, stabbings and laceration with glass (Robbs et al 1983). Vertebral artery injuries appear to be secondary to blunt trauma (Dragon et al 1981), especially road traffic accidents. The mechanisms of injury include direct trauma to the vessel, hyperextension and rotation of the neck, blunt intra-oral trauma and basilar skull fractures.

The presenting features of cervical vascular trauma include haemorrhage, haematoma, shock and CNS disturbances. Associated injuries frequently occur including trauma to the great vessels, pharynx, oesophagus, trachea, larynx, thyroid gland and thoracic duct (Robbs et al 1983). Neurological deficit may be due to the vascular injury but there may also be an associated spinal cord injury (Dragon et al 1981). Many patients have no signs of vascular trauma.

Experience gained from military surgery suggests that all wounds which penetrate the platysma muscle should be explored (Messac et al 1983, Karlin & Marks 1983). However, the majority of such injuries result from high velocity missiles and this approach may not be appropriate to civilian practice, where the majority of injuries arise from stab wounds (Carducci et al 1986, Ngakane et al 1990). Many authors, however, continue to advocate mandatory neck exploration emphasising the low morbidity and mortality associated with negative neck exploration. The indications for selective neck exploration are: (1) vascular (continuous haemorrhage, diminished or absent pulses, large or expanding haematoma); (2) airway (difficulty breathing, voice change); (3) visceral (difficulty swallowing, subcutaneous emphysema, coughing, spitting or vomiting blood) and; (4) neurological (progressive deficit) (Dunbar et al 1984).

Carotid artery injuries caused by blunt trauma often cause thrombosis and delayed neurological deficit, and are associated with mortality rates of up to 40% (Perry et al 1980). It is important to recognise these injuries early, since restoration of carotid blood flow prior to the onset of irreversible neurological damage is necessary if the mortality is to be reduced. Patients who have severe neurologic deficits associated with alterations in consciousness, and who also have total interruption of prograde carotid flow are not improved by surgery.

Unilateral vertebral artery occlusion in a patient with a normal contralateral vertebral artery is well tolerated (Meier et al 1981, Golueke et al 1987). The exception to this may be an injury to the most distal portion of the vertebral artery which supplies flow to the posterior inferior cerebellar artery and thus to the cerebellum and medulla. Accurate assessment of a vertebral artery injury requires a contralateral vertebral arteriogram (Golueke et al 1987).

The prognosis for patients who have sustained vascular trauma to the head and neck is closely related to neurological status at the time of admission. Overall mortality rates vary from 17.4% to 20.9% (Robbs et al 1983, Dragon et al 1981, Meier et al 1981, Golueke et al 1987).

Thoracic injury

Thoracic injuries are responsible for 25% of trauma deaths (Wilson et al 1977). However, traumatic vascular injuries in the chest are poorly documented in the literature. This may, in part, be due to the fact that prior to present day resuscitative procedures, most patients died immediately from thoracic injury due to massive haemorrhage and exsanguination. Many reports detail only those cases arriving in hospital showing some signs of life. The statistics thus obtained relate to an inherently selected group of trauma victims who did not sustain a rapidly fatal wound.

Thoracic vascular injuries may be divided into injuries to the heart and injuries to the great vessels. Stab wounds are the most common type of injury to the heart, with shock being the predominant feature of presentation. Other clinical signs of cardiac injury are hypotension, distended neck veins, pulsus paradoxus and distant heart sounds. Beck's triad of hypotension, raised central venous pressure and muffled heart sounds is observed in only some patients. Rapid resuscitation is required if patients are to survive. Demetriades & Van der Veen reported a mortality rate of 83% with penetrating heart injuries, but this included patients who were dead on arrival at hospital (1983). If the latter are excluded, the mortality rate was 28%. They suggested that the most important single factor operating in determining survival was the time taken to reach medical attention (Demetriades & Van der Veen 1983, Bolanowskin et al 1973). Improved survival rates following penetrating cardiac injuries have resulted from the development of sophisticated pre-hospital systems and trauma centres.

Recognition and standardisation of management of blunt cardiac injuries have been slower to evolve. Blunt trauma to the heart may result in cardiac contusion, or rupture of the heart which may have an associated pericardial injury allowing blood flow into the thoracic cavity. Rupture of the heart is a cause of death in up to 65% of cases of blunt thoracic trauma (Shorr et al 1987). Presenting features include arrhythmia, cardiac tamponade, exsanguination and acute cardiac failure (Wilson et al 1977, Shorr et al 1987). ECG and cardiac enzymes are of limited use in the acute situation with severe cardiovascular trauma. However, they may be of considerable benefit in the diagnosis of less severe cardiac trauma. Myocardial contusion may be indicated by ECG changes including ST changes, arrhythmia and heart block (Gay 1982).

Major vessel injuries resulting from thoracic trauma also have a high mortality rate, due to massive haemorrhage and exsanguination. In a review by Rich & Spencer (1978), fewer than 20 reported successful repairs of acute injuries of the intrathoracic great vessels had been documented. Improved surgical techniques, and more advanced paramedical resuscitation has lead to an increased number of survivors.

Aortic transection, just distal to the left subclavian artery, is the commonest major vessel injury produced by blunt trauma to the chest (45%). Approximately 23% of traumatic aortic transections occur in the ascending aorta and are within the aortic arch. The lethality of aortic rupture is emphasised by the fact that only 20% of patients survive the initial injury (Shorr et al 1987, Gay 1982, Wilson et al 1978).

Innominate vascular injuries occur in patients sustaining low cervical or mediastinal trauma; most innominate arterial and venous injuries result from penetrating trauma. They are frequently associated with other local vascular injuries. Trauma to the innominate vessels is uncommon but is one of the most frequent vascular injuries associated with injuries to the thoracic outlet (Graham et al 1982). Controversy surrounds the incidence of great vessel injury in association with radiologically defined fractures of the first and second rib. Wilson et al found that patients who sustain a fracture of either the first or second rib have severe injuries usually involving multiple systems (1978). There was either haemothorax, pneumothorax, lung contusion, or flail chest in 73% of patients with first rib fractures. 6% of patients had associated vascular injuries (including subclavian and vertebral artery laceration) and 30% had associated cardiac injury. Fisher et al also concluded that the occurrence of aortic/brachiocephalic injuries together with inlet rib fractures is purely coincidental (1982).

Subclavian artery injuries represent 1–5% of the total experience, with arterial trauma reported in either civilian or military practice (Graham et al 1980, Busuttill & Acker 1982). The vast majority of the reported cases are consequences of penetrating subclavian artery injury. These are up to 50 times more common than blunt subclavian artery injuries (Shorr et al 1987). It is important to recognise subclavian artery injury, as delay in diagnosis may lead to secondary embolic events resulting in palmar and digital ischaemia (James et al 1979).

Thoracic vascular injury may rarely be a consequence of oesophageal perforation; 86 cases of aortic injury from an ingested object have been reported, with no survivors (Scher et al 1990). In most cases, a ‘signal haemorrhage' was the first indication of a vascular component to oesophageal perforation. Without treatment, terminal exsanguinating haemorrhage ensued within hours to days.

Abdominal and pelvic injuries

Vascular injury is the major cause of death following abdominal trauma. Mortality rates are high (30–70%) due to massive haemorrhage (Canizaro & Pessa 1990, Ekbom et al 1981, Millikan & Moore 1985). The commonest causes of aortic injury are gunshot wounds, stabbings and blunt abdominal trauma (Canizaro & Pessa 1990). Many patients present with severe hypovolaemic shock and are moribund on admission to hospital. Other clinical features include absent bowel sounds, abdominal distension or a palpable mass. Any patient admitted with penetrating abdominal trauma and profound haemorrhagic shock should be suspected of having an aortic injury or other major vascular injury (Canizaro & Pessa 1990, Ekbom et al 1981, Millikan & Moore 1985).

Blunt aortic trauma is uncommon. This is probably due to the highly protected location of the aorta in the retroperitoneum. Blunt trauma must be severe in order to cause injury to the aorta. Berquist & Takolander suggested that a pressure rise of between 1000 and 2500 mmHg is necessary to result in a blunt aortic injury in the abdomen (1981). The mortality rate from aortic injury is very high. This is because the rate of aortic haemorrhage exceeds the ability to restore blood volume, and shock becomes irreversible (Millikan & Moore 1985). It is therefore necessary to achieve tamponade of the aortic injury early and repair the injury.

Injuries to the inferior vena cava are similar to those of the aorta in several respects. Most are due to penetrating trauma and these have a high mortality rate. The majority of deaths occur from exsanguination due to difficulty in controlling a brisk flowing low pressure system (Turpin et al 1977). Bleeding from a thin-walled vena cava is not easily controlled, and application of vascular clamps to a bleeding site can often aggravate the injury. Three factors appear to have the greatest influence on mortality: (1) presence of shock on arrival at the emergency department: (2) associated intraabdominal vascular trauma, and; (3) location of the vena cava injury (Kudsk et al 1984, Millikan et al 1983). The retrohepatic inferior vena cava appears to be the most lethal site of injury due to the difficulty of exposure in that area (Kudsk et al 1984, Millikan et al 1983).

Renal arteries and veins may be damaged with abdominal trauma. The majority of cases result from rapid deceleration-type blunt injuries. It is thought that sudden displacement of the kidney from a relatively immobile aorta stretches the vascular pedicle producing a tear in the somewhat inelastic intima with resultant subintimal dissection and/or thrombosis (Ernst & Windsor 1981).

Associated injuries are present in many, if not all, patients with aortic or inferior vena cava trauma. They include visceral or other vascular injuries. The mortality rate increases with increasing numbers of associated non-vascular injuries (Ekbom et al 1981). The mortality rate also correlates with the number of vessels injured, ranging from 29% for one or two injured vessels to 100% for four or more (Halpern & Aldrete 1979). Overall, factors influencing mortality include mechanism and location of injury, presence of shock, associated vascular and visceral injuries and delay in onset of treatment (Cohen et al 1980, Borman et al 1982).

The internal iliac artery is the principal vessel supplying blood to the walls and viscera of the pelvis, external genitalia, musculature of the buttocks, and medial side of the thigh. Damage to this vessel may result in massive haemorrhage. The patient will therefore present with hypotensive shock. The importance of restoring vascular integrity after vascular trauma in the lower abdomen or pelvis has been substantiated by military surgical experiences with these injuries in war (Landreneau et al 1989, Ryan et al 1982). The high frequency of other abdominal injuries and associated haemorrhagic shock contribute to the significant morbidity and mortality seen with iliac arterial trauma. Bowel and genitourinary tract injuries are noted to occur in 70% of cases.

Paediatric arterial injury

Arterial injury in children poses a significant challenge even to experienced vascular surgeons. Children are intolerant of blood loss, carry an increased anaesthetic risk and require a high level of technical expertise (Meagher et al 1979). The management of penetrating trauma is straightforward but blunt trauma may pose a dilemma in the paediatric patient. Arterial spasm leading to loss of distal pulses may occur in up to 41% of paediatric patients following blunt trauma (Mills & Robbs 1991). Direct arterial puncture for arteriography is hazardous in children but intravenous DSA may identify those in whom surgery is unnecessary (Fabian et al 1984). Failure to restore a normal blood supply to the limbs in children may have serious long-term consequences. These include limb growth disparity, and bone age retardation (Whitehouse et al, 1976).

CONCLUSIONS

Vascular trauma is one of the most challenging problems in modern surgery. In fact vascular trauma is now commonly managed by multidisciplinary teams consisting of paramedics, accident and emergency specialists, radiologists, vascular, orthopaedic and plastic surgeons, anaesthetists and intensive care specialists. All have a role to play and the best results can only be achieved by the coordinated efforts of all members of the team. A high index of suspicion of injury and a comprehensive, aggressive approach to resuscitation and treatment, based on a full understanding of the pathophysiology of trauma and its consequences is required in the management of vascular trauma. The principles of management of the vascular injury per se have been established since the time of the Korean War, but an appreciation of the local and, more importantly, the systemic injuries caused by reperfusion of ischaemic tissue is relatively recent. Improved management of these sequelae to injury is improving the outcome for patients with complex vascular injuries. The challenges for the future are: (1) rapid diagnosis of vascular injury; (2) adequate resuscitation and transfer of the patient to centres with appropriate teams to deal with these complex injuries; (3) reduction of the incidence of revascularisation failure and reperfusion injury and; (4) improved rehabilitation.

REFERENCES

Adar R, Scharmek A, Khodadadi J et al 1980 Arterial combat injuries of the upper extremity. Journal of Trauma 20: 297–302

Adiseshiah M, Round J M, Jones D A 1992 Reperfusion injury in skeletal muscle: a prospective study in patients with acute limb ischaemia and claudicants treated by revascularization. British Journal of Surgery 79: 1026–1029

Ashworth E M, Dalsing M C, Glover J L et al 1988 Lower extremity vascular trauma: a comprehensive approach. Journal of Trauma 28: 329–333

Barkun J S, Terazza O, Daignault P et al 1988 The fate of venous repair after shock and trauma. Journal of Trauma 28: 1322–1329

Bergentz S E, Berquist D, Ericcson B F 1983 Vascular trauma. Acta Chirurgica Scandinavica 149: 1–10

Berquist D, Takolander R 1981 Aortic occlusion following blunt trauma of the abdomen. Journal of Trauma 21: 319–322

Berquist D, Helfer M, Jensen N et al 1987 Trends in vascular trauma during 30 years. Acta Chirurgica Scandinavica 153: 417–422

Bishara R A, Pasch A R, Lim L T et al 1986 Improved results in the treatment of civilian vascular injuries associated with fractures and dislocations. Journal of Vascular Surgery 3: 707–711

Blacklay P F, Duggan E, Wood R F M 1987 Vascular trauma. British Journal of Surgery 74: 1077–1083

Blaisdell F W, Lim R C, Amberg J R et al 1966 Pulmonary microembolism: a cause of morbidity and death after major vascular surgery. Archives of Surgery 93: 776–786

Blumhoff R J, Powell T, Johnson G Jr 1982 Femoral venous trauma in a university referral centre. Journal of Trauma 22: 703–705

Bolanowskin P J P, Swaminathan A P, Neville W E et al 1973 Aggressive surgical management of penetrating cardiac injuries. Journal of Thoracic Cardiovascular Surgery 66: 52–58

Border J R 1992 Multiple systems organ failure. Annals of Surgery 216: 111–116

Borman K R, Aurbakken C M, Weigelt J A 1982 Treatment priorities in combined blunt abdominal and aortic trauma. American Journal of Surgery 114: 728–732

Busuttill R W, Acker B 1982 Management of injuries to the brachiocephalic vessels. Surgery, Gynecology and Obstetrics 154: 737–743

Cambria R A, Anderson R J, Dikdan G et al 1991 The influence of arachidonic acid metabolites on leucocyte activation and skeletal muscle injury after ischaemia and reperfusion. Journal of Vascular Surgery 14: 549–556

Canizaro P C, Pessa M E 1990 Management of massive haemorrhage associated with abdominal trauma. Surgical Clinics of North America 70: 621–634

Carducci B, Lowe R A, Dalsey W 1986 Penetrating neck trauma: consensus and controversies. Annals of Emergency Medicine 15: 208–215

Cikrit D F, Dalsing M C, Bryant B J et al 1990 An experience with upper extremity vascular trauma. American Journal of Surgery 160: 229–233
Cohen D, Johansen K, Cottingham K et al 1980 Trauma to major visceral veins: an underemphasized cause of accident mortality. Journal of Trauma 20: 918–932
Connell J 1962 Vascular trauma. Australian and New Zealand Journal of Surgery 32: 42
Creagh T A, Broe P J, Grace P A, Bouchier-Hayes D J 1991 Blunt trauma-induced upper extremity vascular injuries. Journal of the Royal College of Surgeons of Edinburgh 36: 158–160
Davis J M, Zimmerman R A 1983 Injury of the carotid and vertebral arteries. Neuroradiology 25: 55–69
DeBakey M D, Simeone F A 1946 Battle injuries of the arteries in World War Two: an analysis of 2471 cases. Annals of Surgery 123: 534–579
Demetriades D, Van der Veen B W 1983 Penetrating injuries of the heart: experience over two years in South Africa. Journal of Trauma 23: 1034–1041
Dragon R, Saranchak H, Lakin P et al 1981 Blunt injuries to the carotid and vertebral arteries. American Journal of Surgery 141: 497–500
Drapanas T, Hewitt, R L, Weichert R F et al 1970 Civilian vascular injuries: a critical appraisal of three decades of management. Annals of Surgery 172: 25–60
D'Sa Barros A A B 1994 Vascular trauma. In: Galland R B, Clyne C A C (eds) Clinical problems in vascular surgery. Edward Arnold, London, pp 166–179
Dunbar L L, Adkins R B, Waterhouse G 1984 Penetrating injuries to the neck. American Surgeon 50: 198–204
Ekbom G A, Towne J B, Majewski J T et al 1981 Intra-abdominal vascular trauma – a need for prompt operation. Journal of Trauma 21: 1040–1044
Elkin, D C, DeBakey M E 1955 Surgery in world war two. Vascular surgery. Office of the Surgeon General Department of the Army, Washington DC
Enge L, Aakhus T, Evensen A 1975 Angiography in vascular injuries of the extremities. Acta Radiologica Diagnostica 15: 193–199
Ernst D, Windsor C W O 1981 traumatic renal artery occlusion producing hypertension. British Journal of Surgery 68: 19–20
Fabian T C, Turkleson M L, Connelly T L et al 1982 Injury to the popliteal artery. American Journal of Surgery 143: 225–228
Fabian T C, Reiter C B, Gold R E et al 1984 Digital venous angiography: a prospective evaluation in peripheral arterial trauma. Annals of Surgery 199: 710–714
Feliciano M D, Bitondo C G, Mattox K L et al 1984 Civilian trauma in the 1980's. Annals of Surgery 199: 717–723
Fisher R G, Ward R E, Ben-Menachem Y et al 1982 Arteriography and the fractured first rib: too much for too little. American Journal of Radiology 138: 1059–1062
Gay W 1982 Blunt trauma to the heart and great vessels. Surgery 91: 507–509
Gelberman R H, Blasingame J P, Fronek A et al 1979 Forearm arterial injuries. Journal of Hand Surgery 4A: 401–408
Godina M 1986 Early microsurgical reconstruction of complex trauma of the extremities. Plastic and Reconstructive Surgery 78: 285–292
Golledge J, Fligelstone L J, Scriven M W, Lane I F 1995 Vascular trauma in civilian practice. Annals of the Royal College of Surgeons of England 77: 417–420
Golueke P, Sclafani S, Phillips T et al 1987 Vertebral artery injury – diagnosis and management. Journal of Trauma 27: 856–865
Gomez G A, Kreis D K, Ratner L et al 1986 Suspected vascular trauma of the extremities: the role of arteriography in proximity injuries. Journal of Trauma 26: 1005–1008
Grace P A 1994 Ischaemia reperfusion injury. British Journal of Surgery 81: 637–647
Graham J M, Feliciano D V, Mattox K J et al 1980 Management of subclavian vascular injuries. Journal of Trauma 20: 537–544
Graham J M, Mattox K J, Feliciano D V et al 1982 Vascular injuries of the axilla. Annals of Surgery 195: 232–238
Graham J M, Feliciano D V, Mattox K J et al 1982 Innominate vascular injury. Journal of Trauma 22: 647–655
Gregory R T, Gould R J, Pedet M et al 1985 The Mangled Extremity Syndrome (MES): a severity grading system of multisystem injury of the extremity. Journal of Trauma 25: 1147–1150
Haimovici H 1979 Muscular, renal and metabolic complications of acute arterial occlusions; myonephropathic-metabolic syndrome. Surgery 85: 461–468

Haimovici H 1990 Arterial embolization with massive ischaemic myopathy and myoglobinuria. Surgery 47: 739–747
Halpern N B, Aldrete J S 1979 Factors influencing mortality and morbidity from injuries to the abdominal aorta and inferior vena cava. American Journal of Surgery 137: 384–388
Hardin W D, O'Connell R C, Adinolfi M F et al 1985 Traumatic arterial injuries of the upper extremity: determinants of disability. American Journal of Surgery 150: 266–270
Harris G D, Nagle D J, Lewis V L et al 1987 Accelerating recovery after trauma with free flaps. Journal of Trauma 27: 849–855
Hollerman J J, Fackler M L, Coldwell D M, Ben-Menachem Y 1990 Gunshot wounds 1: bullets, ballistics, and mechanisms of injury. American Journal of Radiology 155 (4): 685–690
Howe H R, Poole G V, Hansen K J et al 1987 Salvage of lower extremities following combined orthopaedic and vascular trauma. American Surgeon 53: 205–208
James E C, Kluri N T, Fedde C W et al 1979 Upper limb ischaemia resulting from arterial thromboembolism. American Journal of Surgery 137: 739–744
Johansen K H, Daines M, Helfet D et al 1990 Objective criteria accurately predict amputation following lower extremity trauma. Journal of Trauma 30: 568–573
Jones W G, Perry M O, Bush H L 1989 Changes in tibial venous blood flow in the evolving compartment syndrome. Archives of Surgery 124: 801–804
Karlin R M, Marks C M 1983 Extra-cranial carotid artery injury. American Journal of Surgery 146: 225–227
Keeley S B, Snyder W H, Weigelt J A 1983 Arterial injuries below the knee: fifty-one patients with 82 injuries. Journal of Trauma 23: 285–292
Khouri R K, Shaw W W 1989 Reconstruction of the lower extremity with microvascular free flaps: a 10 year experience with 304 consecutive cases. Journal of Trauma 29: 1086–1094
Kjellstrom T, Risberg B 1980 Vascular trauma. Acta Chirurgica Scandinavica 146: 261–265
Kram H B, Shoemaker W C 1984 Diagnosis of major peripheral arterial trauma by transcutaneous oxygen monitoring. American Journal of Surgery 147: 776–780
Kudsk K A, Bongard F, Lim R C Jr 1984 Determinants of survival after vena cava injury. Archives of Surgery 199: 1009–1012
Lambert R 1762 An account of a new method of treating an aneurysm (a paper read in June 1761). Medical Observations and Enquiries 2: 360–364
Landreneau R J, Mitchum P, Fry W J 1989 Iliac arterial transposition. Archives of Surgery 124: 978–981
Lau J M, Mattox K L, Beall A C et al 1979 Use of substitute conduits in traumatic vascular surgery. Journal of Trauma 17: 541–546
Lee R E, Obeid F N, Horst H M et al 1985 Acute penetrating arterial injuries of the forearm. American Surgeon 51: 318–324
Lennon G M, Ryan P C, Fitzpatrick J M 1993 Ischaemia-reperfusion injury in the rat kidney: effect of a single dose of sodium bicarbonate. British Journal of Surgery 80: 112–114
McCabe C J, Ferguson C M, Ottinger L W 1983 Improved limb salvage in popliteal artery injuries. Journal of Trauma 23: 982–985
McCormick T M, Burch B H 1979 Routine angiographic evaluation of neck and extremity injuries. Journal of Trauma 19: 384–387
McCutchan H J, Schwappach J R, Enquist E G et al 1990 Xanthine oxidase-derived H_2O_2 contributes to reperfusion injury of ischaemic skeletal muscle. American Journal of Physiology 258: H 1415–1419
McDonald E J, Goodman P C, Winestock D P 1975 Clinical indications for arteriography in trauma of the extremity. Radiology 166: 45–47
MacFarlane C, Boffard K D, Wilkinson A E 1989 Emergency room arteriography: a useful technique in the assessment of peripheral vascular injuries. Journal of the Royal College of Surgeons of Edinburgh 34: 310–313
McNutt R, Seabrook G R, Schmitt D D et al 1989a Blunt tibial artery trauma: predicting the irretrievable extremity. Journal of Trauma 29: 1624–1627
McNutt R, Seabrook G R, Schmitt D D et al 1989 Blunt tibial artery trauma: predicting the irretrievable extremity. Journal of Trauma 29: 1624–1627
Makins G H 1919 On gunshot wounds to the blood vessels. John Wright, Bristol
Marin M L, Veith F J, Panetta T F et al 1993 Percutaneous transfemoral insertion of a stented graft to repair a traumatic femoral arteriovenous fistula. Journal of Vascular Surgery 18: 299–302

Marsen F A, Winquist R A, Krugmire R B 1980 Diagnosis and management of compartmental syndromes. Journal of Bone and Joint Surgery 62: 286
Mathieu D, Wattell F, Bouchour G et al 1990 Post-traumatic limb ischaemia: prediction of final outcome by transcutaneous oxygen measurements in hyperbaric oxygen. Journal of Trauma 30: 307–314
Mattox K J, Feliciano D V, Burch J et al 1989 5760 cardiovascular injuries in 4459 patients. Annals of Surgery 209: 698–707
Meagher D P, Defoe W W, Mattox K L et al 1979 Vascular trauma in infants and children. Journal of Trauma 19: 532–536
Meek A C, Robbs J V 1984 Vascular injury with associated bone and joint trauma. British Journal of Surgery 71: 341–344
Meier D E, Brink B E, Fry W J 1981 Vertebral artery trauma – acute recognition and treatment. Archives of Surgery 116: 236–239
Mendelson J A 1991 The relationship between mechanisms of wounding, and principles of treatment of missile wounds. Journal of Trauma 31 (9): 1181–1202
Messac E, Siram S M, Lefall L D 1983 Penetrating neck wounds. American Journal of Surgery 145: 263–265
Meyer J, Walsh J, Schuler J et al 1987 The early fate of venous repair after civilian vascular trauma: a clinical, haemodynamic and venographic assessment. Annals of Surgery 206: 458–464
Millikan J S, Moore E E, Cogbill T H et al 1983 Inferior vena cava injuries – a continuing challenge. Journal of Trauma 23: 217
Millikan J S, Moore E E 1985 Critical factors in determining mortality from abdominal aortic trauma. Surgery, Gynecology and Obstetrics 160: 313–316
Mills R P, Robbs J V 1991 Paediatric arterial injury: management options at the time of injury. Journal of the Royal College of Surgeons of Edinburgh 36: 13–17
Montgomery A M, Ireland J 1935 Traumatic segmental arterial spasm. Journal of the American Medical Association 105: 1941–1946
Mozersky D J, Buckley C J, Hagwod C O et al 1973 Ultrasonic evaluation of the palmar circulation. American Journal of Surgery 126: 810–812
Mubarak S J, Hargens A R 1983 Acute compartment syndromes. Surgical Clinics of North America 63: 5–39
Nandi P, Ong G B 1978 Foreign body in the oesophagus: review of 2394 cases. British Journal of Surgery 65: 5–9
Ngakane H, Muckart D J J, Luvuno F M 1990 Penetrating visceral injuries of the neck: results of a conservative management policy. British Journal of Surgery 77: 908–910
Nichols J S, Lillehei K O 1988 Nerve injury associated with acute vascular trauma. Surgical Clinics of North America 68(4): 837–853
Norman D, Ulloa N, Brandt-Zawadzki M et al 1985 Intra-arterial digital subtraction imaging cost considerations. Radiology 156: 33–35
Orcutt M B, Levine B A, Gaskill H V III et al 1985 Iatrogenic vascular injury. Archives of Surgery 120: 384–385
Orcutt M B, Levine B A, Gaskill H V et al 1986 Civilian vascular trauma of the upper extremity. Journal of Trauma 26: 63–67
O'Shaughnessy M, O'Riordain D S, McCann J et al 1991 Consequences of radial and ulnar artery ligation following trauma. British Journal of Surgery 78: 735
Peacock J B, Proctor H J 1977 Factors limiting extremity function following vascular injury. Journal of Trauma 17: 532–535
Peck J J, Eastman B, Bergan J J et al 1990 Popliteal vascular trauma: a community experience. Archives of Surgery 125: 1229–1244
Perry M O, Snyder W H, Thal E R 1980 Carotid artery injuries caused by blunt trauma. Annals of Surgery 192: 74–77
Perry M O 1988 Compartment syndromes and reperfusion injury. Surgical Clinics of North America 68: 853–864
Raju S 1983 Venous insufficiency of the lower limb and stasis ulceration. Annals of Surgery 197: 688–697
Ransom K J, Shatey C H, Soderstrom C A et al 1981 Management of arterial injuries in blunt trauma of the extremity. Surgery, Gynecology and Obstetrics 153: 341–346
Reed M K, Lowry P A, Myers S I 1990 Successful repair of pediatric popliteal artery trauma. American Journal of Surgery 160: 288–290

Reiche F A, Golsorkhi M 1980 Diagnosis and management of penetrating arterial and venous injuries in the extremities. American Journal of Surgery 140: 365–367
Rich N L, Hughes C N 1969 Vietnam vascular registry: a preliminary report. Surgery 65: 218–226
Rich N M, Spencer F C 1978 Vascular trauma. W B Saunders, Philadelphia
Risberg B 1976 Abdominal stab wounds. Acta Chirurgica Scandinavica 12: 589
Robbs J V, Baker L W 1978a Major arterial trauma: review of experience with 267 injuries. British Journal of Surgery 65: 532–538
Robbs J V, Baker L W 1978b Major arterial trauma: a review of experience with 2677 injuries. British Journal of Surgery 65: 532–538
Robbs J V, Human R R, Rajarithnam P et al 1983 Neurological deficit and injuries involving the neck arteries. British Journal of Surgery 70: 220–222
Robbs J V, Baker L W 1984 Cardiovascular trauma. Current Problems in Surgery 21: 1–87
Rodgers C M, Ketch L L 1988 Management of associated soft tissue injury. Surgical Clinics of North America 68: 823–835
Ross S E, Ransom K J, Shatney C H 1985 The management of venous injuries in blunt extremity trauma. Journal of Trauma 25: 150–153
Ryan W, Snyder W III, Bell T et al 1982 Penetrating injuries of the iliac vessels: early recognition and management. American Journal of Surgery 144: 642–645
Saletta J D, Lowe R J, Lim L T 1976 Penetrating injuries to the neck. Journal of Trauma 16: 579
Samson R, Pasternak B M 1980 Traumatic arterial spasm – rarity or nonentity? Journal of Trauma 20: 607–609
Scher R L, Tegtmeyer C J, McLean W C 1990 Vascular injury following foreign body perforation of the oesophagus. Annals of Otology and Rhinology 99: 698–702
Sharma P V P, Babu S C, Shah P M et al 1985 Changing patterns in civilian arterial injuries. Journal of Cardiovascular Surgery 26: 7–11
Shorr R M, Crittenden M, Indek M et al 1987 Blunt thoracic trauma: analysis of 515 patients. Annals of Surgery 206: 200–205
Sibbitt R, Palmaz J, Garaa F et al 1986 Trauma of the extremities: a prospective comparison of digital and conventional angiography. Radiology 160: 179–182
Smith P L, Lim W N, Ferris E J et al 1981 Emergency arteriography in extremity trauma: assessment of indications. American Journal of Radiology 137: 803–807
Snyder W H III, Thal E R, Bridges R A et al 1978 The validity of normal arteriography in penetrating trauma. Archives of Surgery 113: 424–426
Snyder W H 1982 Vascular injuries near the knee: an updated series and overview of the problem. Surgery 91: 502–506
Snyder W H 1988 Popliteal and shank arterial injury. Surgical Clinics of North America 68: 787–807
Thomas W E G, Baird R N 1983 Arterial injuries in two Bristol hospitals from 1974–1980. Injury 15: 30–34
Turpin I, State D, Schwartz A 1977 Injuries to the inferior vena cava and their management. American Journal of Surgery 134: 25–32
Visser P A, Hemreck A S, Pierce G E et al 1980 Prognosis of nerve injuries incurred during acute trauma to peripheral arteries. American Journal of Surgery 140: 596–599
Weaver A, Rosenthal R E, Waterhaus G et al 1983 Combined skeletal and vascular injuries of the lower extremities. American Surgeon 5: 189–197
Weiss S J 1989 Tissue destruction by neutrophils. New England Journal of Medicine 320: 365–376
Welbourne C R B, Young Y 1992 Endotoxin, septic shock and acute lung injury: neutrophils, macrophages and inflammatory mediators. British Journal of Surgery 79: 998–1003
Whelan T J, Burkholder W E, Gomez C A 1968 Management of war wounds. Advances in Surgery 3: 227–350
Whitehouse W M, Coran A G, Stanley J C et al 1976 Pediatric vascular trauma. Archives of Surgery 111: 1269–1275
Williams N, Flanagan A, Lynch G et al 1986 Neurovascular traction injuries to the upper limb: management and prognosis. Irish Medical Journal 79(11): 320–321
Wilson R F, Murray C, Antonenko D R 1977 Non-penetrating thoracic injuries. Surgical Clinics of North America 57: 17–35

Wilson M W, Thomas A N, Goodman P C et al 1978 Severe chest trauma. Archives of Surgery 113: 846–849

Wilson R G, Allsopp R H, Dickinson P H et al 1986 External vascular trauma. Journal of the Royal College of Surgeons of Edinburgh 31: 72–75

Yu Y J, Cooper D R, Wellenstein D E et al 1983 Cerebral angiitis and intracerebral haemorrhage associated with metamphetamine abuse. Journal of Neurosurgery 58: 109–111

Yu Y J, Cooper D R, Wellenstein D E et al 1987 Cerebral vasculitis associated with cocaine abuse. Journal of the American Medical Association 258: 2104–2107

10. Abdominal injuries

Barry Jones Yunus Gul

The principal mechanisms of abdominal injury are by either blunt or penetrating trauma. Road traffic accidents are the cause of the majority of blunt injuries whereas violent assault is responsible for most of the penetrating injuries.

BLUNT TRAUMA

Blunt trauma causes injury to intra-abdominal organs by three distinct mechanisms:

- Rapid deceleration resulting in shearing forces. This causes tears in vascular pedicles and at points of attachment of solid organs.
- Compression injury often affects organs that are fixed, such as the pancreas or duodenum.
- Bursting injuries occur as a result of rapidly increasing intra-abdominal pressure frequently affecting hollow viscera.

PENETRATING TRAUMA

Stab wounds and gunshot wounds comprise the majority of penetrating injuries. There are marked differences between the type and extent of injury caused by ballistic trauma compared to stab injuries. An understanding of ballistic trauma facilitates the management of gunshot victims.

The kinetic energy dissipated by a missile in the tissues determines the degree of tissue damage. Kinetic energy equals half the mass of the bullet by the square of its velocity. Factors affecting the velocity include the distance from the gun, the length of the gun barrel, air/wind resistance, gun barrel and bullet design.

A bullet is stabilised in flight by the spin imparted to it by the rifling on the gun barrel. This helps it overcome its tendency to tumble in flight. The degree to which a projectile tumbles depends on its design and spin. This tumbling or deviation is referred to as 'yaw'.

On impact with a target, the spin of a missile is diminished. The greater the yaw angle on impact, the sooner the missile will tumble within the tissues causing more rapid deceleration and greater dissipation of kinetic energy. If a bullet tumbles and decelerates too early, most of its kinetic energy will be dissipated in the superficial tissues. More stable high velocity bullets decelerate and tumble in the deeper tissues.

An important determinant of tissue damage is the amount of cavitation induced by the passage of the missile through the tissues. All missiles produce temporary cavitation due to the elastic recoil of tissues. For a more detailed analysis of gunshot ballistics refer to Chapter 3.

HEPATIC INJURY

The liver is the most frequently injured abdominal organ. It is second only to spleen in frequency of injury in blunt trauma and is second to small bowel in terms of susceptibility to penetrating trauma. In blunt trauma, liver injury occurs in 20–45% of cases (Alho et al 1978) and is involved in 40% of penetrating injuries (Feliciano & Pachter 1989). Fractures of the lower right ribs carry a 10% risk of hepatic injury.

Mechanisms of injury fall clearly into blunt and penetrating types. The relative proportions of these two mechanisms in a given clinical setting depends on social and cultural factors. In reports from Cambridge UK and Toronto, blunt trauma accounted for 95% of liver injuries (Watson et al 1991, Hanna et al 1991) whereas in Texas, 75% of liver injuries were due to penetrating trauma (Feliciano et al 1986). In Edinburgh the split was more evenly divided with 60% of hepatic injuries caused by blunt trauma and 40% by penetrating injury (John et al 1992).

Classification

There are several systems in use for classifying liver trauma. The system proposed by the American Association for Surgical Trauma (AAST) is recommended (Table 10.1) (Moore et al 1989). This is detailed and part of a consistent organ injury scaling system. The classification devised by Calne et al (1982) is easier to remember but is less comprehensive and, outside the UK, is supplanted by the AAST system (see below) (Table 10.2).

A further classification of hepatic injury based on CT scan appearances proposed by Mirvis et al (1989) may help distinguish injuries needing operative intervention from those which may be managed conservatively (Table 10.3).

Aetiology

The relative incidence of blunt versus penetrating trauma varies from place to place (vide supra). Motor vehicle accident is the single most important cause of blunt liver trauma. Up to 90% of blunt hepatic injuries are caused by road traffic accidents (Rivkind et al 1989). Consequently patients are

Table 10.1 AAST Liver injury scale (Moore et al 1989)

Grade*	Type	Injury	ICD-9	AIS 85	AIS 9
I	Haematoma	Subcapsular, non-expanding, < 10% surface area	864.01 864.11	2	2
	Laceration	Capsular tear, non-bleeding, < 1 cm parenchymal depth	864.02 864.12	2	2
II	Haematoma	Subcapsular, non-expanding, 10-50% surface area; intraparenchymal, non-expanding, <2 cm in diameter	864.01 864.11	2	2
	Laceration	Capsular tear, active bleeding, 1–3 cm parenchymal depth, <10 cm in length	864.03 864.13	2	2
III	Haematoma	Subcapsular, >50% surface area or expanding; ruptured subcapsular haematoma with active bleeding; intraparenchymal haematoma >2 cm or expanding		3	3
	Laceration	>3 cm parenchymal depth	864.04 864.14	3	3
IV	Haematoma	Ruptured intraparenchymal haematoma with active bleeding		3	4
	Laceration	Parenchymal disruption involving >50% of hepatic lobe	864.04 864.14	4	4
V	Laceration	Parenchymal disruption involving >50% of hepatic lobe		5	5
	Vascular	Juxtahepatic venous injuries i.e. retrohepatic vena cava/major hepatic veins		5	5
VI	Vascular	Hepatic avulsion			6

* Advance one grade for multiple injuries to the same organ

often multiply injured. Head and thoracic injuries are commonly associated with blunt hepatic trauma (Watson et al 1991, Rivkind et al 1989). The severity of brain injury correlates approximately with the grade of hepatic injury and is the single most important determinant of outcome.

Other commonly associated injuries include those to the spleen, pancreas, kidney, duodenum, diaphragm and long bone (fractures). These have not been found independently to contribute to the mortality rate (Rivkind et al 1989) but will increase the Injury Severity Score (ISS) (Baker et al 1974).

Table 10.2 Surgical grading of liver injury (Calne et al 1982)

Grade I	Capsular tear, no parenchymal damage Minor bleeding which stops spontaneously or with a few simple sutures
Grade II	Parenchymal damage Careful suturing secures haemostasis
Grade III	Parenchymal damage Major haemorrhage from intrahepatic arteries or veins threatening life-producing shock
Grade IV	Parenchymal damage Tear of inferior vena cava or major hepatic vessels

Table 10.3 Computed tomographic scan grading of liver injury (Mirvis et al 1989)

Grade I	Capsular avulsion: superficial laceration <1 cm deep Subcapsular haematoma of < 1cm maximum thickness Periportal blood tracking only
Grade II	Lacerations 1–3 cm deep Central/subcapsular haematoma 1–3 cm diameter
Grade III	Lacerations >3 cm deep Central subcapsular haematoma >3 cm diameter
Grade IV	Massive central subcapsular haematoma >10 cm Lobar tissue destruction (maceration) or devascularisation
Grade V	Bilobular tissue destruction (maceration) or devascularisation

Penetrating injuries to the liver are associated with a lower median ISS and a lower complication rate and mortality rate (John et al 1992).

Diagnosis

Clinical evaluation retains a central role in the management of abdominal trauma. It does not, however, provide sufficient sensitivity on its own having, at best, accuracy of 65% (Powell et al 1982). This is further reduced where cerebration is impaired due to injury, alcohol or drugs.

Diagnostic peritoneal lavage

Collective experience indicates that diagnostic peritoneal lavage (DPL) has an accuracy of 97.3% with a false positive rate of 1.4% and a false negative rate of 1.3% (Powell et al 1982, Fischer et al 1978). Some centres rely on 'macroscopic' DPL, that is, they do not resort to microscopic evaluation of the aspirate (John et al 1992). It is generally accepted that DPL substantially augments clinicians acumen in evaluating the injured abdomen.

CT scanning

Further diagnostic evaluation is dictated by the patient's condition. In the haemodynamically stable patient CT scanning is a useful adjunct and in certain cases may obviate laparotomy (Mirvis et al 1989). In some cases CT scan may counterbalance the increase in non-therapeutic laparotomy which would occur if DPL was relied upon in isolation. The limitations of CT scanning are its inability to eliminate hollow viscus rupture (Rehm et al 1989). Some investigators have found a poor correlation between CT appearances and operative findings, with CT overestimating the grade of injury in about 40% of cases and underestimating the grade in a further 40% compared to operative findings (Croce et al 1991).

Ultrasound

Ultrasound evaluation may also be beneficial especially on a serial basis. Its precise role is not as yet clear as it remains to be determined if it alters management decisions. It is not as sensitive as DPL (Gruessner et al 1989) and does not at present have the resolution to outrule certain injuries. As such it cannot 'overrule' a positive DPL. A major advantage lies in its portability so that it can be used in emergency operating without compromising resuscitation measures.

Management

Treatment is dictated by the grade of injury, the physiological condition of the patient and associated injuries. Management has changed over the years and more recently has reverted from an aggressive approach to surgical restraint.

Non-operative management may be attempted initially in haemodynamically stable patients with AAST Grades I and II injuries. Over half of these patients will subsequently require some form of intervention (Watson et al 1991). This, however, will often be percutaneous drainage of collections.

Drainage

Active bleeding has stopped in about 50% of cases by the time laparotomy is undertaken and therefore drainage only is required. It is not recommended to suture areas that are not actively bleeding (Trunkey et al 1974). Closed active drainage is preferable as this has a lower infection rate than open drainage (Penrose/Yeats) (0% versus 14%) (Noyes et al 1988). Combining closed suction systems with open passive systems is not recommended as this is associated with an infection rate of 22.5%. Feliciano & Pachter (1989), in an extensive review, conclude that where haemostasis is satisfactory and there is no apparent bile leakage drainage is unnecessary.

Where prolonged, high volume drainage is anticipated, e.g. in the presence of coagulopathy, resection of a portion of the 12th rib may be necessary.

Suturing/haemostatic agents

Localised areas of active bleeding may be managed by liver suture, haemostatic agents and drainage. Where the area is shattered or devitalised, formal resectional debridement of the area may be undertaken using the finger fracture technique combined with the Pringle manoeuvre.

Anatomical lobectomy vs packing

Anatomical hepatic lobectomy may be required where blood loss is not controlled by suturing, resectional debridement or hepatic artery ligation. Popularity for this option has waned in favour of hepatic artery ligation combined with perihepatic packing. Anatomical lobectomy for trauma carries a high mortality rate, in some cases approaching 60% (Defore et al 1976). Packing carries a mortality rate of around 30% (Feliciano et al 1990) but there is wide variation in mortality rates reported in the literature, ranging from 10% (Feliciano et al 1981) to 57% (Ivatury et al 1986). In the same publication Peitzman, Udekwu and Iwatsuki report a mortality rate for anatomical lobectomy of 30% (1990). In experienced hands the mortality rate associated with formal lobectomy approaches that of packing. However, most surgeons do not encounter a large volume of major liver trauma and the literature suggests that in the absence of special expertise in the area, packing is the safer option.

Intra-abdominal abscess is the main complication associated with packing occurring in 20% (Cue et al 1990) to 35% (Ivatury et al 1986) of cases.

Mesh hepatorrhaphy

More recently, mesh hepatorrhaphy has been advocated as a form of compressive therapy in major blunt liver trauma (Stevens et al 1991). This is a development of the technique initially developed for splenic conservation (Delany et al 1985) and involves wrapping the injured lobe or the entire liver in a polyglycolic acid mesh which is secured to the falciform ligament. Reed et al report satisfactory experience with the technique. The mortality rate from 20 patients treated to date is 25% for lobar injuries with an intra-abdominal infection rate of 8%. The technique is less successful for juxtacaval injuries (Reed et al 1992).

Complications

Retrohepatic injury

Retrohepatic venous injuries pose a serious surgical challenge. Access to secure haemostasis is the main problem. Options include intracaval shunting, total hepatic vascular isolation (Heaney et al 1966) and packing. Beal advocates packing and in a study that included 14 hepatic vein and six retrohepatic caval injuries had no mortality due to uncontrolled haemorrhage.

Extrahepatic biliary injury

The extrahepatic biliary system may be injured either by penetrating or blunt trauma. An important consideration in penetrating injuries to the axial biliary system is the presence of associated vascular injury, especially involving the hepatic artery and/or the portal vein. Prompt vascular control is essential otherwise mortality is high.

Partial disruption of a duct may be repaired either by direct re-anastomosis or with a patch. Complete disruptions will commonly develop a stricture if direct re-approximation is attempted. Enteroductal diversion is preferred in these cases (Busuttil et al 1980). It is not clear if a T-tube is definitely beneficial, except where the patient is unfit for formal repair/diversion.

Simple drainage is not advisable where there is a major biliary injury due to the high risk of stricture.

Blunt hepatic injury attracts a higher morbidity and mortality than penetrating trauma. The disparity in morbidity and mortality is well illustrated by Table 10.5 which summarises the experience of John et al 1992. The intra-abdominal sepsis rate in this report is lower than expected compared to other reviews, where between 20% and 35% of patients with blunt injury developed intra-abdominal sepsis. Other specific complications not listed in Table 10.5 include pancreatitis (6%) and pancreatic pseudocyst (<2%). Furthermore blunt trauma may be associated with significant injury in other systems (Table 10.4). Brain injury is the most significant associated injury in terms of effect on outcome (Rivkind et al 1989).

Haemobilia may complicate either blunt or penetrating injuries and can be managed by angiographic embolisation (Heimbach et al 1978).

Extensive devascularising injuries may cause hepatic failure, requiring hepatic transplantation (Angstadt et al 1989).

Table 10.4 Numbers of patients with additional major injuries (Rivkind et al 1989)

	Grade II	Grade III	Grade IV	Non-operative	Total
Head	6	6	2	1	15
Chest	4	5	14	3	26
Diaphragm rupture	1	3	1	0	5
Spleen	4	7	4	0	15
Other intra-abdominal injury	2	3	3	4	12
Long bone fracture	5	6	3	3	17

Table 10.5 Complications in 66 patients undergoing surgery for liver injury (John et al 1992)

	Simple		
	Penetrating (n=24)	Blunt (n=27)	Complex (n=15)
Biliary fistula/bile leak	0	1	3
Progressive jaundice	0	3	2
Coagulopathy	0	3	1
Rebleeding	1	1	1
Intra-abdominal sepsis	0	0	2
Protracted ileus	1	2	0
Chest complications	8	15	7
Wound infection	1	0	1
Deep vein thrombosis	0	0	3
Pyrexia of unknown origin	1	1	0
Renal failure	0	0	1
Death	0(0)	3(11)	6(40)
Complication rate in survivors (%)	46	79	79

SPLENIC INJURY

The spleen is the most frequently injured abdominal organ by blunt trauma. Motor vehicle trauma is the most common aetiology and consequently there is a high incidence of associated injuries including those to head, chest and limbs. Additionally, associated intra-abdominal injuries are common, including hepatic, renal, diaphragmatic, intestinal and mesenteric (Kidd et al 1987, Splenic Injury Study Group 1987). Penetrating injuries to the spleen have an associated injury in 94% of cases (Splenic Injury Study Group 1987). Overall, between 60% and 75% of cases are due to blunt trauma (Milliken et al 1982, Nallathambi et al 1988). In children this rises to 97% (King et al 1981).

Classification

The classification compiled by the AAST is recommended (Table 10.6) (Moore et al 1989).

Splenic function

A better understanding of splenic function has changed the emphasis in splenic trauma towards conservation. The spleen has important haematological and immunological functions which can be summarised as follows:

1. The spleen filters senescent or effete blood cells by exposing them to a relatively hostile (hypoxic, acidotic) environment. Splenectomy is

Table 10.6 Splenic injury scale

Grade	Type	Injury
I	Haematoma	Subcapsular, non-expanding, <10% surface area
	Laceration	Capsular tear, non-bleeding, <1 cm deep
II	Haematoma	Subcapsular, non-expanding, 10–50% surface area
		Intraparenchymal non-expanding, <2 cm diameter
	Laceration	Capsular tear, active bleeding, 1–3 cm deep, does not involve trabecular vessel
III	Haematoma	Subcapsular, >50% surface area or expanding Ruptured subcapsular haematoma with active bleeding Intraparenchymal haematoma, >2 cm expanding
	Laceration	>3 cm deep or involving trabecular vessels
IV	Haematoma	Ruptured intraparenchymal haematoma with active bleeding
	Laceration	Laceration involving segmental or hilar vessels producing major devascularisation (>25% of spleen)
V	Laceration	Completely shattered spleen
	Vascular	Hilar vascular injury which devascularises spleen

associated with erythrocytosis, where many of the erythrocytes may be abnormal (increased membrane pitting) and thrombocytosis, which may carry an increased risk of pulmonary thrombo-embolism (Pimpl et al 1989).

2. The spleen is a source of IgM and opsonins, important in the clearance of encapsulated bacteria from the circulation. Splenectomy increases the risk of both minor and overwhelming infection (vide infra).

Diagnosis

A high index of suspicion is required in blunt trauma cases. Clinical examination has been found to have an accuracy of only 65% (Powell et al 1982). DPL has a sensitivity of up to 98% but is non-specific and can result in non-therapeutic laparotomies in up to 25% of cases (Sonderstrom et al 1980).

Further investigation depends on the stability of the patient. Contrast CT scanning is the investigation of choice. Some investigators believe that CT scanning can be used to rationalise which patients can be successfully treated by non-operative means (Buntain & Gould 1985, Cogbill et al 1989) although this is not supported by the findings of Mirvis et al (1989). Additionally, CT scanning may identify other intra-abdominal injuries but should not usurp standard clinical/haemodynamic evaluation (Resciniti et al 1988).

Scintigraphy, again, requires a stable patient and is particularly useful in children with suspected splenic injury with a specificity of 80% (Mishalany et al 1982). Isotope scanning also gives a baseline of splenic function.

Ultrasonography is frequently used because of accessibility and, though intraperitoneal blood can accurately be detected, it has neither the sensitivity of DPL nor the specificity of CT scanning.

Management

Current approaches emphasise the importance of splenic conservation although this must be kept in perspective. Luna & Dellinger (1987) report that the incidence of Overwhelming Post Splenectomy Infection (OPSI) may be overestimated for trauma patients by a factor of 10–20, as many of the reports included patients undergoing splenectomy for reticulo-endothelial diseases. They suggest that the hazards of the multiple blood transfusions often required in splenic salvage surgery and non-operative management may exceed the risks of an expeditious splenectomy.

Non-operative management

Non-operative management has been particularly successful in children with good outcomes in over 90% of cases (Kakkasseril et al 1982, Wesson et al 1981) (Table 10.7). The splenic capsule is thicker in childhood and contains myoepithelial cells which may allow it to contract when torn.

The criteria for non-operative management for both children and adults are:

- Blunt trauma only – penetrating trauma has an associated injury rate of 94%
- Isolated splenic injury Grades I to III
- Haemodynamic stability
- Clear cerebration.

Cogbill et al (1989) found that only 13.5% of adults fulfilled the above criteria. The outcome of non-operative management in adults varies considerably (Table 10.8). Cogbill et al suggest that a successful outcome is more likely when the injury is caused by low energy impact and the grade of injury is I or II. For at least 48 hours after the patient has been stabilised during non-operative management, he must be prepared for emergency surgery if the clinical situation so dictates.

From their compilation of results from the literature, Shackford & Molin (1990) found that 12.7% of adults were suitable for non-operative treatment and, of these, 69% had a successful outcome. A splenectomy was required in 81% of those who were unsuccessfully managed. Overall,

Table 10.7 Management of paediatric splenic injury: operative and non-operative (selective literature review) (Shackford & Molin 1990)

Author	Year	No	Splenectomy	Splenorrhaphy	Fail splenorrhaphy	Observed	Fail observation	Salvaged	Salvaged (%)
Burrington	1977	10	2	8	0	0	*	8	80
Wesson	1981	63	15	4	0	51	7	48	76
Cohen	1982	58	16	0	*	44	2	42	72
Kakkasseril	1982	28	4	3	0	28	7	24	86
Gourevitch	1986	25	2	19	0	4	0	23	92
Muehrcke	1987	24	5	1	0	18	0	23	96
Total		208	44	35	0	145	16	168	81

* Data not available or not applicable

however, the splenic salvage rate was 75%. Clearly this should not be directly compared to salvage rates for operative management as the grades of injury are not comparable. It is not clear whether non-operative management confers a better salvage rate than operative intervention in similar grades of injury. Luna & Dellinger (1987) point to the poor salvage rate for failed non-operative management (81%) as well as the risks attending excessive blood transfusion, and recommend early surgical intervention. Cogbill et al (1989) reject this based on their success rate of 83%, so that even if 80% of the unsuccessful 17% need splenectomy, this remains an excellent salvage rate.

It is not clear if the injured spleen remains more susceptible to repeat injury. Wesson et al (1981) recommend restricted activities for up to 3 months after the injury whereas Shackford & Molin (1990) state that no such restriction is necessary.

Operative management

Although major emphasis is now placed on splenic conservation, it must be stated that splenectomy remains an expeditious and life-saving procedure. Contra-indications to splenic repair include:

Table 10.8 Ultimate splenic outcome of adult non-operative management (selective literature review)

Author	Year	Observed	Fail observed	Splenectomy	Salvaged	Salvaged (%)
Morgenstern	1983	17	0	*	17	100
Malangoni	1984	10	7	6	4	40
Askergren	1984	4	0	*	4	100
Bitseff	1984	30	21	18	12	40
Mahon	1985	11	8	8	3	27
Andersson	1986	13	0	*	13	100
Johnson	1986	11	2	0	11	100
Moss	1987	7	2	2	5	71
Wiebke	1987	10	3	3	7	70
Resciniti	1988	27	10	10	17	63
Nallathambi	1988	9	7	6	3	33
Cogbill	1989	72	12	5	67	83
Molin	1989	16	2	2	14	88
Total		237	74	60	177	75

* Data not applicable

Table 10.9 Management of paediatric splenic injury: operative management only (selective literature review)

Author	Year	No.	Blunt (%)	Splenectomy	Splenorrhaphy	Fail splenorrhaphy*	Salvaged	Salvaged (%)
Shackford	1981	85	90	42	43	0	43	51
Oakes	1981	24	83	2	20	1	19	66
Guiliano	1981	92	!	59	33	0	33	35
Pachter	1981	27	74	3	24	0	24	88
Traub	1982	272	93	231	41	0	41	15
Barrett	1983	36	50	18	18	0	18	50
Moore	1984	200	69	115	87	2	85	42
Feliciano	1985	305	52	169	137	1	136	45
Wetzig	1986	80	98	60	20	0	20	25
Kreis	1987	85	60	43	42	1	42	49
Lange	1988	33	57	11	22	0	22	66
Total		1239	73	753	487	5	483	39

* Required re-operation for haemorrhage, at which time the spleen was either removed or repaired

! Data not available

- Multiple injuries with haemodynamic instability
- Grade V injuries
- Gross peritoneal soiling due to associated ruptured viscus
- Rupture of a diseased spleen
- Age: a less aggressive approach to splenic salvage is reasonable in older adults.

Operative options for splenic salvage depend on the grade of injury and include:

- Application of topical haemostatic agents (Gelfoam, Surgicel, fibrin glue etc.)
- Suturing using atraumatic needles and collagen sutures often combined with patching using omentum or haemostatic agents
- Partial splenectomy where there is devascularisation of a pole or segment
- Polyglycolic acid mesh or bag in which the entire spleen can be enclosed (Lange et al, 1989)
- Ligation of the splenic artery where repair is otherwise not feasible may secure haemostasis, but it is not clear if this confers an advantage, immunologically, over splenectomy.

The results of operative intervention are summarised by Table 10.9.

Where splenectomy is necessary, most surgeons will attempt autotransplantation of splenic tissue to the omentum or abdominal wall. There is experimental evidence to support this practice (Perry 1988), and there is clinical evidence that autotransplanted tissue retains some reticulo-endothelial function (Traub & Perry 1981) although it is disputed if this provides any protection against OPSI (Moore et al 1983).

Detection of splenic function

Detection of splenic function after injury can be problematic where there is autotransplantation or the possibility of splenosis. Scintigraphy lacks the sensitivity to detect small areas of extra-anatomical activity. The detection of Howell-Jolly bodies, erythrocytosis, thrombocytosis etc. would clearly suggest absent function. A sensitive test for haematological function is scanning electron microscopy for erythrocyte membrane pitting (Jones et al 1991).

Immunological function can be crudely assessed using serum IgG, IgM and IgA levels along with complementary, C3 and C4 assays (Tricarico et al 1993). More specific and sensitive indices of splenic immunological function include total T-cell counts, double positive helper inducer T-cells and phytohaemagglutinin induced proliferation, all of which have been found to be impaired in splenectomised children (Kreuzfelder et al 1991).

Complications

Sepsis

Splenectomy is associated with a high incidence of pulmonary complications as well as subphrenic abcess in up to 13% of cases.

Infection remains the principal concern after splenectomy. Overwhelming Post Splenectomy Infection (OPSI), first described by King & Schumaker (1952), has been the main incentive for splenic preservation. Originally documented where splenectomies were performed for haematological disorders in children, it has been recognised as a distinct risk where splenectomy is performed for trauma in both adults and children. In addition to the distinct entity of OPSI, there is an increased risk of other major infections and of minor infections in asplenic patients (Green et al 1986).

There is considerable variation in estimates of the risk of sepsis. The risk of OPSI or serious infection may be as high as a 5.9% lifetime risk (Green et al 1986), although most estimates are lower. Luna & Delinger suggest that estimates of 1–2% are exaggerated and the true incidence is around 0.2% for otherwise healthy adults.

Other septic complications are increased in asplenic patients. Hebeler et al (1982) found an infection rate of 23% in splenectomised patients compared to 10.7% in patients who had splenic preservation. These groups were not however comparable in terms of injury severity. Willis et al (1986) found no difference in the rate of sepsis in patients who had splenectomy for trauma compared to patients who underwent laparotomy for other injuries but with comparable ISS. This finding conflicts directly with that of Green et al (1986) for similar groups of patients. Green estimated the risk of septicaemia in splenectomised patients to be 140 times that of a normal population. Pimpl et al (1989) similarly found the risk of death due to severe sepsis to be higher in splenectomised patients than in comparable laparotomy patients.

It is recommended that asplenic patients be vaccinated against pneumococcus (Caplan et al 1983) although this does not confer full immunity. Consequently penicillin prophylaxis for at least 3 years post-splenectomy is recommended (Ludtke et al 1989).

Pulmonary

Pulmonary complications include atelectasis, pneumonia and pleural effusion, which occur in up to 38% of cases (Traub & Perry 1981, Splenic Injury Study Group 1987).

Subphrenic abscess

The risk of subphrenic abscess increases with multiple intra-abdominal injuries. The incidence ranges from 1% to 13% (Hebeler et al 1982, Moore et al 1984) and is not influenced by the use of drains (Ludtke et al 1989).

Delayed rupture

Delayed splenic rupture was defined by McIndoe as haemorrhage due to the sudden release of a previously contained subcapsular haematoma more than 48 hours after blunt abdominal trauma. In this study, 87% of delayed ruptures occurred within 14 days and 97% within 21 days (McIndoe 1932). The incidence was estimated to be around 15% (Sizer et al 1966). Improved diagnosis, specifically DPL, resulted in a reduction in incidence to 2% (Olsen & Polley 1977, Benjamin et al 1976), suggesting that delayed rupture in most cases was, in fact, delayed diagnosis. Black et al (1992) conclude that subcapsular haematoma is not a predictor for delayed rupture and can be safely managed conservatively if there is no hilar involvement.

PANCREATIC INJURY

Pancreatic injuries are associated with a significant mortality and morbidity and may present with complications posing problems of a high magnitude to the surgeon.

Trauma of the pancreas accounts for approximately 5% of all abdominal injuries. Approximately 70% of pancreatic injuries are secondary to penetrating injuries, the rest attributable to blunt trauma.

The task facing the surgeon dealing with traumatic pancreatic injuries is fourfold:

1. Early diagnosis or recognition of pancreatic injury
2. Identification and management of associated injuries which may be life-threatening
3. Identification of pancreatic ductal disruption
4. Suitable operative management to control exocrine secretion of pancreas while conserving pancreatic tissue.

Classification

There have been numerous classifications of pancreatic injuries over the last two decades. Lucas (1977) used a classification system based on location and severity of injury.

1. Contusions, peripheral laceration, intact ductal system
2. Distal laceration, transection, disruption, suspected ductal disruption, no duodenal injury
3. Proximal laceration, transection, suspected ductal injury, no duodenal injury
4. Severe combined pancreaticoduodenal injury.

More recently, pancreatic injury has been classified based on the Organ Injury Scaling Committee of the American Association for the Surgery of Trauma (Moore et al 1990) (Table 10.10).

Table 10.10 Pancreatic injury classification (Moore et al 1990)

Grade	Type	Injury
1	Haematoma Laceration	Minor contusion without duct injury Superficial laceration without duct injury
2	Haematoma Laceration	Major contusion without duct injury or tissue loss Major laceration without duct injury or tissue loss
3	Laceration	Distal transection or parenchymal injury with duct injury
4	Laceration	Proximal transection or parenchymal injury involving ampulla
5	Laceration	Massive disruption of pancreatic head

Aetiology

Blunt injury

Pancreatic injuries occur in 2–3% of patients who suffer from blunt abdominal trauma (Robey et al 1982). Road traffic accidents account for the majority of blunt pancreatic injuries, the most common cause being compression of the pancreas against the steering wheel (Northrup & Simmons 1972). Blunt forces acting on the pancreas may cause either contusions or injury of greater severity in the form of transection of a major duct with or without concomitant transection of the gland.

Penetrating injury

This form of injury is usually diagnosed earlier but can be life-threatening because of the higher incidence of associated injuries especially to surrounding major vascular structures.

Stab wounds and gunshot wounds account for the majority of cases of penetrating pancreatic injuries. Ivatury et al (1990) had a series of 103 patients with penetrating pancreatic injuries of which 69% had sustained gunshot wounds, while 31% had received stab wounds. 40% of the injuries were localised to the region of the head of the pancreas, the rest affecting the body and tail.

Diagnosis

This may be extremely difficult in view of the retropancreatic location of the pancreas. Letton & Wilson (1959) also attributed this to the absence of an activating agent of the pancreatic enzymes in isolated injuries, and a decrease in pancreatic secretion after significant trauma involving the gland.

Even patients with complete transection of the pancreatic duct may be asymptomatic for months following the initial insult as reported by Bach & Frey (1979) and Berni et al (1982).

Serum amylase estimation is not a reliable indicator of pancreatic injury but remains a useful screening investigation. Berni et al (1982), in their review of traumatic pancreatic injuries, found the serum amylase elevated in 66% of blunt pancreatic injuries compared to 10% in those with penetrating injuries. Olsen (1973) found that up to one-third of patients with a pre-operative elevation of serum amylase had no significant intra-abdominal injury while Moretz et al (1975) found no correlation between pancreatic injury or its severity and serum amylase elevation following blunt trauma.

CT scan may have a role in the initial evaluation of the stable patient with suspected pancreatic injury. Jeffrey et al (1983) correctly diagnosed 11 of 13 patients with proven pancreatic injuries using computed tomography and emphasised the difficulty in diagnosis in selected patients when scanned soon after their injuries.

Peritoneal lavage may give false negative results in pancreatic injuries because of retroperitoneal location of the pancreas, but amylase estimation of the aspirate may be of value (Lempinen 1981).

Endoscopic retrograde cholangiopancreatography (ERCP) is helpful in identifying ductal injury and delineating ductal anatomy pre-operatively in the stable patient especially when presentation is delayed. Hall et al (1986) used the technique successfully in identifying the presence of ductal rupture and its location in four children with delayed presentation. No difficulty was experienced in cannulating the papilla of Vater in this age group.

An intra-operative pancreatogram will outline the ductal system in cases of suspected major ductal injury. The procedure can be performed either via the proximal pancreatic duct at the ampulla of Vater through a duodenotomy, or through the amputated tail of the pancreas by cannulating the distal pancreatic duct. Transduodenal pancreatography using a fibre-optic duodenoscope was advocated by Gougeon et al (1976) to determine ductal injury intra-operatively.

Management

This depends on the severity and location of injury involving the pancreas.

Grades 1 and 2 (Lucas Grade 1)

External drainage, which is a conservative form of management, is the favoured treatment for Grade 1 and Grade 2 injuries where the main pancreatic duct is intact.

Approximately 75% of patients in Jones's series of 450 patients with pancreatic injuries (1985) were managed by means of external drainage. The morbidity and mortality in three series of pancreatic injuries employing external drainage solely are outlined in Table 10.11.

All three authors favoured conservatism in their review on management of pancreatic injuries. Jones (1985) and Ivatury (1990) also noted a tendency towards more conservative management in the latter part of their series, with an improved outcome in mortality and morbidity rates.

Grade 3 (Lucas Grade 2)

Distal pancreatectomy is the procedure usually reserved for Type 3 injuries. The results of a multicentre review by Cogbill et al (1991) on 74 patients who underwent distal pancreatectomy for trauma is shown in Table 10.12.)

Jones (1985) reported on 71 patients who underwent distal pancreatectomy, 23 of whom had a Roux-en-Y anastomosis. The results are shown in Table 10.13. Of the five deaths associated with distal pancreatectomy and a Roux-en-Y anastomosis, only one death was related to the pancreatic injury.

Table 10.11 Morbidity and mortality in pancreatic injuries using only external drainage

	Mechanism	Patients	External drainage	Fistula	Abscess	Death	Early death
Jones (1985)	B/P	450	342	10	14	25	15
Sorensen (1986)	P	41	20	0	0	2	0
Ivatury (1990)	P	76	47	0	11	0	4

B = Blunt; P = Penetrating

Table 10.12 Distal pancreatectomy in 74 patients

No. of patients	74
Mechanism:	
Blunt	40 (54%)
Penetrating	33 (46%)
Mortality	9 (12%)
Intra-abdominal abscess	24 (32%)
Pancreatic fistula	10 (14%)
Endocrine insufficiency	1 (1%)

Table 10.13 Distal pancreatectomy in 71 patients with Roux-en-Y anastomosis in 23

	Patients	Fistula	Pseudocyst	Abscess	Death >48 hrs
Distal pancreatectomy	48	2	–	4	3
Distal pancreatectomy + Roux-en-Y anastomosis	23	–	–	1	5

In Cogbill et al's (1991) review, the spleen was left intact in 53% of 32 patients in whom there was no injury to the spleen.

In a smaller series, Robey and colleagues (1982) reported the successful outcome in three of four patients with blunt pancreatic injury who were treated with distal pancreatectomy without a concomitant splenectomy. This would appear favourable in appropriate circumstances since it eradicates the potential complication of postsplenectomy sepsis.

Cogbill et al (1991) also concluded that pancreas-related complications frequently occurred following distal resection regardless of the method of pancreatic closure employed (suture or staple).

Grade 4 (Lucas Grade 3)

The procedures employed in this grade of injury include distal pancreatectomy, Roux-en-Y pancreaticojejunostomy or external drainage, especially where the main pancreatic duct is uninjured.

Jurkovich & Carrico (1990) stressed the importance of delineating the main pancreatic duct in proximal pancreatic injuries. Smego et al (1985), however, emphasised the problem of accurately identifying the presence of ductal injury at operation, even with the various techniques available. Berni and colleagues (1982) reported a decrease in complication rate from 55% to 15% in two sequential groups of patients after the introduction of intra-operative pancreatography.

Jones's (1985) results in performing a distal pancreatectomy with a Roux-en-Y anastomosis at the proximal end of the pancreas yielded five deaths (one pancreas-related) and one intra-abdominal abscess out of a total of 23 patients. Eleven patients simply had a Roux-en-Y anastomosis fashioned over the injury with the development of five intra-abdominal abscesses and one death. The author commented that this technique was more successful for injuries with an intact posterior pancreatic capsule, but was associated with a high morbidity rate (45%) and had rarely been used since the late 70s.

Grade 5 (Lucas Grade 4)

This injury is more common in penetrating forms of trauma and is fortunately rare. It is usually associated with other injuries.

Feliciano et al's (1987) management of 129 patients with combined pancreatoduodenal injuries is shown in Table 10.14.

In the 108 patients surviving for more than 48 hours, the most common pancreatoduodenal complication was the formation of a pancreatic fistula (26%). The duodenal fistula rate was 6.5% while 17% of patients developed an intra-abdominal abscess.

Duodenal diverticulisation, a diversionary procedure, was performed in five patients in Jones's (1989) group of 450 patients with the development of a major complication in all five. Berne et al (1974), with their larger

Table 10.14 Management of 129 patients with pancreatoduodenal injuries

Procedure		No. (%)	Mortality
Simple repair/drainage		31 (24)	29%
Duodenal repair or resection; pancreatic repair, distal resection or Roux-en-Y; +/- pyloric exclusion; drainage:		79 (61.2)	22%
with exclusion	68		
without exclusion	11		
Pancreaticoduodenectomy		13 (10.1)	46%
Whipple	10		
Total	3		
None		6 (4.7)	100%

series of 50 patients with combined pancreatic and duodenal injuries who underwent the above procedure, reported a 16% mortality rate and a fistula rate of 14%.

Pyloric exclusion, a modification of duodenal diverticulisation, was introduced by Vaughan et al (1977). There was a total of 75 patients in their report with combined pancreatic and duodenal injuries. The mortality rate was 19% with a morbidity rate of 12%.

Pancreaticoduodenectomy is a major and uncommon procedure that has been associated with a high mortality. Oreskovich & Carrico (1984) performed ten such procedures (out of 117 patients with identifiable pancreatic injuries) where there was a non-reconstructable injury of the ampulla or combined pancreatic and duodenal devascularisation injury, with no mortality reported. They attributed this to careful selection criteria for this operative procedure. Feliciano and colleagues' (1987) experience of 13 patients who had a pancreatoduodenectomy performed yielded a 46% mortality rate.

A Whipple procedure for pancreatoduodenal trauma carries a high mortality and should be reserved for patients who are clinically stable (Lewis et al 1991).

Feliciano et al (1987) in their experience of 129 patients treated for combined pancreatoduodenal trauma concluded that with severe devascu-

Table 10.15 Complications following trauma to the pancreas

	Patients	Pancreatic fistula	Pancreatic abscess	Pseudocyst
Jones (1985)	450	13	14	3
Leppaniemi (1988)	43	5	–	2
Ivatury (1990)	76	4	9	–

larising injuries of the duodenum, and where the main duct in the head of the pancreas was transected or the ampulla of Vater destroyed, then either a Roux-en-Y drainage or a Whipple's procedure could be considered when the patient was stable. Otherwise, a conservative resection, pyloric exclusion with gastrojejunostomy, and drainage should be performed.

Complications

The significant complications that occur following trauma to the pancreas are the development of a pancreatic fistula, an intra-abdominal or pancreatic abscess, or a pseudocyst. Other associated complications include pancreatitis, haemorrhage and endocrine/exocrine insufficiency.

Table 10.15 outlines some of the complications experienced in three different series. Leppaniemi et al (1988) reported a pancreatic complication rate which varied between 8% and 33% in his review of the subject.

Jones (1985) noted an overall mortality rate of 18% secondary to pancreatic trauma in a collective review of 1462 cases from centres which reported more than 100 cases.

GASTRIC INJURIES

Injuries to the stomach occur in up to 20% of cases of penetrating wounds to the lower thoracic cage and upper abdomen (Nance & Cobin 1969, Blaisdell & Trunkey 1982). Blunt trauma on the other hand is an uncommon but serious cause of injury involving the stomach. Less than 2% of blunt abdominal injuries lead to gastric trauma (Brunsting & Morton 1987). The stomach, anatomically situated in the left upper quadrant underneath the protection of the lower thoracic cage is well shielded from trauma. It has a rich blood supply with reliable anastomosis enabling primary repair of gastric injuries in most circumstances without the worry of non-healing or complications associated with the repair.

Aetiology

Mechanism of gastric injury:

- Penetrating
    - stab wounds
    - ballistic
- Blunt
    - direct force
    - deceleration.

Penetrating injuries involving the stomach can range from stab wounds or low-velocity gunshot wounds to high-velocity weaponry. High-velocity ballistic wounds, especially if shot from close range can cause extensive trauma or tissue damage.

Automobile or vehicular trauma account for the majority of cases of blunt gastric injuries (Brunsting & Morton 1987, Courcy et al 1984). Other causes that have been implicated in this form of injury include cardiopulmonary resuscitation, direct violence and falls.

Direct compression of the stomach against the vertebral column is one of the mechanisms involved in blunt gastric trauma. Deceleration injuries may give rise to tears at points of fixation such as at the gastro-oesophageal junction, pylorus or even where gastric adhesions are present (Courcy et al 1984, Durham 1990). Yajko et al (1975) mentioned the following predisposing factors which may lead to gastric injury in blunt abdominal trauma: a full stomach, a competent gastro-oesophageal and pyloric sphincter, gaseous distension of the stomach, pathological change in the stomach wall and ingestion of a large amount of fluid or sodium bicarbonate.

The sites of the stomach most commonly involved by blunt rupture are in decreasing frequency the anterior wall, greater curvature, lesser curvature and the posterior wall (Brunsting & Morton 1987).

Table 10.16 outlines the cause of stomach injuries in Wilkinson's (1989) prospective study of 1214 patients who underwent laparotomy secondary to abdominal trauma, of which 95 patients (8%) were found to have gastric trauma.

Diagnosis

Apart from a careful history and physical examination, routine investigations that are normally performed include radiological investigations of the chest and abdomen. Resuscitative procedures should take precedence depending on the patient's clinical status and are performed accordingly, taking into account any associated injuries which may be life-threatening.

Penetrating wounds are usually diagnosed at laparotomy and formal exploration is the norm for abdominal gunshot wounds. Heselson (1970) used laparoscopy to assess 11 patients with stab wounds to the abdomen and avoided laparotomy in six of them based on his laparoscopic findings.

Table 10.16 Causes of stomach injuries (Wilkinson 1989)

Patients	Injury	
15	Blunt	
	motor vehicle	14
	assault	1
80	Penetrating	
	ballistic	53
	stab	27

Since then there have been numerous reports of its role in the assessment of patients with abdominal trauma. Ivatury and colleagues (1993) recently recommended its use for penetrating injuries in the form of tangential stab and gunshot wounds to avoid unnecessary laparotomy.

Thal (1977) recommended that stab wounds of the abdomen in patients who are clinically stable should be explored under local anaesthesia followed by a peritoneal lavage, if there is any evidence that the peritoneum is breached. In a later study Thal (1984) recommended the continued use of a red blood cell count of greater than 100 000 mm^3 during peritoneal lavage as an indication for laparotomy. There was a 1.9% false–positive and 4.2% false–negative lavage in his series of 213 patients with stab wounds to the lower chest and abdomen. Whereas the sensitivity of diagnostic peritoneal lavage (DPL) can be improved by lowering the red blood cell count, it must be emphasised that there is no substitute for repeated clinical monitoring and evaluation in avoiding unnecessary morbidity as a result of missed injuries. Peritoneal lavage is also useful as a confirmatory procedure denoting gastric injury when gastric aspirate is yielded (Vassy et al 1975). A bloody aspirate via a nasogastric tube may be diagnostic of gastric injury (Durham 1990).

Brunsting & Morton (1987) emphasised that patients with blunt gastric injuries usually exhibit clinical signs of peritonism and are frequently shocked on admission. They further pointed out that pneumoperitoneum on radiological examination is absent in 16–66% of cases. Diagnosis or abdominal examination may be made more difficult by associated injuries especially in blunt gastric injuries.

Management

Following resuscitative measures, a few procedures that may be helpful in the management of gastric injuries include nasogastric tube insertion which, apart from aiding diagnosis, is therapeutic in decompressing the stomach.

The principles of operative management of gastric injuries are outlined below.

- Adequate exposure
- Haemostasis
- Meticulous exploration (including surrounding organs)
- Debridement/resection of devitalised tissue
- Two-layered repair of gastric wound
- Peritoneal toilet.

The stomach must be thoroughly examined if injuries are not to be missed. Careful and thorough exploration for associated injuries involving the liver, spleen, diaphragm and the rest of the gastrointestinal tract is vital in avoiding unnecessary morbidity and mortality. Associated abdominal

Table 10.17 Associated abdominal injuries (Wilkinson 1989)

	Blunt	Penetrating	Total
Liver	5	35	40
Spleen	8	18	26
Small bowel	2	21	23
Large bowel	0	16	16
Pancreas	2	10	12
Diaphragm	4	29	33
Total	21	129	150

injuries in Wilkinson's (1989) experience of 95 patients with gastric trauma is listed in Table 10.17.

Following adequate debridement of the gastric wound, repair of the defect is usually performed using a two-layered closure. A pyloroplasty may be required in repairing defects involving the pylorus. Extensive injuries of the stomach requiring resection are rare and usually associated with vascular damage. Durham (1990) noted only a 2% gastric resection rate of 243 penetrating gastric injuries in the Parkland Memorial Hospital experience. The other 98% underwent simple repair of their gastric injuries.

Morbidity and mortality

The complication and death rates vary between penetrating and blunt gastric injuries. The mortality in blunt gastric trauma may be as high as 50%, as in Brunsting & Morton's (1987) series, with a variation of 0–66% recorded in other reports (Siemens & Fulton 1977, Courcy et al 1984, Semel & Fritelli 1981). Durham (1990) reported a 14% mortality rate and 27% morbidity rate in penetrating injuries of the stomach.

Box 10.1 Complications of gastric injuries

Wound infection
Gastric fistula
Intra-abdominal abscess
Gastrointestinal haemorrhage
Suture line leak
Empyema/pulmonary infections
Outflow obstruction
Missed injuries

Complications that may be associated with gastric injuries are summarised in Box 10.1.

The complications listed in Brunsting & Morton's (1987) report on their personal series of six cases of blunt gastric trauma and additional cases, from a review of English language publications over a 56-year period (1930–1986) is shown in Table 10.18

Intra-abdominal abscesses are common after blunt gastric injuries as demonstrated by Brunsting & Morton (1987) in their review of the literature, which yielded a 52% rate. Stone & Hester (1973) observed a 19% incidence of postoperative intra-abdominal collection in contaminated cases of perforated gastric ulcers versus a 3% incidence in clean cases of penetrating gastric perforations, which may explain the higher incidence of contamination in blunt gastric trauma, especially with a full stomach. Penetrating gastric trauma rarely gives rise to intra-abdominal collection. Durham's (1990) report on the Parkland series of 243 patients with penetrating injuries of the stomach demonstrated a less than 1% incidence of intra-abdominal collection.

Pulmonary infections such as empyema may result when simultaneous injury of the stomach and diaphragm occur. Villalba et al (1979) in a review of patients with penetrating injuries to the chest found a 1.3% incidence of empyema. The authors cited diaphragmatic injury as a risk factor in the development of a collection in the pleural cavity, and mentioned the stomach as a common associated intra-abdominal organ injured, in their study.

Postoperative haemorrhage in gastric trauma may be from the wound suture line repair or more commonly from disruption of the short gastric vessels or iatrogenic splenic injury. Postoperative gastric obstruction is rare following repair of gastric injuries, due to the large diameter lumen of the stomach. However, this complication may develop at the gastro-oesophageal junction and the pylorus if the lumen is compromised in surgical repair.

Table 10.18 Complications of blunt gastric injuries (from Brunsting & Morton 1987)

Complications	Patients (n=25)
Abdominal abscess	13 (52%)
Pulmonary infection	10 (40%)
Wound infection	5 (20%)
GI bleeding	5 (20%)
Gastrocutaneous fistula	4 (16%)

DUODENAL INJURIES

Traumatic injuries of the duodenum, among enteric injuries, remain the most difficult to manage. Complicated duodenal wounds are associated with a high mortality but nevertheless, there has been a steady decline in morbidity and mortality rates over the years, largely attributable to the improvement in care of the critically ill patient. Furthermore, because of its anatomical location, duodenal injuries frequently occur in association with other injuries, increasing the complexity of the overall management, especially when there is pancreatic involvement (Frey 1982, Flint et al 1980). Careful consideration should be given to the above factors, including the nature of duodenal trauma, when managing or selecting a suitable operative procedure for duodenal injuries.

Aetiology

Penetrating duodenal injuries predominate over those caused by blunt trauma. In Snyder et al's (1980) review of 247 patients with duodenal trauma, 193 cases (78%) were due to penetrating injuries. Gunshot wounds (>75%) predominated as the leading cause of injury in his series of penetrating duodenal wounds, followed by stab wounds and shotgun wounds in decreasing order.

Blunt injuries to the abdomen are rare but potentially serious causes of duodenal trauma. Cox's (1984) analysis of 870 patients requiring laparotomy due to blunt abdominal trauma over a 5-year period yielded only a single case of duodenal rupture (0.01%) and six cases of paraduodenal haematomas. Motor vehicle accidents including pedestrian injuries (85%) dominate as the prime cause of blunt duodenal injuries in Weigelt's (1990) review of six recent series. Falls accounted for 6% of the injuries while 9% were due to miscellaneous forms of injury.

Cogbill et al's (1990) multicentre review of 164 duodenal injuries demonstrated 62% of the injuries as being secondary to penetrating trauma, the rest attributable to blunt trauma.

The modes of injurious disruption caused by blunt duodenal trauma are crushing, bursting, or shearing forces. A crushing injury is caused by direct compression of the duodenum against the vertebral column, while shearing type injuries are usually secondary to deceleration trauma. A bursting type injury results from a sudden increase in intraluminal pressure, secondary to a closed loop obstruction formed between an external force applied and an anatomical structure at either end.

Intramural haematoma is a form of blunt duodenal trauma which is due to accumulation of blood in the submucosal layer of the duodenal wall. The cause of intramural haematoma in children is most often play-related, while road traffic accidents account for the majority of cases in adults. Trivial forces in patients with a coagulation defect may lead to the formation of an intramural duodenal haematoma. Wooley et al (1978) and Jewett and colleagues (1988) noted that child abuse should be ruled out as a cause in this form of injury.

Diagnosis

While the introduction of diagnostic peritoneal lavage by Root and colleagues (1965) has revolutionised the diagnosis of traumatic injuries to intra-abdominal organs, the diagnosis of blunt trauma, especially to retroperitoneal structures such as part of the duodenum, remains difficult and less clear in comparison to penetrating injuries.

The patient may not exhibit physical signs on initial examination in blunt duodenal trauma because of the duodenum's retroperitoneal location. The delay in diagnosis in such cases results in increased morbidity and mortality with bile and pancreatic enzymes spillage involved in the pathological process.

Apart from an erect chest X-ray and plain abdominal films, other radiological investigations of help when duodenal or other upper gastrointestinal injuries are suspected is a gastrograffin study. A CT scan with contrast may give a better resolution. Kunin et al (1993) concluded in their retrospective study of a small group of patients with duodenal trauma that a CT scan was helpful in differentiating duodenal perforation from haematoma without perforation.

Laboratory investigation, apart from baseline full blood count and urea and electrolyte, that may be helpful is serum amylase estimation. 53% of the 247 patients in Snyder et al's (1980) series had an elevated serum amylase. An elevated white cell count (>10 000) may also be present.

DPL, in injury of the intraperitoneal segment of the duodenum may yield bile or enteric contents.

In blunt duodenal trauma, blood may be aspirated on lavage. There is no doubt that this technique has improved detection of blunt duodenal injury as demonstrated by Snyder and colleagues (1980) and DeMars et al (1979).

Classification

There is a range of surgical procedures that are employed in the treatment of duodenal injuries depending upon their severity. The organ injury classification for the duodenum based on the Organ Injury Scaling (OIS) Committeee of the American Association for the Surgery of Trauma is outlined in Table 10.19 (Moore et al, 1990).

Management

The methods employed in the surgical management of duodenal trauma are as follows:

- No repair
- Simple repair (Duodenorrhaphy) +/– tube decompression
- Serosal patch
- Pyloric exclusion
- Diverticulisation
- Resection and anastomosis
- Roux-en-Y duodenojejunostomy
- Pancreaticoduodenectomy (combined injuries or non-reconstructable injuries involving ampulla).

Table 10.20 below outlines the operative management employed in eight trauma units in the 5-year multicentre review involving 164 duodenal injuries by Cogbill et al (1990).

Several factors have been identified as affecting the severity of a duodenal wound. These are summarised below (Lucas & Ledgerwood 1975, Heitsch et al 1976, Graham et al 1979, Snyder 1980):

- Delay in treatment
- Size of duodenal wound
- Site of duodenal injury. Increased morbidity if 1st or 2nd part of duodenum affected
- Associated common bile duct injury
- Associated pancreatic injury
- Associated injury of the proximal main pancreatic duct.

Mild contusion injuries of the duodenum do not require any repair. Over 70% of duodenal injuries can be treated by simple duodenorrhaphy and debridement. Eighty-seven of 105 (83%) patients with duodenal injuries who survived for more than 48 hours in Shorr et al's (1987) series were treated with primary repair of the duodenal wound with placement of

Table 10.19 Duodenum injury classification

Grade	Type	Injury
I	Haematoma	Involving single portion of duodenum
	Laceration	Partial thickness, no perforation
II	Haematoma	Involving more than one portion
	Laceration	Disruption <50% of circumference
III	Laceration	Disruption 50–75% circumference of D2
		Disruption 50–100% circumference of D1, D3, D4
IV	Laceration	Disruption >75% circumference of D2
		Involving ampulla or distal common bile duct
V	Laceration	Massive disruption of duodenopancreatic complex
	Vascular	Devascularisation of duodenum

D1, D2, D3, D4 = 1st, 2nd, 3rd or 4th part of duodenum respectively

Table 10.20 Operative management of duodenal injuries

Procedure	Patients
Duodenorrhaphy (with duodenostomy)	90 (55%)
Pyloric exclusion (with duodenostomy)	27 (16%)
Duodenostomy	1 (1%)
Duodenojejunostomy	4 (2%)
Pancreatoduodenectomy	5 (3%)
Drain intramural haematoma	3 (2%)
No duodenal procedure	25 (15%)
Died before repair	8 (5%)
Other	1 (1%)

Penrose drains lateral to the duodenum. An isolated duodenal injury was present in 20% of the patients. This method of management was successful in all but one patient who had multiple injuries and succumbed to multiple system organ failure.

The different methods of duodenal decompression are outlined below:

- Antegradely via stomach
- Directly through duodenum
- Retrogradely via jejunum.

Tube decompression may be used on a selective basis in conjunction with any form of the repairs mentioned above. Stone & Fabian (1979) managed 73% of 321 patients with traumatic duodenal injuries with tube decompression, with the development of only one (0.5%) fistula. Hasson et al (1984) in their literature review of 563 cases of penetrating duodenal trauma reported a fistula rate of only 2.3% when decompression was used, compared to a 11.8% fistula rate in repairs without decompression. Their series also demonstrated a lower fistula rate when the decompression tube was placed retrogradely via the jejunum rather than being placed via the duodenum (0.4% vs. 19.4%). Furthermore they found that the overall mortality was much higher when decompression was not used compared to when no decompression was employed (9.0% vs. 19.4%). They also revealed a striking difference in the mortality of patients with a duodenal fistula between decompressed and nondecompressed repairs (14.3% vs. 41.9%), and therefore recommended the above procedure in duodenal injuries, citing the presence of a controlled fistula, should one occur with decompressive injuries, as being favourable compared to an uncontrolled fistula.

Snyder et al (1980) failed to demonstrate any difference in duodenal morbidity rates whether or not decompression was employed with duodenorrhaphy. Duodenal tube decompression was performed in 101 of 190 patients who had duodenorrhaphy in Snyder's series. Duodenal fistulas developed in 9% and the mortality was 4%. Ivatury and colleagues (1985) found that the use of decompressive enterostomy increased the morbidity rate in a review of 100 consecutive patients with penetrating duodenal trauma.

Segmental resection and anastomosis of duodenal wounds is performed whenever possible, but this procedure is redundant in injuries of the second part of the duodenum, because of the anatomical complexity in this region associated with the pancreatic and common bile ductal structure.

Pyloric exclusion and duodenal diverticulisation are diversionary procedures that exclude the normal flow of gastric chyme from contact with the duodenal wound, in an attempt to protect the duodenal suture line. Both these procedures substitute a potential lateral fistula to an end fistula. Pyloric exclusion may either be temporary or permanent with a gastrojejunostomy fashioned, and if permanent exclusion is selected, nonabsorbable sutures are then used to close the pylorus. Stomal ulcers are a complication of pyloric exclusion (Vaughan et al 1977), even though Martin and colleagues (1983) had a marginal ulceration rate of only 3% in their series of 128 patients treated with the above procedure.

Duodenal diverticulisation was first described by Berne and colleagues in 1968. The procedure essentially consists of an antrectomy, tube duodenostomy, vagotomy and gastroenterotomy following repair of the duodenal wound. In Berne et al's (1974) later series of 50 patients, there was a mortality rate of 7% among 45 patients who survived for more than 48 hours undergoing duodenal diverticulisation for combined pancreaticoduodenal injury. There was a total of 12(24%) fistulas, 14% of which were duodenal fistulas, the rest being pancreatic fistulas.

Pancreaticoduodenectomy is a major procedure usually reserved for combined injuries of the duodenum, biliary tree and the pancreas, where the blood supply of the injured organ may be compromised. The above form of injury which is at the severe end of the injury spectrum usually constitutes less than 1% of the patients who undergo exploratory laparotomy for trauma (Oreskovich & Carrico 1984). This form of surgical management is further dealt with in the section on pancreatic trauma. Snyder et al's (1980) series of seven patients who underwent this procedure yielded an adjusted mortality rate of 14%.

Morbidity and mortality

Morbidity associated with duodenal trauma may be sepsis-related in the form of a wound infection, intra-abdominal abscess or septicaemia. Other complications include haemorrhage, pancreatitis, bowel obstruction and most importantly the development of duodenal fistulas.

Snyder et al (1980) identified four factors which increased the likelihood for complication in duodenal injuries:

- Missile or blunt injury
- Injury of the 1st or 2nd part of the duodenum
- Delay in operation of >48 hours following injury
- Adjacent CBD injury.

The duodenal-related complications in 39 patients who survived the initial operation in Cogbill et al's (1990) multicentre review is outlined in Table 10.21.

Duodenal fistula remains a serious and troublesome complication associated with duodenal injuries. The duodenal fistula rate is usually less than 14% and the rate is usually taken to measure morbidity related to the duodenal wound (Weigelt 1990). The mortality of patients with duodenal fistulas has been reported to be between 20% and 40% (Flint et al 1980, Kelly et al 1978, Stone & Fabian 1979). The six patients who developed a duodenal fistula (>50 ml drainage per day for > 7 days) in Cogbill's series were three who had a pyloric exclusion performed; two following duodenorrhaphy, and one following drainage of an intramural haematoma. The fistulas resolved without treatment in the pyloric exclusion group; required reoperation with a pyloric exclusion in the primary repair group; and the final patient required a duodenal resection and duodenojejunostomy in the management of the fistula. None of the six patients died.

Weigelt (1990) quoted a mortality rate of between 13% and 28% in his review of duodenal trauma. This figure was dramatically reduced by almost half when mortality from haemorrhagic shock was excluded. Death attributable directly to duodenal injury is less than 6% in most reported series. Haemorrhagic shock is the leading cause of death especially in the early period, and associated injuries play a major role in the

Table 10.21 Duodenal-related complications

Complications	Patients
Intra-abdominal abscess	22 (16%)
Duodenal fistula	6 (4%)
Duodenal dehiscence	5 (3.6%)
Pancreatic fistula	4 (3%)
Biliary fistula	1 (1%)
Duodenal obstruction	1 (1%)
Total	39

mortality rate which explains the higher figures in blunt duodenal, trauma in comparison to penetrating injuries. In Cogbill et al's (1990) review of 164 duodenal injuries, there were 30 (18%) deaths. Twenty-two (73%) were secondary to uncontrollable haemorrhage and only two deaths were duodenal-related. The latter two patients both died of duodenal wound repair dehiscence and subsequent sepsis.

Duodenal injuries, if diagnosed early and managed correctly using the many surgical techniques available, give acceptable mortality and morbidity rates. Further prospective evaluation of duodenal injuries and the different surgical techniques employed depending on injury severity will serve as helpful guidelines to the surgeon managing traumatic duodenal injuries.

SMALL BOWEL INJURIES

The small intestine is the commonest part of the bowel involved in intra-abdominal injuries, and has exceeded the liver in becoming the most frequently injured organ in penetrating abdominal injuries. Traumatic injuries secondary to blunt abdominal trauma relegates the small bowel below the liver and spleen in terms of frequency.

Aetiology

Penetrating injuries account for 90% of small bowel trauma in comparison to blunt trauma. Blunt abdominal trauma causes small bowel injury in 5–15% of cases (Dauterive et al 1985).

- **Penetrating**
  Ballistic wounds from firearms and stab wounds are the main perpetrators in this form of injury. The mobility of the small intestine spares it occasionally from injury in stab wounds (Stevens & Maull 1990).
- **Blunt**
  This is usually associated with more severe injuries. Most are secondary to road traffic accidents and associated multi-organ injury is common. Three mechanisms of injury have been described.
  - *Crushing*
    The intestine in this mechanism is crushed between the anterior abdominal wall and the vertebral column.
  - *Bursting*
    A sudden increase in intraluminal pressure in the bowel which is fluid-filled, causing punctate or slit-like perforations on the antimesenteric border e.g., seatbelt injury
  - *Shearing*
    Disruption caused by acceleration/deceleration forces at or near a fixed point such as the duodenojejunal flexure and ileocaecal valve or bowel restricted by adhesions. May cause tears of bowel wall or avulsion-type injuries of mesentery.

Table 10.22 outlines the type of small bowel injuries in the review by Dauterive et al (1985) who identified 60 patients with major intestinal injuries out of 196 patients with an injury to the small bowel, colon or mesentery. These patients were identified out of 870 patients who underwent a laparotomy secondary to blunt abdominal trauma. Major injuries were defined as (1) transmural perforation or transection of the bowel; (2) mesenteric injury resulting in ischaemic bowel requiring resection; (3) contusions of the bowel wall with seromuscular damage requiring resection and; (4) injury of the mesenteric root resulting in a tear of the superior mesenteric artery or vein or both.

Table 10.23 outlines the location of small intestinal injury (inc. duodenal wounds) in Donohue et al's (1985) review of 163 patients treated for blunt and penetrating small bowel trauma over a 4½ year period.

The jejunum, in Donohue et al's (1985) review was the most frequently injured portion of small bowel in patients with penetrating injuries. The frequency of multiple small bowel segments involved in the injurious process also increased from blunt to penetrating trauma.

Diagnosis

Hollow viscus injuries such as in the small intestine, especially when occurring in isolation, can present a diagnostic dilemma. This difficulty is compounded in patients with blunt intestinal injury. Distal small bowel injury, with a near neutral pH of leaking contents produces less of a chemi-

Table 10.22 Types of small bowel injuries (Dauterive et al 1985)

Injury	Patients
Perforation/transection	30*
Devascularisation	34**
Severe contusion	0

* Includes 2 duodenal perforations
** Includes 10 mesenteric root injuries

Table 10.23 Location of small intestinal injuries (Donohue et al 1985)

Type	Duodenum	Jejunum	*Small bowel	Ileum	Multiple
Blunt	50%	43%	7%	4%	14%
Stab	18%	53%	12%	9%	18%
Firearm	30%	44%	30%	26%	26%
Total	25%	44%	16%	15%	20%

* Indicates exact location of injury not specified

cal peritoneal irritation compared to upper small intestinal injury, and thus delayed presentation may be seen in lower ileal injuries (Anderson & Ballinger 1979).

Routine laboratory investigations such as haemoglobin, white cell count and amylase estimations, and standard radiological examinations such as an erect chest X-ray and plain film of the abdomen, have a low threshold in achieving a diagnosis of small bowel injury. Fewer than 40% of patients with blunt rupture of the small intestine demonstrate pneumoperitoneum on radiological investigations (Duncan 1956).

Diagnostic peritoneal lavage is a useful test in the evaluation of a patient with penetrating and particularly blunt abdominal trauma especially when the clinical findings are equivocal in a haemodynamically stable patient (Root et al 1967, Thompson & Moore 1983, Moore & Marx 1985). Standard measurement of red blood cell count (>10 000/mm^3) and white cell count (>500/mm^3) on lavage may not be reliable in isolated hollow viscus injuries. McAnena et al (1991) recommended the measurement of amylase (>20 iu/L) and alkaline phosphatase (>3 iu/L) on peritoneal lavage as reliable predictors of small bowel injury. 22% of patients in their series had a laparotomy performed based on the above findings, confirming occult small bowel perforations.

Water soluble contrast radiography may be of benefit in confirming a perforation of the upper small intestine when doubt remains about a possible injury following other negative diagnostic tests (Rouse et al 1984).

Computed tomography (CT) may be a useful tool in the evaluation of a patient with blunt abdominal trauma even though its reliability in detecting bowel injuries has been questioned (Cook et al 1986, Marx et al 1985). Sherck et al (1994) reviewed 883 patients who had an abdominal CT performed because of equivocal physical findings and reported satisfactory results in the form of a sensitivity of 92% and a specificity of 94% by this investigatory mode. The negative and positive predictive values were 100% and 30% respectively.

Laparoscopy is a useful tool in the evaluation of patients with penetrating or blunt trauma, particularly in avoiding unnecessary laparotomy. In this context, it is especially valuable in obese patients with tangential gunshot wounds (Sosa et al 1992). However, caution and expertise is also required in interpreting laparoscopic findings in this setting. Ivatury et al (1993) demonstrated only an 18% sensitivity rate in detecting hollow viscus injury with laparoscopy in their study of 100 patients with penetrating abdominal trauma.

Classification

Based on the Organ Injury Scaling Committee of the American Association for the Surgery of Trauma, the following classification Table 10.24 has been recommended for small bowel injuries (Moore et al 1990).

Management

Stevens & Maull (1990) outlined the principles of operative management as follows:

1. Debridement of devitalised tissue
2. Liberal irrigation of the peritoneal cavity
3. Restoring bowel continuity and function.

Serosal tears are managed by inversion using Lembert sutures in a transverse axis.

Single small perforations are primarily closed transversely following debridement. Single-layer closure is adequate and has the advantage of not compromising the bowel lumen. Two perforations in close proximity may also be repaired primarily with resection of the bridging tissue and the defect closed in a transverse fashion (Stevens & Maull 1990). Large perforations on the mesenteric border or multiple perforations in a short segment of bowel require resection and primary anastomosis (Anderson & Ballinger 1979, Shires et al 1994).

Contusion injury of the small bowel is managed depending on its size. If less than 1 cm, it can be inverted as in serosal tears. Otherwise, debridement and primary closure are necessary. Major or large-sized contusion injuries require resection and primary anastomosis. Anastomoses should only be made with bowel ends of unquestionable viability.

Lacerations of the small bowel may be closed primarily depending on length. Difficulty implementing this technique exists with long linear lacerations, which should be resected.

Transection or avulsion injuries of the intestine or mesentery are treated with resection and primary anastomosis because of compromised blood supply. Large mesenteric haematomas (>2 cm) require exploration if expanding or uncontained. Rarely, the superior mesenteric artery needs to be isolated when bleeding is uncontrolled. Repair of the superior mesenteric artery is required in the rare instance of its involvement in the injurious process. This is a major undertaking in which a vascular surgeon should be involved.

Table 10.24 Small bowel injury classification

Grade	Type	Injury
I	Haematoma Laceration	Contusion or haematoma without devascularisation Partial thickness, no perforation
II	Laceration	Laceration <50% of circumference
III	Laceration	Laceration >/= 50% of circumference without transection
IV	Laceration	Transection of the small bowel
V	Laceration Vascular	Transection of the small bowel with segmental tissue loss Devascularised segment

The type of intestinal repair employed in Donohue et al (1985) series is shown in Table 10.25.

Morbidity and mortality

Factors such as delay in diagnosis and thus initiation of treatment, concomitant multi-organ injury and extent of damage to the small bowel have all been implicated in affecting morbidity and mortality rates.

Donohue et al (1985) reported 11 deaths (7% mortality) in their review of 163 patients with small bowel injuries. There was a 21% blunt trauma mortality rate compared with 7% in the penetrating trauma group. The authors stressed that five of the six deaths in the blunt trauma group and two of the five deaths in the penetrating injury group included duodenal injuries. The type of trauma and cause of death in Donohue's review are shown in Table 10.26.

Wounds in the terminal part of the small intestine have a higher potential for bacterial contamination following injury compared to more proximally placed wounds. Overall, septic complications are fewer than those

Table 10.25 Intestinal repairs (Donohue et al 1985)

Repair	Blunt	Stab	Firearm
None	2	1	*2
Simple closure			
jejunum	5	51	11
small bowel	1	9	9
ileum	2	9	11
Resection			
jejunum	5	5	16
small bowel	0	1	11
ileum	2	1	13

* Intraoperative death

Table 10.26 Types of small bowel injury and cause of death (Donohue et al 1985)

Trauma	No.	Cause of death
Blunt	3	Sepsis
	2	Anoxic brain death
	1	Haemorrhage
Stab	1	Multiple organ failure
Firearm	3	Haemorrhage
	1	Multiple organ failure
Total	11 (7%)	

seen in large bowel injuries and fistula formation far less than that experienced in duodenal trauma.

The complication rate reported by Donohue et al (1985) was 41%, 22% and 33% respectively for blunt, stab and firearm injuries. Complications were commoner in those with multiple injuries. The most frequent complication reported was that of an infective element. Other complications included postoperative ileus or obstruction, haemorrhage and iatrogenic injuries.

COLONIC AND RECTAL INJURIES

The challenging aspect of intraperitoneal colonic injury is mainly related with its far-reaching potential for the development of complications ranging from septic manifestations to problems related with diversionary ostomies and later closure.

Colostomy became the standard surgical procedure performed for colonic injuries by the end of the Second World War. It was not until the 1950s that primary repair of colonic injuries gained recognition when favourable reports of the procedure were published. Further support for primary repair has been established since then and this has propelled its utilisation in colonic injuries on a more frequent basis. Exteriorised repair, despite early encouraging reports by Kirkpatrick (1977) and Okies et al (1972), is losing popularity and only performed occasionally.

The mortality rate, which stood at approximately 60% in the First World War and 30% in the Second World War, currently stands at 5%.

Aetiology

The majority of injuries involving the colon are the result of penetrating trauma in the form of either stab or ballistic wounds. The latter mode of injury can be further subdivided into gunshot and shotgun wounds. Other forms of penetrating trauma are those encountered in a military setting where high-velocity missiles and shrapnels cause more extensive damage.

Colonic injury secondary to blunt abdominal trauma is less common, Levison et al (1977) having reported an incidence of less than 5%. Large bowel injuries caused by blunt forces are encountered in approximately 2–15% of cases (Burch et al 1991, Flint et al 1981). Road traffic accidents account for the majority of cases of blunt colonic trauma. Ross et al (1992), in their retrospective review of 286 patients with blunt colonic trauma, identified approximately 90% of cases as being secondary to some form of vehicular or pedestrian related injury.

Injuries to the colon may range from simple seromuscular tears or haemorrhagic contusion to more severe full thickness or devascularising injuries from mesenteric damage (Table 10.27).

Intraluminal injuries of the colon may also occur though less commonly. Iatrogenic injuries from colonoscopic examinations may cause colonic perforations, as can radiological examination of the large bowel using contrast medium, especially in certain pathological conditions.

Diagnosis

The diagnostic principles and tests employed in colonic injuries are usually as for small bowel injuries. Difficulties are usually experienced with blunt trauma as demonstrated by Ross et al (1992), who only diagnosed 5% of blunt colonic injuries pre-operatively in their multicentre review involving 286 patients with colonic trauma.

Furthermore, associated injuries in blunt abdominal trauma, such as in a patient with a head injury or in intoxicated patients, may complicate the diagnosis. Abdominal paracentesis and CT scans may not be reliable in this clinical setting as confirmed by numerous authors (Ross et al, 1992, Howell et al 1976, Donohue et al 1987).

Classification

The following classification has been recommended for colonic injuries by the American Association for the Surgery of Trauma through their Organ Injury Scaling Committee (Moore et al 1990).

Surgical management

Primary repair

This procedure has gained widespread popularity in recent years since it was reintroduced by Woodhall & Oschner (1951). Primary repair of colonic wounds involves simple closure of a serosal tear or small perforation. Resection of an involved colonic segment with primary anastomosis has also been included in this mode of treatment, and its employment is mentioned where applicable.

Table 10.27 Colonic injury classification

Grade	Type	Injury
1	Haematoma Laceration	Contusion or haematoma without devascularisation Partial thickness, no perforation
2	Laceration	< 50% of circumference
3	Laceration	>/= 50% of circumference without transection
4	Laceration	Transection of the colon
5	Laceration	Transection of the colon with segmental tissue loss
6	Vascular	Devascularised segment

Stone & Fabian (1979) used many exclusion criteria in their recommendation of the procedure following a randomised prospective study involving 268 patients which included:

- Blood pressure of less than 80/60 mmHg
- Intraperitoneal blood loss of more than 1000 ml
- Injury to more than two intra-abdominal organs
- Significant contamination of the peritoneal cavity with faeces
- Treatment delay of >8 hours from time of injury
- Colonic trauma requiring resection
- Destruction of a major part of the abdominal wall in the ensuing trauma.

Almost half the patients in their study group were excluded following application of the above criteria. The remaining 139 patients were divided into two groups, one of which was treated with primary repair while the other group with either primary closure protected by a proximal diverting colostomy or exteriorisation. The morbidity and mortality were both significantly lower in the group treated by primary closure.

However, the above rigid exclusion criteria were not reproduced in subsequent reports (George et al 1988, Burch et al 1991, Levison et al 1990). Chappuis et al (1991) even concluded in a recent study that virtually all patients with penetrating civilian injuries could be safely managed by primary repair. George and colleagues (1989), in their prospective trial of penetrating intraperitoneal colonic injuries involving 102 non-selected patients, found that primary repair was a safe option in virtually all (93%) but a few cases. Eighty-three patients in their study had primary closure performed while 12 patients had segmental colonic resection and anastomosis. Only one suture line leak developed in the anastomosis group. They concluded that the method of colon wound management, location and mode of injury, the presence of a low blood pressure (<90 mmHg systolic) and age did not significantly contribute to sepsis.

Burch et al (1991) performed primary repair in 61% of 614 patients over a ten-year period. Colostomy was employed in 28% of patients while 8.3% had exteriorised repair. They found that the probability of an adverse outcome was twice as great for both colostomy and exteriorised repair in comparison to primary repair, after analysing independent risk factors and calculating odds ratio for the above procedures. Ross et al (1992), in their multicentre review of 286 patients with blunt colonic trauma, also reported a successful outcome in utilising primary repair or non-surgical management which was employed in 65% of the patients. Bugis et al (1982), in their retrospective review of 28 patients of which a higher than usual number of patients (57%) had blunt injuries to the colon, managed 88% of patients with penetrating injuries and 59% of those with blunt injuries with primary repair. They advocated this form of repair based on a colon-related morbidity rate of 6%. The results, however, are inconclusive because of the small number of patients and the retrospective nature of the study.

Ross et al (1992) highlighted the fact that the rate of primary repair for full thickness blunt injuries of the colon has not shown a similar rise as for penetrating injuries. Falcone et al (1992) suggested the use of primary repair or anastomosis in combination with an intracolonic bypass as an alternative to an ostomy in intraperitoneal colorectal trauma. Theirs was a randomised prospective study which, even though it showed promising results, comprised only 22 patients.

Colostomy

Diversionary stomas will always play a role in the management of traumatic colonic injuries as this avoids the possibility of an anastomotic leak, which is a major source of sepsis or death. There is little doubt about its safety in a good clinical setting.

It does, however, have its own attendant morbidity, as stated by Jordan (1989) and Pachter et al (1990), the latter of whom addressed complications associated with colostomy closure and its impact on health care costs. Retrospective studies have a pitfall in demonstrating morbidity associated with colostomies since this procedure is usually reserved for those patients with more serious injuries.

Chappuis and colleagues (1991), in their prospective randomised trial of 56 patients with penetrating colon injuries, produced data demonstrating equal incidence of complications between two groups of patients treated with either a diversionary stoma or primary repair (or resection). The two groups of patients were similar in respect of grade of colon injury according to colon injury severity (CIS) score and location of injury. The incidence of intra-abdominal abscess was 14% in the diversion group and 11% in the primary repair group.

Concerning colostomy closure, Crass et al (1987) demonstrated a 5% overall complication rate in their study of 75 patients who underwent the procedure, in comparison to Parks & Hastings (1985) who recorded a 36% complication rate in their series of 83 patients. Thal & Yeary (1980) also produced favourable results associated with colostomy closure, recording a 10.2% complication rate in their group of 139 patients in which all the wounds were left open.

Exteriorised repair

This technique has largely been abandoned despite earlier favourable reports (Okies et al 1972, Burdette 1985) because of its complication rate and the meticulous technique and attention to detail that is required in the postoperative period. Close and regular observation of the exteriorised repair is also required by both the medical and nursing staff which can be demanding in a busy unit. Flint and colleagues (1981) reported a 50%

morbidity rate associated with exteriorised repair while Thompson & Moore (1982), in their series of 32 patients who had the above procedure performed, had to convert half of these to a colostomy.

Morbidity and mortality

It is generally accepted that multiple factors working in concert affect morbidity and mortality in traumatic colonic injuries. Huber & Thal (1990) highlighted a number of these, a few of which are outlined in Box 10.2.

The number and severity of associated injuries have been repeatedly shown to influence the outcome for patients with colonic trauma. Moore et al (1981) used the Penetrating Abdominal Trauma Index (PATI) score to demonstrate that higher morbidity and mortality are to be expected when the total PATI score is greater than 25. The CIS (Table 10.28), which is that part of PATI relating to the colon, and the grading system described by Flint et al (1981) are other indices denoting injury severity which are used to grade colonic injuries (Table 10.29).

However, there have been conflicting reports regarding the above scoring systems and their individual or combined use in helping to decide whether a procedure such as primary repair can be performed with safety. Nelken & Lewis (1989) found that of the injury severity indices that they examined, the PATI was most reliable in predicting complications, and most helpful in identifying patients who could undergo primary repair of their colonic injury.

They further found that when the PATI and the Injury Severity Score (ISS) were less than 25 and the Flint score was either 2 or less, primary closure resulted in fewer complications than colostomy. George et al (1989) utilised primary repair in 45% of their patients who had a PATI of greater than 25 satisfactorily without any suture leaks.

George et al (1989) and Nelken & Lewis (1989) also reported that the degree and number of blood transfusions were significant factors in the development of septic complications. A higher incidence of complications was predicted where four more units of blood were transfused. The presence of shock on presentation has not been conclusively shown to affect

Box 10.2

Age
Mechanism of injury
Associated injuries
Delay between injury and repair
Blood transfusion requirements/presence of shock
Extent or grade of colonic injury
Faecal contamination
Location of colonic injury

the outcome of surgery. George et al (1989), in their prospective series of 102 patients, failed to demonstrate any relationship between the development of postoperative sepsis and the presence of shock.

The site of colonic injury is now not deemed to be a major factor in predicting outcome or morbidity, nor in the choice of surgical intervention. It has also been advocated that right and left-sided colonic injuries should be treated similarly (Thompson et al 1981, Dang et al 1982, Demetriades et al 1985), unlike previously when diversionary procedures were considered for left-sided injuries. Thompson et al (1981), in a retrospective study consisting of 105 patients with penetrating colonic injuries, found no difference in the morbidity and mortality between two groups with either left or right-sided colonic injuries. Demetriades et al (1985), in a retrospective study of 134 cases of penetrating colonic injuries, found a similar complication rate of 11% in patients with left-sided colonic trauma treated with primary repair, compared to those with right-sided injuries treated similarly. There was also no statistical difference in the complication rate of patients treated with colostomy between the two anatomical sites.

As can be predicted, septic complications form a major part of the morbidity in colonic trauma, either as intra-abdominal abscesses or collections and anastomotic leaks which can lead to the development of multi-system organ dysfunction or failure and ultimately death. Wound infection is also common, especially when there is significant contamination. Complications, however, should be expected and dealt with in an aggressive manner to provide a good outcome (Falcone & Carey, 1988).

The mortality rate of civilian colonic trauma now stands at below 10%. Blunt colonic trauma, as expected, results in a higher mortality rate compared to penetrating injuries.

Table 10.28 Colon injury severity score (CIS)

Grade	Type
1	Serosal tear
2	Single wall injury
3	Injury involving < 25% of the wall
4	Injury involving > 25% of the wall
5	Injury involving colon wall and its blood supply

Table 10.29 Flint severity score

Grade	Type
1	Isolated colon injury, no shock, minimal delay, minimal contamination
2	Through perforations or lacerations, moderate contamination
3	Severe tissue loss, devascularisation, heavy contamination

More prospective evaluation of the various techniques in different clinical settings is required to establish the role of primary repair as the dominant mode of surgical intervention in colonic trauma.

RECTAL INJURIES

Aetiology

This is via either penetrating or blunt forms of injury. Iatrogenic injuries secondary to therapeutic anorectal surgical procedures, and urologic and gynaecological operations also account for a substantial part of trauma in this region. Inserted or ingested foreign bodies may also cause anorectal injuries.

Penetrating injuries are commoner than blunt rectal injuries. Bostick et al (1993) reviewed 28 patients with extraperitoneal rectal injuries, all of which were secondary to penetrating gunshot injuries, while Renz et al's (1993) prospective study of 30 patients with rectal trauma revealed 90% of the injuries as being secondary to penetrating gunshot wounds. Other forms of penetrating injuries include stab wounds and impalement injuries. Blunt trauma is usually secondary to vehicular accidents and falls.

Classification

The classification of rectal injuries is essentially similar to that of colonic injuries, using the Organ Injury Scaling (OIS) Committee of the American Association for the Surgery of Trauma (Moore et al 1990) except for Grade 4 injuries which are classified as: full thickness laceration with extension into the perineum.

Diagnosis

Apart from the importance of physical examination, specific investigations such as proctosigmoidoscopy and radiological studies may be helpful. Bostick et al (1993) had a 75% positive diagnostic rate on rectal examination compared to an 81% rate on proctosigmoidoscopy. Mangiante et al (1986) discovered blood on anorectal examination in 80% of patients in their series of penetrating rectal gunshot wounds.

Management

This depends on the injury severity and other injuries sustained. While certain procedures have been proved to be effective and safe, the question of distal rectal irrigation has given rise to controversy. More recent studies have disclaimed its routine use as a method of reducing septic complications.

Ivatury et al (1991) performed a retrospective study on 54 patients who sustained penetrating rectal injuries and concluded that colostomy and presacral drainage were the most important components of operative management. This procedure was employed in 43 patients with or without repair of the rectal injury. Almost half of these patients had a rectal washout performed and the incidence of pelvic abscess was identical in both groups of patients (4.7% in washout group; 4.5% in no-washout group). They further surmised that small and isolated injuries of the rectum could be repaired primarily without faecal diversion.

Bostick et al (1993), in their retrospective review of 28 penetrating gunshot rectal injuries, performed a faecal diversion procedure in all their patients, with presacral drainage employed in almost 90% of the patients. Distal irrigation was performed in only 46% of the patients and primary repair in 32% of patients. They inferred from their results that the routine employment of distal rectal washout was not established. They further concluded that primary repair of the rectum had no effect on morbidity and mortality.

Carpenter et al (1990) avoided the use of a diverting stoma in nine patients with severe colonic or rectal trauma by utilising an intracolonic bypass tube successfully.

Iatrogenic injuries

Both diagnostic and therapeutic procedures may cause injuries of the anorectum. Therapeutic procedures in this context not only encompass anorectal surgical procedures, but also include urological and gynaecological surgery in the proximity of this anatomical region. Flechner & Spalding (1982) reported approximately a 4% incidence of rectal trauma following radical cystectomy.

Diagnostic procedures which may cause rectal injury include barium enema studies. Hakim et al (1992) reported on five colorectal procedures out of 13 000 barium studies performed in the Mayo Clinic between 1977 and 1986. Three of the cases were rectal perforations, two of which were managed conservatively and one of which required a proximal diversion. They concluded in their study that extraperitoneal rectal perforations could be managed conservatively in selected patients, emphasising the need for early diagnosis and equally prompt treatment.

Insertion of rectal thermometers, especially in the paediatric age group can also cause rectal perforations, as reported by Horwitz & Bennett in 1976.

REFERENCES

Hepatic and splenic injury

Alho A, Karaharju O, Kallio E 1978 Blunt hepatic injury. Annales Chirurgiae et Gynaecologiae 67: 66

Angstadt J, Jarrell B, Moritz M et al 1989 Surgical management of severe liver trauma: a role for liver transplantation. Journal of Trauma 29: 606
Baker S P, O'Neill B, Haddon W et al 1974 The injury severity score: a method for describing patients with multiple injuries. Journal of Trauma 14: 187
Beal S C, Ward R E 1989 Successful atrial caval shunting in the management of retrohepatic venous injuries. American Journal of Surgery 158: 409
Benjamin C I, Engrav L H, Perry J F 1976 Delayed rupture or delayed diagnosis of rupture of the spleen. Surgery, Gynecology and Obstetrics 142: 171
Black J J, Sinow R M, Wilson S E et al 1992 Subcapular haematoma as a predictor of delayed splenic rupture. American Surgeon 58(12): 732
Buntain W L, Gould H R 1985 Splenic trauma in children and techniques of splenic salvage. World Journal of Surgery 9: 398
Busuttil R W, Kitahama A et al 1980 Management of injuries to portahepatitis. Annals of Surgery 191: 641
Calne R Y, Wells F C, Forty J 1982 Twenty-six cases of liver trauma. British Journal of Surgery 69: 365
Caplan E S, Boltansky H, Snyder M J et al 1983 Response of traumatized patients to immediate vaccination with polyvalent pneumococcal vaccination. Journal of Trauma 23: 801
Cogbill T H, Moore E E et al 1989 Nonoperative management of blunt splenic trauma: a multicentre study. Journal of Trauma 29: 1312
Croce M A, Fabian T C, Kudski K A et al 1991 AAST Organ Injury Scale: correlation of CT-graded liver injuries and operative findings. Journal of Trauma 31: 806
Cue J I, Cryer H G, Miller F B et al 1990 Packing and planned re-exploration for hepatic and retroperitoneal haemorrhage. Journal of Trauma 30: 1007
Defore W W, Mattox K L, Jordan G L et al 1976 Management of 1590 consecutive cases of liver trauma. Annals of Surgery 111: 493
Delany H M, Rudavesky A Z, Lan S 1985 Preliminary clinical experience with the use of absorbable mesh splenorrhaphy. Journal of Trauma 25: 909
Feliciano D V 1990 In: Simmons R L, Udekwu A O (eds) Packing in major liver surgery. Debates in Clinical Surgery vol 1. Year Book Medical Publishers, Chicago
Feliciano D V, Mattox K L, Burch J M et al 1986 Packing for control of hepatic haemorrhage. Journal of Trauma 26: 738
Feliciano D V, Pachter H L 1989 Hepatic trauma revisited. Current Problems in Surgery 26: 459
Feliciano D V, Mattox K L, Jordan G L et al 1981 Intraabdominal packing for control of hepatic haemorrhage – a reappraisal. Journal of Trauma 21: 285
Fischer R P, Beverlin B C, Engrav L H et al 1978 Diagnostic peritoneal lavage: 14 years and 2586 patients later. American Journal of Surgery 136: 701
Green J B, Shackford S R et al 1986 Late septic complications in adults following splenectomy for trauma. Journal of Trauma 29: 999
Gruessner R, Mentges B, Duber C H et al 1989 Sonography versus peritoneal lavage in blunt abdominal trauma. Journal of Trauma 29: 242
Hanna S S, Pagliarello G, Taylor G et al 1991 Blunt liver trauma at Sunnybrook Medical Centre: a 13-year experience. HPB Surgery 4: 49
Heaney J P, Stanton W R, Halbert D S et al 1966 An improved technique for vascular isolation of the liver. Annals of Surgery 163: 237
Hebeler R F, Ward R E, Miller P W et al 1982 The management of splenic injury. Journal of Trauma 22: 492
Heimbach D M, Ferguson G S, Harley J D et al 1978 Treatment and traumatic hemobilia with angiographic embolization. Journal of Trauma 18: 221
Ivatury R R, Nallthambi M, Gundez Y et al 1986 Liver packing for uncontrolled haemorrhage – a reappraisal. Journal of Trauma 26: 744
John T G, Greig J D, Johnstone A J et al 1992 Liver trauma: a 10-year experience. British Journal of Surgery 79: 1352
Jones B J, Daly M, Delaney P V 1991 Torsion of the spleen managed by splenopexy. British Journal of Surgery 78: 887
Kakkasseril J S, Stewart D, Cox J A et al 1982 Changing treatment of paediatric splenic trauma. Archives of Surgery 117: 758

Kidd W T, Lui R C, Khoo R et al 1987 The management of blunt splenic trauma. Journal of Trauma 27: 977

King H, Schumaker H B 1952 Splenic studies: susceptibility to infection following splenectomy performed in infancy. Annals of Surgery 136: 239

King D R, Lobe T E, Hoase G M et al 1981 Selective management of the injured spleen. Surgery 90: 677

Kreuzfelder E, Obertacke U, Erhard J et al 1991 Alterations of the immune system following splenectomy in childhood. Journal of Trauma 31: 358

Lange D A, Robin A P, Andrews J R et al 1989 Selective management of anterior abdominal stab wounds. Journal of Trauma 29: 1684

Ludtke F A, Mack S C, Schuff-Werner P et al 1989 Splenic function after splenectomy for trauma. Role of autotransplantation and splenosis. Acta Chirurgica Scandinavica 155: 533

Luna, Dellinger 1987 Non-operative observation therapy for splenic injuries: a safe therapeutic option? American Journal of Surgery 153: 462

McIndoe A H 1932 Delayed haemorrhage following traumatic rupture of the spleen. British Journal of Surgery 20: 249

Milliken J S, Moore E E, Moore G E et al 1982 Alternatives to splenectomy in adults after trauma. American Journal of Surgery

Mirvis S E, Whitley N O, Vainwright J R et al 1989 Blunt hepatic trauma in adults: CT-based classification and correlation with prognosis and treatment. Radiology 171: 27, 33

Mishalany H G, Miller J H, Woolley M M et al 1982 Radioisotope spleen scan in patients with splenic injury. Archives of Surgery 117: 1147

Moore E E, Shackford S R, Pachter H L 1989 Organ injury scaling: spleen, liver and kidney. Journal of Trauma 29: 1664

Moore F A, Moore E E, Moore G E et al 1984 Risk of splenic salvage following trauma: analysis of 200 adults. American Journal of Surgery 148: 800

Moore G E, Stevens R E, Moore E E, Aragon G E et al 1983 Failure of splenic implants to protect against fatal postsplenectomy infection. American Journal of Surgery 146: 413

Nallathambi M N, Ivatury R R, Waprin I et al 1988 Nonoperative management vs early operation for blunt splenic trauma in adults. Surgery, Gynecology and Obstetrics 166: 252

Noyes L D, Doyle D J, McSwain N E 1988 Septic complications associated with the use of peritoneal drains in liver trauma. Journal of Trauma 28: 337

Olsen W R, Polley T Z 1977 A second look at delayed splenic rupture. Archives of Surgery 112: 422

Perry J F Jr 1988 Injuries of the spleen. Current Problems in Surgery 25: 749

Pimpl W, Dapunt O, Kaindl H et al 1989 Incidence of septic and thromboembolic-related deaths after splenectomy in adults. British Journal of Surgery 76: 517

Powell D C, Bivins B A, Bell R M 1982 Diagnostic peritoneal lavage. Surgery, Gynecology and Obstetrics 155: 257

Reed R L, Merrell R C, Meyers W C et al 1992 Continuing evolution in the approach to severe liver trauma. Annals of Surgery 216: 524

Rehm C G, Sherman R, Hinz T W 1989 The role of CT scan in evaluation for laparotomy in patients with stab wounds of the abdomen. Journal of Trauma 29: 446

Resciniti A, Fink M P, Ratapoulos V et al 1988 Nonoperative treatment of adult splenic trauma: development of a CT scoring system. Journal of Trauma 28: 828

Rivkind A I, Siegel J H, Dunham C M 1989 Patterns of organ injury in blunt hepatic trauma and their significance for management and outcome. Journal of Trauma 29: 1398

Shackford S R, Molin M 1990 Management of splenic injuries. Surgical Clinics of North America 70: 595

Sizer J S, Wayne E R, Frederic P L 1966 Delayed rupture of the spleen. Review of the literature and report of six cases. Archives of Surgery 92: 362

Sonderstrom C A, Dupriest R W, Cowley R A 1980 Pitfalls of peritoneal lavage in blunt abdominal trauma. Surgery, Gynecology, Obstetrics 151: 513

Splenic Injury Study Group 1987 Splenic injury: a prospective multicentre study on nonoperative and operative treatment. British Journal of Surgery 74: 310

Stevens S L, Maull K L, Enderson B L et al 1991 Total mesh wrapping for parenchymal liver injuries – a combined experimental and clinical study. Journal of Trauma 31:1103

Traub A C, Perry J F 1982 Splenic presentation following splenic trauma. Journal of Trauma 22: 496

Traub A C, Perry J F 1981 Injuries associated for splenic trauma. Journal of Trauma 21: 840

Tricarico A, Sicoli F, Calise F et al 1993 Conservative treatment in splenic trauma. Journal of the Royal College of Surgeons of Edinburgh 38: 145
Trunkey D, Shires G T, McClelland R N 1974 Management of liver trauma in 811 consecutive patients. Annals of Surgery 179: 722
Watson C J, Caine R Y, Padhani A R et al 1991 Surgical restraint in the management of liver trauma. British Journal of Surgery 78: 1071
Wesson D E, Filler R M, Ein S H et al 1981 Ruptured spleen – when to operate. Journal of Paediatric Surgery 16: 324
Willis B K, Deitch E A, McDonald J C et al 1986 The influence of trauma to the spleen on postoperative complications and mortality. Journal of Trauma 26: 1073

Pancreatic injury

Bach R D, Frey C F 1979 Diagnosis and treatment of pancreatic trauma. Current Problems in Surgery 16(12): 1–59
Berne C J, Donovan A J, White E J et al 1974 Duodenal 'diverticulization' for duodenal and pancreatic injury. American Journal of Surgery 127: 503–507
Berni G A, Bandyk D F, Oreskovich M R, Carrico C J 1982 Role of intraoperative pancreatography in patients with injury to the pancreas. American Journal of Surgery 143(5): 602–605
Cogbill T H, Moore E E, Morris J A Jr, Hoyt D B, Jurkovich G J et al 1991 Distal pancreatectomy for trauma: a multicenter experience. Journal of Trauma 31(12): 1600–1606
Feliciano D V, Martin T D, Cruse P A, Graham J M et al 1987 Management of combined pancreatoduodenal injuries. Annals of Surgery 205(6): 1600–1606
Gougeon F W, Legros G, Archambault A et al 1976 Pancreatic trauma: a new diagnostic approach. American Journal of Surgery 132: 400–402
Hall R I, Lavelle M I, Venables C W 1986 Use of ERCP to identify the site of traumatic injuries to the main pancreatic duct in children. British Journal of Surgery 73(5): 411–412
Ivatury R R, Nallathambi M, Rao P, Stahl W M 1990 Penetrating pancreatic injuries: analysis of 103 consecutive cases. The American Surgeon 56(2): 90–95
Jeffrey R B, Federle M P, Creass R A 1983 Computed tomography of pancreatic trauma. Radiology 147(5): 491–494
Jones R C 1985 Management of pancreatic trauma. The American Journal of Surgery 150: 698–704
Jurkovich G J, Carrico C J 1990 Pancreatic trauma. Surgical Clinics of North America 70(3): 575–593
Lempinen M 1981 Management of major abdominal trauma: pancreas. In: Carter D, Polk H C Jr (eds) Surgery I; trauma. Butterworths, London, pp 117–128
Leppaniemi A, Haapiainen R, Kiviluoto T et al 1988 Pancreatic trauma: acute and late manifestations. British Journal of Surgery 75: 165–167
Letton A H, Wilson J P 1959 Traumatic severance of pancreas treated by Roux-en-y anastomosis. Surgery, Gynecology and Obstetrics 109: 473
Lewis G, Knottenbelt J D, Krige J E 1991 Conservative surgery for trauma to the pancreatic head: is it safe? Injury 22(5): 372–374
Lucas C E 1977 Diagnosis and treatment of pancreatic and duodenal injury. Surgical Clinics of North America 57: 49–65
Moore E E, Cogbill T H, Malangoni M A et al 1990 Organ injury scaling II: pancreas, duodenum, small bowel, colon and rectum. Journal of Trauma 30: 1247
Moretz J A, Campbell D P, Parker D E, Williams G R 1975 Significance of serum amylase level in evaluating pancreatic trauma. American Journal of Surgery 130: 739–741
Northrup W F, Simmons R C 1972 Pancreatic trauma: a review. Surgery 71: 27–43
Olsen W R 1973 The serum amylase in blunt abdominal trauma. Journal of Trauma 13: 200–204
Oreskovich M R, Carrico C J 1984 Pancreaticoduodenectomy for trauma: a viable option. American Journal of Surgery 147: 618–623
Robey E, Mullen J T, Schwab C W 1982 Blunt transection of the pancreas treated by distal pancreatectomy, splenic salvage and hyperalimentation. Annals of Surgery 196: 695–699
Smego D R, Richardson J D, Flint L M 1985 Determinants of outcome in pancreatic trauma. Journal of Trauma 25: 771
Sorensen V J, Obeid F N, Horst H M et al 1986 Penetrating pancreatic injuries, 1978–1983. American Surgeon 52: 354–358

Gastric injuries

Blaisdell F W, Trunkey D D 1982 Trauma management. In: Abdominal trauma. Thieme-Stratton, New York, pp 77–86
Brunsting L A, Morton J H 1987 Gastric rupture from blunt abdominal trauma. Journal of Trauma 27: 887–891
Courcy P A, Soderstrom C, Brotman S 1984 Gastric rupture from blunt trauma: a plea for minimal diagnostics and early surgery. American Surgeon 50: 424–427
Demos N J, Poticha S M 1964 Gastric rupture occurring during external cardiac resuscitation. Surgery 55: 364–366
Durham R 1990 Management of gastric injuries. Surgical Clinics of North America 70(3): 517–527
Heselson J 1970 Peritoneoscopy in abdominal trauma. South African Journal of Surgery 8: 53
Ivatury R R, Simon R J, Stahl W M 1993 A critical evaluation of laparoscopy in penetrating abdominal trauma. Journal of Trauma 34: 822–828
Nance F C, Cobin I 1969 Surgical judgement in the management of stab wounds to the abdomen: a retrospective and prospective analysis based on a study of 600 stabbed patients. Annals of Surgery 170: 569
Semel L, Fritelli G 1981 Gastric rupture from blunt abdominal trauma. New York State Journal of Medicine 81: 938–939
Siemens R A, Fulton R L 1977 Gastric rupture as a result of blunt trauma. Annals of Surgery 43: 229
Stone H H, Hester T R Jr 1973 Incisional and peritoneal infection after emergency celiotomy. Annals of Surgery 177: 669
Thal E R 1977 Evaluation of peritoneal lavage and local exploration in lower chest and abdominal stab wounds. Journal of Trauma 17: 642–648
Thal E R 1984 Peritoneal lavage: reliability of RBC count in patients with stab wounds to the chest and abdomen. Archives of Surgery 119: 579–584
Vassy L E, Klecker R L, Koch E et al 1975 Traumatic gastric rupture in children from blunt trauma. Journal of Trauma 15: 184–186
Villalba M, Lucas C E, Ledgerwood A M et al 1979 The aetiology of post-traumatic empyema and the role of decortication. Journal of Trauma 19: 414
Wilkinson A E 1989 Injuries of the stomach: an analysis of 95 cases. South African Journal of Surgery 27: 59–60
Yajko R D, Seydel F, Trimble C 1975 Rupture of the stomach from blunt abdominal trauma. Journal of Trauma 15: 177–183

Duodenal injury

Berne C J, Donovan A J, Hagen W E 1968 Combined duodenal pancreatic trauma: the role of end-to-side gastrojejunostomy. Archives of Surgery 96: 712–722
Berne C J, Donovan A J, White E J, Yellin A E 1974 Duodenal 'diverticulization' for duodenal and pancreatic injury. American Journal of Surgery 127: 503–507
Cogbill T H, Moore E E, Feliciano D V, Hoyt D B, Jurkovich G J, Morris J A et al 1990 Conservative management of duodenal trauma: a multicenter perspective. Journal of Trauma 30: 1469–1475
Cox E 1984 Blunt abdominal trauma. Annals of Surgery 199: 467–474
DeMars J J, Bubrick M P, Hitchcock C R 1979 Duodenal perforation in blunt abdominal trauma. Surgery 86: 632
Federle M P, Crass R A, Jeffrey R B et al 1982 Computed tomography in blunt abdominal trauma. Archives of Surgery 117: 645–650
Flint L M, McCoy M, Richardson J D, Polk H C Jr 1980 Duodenal injury: analysis of common misconceptions in diagnosis and treatment. Annals of Surgery 191: 697
Frey C 1982 Trauma to the pancreas and duodenum. In: Blaisdell F W, Trunkey D D (eds) Trauma management. Abdominal trauma. Thieme-Stratton, New York, vol 1: 87–122
Graham J M, Mattox K L, Vaughan G D III et al 1979 Combined pancreatoduodenal injuries. Journal of Trauma 19: 340–345
Hasson J E, Stern D, Moss G S 1984 Penetrating duodenal trauma. Journal of Trauma 24(6): 471–474
Heitsch R C, Knutson C O, Fulton R L et al 1976 Delineation of critical factors in the treatment of pancreatic trauma. Surgery 80: 523–529

Ivatury R R, Nallathambi M, Gaudino J, Rohman M, Stahl W M 1985 Penetrating duodenal injuries: analysis of 1000 consecutive cases. American Surgeon 202(2): 153–158
Jewett T C, Caldarola V, Karp M P et al 1988 Intramural haematoma of the duodenum. Archives of Surgery 123: 54–58
Kelly G, Norton L, Moore G et al 1978 The continuing challenge of duodenal injuries. Journal of Trauma 18: 160–165
Kunin J R, Korobkin M, Ellis J H et al 1993 Duodenal injuries caused by blunt abdominal trauma: value of CT scanning in differentiating perforation from haematoma. American Journal of Roentgenology 160(6): 1221
Lucas C E, Ledgerwood A M 1975 Factors influencing outcome after blunt duodenal injury. Journal of Trauma 15: 839
Martin T D, Feliciano D V, Mattox K L, Gordon G L Jr 1983 Severe duodenal injuries. Archives of Surgery 118: 631–635
Moore E E, Cogbill T H, Malangoni M A et al 1990 Organ injury scaling II: pancreas, duodenum, small bowel, colon and rectum. Journal of Trauma 30: 1247
Oreskovich M R, Carrico C J 1984 Pancreaticoduodenectomy for trauma: a viable option. American Journal of Surgery 147: 618–623
Root H D, Hauser C W, McKinley C R et al 1965 Diagnostic peritoneal lavage. Surgery 57: 633
Shorr R M, Greaney G C, Donovan A J 1987 Injuries of the duodenum. American Journal of Surgery 154: 93–98
Snyder W H III, Weigelt J A, Watkins W L, Bietz D S 1980 The surgical management of duodenal trauma: precepts based on a review of 247 cases. Archives of Surgery 115: 422–429
Stone H H, Fabian T C 1979 Management of duodenal wounds. Journal of Trauma 19(5): 334–339
Vaughan G D III, Frazier O H, Graham D Y, Mattox K L, Petmecky F F, Jordan G L Jr 1977 The use of pyloric exclusion in the management of severe duodenal injuries. American Journal of Surgery 134: 785–790
Weigelt J A 1990 Duodenal injuries. Surgical Clinics of North America 70(3): 529–539
Wooley M M, Mahour G H, Sloan T 1978 Duodenal haematoma in infancy and childhood. American Journal of Surgery 136: 8–14

Small bowel injury

Anderson C B, Ballinger W F 1979 Abdominal injuries. In: Zuidema, Rutherford, Balinger W F (eds) Management of trauma, 3rd edn. W B Saunders, Philadelphia, pp 429–482
Cook D E, Walsh J W, Vick C W et al 1986 Upper abdominal trauma: pitfalls in CT diagnosis. Radiology 159: 65–69
Dauterive A H, Flancbaum L, Cox E F 1985 Blunt intestinal trauma. Annals of Surgery 201: 198–203
Donohue J H, Crass R A, Trunkey D D 1985 The management of duodenal and other small intestinal trauma. World Journal of Surgery 9: 904–913
Duncan J T 1956 Rupture of the small intestine through the intact abdominal wall without associated intraperitoneal injury. American Surgeon 22: 1215
Ivatury R R, Simon R J, Stahl W M 1993 A critical evaluation of laparoscopy in penetrating abdominal trauma. Journal of Trauma 34: 822–828
Marx J A, Moore E E, Jordan R C et al 1985 Limitations of computerized tomography in the evaluation of acute abdominal trauma: a prospective comparison with diagnostic peritoneal lavage. Journal of Trauma 25: 933
McAnena O J, Marx J A, Moore E E 1991 Peritoneal lavage enzyme determinations following blunt and penetrating abdominal trauma. Journal of Trauma 31: 1161–1164
Moore E E, Cogbill T H, Malangoni M A et al 1990 Organ injury scaling II: pancreas, duodenum, small bowel, colon and rectum. Journal of Trauma 30: 1247
Moore E E, Marx J A 1985 Penetrating abdominal trauma: rationale for exploratory laparotomy. Journal of American Medical Association 253: 2705–2708
Root H D, Keizer P J, Perry J F 1967 Peritoneal trauma: experimental and clinical studies. Surgery 62: 679–685
Rouse T, Collin J, Daar A 1984 Isolated injury to the intestine from blunt abdominal injury. British Journal of Accident and Surgery 16: 131–133

Sherck J, Shatney C, Sensaki K, Selivanov V 1994 The accuracy of computed tomography in the diagnosis of blunt small bowel perforation. American Journal of Surgery 168: 670–675
Shires G T, Thal E R, Jones R C, Shires G T III, Perry M O 1994 Trauma: small intestine. In: Principles of surgery. McGraw Hill, Singapore
Sosa J L, Sims D, Martin L, Zeppa R 1992 Laparoscopic evaluation of tangential abdominal gunshot wounds. Archives of Surgery 127: 109–110
Stevens S L, Maull K I 1990 Small bowel injuries. Surgical Clinics of North America 70: 541–560
Thompson J S, Moore E E 1983 Peritoneal lavage in the evaluation of penetrating abdominal trauma. Surgery, Gynecology and Obstetrics 153: 861–863

Colonic and rectal injury

Bostick P J, Johnson D A, Heard J F et al 1993 Management of extraperitoneal rectal injuries. Journal of National Medical Association 85: 460–463
Bugis S P, Blair P W, Letwin E R 1982 Management of blunt and penetrating colonic injury. American Journal of Surgery 163: 547–550
Burch J M, Martin R R, Richardson R J et al 1991 Evolution of the treatment of the injured colon in the 1980s. Archives of Surgery 126: 979–984
Burdette W J 1985 Primary intraperitoneal closure and exteriorization of primarily sutured colon for colon injuries. Surgical Rounds (June): 65–112
Carpenter, Bello J, Sokol T P et al 1990 The intracolonic bypass tube for left colon and rectal trauma: the avoidence of a colostomy. American Surgeon 56: 769
Chappuis C W, Frey D J, Dietzen C D et al 1991 Management of penetrating colon injuries: a prospective randomized trial. Annals of Surgery 213: 492–498
Crass R A, Salbi F, Trunkey D D 1987 Colostomy closure after colon injury: a low morbidity procedure. Journal of Trauma 27: 1237–1239
Dang C V, Peter E T, Parks S N et al 1982 Trauma of the colon. Archives of Surgery 117: 652–656
Demetriades D, Rabinowitz B, Sofianos C et al 1985 The management of colon injuries by primary repair or colostomy. British Journal of Surgery 72: 881–883
Donohue J H, Federle M P, Griffiths B G et al 1987 Computed tomography in the diagnosis of blunt intestinal and mesenteric injuries. Journal of Trauma 27: 11
Falcone R E, Carey L C 1988 Colorectal trauma. Surgical Clinics of North America 68(6): 1307–1318
Falcone R E, Wanamaker S R, Santanello S A, Carey L C 1992 Colorectal trauma: primary repair or anastomosis with intracolonic bypass vs ostomy. Disease of Colon and Rectum 35: 957–963
Flechner S M, Spalding J T 1982 Management of rectal injury during cystectomy. Urology 19: 143
Flint L M, Vitale G C, Richardson J D, Park H C 1981 The injured colon: relationship of management to complications. Annals of Surgery 193: 619–623
George S M, Fabian T C, Mangiante E C 1988 Colon trauma: further support for primary repair. American Journal of Surgery 156: 16–20
George S M, Fabian T C, Voeller G R, Kudsk K A, Mangiante E C, Britt L G 1989 Primary repair of colon wounds. Annals of Surgery 209(6): 728–734
Hakim N S, Sarr M G, Bender C E et al 1992 Management of barium enema induced colorectal perforation. American Surgeon 58: 673–676
Horwitz M A, Bennett J V 1976 Nursery outbreak of peritonitis with pneumoperitoneum probably caused by thermometer-induced rectal perforation. American Journal of Epidemiology 104: 632
Howell H S, Baritzal J F, Freeark R J 1976 Blunt trauma involving the colon and rectum. Journal of Trauma 16: 624
Ivatury R R, Licata J, Gunduz Y et al 1991 Management options in penetrating rectal injuries. American Surgeon 57: 50–55
Jordan G L Jr 1989 Editorial comment: Livingston D H, Miller F B, Richardson J D Are the risks after colostomy closure exaggerated? American Journal of Surgery 158: 20
Kirkpatrick R J, Rajpal S G 1975 The injured colon: therapeutic considerations. American Journal of Surgery 129: 187–191

Kirkpatrick J R 1977 The exteriorized anastomosis: its role in surgery of the colon. Surgery 82: 362–365

Levison M A, Thomas K K, Wiencek R G et al 1990 Management of the injured colon: evolving practice at an urban trauma centre. Journal of Trauma 30: 247–253

Mangiante E C, Graha A D, Fabian T C 1986 Rectal gunshot wounds. American Surgeon 52: 37

Moore E E, Cogbill T H, Malangoni M A et al 1990 Organ injury scaling: II. Pancreas, duodenum, small bowel, colon, and rectum. Journal of Trauma 30: 1427

Moore E E, Dunn E L, Moore J B et al 1981 Penetrating abdominal trauma index. Journal of Trauma 21: 438–445

Nelkin N, Lewis F 1989 Influence of injury severity on complication rates after primary closure or colostomy for penetrating colon trauma. Annals of Surgery 209(4): 439–447

Okies J E, Bricker D L, Jordan G L, Beall A C, DeBakey M E 1972 Exteriorized primary repair of colon injuries. American Journal of Surgery 124: 807–810

Pachter H L, Habullah J J, Corcoran T A, Hofstetter S R 1990 The morbidity and financial impact of colostomy closure in trauma patients. Journal of Trauma 30: 1510–1513

Parks S E, Hastings P R 1985 Complications of colostomy closure. American Journal of Surgery 149: 672–675

Renz B M, Feliciano D V, Sherman R 1993 Same admission colostomy closure (SACC): a new approach to rectal wounds. A prospective study. Annals of Surgery 218: 279

Ross S E, Cobean R A, Hoyt D B et al 1992 Blunt colonic injury: a Multicenter Review. Journal of Trauma 33: 379–384

Stone H H, Fabian T C 1979 Management of perforating colon trauma: randomization between primary closure and exteriorization. Annals of Surgery 190: 430–443

Thal E R, Yeary E C 1980 Morbidity of colostomy closure following colon trauma. Journal of Trauma 20: 287–291

Thompson J J, Moore E E, Moore J B 1981 Comparison of penetrating injuries of the right and left colon. Annals of Surgery 193(4): 414–418

Thompson J S, Moore E E 1982 Factors affecting the outcome of exteriorized colon repairs. Journal of Trauma 22: 403–406

Woodhall J P, Oschner A 1951 The management of perforating injuries of the colon and rectum in civilian practise. Surgery 29: 305–320

11. Urological injuries

Barry Jones

Injuries to the urological tract involve a complex array of problems and require a versatile range of technical skills in order to be optimally managed. In addition to challenges related to function and anatomical continuity, serious quality of life and psychological issues arise where continence or erectile function has been compromised. The frequent occurrence of associated non-urological injuries frequently requires a multidisciplinary approach in addition to a high level of competence in the principles of trauma management on the part of the urological surgeon.

The majority of urological injuries are caused by motor vehicle trauma, malicious assault or iatrogenic mishaps and consequently will frequently attract litigation. Meticulous documentation of treatment and follow-up are essential. A high level of communication with the patient, to ensure realistic expectations and good compliance where treatment events are potentially multiple, is vital.

BLADDER INJURIES

Although generally well protected, the bladder is prone to injury in certain well recognised circumstances. Typically, the full bladder is more vulnerable to injury. The categories of bladder injury are shown in Table 11.1.

Table 11.1 Bladder injury (Carroll & McAninch 1984)

Category	Patients (%)
Blunt (non-penetrating)	63
Penetrating	25
Spontaneous	2
Iatrogenic	
Gynaecologic surgery	8
Long-term Foley catheter	2
Total	100

Table 11.2 Urological injury classification

Grade	Type
1	Contusion
2	Laceration (penetrating)
3	Rupture (bursting)
4	Complicated (associated with other injuries or underlying urological pathology)

Table 11.3 Blunt bladder injury (Carroll & McAninch 1984)

Type	Patients (%)
Extraperitoneal	63
Intraperitoneal	25
Combined	12
Total	100

The anatomical classification of blunt bladder trauma is shown in Table 11.3.

Blunt injury

Blunt trauma is the most common mechanism of injury to the bladder, accounting for up to 80% of all bladder injuries. Motoring accidents cause over 80% of significant blunt injury to the bladder (excluding minor injuries such as exercise-related bladder contusions). The next most frequent aetiology is physical assault.

In bladder ruptures caused by road accidents there is a high incidence of associated injury. Up to 70% such cases have associated pelvic fractures (Brosman & Paul 1976) and in one review 93% of bladder ruptures also had injury to other organs. Clearly the mechanism of trauma is a major consideration in this respect.

Table 11.4 Rupture with blunt injury (Carroll & McAninch 1984)

Area	Patients (%)
Dome	34
Lateral wall	29
Anterior wall	10
Posterior wall	10
Bladder neck	14

The site of rupture is documented in Table 11.4 in order of frequency.

Spontaneous rupture of the bladder is a rarity. Pre-existing bladder pathology will, however, make a bladder more susceptible to trauma. Predisposing factors include bladder distension due to outflow obstruction or atonic detrusor, or conditions which weaken or reduce the elasticity of the bladder wall such as chronic inflammatory disease, previous radiotherapy or previous enterocystoplasty.

Management

The distinction between extraperitoneal and intraperitoneal rupture has important management implications. The diagnosis is usually made by retrograde cystography combined with the appropriate clinical circumstances.

The prinicipal treatment options for an extraperitoneal rupture are simple urethral catheter drainage and antibiotics, or open surgery. Both Corriere & Harris (1981) and Cass & Ireland (1973) report satisfactory results for conservative management with minimal complications. The main indications for open intervention are an extensive injury, the possibility of a co-existing injury and abscess development. It is not appropriate, therefore, to compare conservative management to open surgery as in the latter group the injury is more severe.

Intraperitoneal ruptures require surgical exploration in most cases. This is because of the high incidence of associated organ injury. Carroll & McAninch (1984) reported a mortality rate of 22% in their review, but all deaths were due to injuries other than the bladder injury. Similarly Peters in his review found that poor outcome was related to co-existing visceral injury. The most frequent associated injuries according to Carroll & McAninch are listed in Table 11.5.

Penetrating injury

Penetrating injuries to the bladder are more commonly associated with physical assault. In anticipation of future legal proceedings, it is essential to keep detailed notes. In American reports, the firearm is the commonest

Table 11.5 Associated organ injury in 13 patients with penetrating injury

Organ	Patients	%
Small bowel	3	23
Colon	3	23
Rectum	2	15
Long bones	1	8
Ureter	1	8

weapon of offence followed by stab wounds and iatrogenic injuries. Countries with more restrictive firearms legislation do not produce these kinds of statistics. Ballistic characteristics of the firearm missile are important in determining the extent of injury. For a more detailed understanding refer to Chapter 4.

Penetrating bladder trauma has a high incidence of associated injuries (see Table 11.5). Compared to blunt trauma, orthopaedic injuries are much less prominent whereas bowel injury is to the forefront. These associated injuries are themselves usually penetrating in nature. Consequently there is a greater imperative to manage penetrating bladder injuries by open exploration.

Iatrogenic bladder injury

Iatrogenic injury to the bladder is common but is usually not of great significance. The bladder is most vulnerable to injury during deep pelvic operations such as abdominoperineal resection or total abdominal hysterectomy. There are three basic types of injury relating to these procedures:

1. **Retractor injury/compression contusion**. Causes haematuria but resolves promptly with no adverse sequelae.
2. **Crush injury**. This is usually caused by inadvertently including a fold of bladder in a heavy haemostat such as a Kocher's forceps. This most commonly occurs when securing the uterine artery as it joins the uterus and proximal vagina at total abdominal hysterectomy. If promptly recognised and rectified, no further action is required. If, however, the overlying detrusor muscle is denuded or appears non-viable, single-layer repair plus postoperative catheter drainage is advisable.
3. **Penetrating injury**. Difficult deep pelvic surgery may be complicated by penetrating injury to the bladder. This can be caused by either sharp or blunt dissection. In the otherwise healthy bladder simple repair and catheter drainage is the treatment of choice. In this case, no long-term consequences occur.

Problems arise either where the injury is unrecognised at the time of surgery or the healing capacity of the bladder is impaired by previous radiotherapy. An unrecognised injury will result in precarious fluid balance postoperatively and a progressive development of pelvic and/or intra-abdominal collection of urine. Equally such an injury may not become manifest while the patient is catheterised, but rather become apparent as abdominal swelling about a week after the operation.

Diagnosis is by retrograde cystography, and treatment depends on the extent of the injury. Usually the injury is localised and discrete and can be managed by defunctioning the bladder for 3–4 weeks, peritoneal aspiration where indicated and antibiotics. It must be confirmed cystographically that the perforation has healed before removing the catheter.

Complications

Vesicovaginal fistulas. The commonest complication of unrecognised or poorly repaired iatrogenic injury to the bladder is the development of a fistula (usually to the vagina in the female). Not surprisingly the operation most frequently associated with vesicovaginal fistulas is abdominal hysterectomy (75%). Vaginal hysterectomy has a lower incidence of VVF. Predisposing factors towards this complication include previous radiotherapy, other causes of pelvic fibrosis, endometriosis, obesity and poor surgical technique. Notwithstanding these risk factors, almost 70% of iatrogenic urinary fistulas occur in their absence (Tancer 1992). In the developed world it is rare for VVF to develop as a complication of prolonged obstructed labour, but it is a common complication in underdeveloped societies.

VVFs are classified as:

- High: above the trigone
- Low: below the trigone
- Complex: either of the above associated with another significant injury e.g., associated ureteric damage.

The details of VVF repair are beyond the scope of this book. Only around 5% of VVFs will heal spontaneously with catheter drainage. The optimal time for repair is 2–4 weeks after the original surgery unless radiotherapy has been previously delivered, in which case most surgeons will wait 6–8 weeks. In general, a transvaginal repair is used for low VVFs and a transabdominal approach for high, large or complex fistulas. The success rate for both approaches is between 85% and 95% 'first time out' for uncomplicated VVFs but drops to 50% on the second attempt and 33% on the third. Complex fistulas, particularly those also involving the rectum, have successful repair rates of around 50% (Elkins, 1994).

Endoscopic bladder injury

The bladder is less vulnerable to endoscopic damage than either the ureter or urethra. In inexperienced hands, the blind introduction, usually under a trabeculation bar of a cystoscope or resectoscope sheath to an empty bladder may result in perforation of the bladder. If promptly recognised and the rest of the procedure is abandoned, this complication is easily managed by a short period of catheterisation. On the other hand, failure to recognise the problem will result in extravasation or intraperitoneal infusion of large volumes of fluid with attendant problems of shock, sepsis etc.

More commonly, the bladder may be perforated during transurethral resection of bladder tumour (TURBT). The risk of this is increased by:

- Thin-walled female bladder
- Repeat resections at the same site

- Tumours in the 'obturator area'
- Resections following radiotherapy
- Tumours on a trabeculation bar
- Failure to evaluate adequately depth of invasion by bimanual examination.

Obturator spasm is prevented by accurately identifying the location of the tumour and, where it is on the lower lateral wall, the use of general anaesthesia with muscle relaxants. The remainder of the risk factors can only be ameliorated by operator experience.

There is no evidence that bladder perforation during TURBT has a negative effect on the natural history of the tumour. Specifically, there is no evidence to support the theoretical possibility of the tumour being upstaged by bladder perforation (Mack et al 1988). Nevertheless, there is a paucity of comprehensive clinical data of the issue.

The management of TURBT perforation of the bladder depends primarily on the site of perforation and to a lesser extent on the depth of perforation. Some urologists advocate immediate open exploration and repair when the perforation is in the intraperitoneal portion of the bladder. Others advocate defunctioning (catheterisation) plus observation where the perforation is discrete and a layer of areolar or adipose tissue can be clearly seen.

Delayed rupture of the bladder may occur following TURBT (Pyrah 1955). This is more likely to occur where an excess of coagulation compared to resection is used, resulting in full thickness necrosis of the bladder wall in that area.

Overall the bladder has remarkable healing capacity. There are no significant specific long-term complications to bladder perforation or contusion where the problem has been promptly recognised and appropriately managed.

Bladder dysfunction following trauma

The impact of spinal cord injury on bladder function will be dealt with in a subsequent section. Radical pelvic surgery may result in disruption of the pelvic autonomic nerves.

Procedures most commonly associated with such disruption are:

- Abdominoperineal resection
- Low anterior resection
- Restorative rectal surgery (pouches)
- Radical hysterectomy (Pavlakis et al 1983, Yalla & Andriole, 1984)

Typically this causes urinary retention. Damage to the hypogastric nerves will sometimes produce poor detrusor accommodation and high filling pressures.

Most of these cases can be managed expectantly but may take up to 6 months to resolve. About a third of cases are left with residual dysfunction. In the older male resolution may be facilitated by transurethral resection of prostate (TURP) and/or bladder neck incision.

Although prospective data are difficult to obtain, it is widely accepted that there is an association between hysterectomy and worsening of irritative urinary symptoms. In addition, patients with documented interstitial cystitis (IC) have been noted to have a higher than expected incidence of previous hysterectomy. It is not clear why this is so but there is some evidence of a neurological disturbance in IC (Jones 1992), and some authors have described IC in terms of a chronic pain syndrome similar to a reflex sympathetic dystrophy.

SPINAL CORD INJURIES (SCI)

The type and severity of urological dysfunction affecting spinal cord injury patients is dependent on the level and severity of cord damage. Although usually described in terms of a discrete lesion at a given level, the lesion will commonly extend one or two cord segments distally and proximally. In blunt trauma, haemorrhagic necrosis mediated possibly by local hypoxia, means that the lesion may be progressive in terms of severity over time after the acute trauma (Osterholm 1974).

The bladder is innervated by both parasympathetic and sympathetic neural systems. The parasympathetic feed derives from sacral cord segments S2, S3 and S4. The sympathetic supply emanates from autonomic nuclei located in the intermediolateral columns of the 10th thoracic to 2nd lumbar segments. The somatic supply to the striated periurethral muscle emanates from the anterior horns of the sacral cord (Elbadawy 1988).

Simplistically, cauda equina lesions and sacral rhizotomies result in a lower motor lesion to the bladder (areflexia), whereas suprasacral lesions result in upper motor lesions (hyper-reflexia with striated sphincter dysenergia). Usually the situation is more complex with combinations of upper and lower motor lesions. This applies especially for lesions at T12/L1.

Phases of SCI

Spinal shock

This occurs where the lesion is above the level of the sacral cord. There is areflexia of the neural functions distal to the lesion including visceral reflexes. The most distal somatic reflexes, such as the anal skin reflex, may persist. The bladder is acontractile and completely refractory to reflex stimulation. There is insensible urinary retention with overflow incontinence. This phase lasts anything from a few hours to several months.

Recovery phase. Reflex activity returns to the undamaged isolated cord segments caudal to the lesion. Usually the most distal somatic reflexes are the first to return. There is a progressive return in uninhibited bladder contractions which are initially low-pressure. This is accompanied by a progressive increase in bladder outlet resistance as evidenced by increased external sphincter closure pressures and bladder neck dysenergia. Voiding is uncoordinated and there are high residual volumes. In 5% of suprasacral lesions the bladder remains areflexic, the reason for which is not clear (Light et al 1985).

Established phase. Bladder outlet pressures increase. Voiding pressures increase due to detrusor hyper-reflexia and vesico-ureteric reflux becomes progressively more marked. Patients with complete suprasacral lesions usually develop reflex micturition by somatic stimulation, e.g. tapping the suprapubic skin. Cervical and high thoracic lesions are further complicated by postural fluctuations in blood pressure resulting in a diuresis when the patient lies down.

Patients with incomplete suprasacral lesions will rarely have normal bladder function. More commonly, they will have uninhibited micturition with sphincter dysenergia and unlike complete lesions, no ability to provoke voiding by reflex stimulation.

Damage to sacral segments or sacral roots

Complete

The bladder becomes atonic and acontractile. Voiding can be achieved by the Valsalva manoeuvre and manual compression. In males, the external sphincter may behave as a functional outflow obstruction.

Incomplete

In these cases the pattern may vary. Typically, the detrusor is acontractile but the outflow resistance may be high due to increased reflex activity in the pelvic floor muscles. In one study, 16% had voluntary micturition, 34% had uninhibited reflex micturition and 50% had straining micturition (Hardy 1974).

Urological complications of SCI

Detrusor spasticity / upper tract dilatation

Occasionally, overactivity of the detrusor may become so severe as to obstruct both intramural ureters. Alternatively, ureteric peristalsis may become inhibited by high intravesical pressures (Butler et al 1971). Either mechanism may result in anuria and renal failure if unrecognised.

Vesico-ureteric (VU) reflux

Most common in suprasacral lesions, VU reflux was found to be present in

60% of SCI patients with renal failure. The overall incidence in SCI patients is between 17% and 25% (Damanski 1965). Persistent VU reflux leads to inevitable damage, whereas transient reflux leads to damage only in a minority of cases. In Hackler's series (1965), 83% of SCI patients with transient VU reflux over a period ranging from 5 to 15 years, had normal or nearly normal renal function.

Upper urinary tract infection (UTI)

The risk of upper tract UTI is increased by the presence of lower tract UTI, vesicoureteric reflux or upper tract calculi. The combination of high pressure VU reflux and upper tract UTI will accelerate renal damage greatly.

Lower urinary tract infection

Recurrent or persistent lower UTI is an ongoing problem in SCI patients due to inefficient voiding, prolonged catheterisation or concomitant calculus disease. Persistent bladder infection can accentuate deterioration in bladder function (Tribe & Silver 1965). The prevalence of bacteriuria, especially with an indwelling catheter, approaches 86% (Perkash & Giroux 1993). It is generally agreed that antibiotics are indicated only in the presence of pyuria. The overall prevalence of significant UTI has been found to be 57.4% (Waites et al 1993). In male patients, the high incidence of epididymo-orchitis (31%) suggests that bilateral vasectomy should be considered.

Urolithiasis

The combination of disordered urological function, infection and altered metabolism make SCI patients especially prone to urolithiasis. Immobility causing hypercalcaemia and dehydration are among the relevant metabolic factors. Prolonged catheterisation encourages encrustation and bladder calculus formation. In one series 8.2% of SCI patients developed urolithiasis, more than half of them within the first 2 years of injury. Stone management is as for ambulatory patients, although the complication rate, particularly those related to sepsis, is significantly higher in SCI patients (Culkin et al 1990).

Urethral erosions and fistulas

Long-term urethral catheters and collection devices can lead to erosion of the ventral surface of the urethra in the male. This occurs most commonly in the bulbous urethra where prolonged pressure from the sitting position against the relatively firm catheter causes pressure necrosis. This can be a difficult management problem as patients with a hyper-reflexic bladder will

Table 11.6 Anterior urethral injury classification

Grade	Injury
1	Contusion, no disruption, no extravasation
2	Laceration, incomplete disruption, some extravasation. Buck's fascia usually intact
3	Complete disruption, distraction of edges <1 cm. Buck's fascia usually disrupted
4	Complete disruption, distraction of edges >1 cm or extensive crush injury on one or both sides of the disruption

not be controlled by mere suprapubic drainage and it may be necessary to formally close the bladder neck.

In females, erosion problems do not occur as frequently. Catheter erosion can produce a vesicovaginal fistula. Prolonged catheterisation may result in the urethra becoming markedly patulous, so that catheter retention and catheter bypassing become a real problem. Compliance with clean self intermittent catheterisation is poor amongst female SCI patients (Timoney et al 1990).

URETHRAL INJURIES

The male urethra is divided (anterior and posterior) by the urogenital diaphragm. In all studies, the posterior urethra is the most frequently injured (70%) compared to the anterior urethra (30%) (Attah et al 1982, Mitchell 1968). These studies do not include instrumentation injuries which more commonly affect the anterior urethra so the overall ratio is probably less skewed.

There is no consensus on the optimal treatment strategies for urethral trauma. The details of the various surgical approaches are beyond the scope of this text.

Anterior urethral injury

Injuries to the anterior urethra are caused by direct trauma which can be blunt (crush) or penetrating (external or internal/iatrogenic). It is unusual for the penile urethra to be injured by penetrating trauma unless it is iatrogenic.

Injuries to the anterior urethra may be classified according to severity based on urethrographic and endoscopic evaluation in Table 11.6.

Treatment and outcome vary considerably with each grade. Grade 1 lesions can be managed expectantly if the patient can micturate easily. If not, or if the patient has significant other injuries, simple suprapubic catheterisation is sufficient. Although the stricture rate is low for Grade 1 injuries, many urologists recommend routine endoscopic evaluation 3–4 months after the injury (Mitchell 1984).

Complications

As a general rule, the higher the grade of injury using the above classification, the more problematic the management and the higher the long-term complication rate. The presence of significant adjacent soft-tissue damage will also compromise outcome.

Stricture. Most of the complications associated with anterior urethral injuries are stricture related. In all but Grade 1 injuries there is a high incidence of stricture formation. Pontes & Pierce's review (1978) suggests that when managed with suprapubic drainage alone, up to 70% of anterior urethral injuries heal without stricture. This is at variance with most other experience where stricturing of some degree has been found to be virtually inevitable (Jenkins et al 1992, Mitchell 1968). It is generally believed that antibiotics reduce the degree of stricturing (Carpinito 1994).

Urinary tract infection etc. Associated with stricture development are attendant complications of urinary tract infection, epididymo-orchitis (c. 10%) and urinary retention. In addition, there is a risk of perineal abscess or cellulitis which is proportional to the degree of perineal soft tissue damage. Other septic complications include septicaemia (3%), haematoma (4%) and wound infection (3%) (Jenkins et al 1992).

Penile distortion. Anterior urethral injuries may be complicated by penile distortion due to fibrosis mimicking Peyronie's disease (Mitchell 1968). This is a rare occurrence. Erectile failure is not a recognised complication of anterior urethral injuries.

Although much debate has occurred as to whether urethral injuries should be managed by immediate early or delayed repair, the decision to make formal surgical repair of anterior urethral injuries should be based on the likelihood or not that the resulting stricture will be manageable by conservative (optical urethrotomy/dilatation) means. The most important determinant factors in this respect are the degree of distraction/disruption of the ends and the degree of associated soft-tissue damage. The timing of formal urethral repair depends on the experience and preference of the surgeon. There is no accepted superior treatment. The overriding management problem, regardless of approach, is that of repeated stenosis which occurs in up to 40% of cases, even when managed by urethroplasty.

Iatrogenic anterior urethral injuries

These injuries occur primarily by injudicious and inexperienced instrumentation typically with a urethral catheter, dilators or endoscopes. Catheter introducers should be used only by clinicians with considerable urological experience. Inexperienced doctors should be encouraged to use the suprapubic approach where any resistance to urethral catheterisation is encountered. Rigid instruments such as dilators or cystoscopes are potentially lethal in inexperienced hands.

The main complications are false passage usually in the bulbous urethra, avulsion tears usually at the external meatus, septicaemia, haematuria, scrotal oedema and necrosis of the scrotal skin. Delayed complications include stricture and epididymoorchitis.

Posterior urethral injury

Injuries to the posterior urethra represent a different spectrum of injury. 90% are associated with pelvic fracture (Lowe et al 1988) and approaching 30% will have an associated bladder rupture (Cass et al 1984).

Although a similar classification as utilised in anterior urethral injuries could be applied to posterior injuries, difficulties arise in interpretation. For instance, Kisner (1958) and McAninch (1981) reported partial disruptions in 16–19% of cases, whereas Mitchell (1968) and Petkovic noted partial tears in 90% and 59% respectively. The consensus figure for partial disruptions based on a compilation on reports was found to be 34% by Webster et al (1983). Both Webster and Mitchell suggest that the disparity in figures from different centres is related to the proportion of primary versus secondary referrals, whereby stop-gap treatment elsewhere may be responsible for converting many partial tears to complete tears by the time they are seen by experts. From the medicolegal point of view this underlines the importance of obtaining an ascending urethrogram before any other urological intervention is attempted. The management and outcome of partial posterior urethral tears is different from those of complete disruptions, so inadvertently converting the former to the latter has detrimental implications for the patient.

The clinical signs of urethral bleeding, urinary retention, perineal haematoma and high-riding prostate gland are well described and generally appreciated. However, where these signs are not so clear, urethrography should still be performed before catheterisation if both anterior and posterior pelvic arches are fractured (Lowe et al 1988).

The classification developed by Colapinto & McCallum (1977) is recommended. Notably in the Grade 3 injury using this classification Sandler et al (1981) have identified different patterns of extravasation and haematoma localisation in that the collection may be either predominantly pelvic or predominantly perineal. The determinant factor appears to be the degree of disruption to the urogenital diaphragm.

It should be noted that the risk of associated urethral injury varies depending on the pattern of pelvic fracture. Fractures of the anterior pelvis especially when combined with posterior disruption carry a high risk of urethral injury (67%), whereas posterior arch injuries on their own have a much lower risk of urethral injury (Lowe et al 1988).

It is beyond the scope of this text to deal with the management of posterior urethral injuries in detail. Again there is no consensus as to the optimal therapeutic modality.

Partial tears

Incomplete injuries can be managed either by endoscopically guided urethral catheterisation or by suprapubic cystostomy. It is recommended that suprapubic catheterisation be achieved either by formal open cystotomy or by ultrasound guided catheterisation.

Complete disruptions

The two main management approaches are primary realignment or simple suprapubic drainage followed by delayed correction. It is suggested with primary realignment that the degree of subsequent stricture formation is not as severe as in delayed management. Against this is the suggestion that the manipulation involved in primary realignment might increase the degree of disruption and thereby increase the risk of impotence and incontinence. Most recent evidence suggests that the incidence of both impotence and incontinence are similar for both primary realignment and delayed repair (Follis et al 1992, Husmann et al 1990).

Complications

Impotence. Erectile impairment is commonly associated with this injury. In most cases it is due to disruption of the neurovascular bundle caused by the initial trauma. Dhabuwala et al (1990) and Herschorn et al (1992) both conclude from their studies that the disruption occurs at the time of impact as distinct from subsequent surgical intervention. There was no increase in erectile dysfunction after delayed intervention in Mark et al's review (1995). Potency may be affected to a variable degree from diminished but adequate tumescence to complete absence of tumescence. The incidence of impotence varies from 20% to 68% in different reports (Mark et al 1995, Follis et al 1992, Crasswell et al 1977, Husmann et al 1990). The scepticism of Mitchell (1984) with respect to the impact of impending litigation on the incidence of erectile dysfunction is noted.

Table 11.7 Renal injury classification

Grade	Type	Injury
1	Contusion Haematoma	Microscopic haematuria, normal IVU and/or ultrasound Subcapsular, non-expanding, non-parenchymal laceration
2	Haematoma Laceration	Perirenal, non-expanding, confined to retroperitoneum Cortical, <1 cm depth, no extravasation on IVU
3	Laceration	Parenchymal, >1 cm depth, no extravasation
4	Laceration Vascular	Extending through cortex, medulla and collecting system Injury to either main renal artery or vein with contained haemorrhage
5	Completely shattered kidney Avulsion from vascular pedicle at hilum which devascularises kidney	

Nevertheless the consensus from most other authorities in the field is that the problem is usually genuine, adequately accounted for by the degree of anatomical disruption in the region.

Incontinence. Continence may be impaired following posterior urethral injury due to direct disruption of the bladder neck, prostate and external sphincter. The degree of incontinence will vary from patient to patient from stress leaks to complete loss of outflow control. The incidence ranges from 2% to 15% dividing equally between stress leakage and more florid incontinence (Mark et al 1995, Husmann 1990).

RENAL INJURIES

The American Association for the Surgery of Trauma through their Organ Injury Scaling committee have proposed the following classification of renal trauma which the authors of this text recommend (Moore et al 1989):

Renal trauma can be caused by either blunt or penetrating injury. About 90% of all renal injuries are caused by blunt trauma (Mee et al 1989). The commonest aetiological events include road accidents, sporting accidents, falls and assaults. Narrod et al (1985) found significant renal injury in 7% of patients undergoing laparotomy for major abdominal trauma. Importantly, 13 of the 14 patients in this series who required nephrectomy were victims of penetrating injury. In contrast to blunt renal injury, penetrating trauma is likely to result in major renal damage in up to 70% of cases (Carroll & McAninch 1985).

Haematuria is the most sensitive indicator of renal trauma. The severity of the haematuria does not correlate with the severity of the renal injury (Bright et al 1978). Further investigation depends on the clinical circumstances. A haemodynamically stable patient who has suffered blunt trauma and has only microscopic haematuria does not need an IVU (Eastham et al 1992). Gross haematuria, local signs, hypotension plus any haematuria, or a paediatric patient with any haematuria are all indications for further investigation (Mee et al 1989, Hardeman et al 1987).

Because penetrating injuries are most likely to cause major renal trauma, all suspected penetrating renal injuries need further investigation.

IVU is the radiological investigation of choice. In a stable patient, a full IVU with tomography is indicated (Mahoney & Persky 1968). Where the results are equivocal a CT scan will detect vascular and associated injuries (Bretan et al 1985, Sclafani & Becker, 1985). Contrast enhanced CT scan will also detect post-traumatic renal artery occlusion (Lupetin et al 1989).

Management

Renal injuries, depending on type and severity, may be managed either by operative intervention or expectantly. Where appropriate, the non-operative approach is preferred (Osias et al 1976, Husmann & Morris,

Table 11.8 Results of renal exploration and type of renal reconstruction (McAninch & Carroll 1991)

	Blunt trauma (31pts)(%)	Stab wound (49pts)(%)	Gunshot (53pts)(%)	Totals (133pts)(%)
Renorrhaphy	11(35.5)	29(59.2)	21(39.6)	61(45.9)
Partial nephrectomy	4(12.9)	7(14.2)	12(22.7)	23(17.3)
Nephrectomy	4(12.9)	4(8.2)	7(13.2)	15(11.3)
Vascular repair only	3(9.7)	4(8.2)	4(7.5)	11(8.2)
Pelvis repair only	4(12.9)	1(2.0)	0	5(3.7)
Vascular and pelvis only	0	0	1(1.9)	1(0.8)
Exploration only	5(16.1)	4(8.2)	8(15.1)	17(12.8)

1990). Generally speaking no difficulty arises in deciding not to operate on a mild renal injury or to explore a severe renal injury. The problem arises most frequently with injuries of intermediate severity. According to Peterson's large series (1977), exploration of injuries with intermediate extravasation leads to an unacceptably high nephrectomy rate (9 out of 13 patients). Cass & Ireland (1973) found that the nephrectomy rate was higher for intermediate injuries caused by blunt trauma (10/15), compared to penetrating trauma (5/15). They concluded that pre-emptive exploration resulted in a lower morbidity but a higher nephrectomy rate. However, Husmann & Morris (1990) report a delayed surgical intervention rate of 13% in stable patients with either Grade 3 or 4 injury managed conservatively, with a 0% delayed nephrectomy rate where the fragments were vascularised. In contrast, where a fragment of the kidney was devascularised, the secondary intervention rate was 83% due to abscess and urinomas.

Indications for exploration

Absolute indications for exploration are:

- Expanding, pulsatile retroperitoneal haematoma (Holcroft et al 1975)
- Vascular pedicle injury in solitary or predominant kidney
- Precarious haemodynamic stability.

Relative indications for exploration include:

- Major lacerations
- Urinary extravasation outside Gerota's fascia (Peterson 1977)
- Laceration with devascularised fragment
- Associated injuries.

Where exploration is indicated, early vascular control has significantly reduced the nephrectomy rate from 40–60% to 18% (McAninch & Carroll 1982).

Results of surgical intervention

The technical details of surgical repair of renal injuries are beyond the scope of this book. The results of surgical intervention are best summarised by Table 11.8 (McAninch et al 1991).

Acute nephrectomy is associated with a mortality approaching 50% but this is due to a high rate of coincident injuries, a high injury severity score, and high rate of serious sepsis, rather than to the nephrectomy per se (Narrod et al 1985).

Complications of conservative management

Most of the delayed complications associated with non-surgical management are related to collections of either urine or blood. These include urinoma, abscess, non-functioning kidney, fistula, hydronephrosis caused by pressure of urinoma, capsular hydrocoele, pyonephrosis and secondary haemorrhage. In addition renal hypertension and arteriovenous fistulas, which are dealt with below, may occur. The exact incidence of the above complications is difficult to quantify.

Osias et al (1976) report an incidence of up to 32% in their review of non-operative management. Despite this, their delayed nephrectomy rate was only 2/75. Husmann & Morris (1990) indicate the importance of a devascularised fragment in significantly increasing the complication rate.

Arteriovenous malformations

AV fistulas may occur as a complication of either penetrating or blunt renal trauma. They present as delayed haematuria up to 3 months after the injury and, untreated, may be recurrent thereafter. Husmann & Morris (1990) noted an incidence of documented AV malformations approaching 14% of Grades 3 and 4 injuries due to blunt trauma managed conservatively. Arteriographic embolisation was successful in resolving half of these, whereas the remainder required open exploration.

In the report by Bernath et al (1983) there were two AV malformations out of 34 patients with penetrating renal trauma managed conservatively. The incidence of AV malformation was not correlated with the severity of renal injury.

Secondary (renal) hypertension

Hypertension is a known complication of renal trauma. The precise incidence is unknown but it appears to be higher for renovascular injury compared to parenchymal damage. In Maggio & Brosnan's series (1978) of renal artery injuries hypertension was found in 57% of cases. Other studies report incidences ranging from 2% to 33% (Cass & Ireland 1973, Grant et al 1971, Maling et al 1976).

Because renal trauma victims are generally young, the onset of premature hypertension is of great significance. Hypertension may be transient in the acute injury phase (Husmann & Morris 1990) or may ensue many years later.

From the medicolegal point of view, it is important to define hypertension secondary to renal trauma. It is generally accepted that to establish a causal link, the onset of hypertension must occur within 5 years of the injury (Glenn & Harvard 1960). Renovascular hypertension is defined as a sustained blood pressure elevation secondary to a physiologically significant renal artery stenosis that is correctable by repair of the lesion or removal of the kidney. It is identified by an elevated ambulatory plasma renin activity followed by a positive single dose Captopril test. If this is positive in the context of renovascular trauma, one should then proceed to selective renal vein sampling with Captopril and ultimately to renal arteriography (Sosa & Darracott Vaughan 1994).

Hypertension due to parenchymal scarring or capsular fibrosis is more difficult to define as the ambulatory plasma renin activity is usually normal (Vaughan et al 1984). Nephrectomy is not recommended unless the traumatised kidney is non-functioning. In poorly functioning kidneys due to trauma with perinephric fibrosis, hypertension was cured or improved in 24/26 patients (Sterns et al 1985).

Iatrogenic renal injury

The commonest area for iatrogenic renal injury to occur is in the treatment of renal stones. Currently renal calculi are most commonly managed either by percutaneous nephrolithotripsy (PCNL) and extracorporeal shockwave lithotripsy (ESWL). Untreated, renal calculi will of themselves cause renal damage and the risk, in the absence of other complications such as obstruction, is proportional to stone burden.

PCNL of necessity causes some renal damage as the tract is usually through renal parenchyma. The impact on renal function appears to be insignificant (Chandoke et al 1992). Even where multiple tracts are utilised the effect appears to be negligible (Marberger et al 1985). PCNL is commonly associated with some degree of haemorrhage but this is usually venous in origin and not of great significance. Occasionally the bleeding is copious and may be arterial in origin requiring transfusion and compromising the procedure (Marberger 1994). There is a reported incidence of delayed haemorrhage of 0.6% following PCNL due to AV malformations (Patterson et al 1985). These are usually manageable by arteriographic embolisation.

ESWL can cause parenchymal contusion (Ryan et al 1991) and perirenal haematomas (Knapp et al 1988) in a dose-related manner. ESWL can lead to a temporary but clinically insignificant reduction in glomerular filtration rate immediately after ESWL which returns to normal within 3 weeks (Kaude et al 1985). Only in excessive doses i.e., doses not usually employed in clinical practice, does ESWL appear to have any effect on the growth and function of the paediatric kidney (Jones et al 1990).

Parenchymal scarring or perirenal haematoma and fibrosis induced by ESWL give rise to the theoretical possibility of ESWL causing renal hypertension. Lingeman & Kulb reported an incidence of 8% following ESWL. Patients with untreated urolithiasis have a higher than expected incidence of hypertension (Knapp & Lingeman 1988). Long-term trials are under way to clarify this but the general opinion at present is that the association between ESWL and de novo hypertension is not well founded.

Long-term effects of nephrectomy

The loss of a kidney invariably causes concern as to the long-term implications of having only one kidney. The bulk of opinion from the literature is that there is no significant long-term effect if all other things are equal. Grossmann et al (1994) noted that 5% of patients had an increase in serum creatinine following unilateral nephrectomy for malignant disease. All of these had an additional risk factor for renal damage including diabetes, hypertension, chronic pyelonephritis and renal artery stenosis.

There is a paucity of information on the long-term effects of unilateral nephrectomy for trauma. Narkun-Burgess et al (1993) followed up ex-servicemen who lost a kidney due to trauma in the Second World War. Mortality at 45 years was the same as normal projections. There was evidence of renal impairment in just under 20% of cases all of which had associated medical conditions mentioned above which can impair renal function. It is not legitimate to extrapolate data on the effects of nephrectomy in the trauma context from studies which include chronic diseases such as renal stone disease or pelviureteric junction obstruction, as in these situations the good kidney has had ample time to adjust. Studies on living related kidney donors are more closely analogous as these patients also lose a previously normal kidney. Anderson et al (1991) found that compensatory hypertrophy of the remaining kidney was complete at 7 days post-nephrectomy. The degree of compensatory hypertrophy was greatest in patients under 30 years old at the time of nephrectomy. There was a small decrease in renal plasma flow at 10 years which was similar to the decrease seen in age-matched normal population.

Sesso et al (1991) found that female gender and increased age were risk factors for reduced glomerular filtration rate and increased serum creatinine following kidney donation.

In conclusion, it appears that the traumatic loss of a kidney has no significant long-term sequelae. However, patients with concurrent diabetes, hypertension chronic pyelonephritis or renal artery stenosis of the remaining renal unit are at risk of renal impairment. Also, compensatory hypertrophy appears to be optimal in young males and occurs least in older females.

URETERIC INJURIES

The ureter is most commonly injured by way of iatrogenic misadventure. It is unusual for the normal ureter to be injured by penetrating trauma. Decelerating blunt trauma may cause ureteric disruption particularly at the level of the pelvi-ureteric junction (Boone et al 1993). The commonest clinical situations in which ureteric injury occur are during radical pelvic surgery and as a complication of ureteroscopic management of calculi. The incidence of perforation during ureteroscopic manipulation has been reported as 31% for proximal calculi, 8% for mid-ureteral and 8% for distal ureteral calculi. Radiological follow-up of these patients revealed a stricture rate of 5.9% compared to 3.5% in patients who had ureteroscopic manipulation without perforation (Stoller et al 1992).

Types of ureteric injury vary enormously and there is no particularly useful system of uniform classification. Factors which determine treatment and outcome include:

- Extent of disruption, i.e. simple perforation, partial disruption or complete disruption.
- Length of ureter directly traumatised or devascularised.
- Level of injury, i.e. intra- or extra-pelvic.
- Timing of recognition: management and outcome varies considerably where the injury is recognised immediately compared to presentation with complications 10 days post injury.

Simple perforations

Simple perforations, especially when they are recognised immediately (usually at ureteroscopy) can be managed successfully by ureteric stenting preferably using a JJ stent (Jones et al 1990). Late presentation occurs with urinoma formation and usually sepsis. In these situations percutaneous or transvaginal drainage is also required.

Partial disruptions

When recognised immediately simple repair with accurate urothelial re-approximation over a ureteric stent is indicated. Where diagnosis is delayed the incised edges may be unsuitable for re-approximation and should be excised. Drainage of concomitant collections is also necessary.

Table 11.9 Testicular injury classification

Grade	Injury
1a	Simple contusion, minimal or no bruising, no haematocoele
1b	Clinically as per Grade 1a but ultrasound appearances of intratesticular haematoma
2	Disruption of tunica albuginea +/– tunica vaginalis, bruising and haematoma
3	Full width disruption of tunica albuginea with amputation or near amputation of lower pole
4	As per Grade 3 with epididymal disruption added
5	Completely disrupted, non-viable testis

Complete disruptions

Complete disruptions require tension-free repair. In the immediate setting this can be achieved by judicious mobilisation and a direct repair of the spatulated ends over a stent. In delayed cases some form of reconstructive procedure is more commonly required. The type of reconstruction depends on the level and length of injury. Generally where the injury is within the true pelvis, reimplantation of the ureter should be possible. Injuries distal to the pelvic brim may require either a psoas hitch or a Boari flap. Injuries proximal to the pelvic brim may require either a transuretero-ureterostomy or a small bowel interposition.

Complications

Stricture. Stricture formation with hydronephrosis is the most significant long-term complication of ureteric injury. Management options include retrograde or antegrade balloon dilatation or proximal reconstruction. Progressive obstruction may be silent so follow-up by IVU is necessary. Urinoma formation may result in fulminant sepsis and therefore require drainage. Vesicoureteric reflux is common following reimplantation but is not a serious problem in adults.

MALE GENITAL INJURIES

Trauma to the penis and scrotum is not rare. As with other injuries the trauma may be blunt or penetrating. In addition the male external genitalia may suffer avulsion injuries, 'fractures', and injuries which are the result of psychosis. The most common injury is blunt scrotal trauma typically caused by sporting misadventure or a deliberate kick.

Testicular injury

Although there is no generally accepted classification of testicular injuries there is a well recognised spectrum of severity summarised by the above classification.

Pre-existing disease such as epididymo-orchitis or tumour render the testis more susceptible to trauma. Undescended testes, particularly when located at the external ring or within the inguinal canal, are more vulnerable to trauma. Furthermore, testicular trauma may be complicated by torsion.

Ultrasound is helpful in evaluating testicular trauma, but has a negative predictive value of 58% (Corrales et al 1993) and therefore cannot be relied upon to avoid surgical exploration. Del Villar et al (1973) found that conservative management resulted in a delayed orchidectomy rate of 48% compared to 5% in patients treated by immediate surgical exploration. Immediate surgical exploration is advisable in all but Grade 1a injuries. The main advantage of ultrasound evaluation is in detecting intratesticular haematoma. These injuries are clinically the same as Grade 1a injuries but have a significant risk of testicular atrophy probably due to pressure necrosis.

Surgical management and outcome depend on the grade of injury. Grade 1b injuries should be explored to decompress the testis and evacuate the haematoma. Grade 2 injuries require simple haemostatic repair of the edges of the tunica albuginea (not closure) and evacuation of the haematoma. Grade 3 and 4 injuries usually require amputation of the non-viable segment and repair of the remaining testis; and in the case of Grade 4 repair of the epididymis. Grade 5 injuries will normally require orchidectomy.

Complications

Sepsis. Penetrating and avulsion injuries are at risk of septic complications such as cellulitis and abcess. Associated injuries such as urethral and spermatic cord lesions should be borne in mind. The most common source of anxiety for the patient and his family is whether there is any effect on fertility. The received knowledge is that with a normal contralateral testis, both endocrine functions and spermatogenesis will not be impaired. However, Nolten et al (1994) recently reported that infertile men have a higher than expected incidence of testicular trauma in their past compared to age-matched, fertile controls, and that oestradiol levels were up to 25% higher in infertile men with a past history of trauma compared to infertile men with no history of testicular trauma.

Penile injury

Minor penile trauma is relatively common but generally is not of major consequence in terms of management or sequelae. Common minor injuries include contusion and haematoma caused by blunt injury to the groin, and minor lacerations usually caused by an altercation with a zipper. Tearing of the frenulum may occur due to over-enthusiastic sexual activity and is more likely to occur and recur where there is an element of chordee. In this situation, frenuloplasty is recommended.

Causes of more significant penile injuries include blunt, sharp and penetrating trauma, degloving injuries and 'fractures'. The important factors impinging on management include the restoration of function, management of associated urethral injuries and the management of psychological disturbance where relevant.

Degloving injuries are often the result of industrial and agricultural accidents where loose clothing gets caught in power take-offs. Skin loss can be extensive though the body of the penis is frequently well preserved. Treatment consists of conservative debridement with skin grafting using scrotal skin where possible. Circumferential degloving may result in lymphoedema distal to the skin loss.

Amputation injuries are frequently the result of psychiatric disturbance, being an attempt at emasculation. Replantation should be undertaken as soon as the patient is stabilised. The warm ischaemia time of the penis is at least 16 hours (Wei et al 1983). Cold ischaemia time should not exceed 72 hours (Henry & Malloy 1994). Simple reattachment of the corpora and urethra results in a viable distal portion but problems with lymphoedema and potency make microsurgical revascularisation and dorsal nerve repair the procedure of choice.

Penetrating trauma includes knife and gunshot injuries. Knife assaults may result in anything ranging from simple laceration to complete amputation. Gunshot injuries may result in complex and extensive soft tissue damage which may include the urethra and scrotum. Where the urethra is involved this should be repaired primarily (Jordan & Gilbert 1985).

'Fractures' or rupture of the corpora cavernosa usually affects the distal third and should be managed by surgical repair of the tunica albuginea (Jallin et al 1980). Associated urethral repair may occur in up to 20% of cases (Nicholaison et al 1983). Surgical management is the treatment of choice as conservative management results in 40% rate of fibrosis and distortion.

REFERENCES

Anderson R G, Bueschen A J, Lloyd L K et al 1991 Short and long-term changes in renal function after donor nephrectomy. Journal of Urology 145: 1

Attah C A, Mbonu O, Anikwe R M 1982 Management of urethral injuries in University of Nigeria Teaching Hospital. Journal of Urology

Bernath A S, Schutte H, Fernandez R R D et al 1983 Stab wounds to the kidney: conservative management in flank penetration. Journal of Urology 129: 467

Boone T B, Gilling P J, Husmann D A 1993 Ureteropelvic junction disruption following blunt abdominal trauma. Journal of Urology 150: 33

Bretan P N, McAninch J W, Faderle M P et al 1985 Renal trauma: re-evaluation of the indications for radiographic evaluation. Journal of Urology 133: 183

Bright T C, White K, Peters P C 1978 Significance of haematuria after trauma. Journal of Urology 120: 455

Brosman S A, Paul J G 1976 Trauma of the bladder. Surgery, Gynecology and Obstetrics 143: 605

Butler E D, Friedland G W, Govan D E 1971 A radiological study of the effect of elevated intravesical pressures on urethral calibre and peristalsis in patients with neurogenic bladder dysfunction. Clinical Radiology 22: 193

Carpinito G A 1994 Lower urinary tract trauma. In: Krana R J, Siroky M B, Fitzpatrick J M (eds) Clinical Urology. J B Lippincott, Philadelphia, p. 688
Carroll P R, McAninch J W 1984 Major bladder trauma: mechanisms of injury and a unified method of diagnosis and repair. Journal of Urology 132: 254
Carroll P R, McAninch J W 1985 Operative indications in penetrating renal trauma. Journal of Trauma 25: 587–593
Cass A S, Ireland G W 1973 Comparison of the conservative and surgical management of the more severe degrees of renal trauma in multiply injured patients. Journal of Urology 109: 8
Cass A S, Gleich P, Smith C 1984 Simultaneous bladder and prostatomembranous urethra disruption from external trauma. Journal of Urology 132: 907
Chandoke P S, Albala D M, Clayman R V 1992 Long-term comparison of renal function in patients with solitary kidneys and/or moderate renal insufficiency undergoing extracorporeal shockwave lithotripsy or percutaneous nephrolithotomy. Journal of Urology 147: 1226
Colapinto V, McCallum R W 1977 Injury to the male posterior urethra in fractured pelvis: a new classification. Journal of Urology 118: 575
Corrales J G, Corbel L, Cipolla B et al 1993 Accuracy of ultrasound diagnosis after blunt testicular trauma. Journal of Urology 150: 1834
Corriere J N, Harris J D 1981 The management of urologic injuries in blunt pelvic trauma. Radiological Clinics of North America 19: 187
Crasswell P O, Farrow G A, Robson C J et al 1977 Traumatic rupture of the supramembranous urethra. Journal of Urology 188: 770
Culkin D J, Wheeler J S, Nemchausky B A et al 1990 Percutaneous nephrolithotomy: spinal cord injury vs. ambulatory patients. Journal of the American Paraplegic Society 13(2): 4–6
Damanski M 1965 Vesico-ureteric reflux in paraplegia. British Journal of Surgery 52: 168
Del Villar R G, Ireland G W, Cass A S 1973 Early exploration following trauma to the testicle. Journal of Trauma 13: 600
Dhabuwala C B, Hamid S, Katsikas B M et al 1990 Impotence following delayed repair of prostatomembranous urethral disruption. Journal of Urology 144: 677
Eastham J A, Wilson T G, Ahlering T E 1992 Radiographic evaluation of adult patients with blunt renal trauma. Journal of Urology 148: 266–267
Elbadawy A 1988 Neuromuscular mechanisms of micturition. In: Yalla S V, Elbadawy A, McGuire E M (eds) The principles and practice of neurourology and urodynamics. Macmillan, New York, ch 1
Elkins T E 1994 Surgery for the obstetric vesicovaginal fistula: a review of 100 operations in 82 patients. Americal Journal of Obstetrics and Gynecology 170: 1108
Follis H W, Koch M O, MacDougall S W et al 1992. Immediate management of prostatomembranous urethral disruptions. Journal of Urology 147: 1259
Glenn J F, Harvard B M 1960 The injured kidney. Journal of the American Medical Association 173: 1189
Grant R P, Gifford R W, Pudvan W R et 1971 Renal trauma and hypertension. American Journal of Cardiology 27: 173
Grossmann H B, Sommerfield D, Konnak J W et al 1994 Long-term assessment of renal function following nephrectomy for Stage 1 renal carcinoma. British Journal of Urology 74(3): 279
Hackler R H, Dalton J J, Bunts R C 1965 Changing concepts in the preservation of renal function in the paraplegic. Journal of Urology 94: 107
Hackler R, Broecker B, Klein F et al 1980 A clinical experience with dantrolene sodium for experimental urinary sphincter hypertonicity in spinal cord injury patients. Journal of Urology 124: 78
Hardeman S, Husmann D A, Chinn H K W et al 1987 Blunt urinary tract trauma: identifying the patients who require radiological studies. Journal of Urology 138: 99–101
Hardy A G 1990 In: Chisholm G D, Fair W R (eds) The scientific foundations of urology. Heinemann, Oxford, p 290
Henry J M, Malloy T R 1994 Treatment of external male genital trauma. In: Krane R J, Siroky M B, Fitzpatrick J M (eds) Clinical Urology. J B Lippincott, Philadelphia, p 1276
Herschorn S, Thissjen A, Radomski S B 1992 The value of immediate or early catheterization of the traumatized posterior urethra. Journal of Urology 148: 1428
Holcroft J W, Trunkey D D, Minagi H et al 1975 Renal trauma and retroperitoneal haematomas: indications for exploration. Journal of Trauma 15: 1045

Husmann D A, Wilson W T, Boone T B et al 1990a Prostatomembranous urethral disruptions: management by suprapubic cystostomy and delayed urethroplasty. Journal of Urology 144: 76

Husmann D A, Morris J S 1990b Attempted conservative management of blunt renal lacerations extending through the corticomedullary junction: short term and long term sequelae. Journal of Urology 143: 682

Jallin A, Wani W A, Rashid P A 1980 Fracture of the penis. Journal of Urology 123: 285

Jenkins B J, Badenoch D F, Fowler C G et al 1992 Long-term results of treatment of urethral injuries in males caused by external trauma. British Journal of Urology 70: 73

Jones B J, Connolly J, Nowlan P et al 1990 The effect of extracorporeal shockwave injury on the function and growth of the paediatric kidney. Journal of Endourology 4(1): 557

Jones B J, Ryan P C, Lyons O et al 1990 Failed ureteroscopy for ureteric calculi: the impact of double J stent on subsequent calculus retrieval. British Journal of Urology 66: 254

Jordan G M, Gilbert D A 1985 Male genital trauma. American Urological Association Update 20: 4

Kaude J, et al 1985 Renal morphology and function immediately after extracorporeal shockwave lithotripsy. American Journal of Radiology 145: 305

Kisner C D 1958 Injuries of the urethra. South African Medical Journal 32: 1105

Knapp P M, Kulb T B, Lingeman J E et al 1988 Extracorporeal shockwave induced perirenal haematoma. Journal of Urology 139: 700

Lechevallier E, Siles S, Ortega J C et al 1993 Comparison by SPECT of renal scars after extracorporeal shockwave lithotripsy and percutaneous nephrolithotomy. Journal of Endourology 7: 465

Light J K, Fagenal J, Beric A 1985 Detrusor areflexia on suprasacral spinal cord injuries. Journal of Urology 134: 295

Lingeman J, Kulb T B 1987 Hypertension following extracorporeal shock wave lithotripsy. Journal of Urology 137: 142A

Lowe M A, Mason J T, Luna G K et al 1988 Risk factors for urethral injuries in men with traumatic pelvic fractures. Journal of Urology 140: 506

Lupetin A R, Mainwaring B L, Daffner R H 1989 CT diagnosis of renal artery injury caused by blunt abdominal trauma. American Journal of Radiology 153: 1065

McAninch J W 1981 Traumatic injuries to the urethra. Journal of Trauma 21: 291

McAninch J W, Carroll P R 1982 Renal trauma: kidney preservation through early vascular control – a refined approach. Journal of Trauma 22: 285

McAninch J W, Carroll P K, Klosterman P W et al 1991 Renal reconstruction after injury. Journal of Urology 145: 932

Mack J, Rammal E, Jaske G 1988 Iatrogenic tumorzellimplantation beim Blasenkarzinom. Urologie 27: 99

Maggio A J, Brosman S 1978 Renal artery trauma. Urology 11: 125

Mahoney S A, Persky L 1968 Intravenous drip nephrotomography in the evaluation of renal injury. Journal of Urology 99: 513–516

Maling T J, Little P J, Maling T M et al 1976 Renal trauma and persistent hypertension. Nephron 116: 173

Marberger M 1994 Percutaneous renal surgery: its role in stone management. In: Krane R J, Siroky M B, Fitzpatrick J M (eds) Clinical Urology. J B Lippincott, Philadelphia, p 262

Marberger M, Stackl W, Hruby W et al 1985 Late sequelae of ultrasonic lithotripsy of renal calculi. Journal of Urology 133: 170

Mark S D, Keane T E, Vandermark R M et al 1995 Impotence following pelvic fracture urethral injury: incidence, aetiology and management. British Journal of Urology 75: 62

Mee S L, McAninch J W, Robinson A L et al 1989 Radiographic assessment of renal trauma: a 10 year prospective study of patient selection. Journal of Urology 141: 1095–1098

Mitchell J P 1968 Injuries of the urethra. British Journal of Urology 40: 649

Mitchell J 1984. In: Urinary tract trauma. Wright, Bristol, p 212

Moore E E, Shackford S R, Pachter H L et al 1989 Organ injury scaling. Journal of Trauma 29: 1664

Narkun-Burgess D M, Nolan C R, Norman J E et al 1993 Forty five year follow-up after uninephrectomy. Kidney International 43(5): 1110

Narrod J A, Moore E E, Posner M et al 1985 Nephrectomy following trauma: impact on patient outcome. Journal of Trauma 25: 842

Nicholaison G, Melamud A, Williams R D et al 1983. Rupture of the corpora cavernosa: surgical management. Journal of Urology 130: 917
Nolten W E, Viosca S P, Korenman S G et al 1994 Association of elevated estradiol with remote testicular trauma in young fertile men. Fertility & Sterility 62: 142
Osias M B, Hale S D, Lytton B 1976 The management of renal injuries. Journal of Trauma 16: 954
Osterholm J L 1974 The pathophysiological response to spinal cord injury: the current status of related research. Journal of Neurosurgery 40: 5
Page J E, Walker W J 1992 Complications attributable to the formation of the track in patients undergoing percutaneous nephrolithotomy. Clinical Radiology 45: 20
Patterson D E, Segura J W, Leroy A J et al 1985 The aetiology and treatment of delayed bleeding following percutaneous lithotripsy. Journal of Urology 133: 447
Pavlakis A J, Siroky M B, Goldstein I et al 1983 Neurologic findings in conus medullaris and cauda equina injury. Archives of Neurology 40: 570
Perkash I, Giroux J 1993 Clean intermittent catheterization in spinal cord injury patients: a follow up study. Journal of Urology 149: 1068
Peters P C 1989 Intraperitoneal rupture of the bladder. Urologic Clinics of North America 16: 279
Peterson N E 1977 Intermediate degree blunt renal trauma. Journal of Trauma 17: 425
Pontes J E, Pierce J M 1978 Anterior urethral injuries: 4 years of experience at the Detroit General Hospital. Journal of Urology 128: 563
Pyrah L N 1955 Spontaneous rupture of the urinary bladder. Proceedings of the Royal Society of Medicine 48: 696
Ryan P C, Jones B J, Nowlan P et al 1991 Piezoelectric shockwave lithotripsy: functional and morphological effects of single and multiple treatments. Journal of Urology 145: 399
Sandler C M, Phillips J M, Harris J D et al 1981 Radiology of the bladder and urethra in blunt pelvic trauma. Radiologic Clinics of North America 19: 195
Sclafani S J, Becker J A 1985 Interventional radiology in the treatment of retroperitoneal trauma. Urology and Radiology 7: 63
Sesso R, Whelton P K, Klag M J 1991 Effect of age and gender on kidney function in renal transplant donors: a prospective study. Clinical Nephrology 40(1): 31
Sosa R E, Darracott Vaughan E 1994 Renovascular and renal parenchymal hypertension. In: Krane R J, Siroky M B, Fitzpatrick J M (eds) Clinical Urology. J B Lippincott, Philadelphia, ch 21: 304
Sterns R H, Rabinowitz R, Segal A J et al 1985 Hypertension caused by chronic subcapsular haematoma. Archives of International Medicine 145: 169–171
Stoller M L, Wolf J S, Hofman R 1992 Ureteroscopy without routine balloon dilatation. Journal of Urology 147: 1238
Tancer M L 1992 Observations on prevention and management of vesicovaginal fistula after total hysterectomy. Surgery, Gynecology and Obstetrics 175: 501
Timoney A G, Shaw J 1990 Urological outcome in female patients with spinal cord injury: the effectiveness of intermittent catheterisation. Paraplegia 28(9): 556–563
Tribe C R, Silver J R 1965 Renal failure in paraplegia. Pitman, London
Vaughan E D, Case D B, Pickering T G et al 1984 Clinical evaluation of renovascular hypertension and therapeutic decisions. Urologic Clinics of North America 11: 393
Waites K B, Canupp K C, DeVivo M J 1993 Epidemiology and risk factors for urinary tract infection following spinal cord injury. Archives of Physical and Medical Rehabilitation 74: 691
Webster G D, Mathes G L, Selli C 1983 Prostatomembranous urethral injuries: a review of the literature and a rational approach to management. Journal of Urology 130: 898
Wei F G, McKee N H, Huerta F J et al 1983 Microsurgical replantation of completely amputated penis. Annals of Plastic Surgery 20: 317
Yalla S V, Rossier A B, Fam B A 1976 Dysenergic vesicourethral responses during bladder rehabilitation. Journal of Urology 115: 575
Yalla S V, Andriole G 1984 Vesicourethral dysfunction following pelvic ablative surgery. Journal of Urology 132: 503

12. Chronic pain syndromes

Chris Glynn

The incidence or prevalence of chronic pain following surgical trauma is not known, as there does not appear to be any epidemiological study designed to address this problem. Chronic pain may be a direct result of the surgery, the result of a recognised complication of the surgery, a result of the complication of the anaesthesia necessary for the surgery or, indirectly, a result of the aggravation of a patient's underlying condition during anaesthesia and surgery or the positioning for the anaesthesia and surgery (Table 12.1). However, it is a consistent reason for referral to the pain clinic and is of the order of 7% of the annual referral to the Oxford Pain Relief Unit, which is one of the biggest units in the United Kingdom.

Chronic pain is an uncommon complication following surgical trauma and therefore individual surgeons do not see it very often and do not readily recognise the problem.

The latest classification of chronic pain (Merskey & Bogduk 1994) shows 18 syndromes of possible pain following surgical trauma, as follows:

- Post-cholecystectomy syndrome
- Iliohypogastric nerve
- Ilio-inguinal nerve
- Genitofemoral nerve
- Lumbar spinal or radicular pain after failed spinal surgery
- Injection neuropathy

Table 12.1 Examples of causes for chronic pain following surgical trauma

	Direct	Indirect
Patient	Known diagnosis	Unknown diagnosis
Anaesthesia	Nerve trauma from regional anaesthesia	Muscle pain
Position	Brachial plexus lesion	Exacerbation of low back pain
Surgery	Predictable complication, e.g. phantom pain	Unpredictable complication, e.g. painful neuroma

- Abdominal cutaneous nerve entrapment syndrome
- Internal mammary artery syndrome
- Post-thoracotomy syndrome
- Post-mastectomy pain syndrome (non-malignant and malignant)
- Dry socket
- Glossopharyngeal pain from trauma
- Hypoglossal pain from trauma
- Secondary trigeminal neuralgia from facial trauma
- Painful scar
- Complex regional pain syndrome 1 (reflex sympathetic dystrophy)
- Complex regional pain syndrome 2 (causalgia)
- Phantom pain
- Stump pain.

If a patient has a pain that he or she did not have before the surgery, he or she may believe that the pain is an indication of something wrong. In addition, these patients may have the belief that the pain is the result of a mistake or negligence during surgery. An attempt has been made to identify psychological differences between pain patients undergoing litigation and pain patients who are not involved in litigation (Dush et al 1994). While this study revealed some differences between these two groups on the Minnesota Multiphase Personality Inventory (MMPI-2), there appears to be some reservation about this interpretation of the MMPI-2. The result of the Harvard medical practice study of hospitalised patients is reassuring for surgeons in that, although 47% of adverse effects occurred during surgery, these adverse events were unlikely to be caused by negligence; 17% surgical compared to 30% non-surgical (Leape et al 1991).

These patients wish to see the surgeon to find out the cause of the pain and to have the pain cured. The patient's belief that the surgeon has made a mistake and the surgeon's unfamiliarity with the problem is a perfect recipe for medicolegal confrontation. The best time to prevent this confrontation is at the first postoperative consultation. In an ideal world the surgeon would give the patient a clear and concise explanation of what the pain means and what the pain does not mean, confirming that the pain is not a result of some misdemeanour and that it will resolve with time. The patient would also be told of the treatment options for the pain, and thus be reassured. Whether or not the patient wishes to have any treatment depends on how serious the pain is for that individual.

The patient's expectation is that he should be able to undergo a surgical operation without any possible complications. Although the surgeon may explain quite clearly the possible complications of a particular operation, human nature is such that most patients believe that they will not have any problems. Indeed a number of patients do not even hear the surgeon's description of the possible complications of an operation; they only hear the possible advantages. Chronic pain following surgery appears to be so uncommon that it would not normally be discussed prior to surgery. Most journalistic articles or presentations about the complications of surgery, are about the unsuspecting patient disadvantaged by medical therapy, from which it is natural to infer that the therapy or the therapist is at fault. These publications generally fail to mention all the successfully treated patients. The patient needs to understand that all therapies have complications and side-effects, and the more invasive and complicated the therapy the greater the potential complications and side-effects. Statistics are all very well, but a complication of one in a million is 100% for the patient unfortunate enough to have that complication.

Pain was responsible for 13% of the claims for medical negligence handled by the Medical Defence Union in 1989–90 (Walker 1994). How many of these 150 cases were a result of surgical trauma was not stated, but pain per se as a cause for claims of medical negligence occurred in approximately one in every eight cases reported to the Medical Defence Union in 1989–90. If the percentage of adverse events in the UK were similar to those reported by the Harvard group, then it could be expected that about half the adverse events would be associated with surgery (Leape et al 1991). If the number of patients seeking litigation were in similar ratio then it might be expected that half of these 150 patients were complaining of pain following surgical trauma. Therefore it is possible that one in 16 patients (6.5%) seeking redress from the medical profession because of pain may be complaining of pain as a result of surgical trauma (Green 1987).

PAIN

Pain has been defined by the International Association for the Study of Pain as 'an unpleasant sensory and emotional experience associated with actual or potential tissue damage or described in terms of tissue damage' (Merskey & Bogduk 1994) (Fig. 12.1). Pain is the prerogative of man because he *perceives* pain. Animals do not, as far as we are aware, perceive pain and therefore pain in animals is called nociception (the response to a noxious stimulus).

This basic difference was reinforced by Pavlov in the early part of this century, when he took dogs and gave them electric shocks before he fed them. Initially this produced a painful response, withdrawal and vocalisation, but after a time the painful response was replaced by a joyful response, salivation (Pavlov 1960). Thus he proved that in dogs the response to a noxious stimulus could be changed from nociception to a joyful response.

This difference between pain and nociception has important connotations when research in animals is extrapolated to man. Pain and nociception are not the same; they are related in some way but the relationship may not always be a direct one. The basis of experimental research into pain had been the relationship between the stimulus and the response in animal models (nociception), and the relationship between the stimulus and the perception of pain in man. However, in only one of three different types of pain; operative, acute and chronic, is this relationship direct and that is in operative pain (Glynn 1988). The experimental models only address one component of pain, the physical response. From the definition of pain discussed earlier, there is also an emotional response involved.

Pain has two components; physical and emotional (Fig. 12.1), whereas nociception has one component, the physical response to the noxious stimulation. The relative contribution of these two components of pain is important to identify when assessing patients for treatment, and the respective roles of these two components are often crucial to a court's decision in the medicolegal assessment of a patient's pain. However, the legal phrase, 'pain, suffering and loss of amenity', suggests that the pain and the suffering are separate, whereas pain has an emotional response that does not always equate with suffering (Fig. 12.1.) It is abnormal for there to be no emotional component. Pain always has an emotional response, hence the clinical and medicolegal question, 'Is the emotional response normal or exaggerated?' In the clinical situation the exaggerated response indicates that the emotional component is significant and therefore requires therapy, and that the earlier this response can be addressed the better the results.

It is not common to be able to address this emotional component without at the same time treating the physical component. Most, if not all, psychological treatment programmes have a physical basis, indeed the outcome assessments of these programmes are nearly all physically based. Thus the difficulty that medicolegal assessors have with the emotional component of pain is not unique, clinicians also have problems in assessing the outcome of their treatment programmes for this component.

For the purposes of this discussion, there are three different types of pain in man. Chronic pain is the most important from the medicolegal

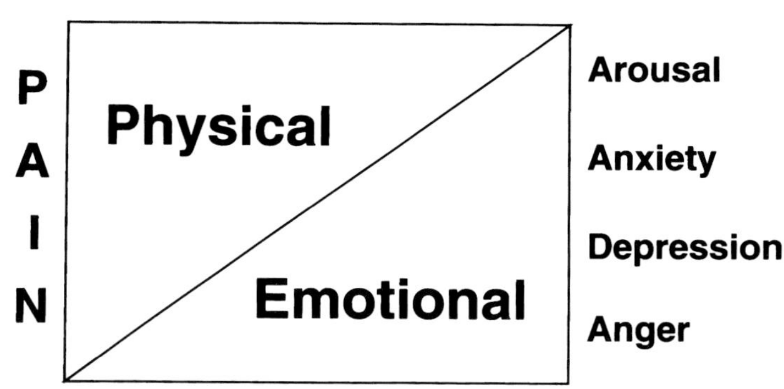

Fig. 12.1 Relationship between the physical and emotional components of pain which vary with time and place. The emotional component may vary as to the relative contributions of each of the four basic mood factors shown.

point of view, but a brief explanation of the other two types of pain (operative and acute) will give the surgeon a better understanding of pain and the problems it creates for the patient, as well as of the problems that it creates for the medical and the legal profession.

Operative and acute pain

The anatomy, neurophysiology, neurochemistry and the emotional response to the three types of pain in man are not the same. For a complete description of these differences the reader is referred to a more definitive text (Melzack & Wall 1993).

Operative pain is the nearest to nociception in animals, which is the patient's response to surgery (a noxious stimulus followed by a response in an almost graded fashion). As most, if not all, surgery is performed under general anaesthesia (therefore the patient's response to the noxious stimulus is assessed by the anaesthetist who infers that the patient is or is not feeling pain), then this as a physical response is nociception not pain. In this situation there is progressive damage and the pain provides some protective function to the organism, i.e. an indication of ongoing damage. The emotional component of operative pain is awareness (arousal). Consult figure 12.2, where the patient is aware during the operation because not enough anaesthetic has been given (Rubin 1993). Such a patient is not necessarily in physical pain but is aware of the operation which is unpleasant and therefore painful.

The second type of pain is acute, and a good example of this is the pain associated with a broken limb which is made worse by movement, stimulus-dependent but not necessarily relieved by rest. The stimulus-dependent pain is protective in that the fracture may heal more quickly and effectively if the limb is rested and immobilised. The stimulus here is related to the response. However, there is another pain associated with the frac-

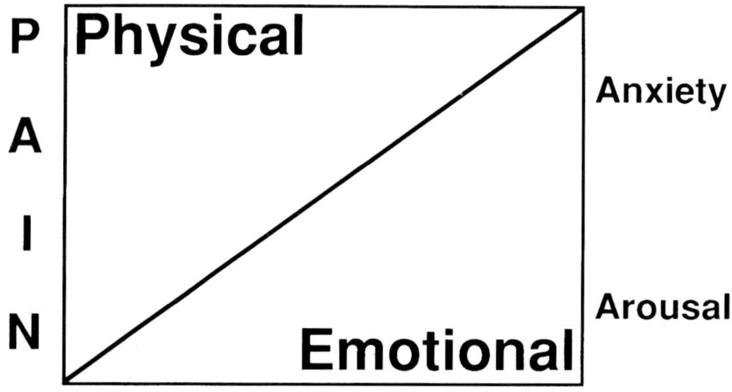

Fig. 12.2 Relationship between the physical and emotional components of operative pain. Arousal (awareness) during anaesthesia is the unpleasant emotional factor in this type of pain.

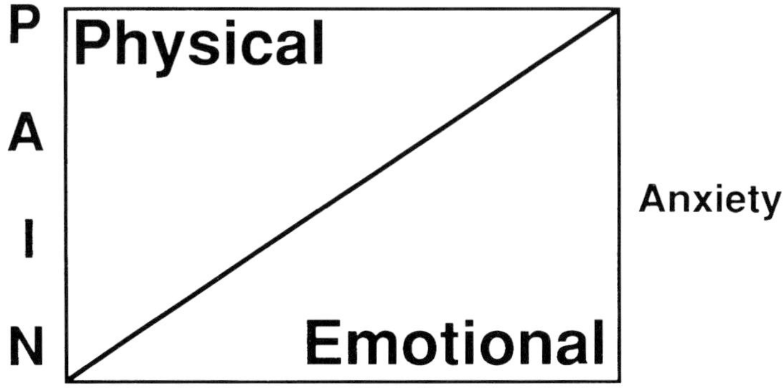

Fig. 12.3 Relationship between the physical and emotional components of acute pain. The unpleasant mood factor associated with acute pain is acute anxiety.

ture. This is the dull aching pain which is not related to any external or obvious stimulus but to the trauma itself, stimulus-independent pain. It is difficult to see a protective function for this stimulus independent pain, apart from reminding the patient of the injury. Postoperative pain is similar in all respects to this, and the stimulus-independent pain may persist and become chronic. Wall (1993) has suggested that chronic pain may be acute pain which persists because of inappropriate treatment. The emotional component of acute pain is acute anxiety about the cause of, and the reason for the pain, acute anxiety is unpleasant and therefore painful (Fig. 12.3). The clinical significance of the acute anxiety varies from patient to patient and is more likely to be related to patient characteristics than to the cause of the pain.

Chronic pain

The third type of pain is chronic pain, where there is no relationship as yet described between the stimulus and the response. If, for example, we take the pain associated with arthritis, there is absolutely no correlation between the pain and the degree of arthritis found on imaging radiographs (Wood 1972). The amount of arthritis found on X-ray is believed to be an indication of the damage to the joint. It is clear from this that the pain and the damage on X-ray are not related. In low back pain, considered to be one of the most common causes of chronic pain responsible for a patient consulting the doctor, there is no relationship between the findings on magnetic resonance imaging and the pain (Deyo 1994, Jensen et al 1994).

Chronic pain appears to have no positive advantages for man; indeed it appears to be totally useless. Furthermore, there is no evidence that animals suffer chronic nociception (pain), thus it is difficult to establish any logical phylogenetic reason for chronic pain. The relationship between nociception and pain is even more tenuous when the animal experiments on acute nociception are extrapolated to chronic pain in man. Pavlov's

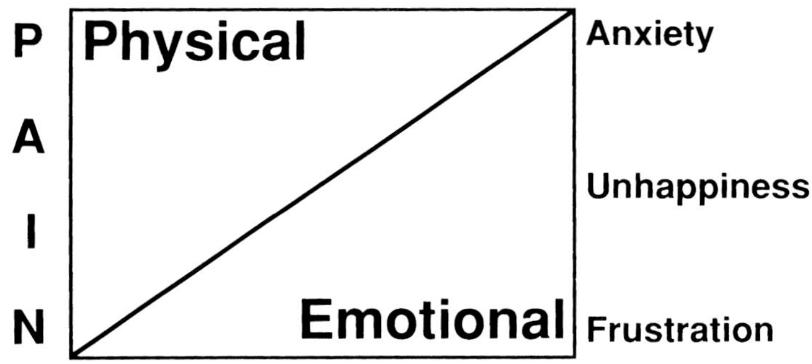

Fig. 12.4 Relationship between the physical and emotional components of chronic pain. The unpleasant mood factors associated with chronic pain are chronic anxiety, unhappiness and frustration (anger).

experiments are even more pertinent because they demonstrate the changes in responses with time, which is an important component of conditioning (Pavlov 1960).

The emotional component of chronic pain is a result of three unpleasant mood factors: chronic anxiety, unhappiness and frustration (Fig. 12.4). The patient with chronic pain is chronically anxious about the medical profession's inability to define clearly the cause of the pain in conjunction with its inability to relieve the pain. Chronic anxiety is unpleasant and therefore painful. The patient with chronic pain is unhappy because of the pain and the effect the pain has on quality of life. Unhappiness is unpleasant and therefore painful. The patient with chronic pain is frustrated by the lack of a clear diagnosis as well as the absence of a cure or even effective therapy. Unrelieved frustration is unpleasant and therefore painful. These emotional responses to chronic pain are always present and are normal. The clinical significance of this component is important to define when planning a therapeutic programme. The nature and composition of these responses to chronic pain are more likely to be related to the individual patient's characteristics than they are to the diagnosis or to the cause of the pain.

The relationship between disability and pain

Patients perceive disability (loss of amenity) as unpleasant (Fig. 12.5) and when disability and pain occur together patients quite often do not differentiate between the two. As far as the patient is concerned both interfere with quality of life, and from the medicolegal aspect it is the effect on quality of life that generally affects the level of award.

Disability has two components, a physical one i.e., the loss of physical ability, and an emotional response to the disability. As is apparent from Figure 12.5 the emotional response to the disability is the same as occurs

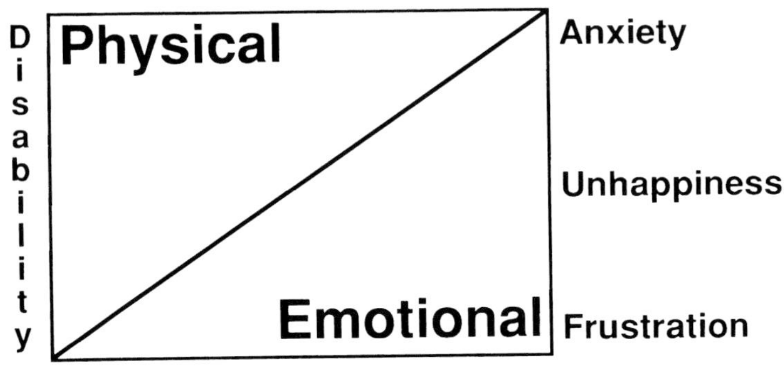

Fig. 12.5 Relationship between the physical and emotional components of disability. It is obvious that there is a significant overlap between the emotional response to chronic pain and disability.

with chronic pain. This is not surprising, as man can only respond emotionally in a limited number of ways. The nature of a patient's emotional response to disability is more likely to be governed by the patient's characteristics than by the disability.

It is important to differentiate between the effect of pain on the quality of life and the effect of disability on the quality of life; they are not the same thing. A postal survey of the relationship between pain relief and the quality of life in patients with neuropathic pain revealed no relationship between pain relief and the quality of life (Glynn & Smith in preparation). In addition, patients with pain and disability who are provided with long-term pain relief do not report an improvement in their quality of life which is still limited by their disability. Indeed, these patients are no better because their expectations are that the relief of pain will also resolve their disability. When pain is the cause of the disability then the relief of pain may improve that patient's quality of life. When assessing patients with chronic pain and disability it is important to be aware of the fact that the two may not be related and to define, where possible, their relationship.

The conclusions of the Harvard medical practice study 1 were that, 'There is a substantial amount of injury to patients from medical management, and many injuries are the result of substandard care.' (Brennan et al 1991). There are no data, however, to support the thesis that the recognised post-surgical chronic pain conditions listed on pages 281–282 are a result of 'substandard care'. For example, there are as many complaints of chronic pain after wound infection as there are associated with no wound infection. Wound infection was the most common adverse event following surgery, reported as 13.6% in the Harvard medical practice study 2 (Leape et al 1991). It is difficult to estimate the prevalence of the categorized post-surgical chronic pain conditions, but they are certainly much less common than the prevalence of wound infection. Both the Harvard studies revealed that there was no correlation between adverse events and negligence claims, nor between negligent adverse events and negligence claims. These data raise the possibility that it is the combination of the patient and the adverse event that leads to litigation. Dush et al (1994), in their psychological profile of litigating and non-litigating pain patients, could not exclude the possibility that the difference found in the psychological profiles in these two groups did not pre-date the litigation. The medicolegal connotations of operative and acute pain will be briefly discussed but the majority of the discussion will centre on chronic pain, as that is believed to be the greater medicolegal problem for surgeons.

OPERATIVE PAIN

Phylogenetically, operative pain is a result of the advancement of science and is most often well controlled with adequate anaesthesia. Prior to the development of anaesthesia, surgery was limited by the lack of adequate pain relief (Thorwald 1957). Operative pain without anaesthesia equates with torture in most situations. In modern society there are rare circumstances where it is conceivable that surgery would be performed without anaesthesia, but it is unlikely that there would, in these situations, be any medicolegal consequences. Operative pain without anaesthesia, therefore, will not be discussed.

The medicolegal consequences of operative pain during general anaesthesia are most likely to involve awareness (Powers 1987, Puxon 1987). Awareness under general anaesthesia may be unpleasant and therefore painful for the patient; part of the emotional component of operative pain, as described above (Fig. 12.2). It is also possible that inadequate anaesthesia can result in pain. The medicolegal consequences of such pain are related to the negligence of the anaesthetist – the physical component (Green 1987). In addition, these patients complain of the emotional trauma associated with their memory of the event. It would appear that neither of these situations, awareness and/or pain during surgery are defensible medicolegally. The difficulty is proving that the patient was, or was not adequately anaesthetised, and as there is no definitive measure of depth of anaesthesia, then there will always be room for debate until there is such a measure (Jones 1989).

ACUTE PAIN

The acute pain following surgical trauma is the expected postoperative pain. This is normal; negligence claims are most likely to be related to the presumed or real mismanagement of pain in the postoperative period. There has been a great deal written about the treatment of postoperative pain and various guidelines have been produced (Commission on Provision of Surgical Services 1990).

Negligence claims for the mismanagement of pain are most likely to be based on the memory of the pain; the emotional response. Situations where there was negligence in dealing with the physical component of postoperative pain relate to the total lack of therapy or inadequate treatment (Gould et al 1992). Medicolegal claims for negligence during the acute postoperative period are more likely to be related to the patient's expectations of pain and pain relief than any other factor (Laing et al 1993), reinforcing the importance of the patient's characteristics in medicolegal confrontation (Dush et al 1994).

CHRONIC PAIN

Chronic pain seems to provide only disadvantages for the patient; it does not appear to be an indication of progressive damage and therefore does not seem to provide any protective function to the organism. It is totally functionless and therefore may be a random error in the system (Glynn 1994). The possible random nature of chronic pain is reinforced by the therapeutic programmes prescribed for patients with chronic pain and the results of these programmes. However, it is almost always chronic pain that the patients complain about and take to court.

Table 12.2 Therapeutic modalities for the treatment of the physical component of chronic pain

Physical
Conventional
Transcutaneous electrical stimulation
Physiotherapy
Unconventional
Acupuncture
Pharmacological
Conventional
Non-narcotic
Narcotic
Unconventional
Anticonvulsants
Antidepressants
Alpha_2 agonists
Injections
Diagnostic
Therapeutic
Operations
Definitive,
i.e. for the cause of the pain
Symptomatic,
i.e. for the management of the pain

Chronic pain by definition includes an element of time, and it is this relationship with time that is important in the medicolegal assessment of chronic pain and its consequences. However, it is also important to ensure that the patient has been adequately assessed and treated for both the physical and emotional components of his or her pain. A brief summary of the therapeutic options available for the two components of chronic pain follows.

Treatment of the physical component (Table 12.2)

The major problem in assessing the outcome of the treatment of patients with chronic pain is that all therapies work some of the time but no therapy works all the time. This unpredictability reinforces the random nature of chronic pain, indeed, the response to treatment is good evidence for belief that chronic pain may be a random error in the sensory nervous system (Horton & May 1993). It is important to ensure that all patients undergoing litigation for chronic pain are made aware of the therapeutic modalities available, because the occasional patient may respond to the therapy and cease litigation. It is often stated that patients undergoing litigation for chronic pain do not respond to treatment but there are few published data to confirm or deny this thesis (Mendelson 1994). The success rate in all patients with chronic pain is low.

The treatment of the physical component of chronic pain may be subdivided into four treatment modalities: physical, pharmacological, injections and surgery.

Physical

The physical therapies are the simplest and so are the most commonly used to treat patients with chronic pain. These therapies, as with all the therapies for chronic pain, may be divided into conventional and unconventional. The conventional therapies are those that are prescribed by the medical profession and therefore should have some degree of medical control. The unconventional therapies are those without medical prescription and therefore do not generally have an element of medical control.

A good example of a conventional physical therapy is physiotherapy, which is prescribed by the medical profession and carried out by paramedically trained physiotherapists. If the therapy fails to relieve the pain the physiotherapist refers the patient back to the referring medical practitioner.

The unconventional physical therapies encompass all those treatments that the patient can organise without necessarily involving the medical profession. The list is almost endless and includes acupuncture, osteopathy, chiropractic, reflexology, etc. There is no doubt that these alternative therapies can be successful, but assessing their effectiveness is difficult.

Pharmacological

The most common way of treating patients with chronic pain is with drugs. The conventional analgesics, NSAIDs, non-narcotic analgesics and narcotic analgesics all have a place in the treatment of these patients. If we take the narcotic analgesics as an example, there are two broad categories where these drugs do not provide effective analgesia:

1. Narcotic insensitive pain: A classical example of this kind of pain is trigeminal neuralgia, which is not affected by large doses of morphine, but completely relieved by the use of anticonvulsants (e.g. carbamazepine).
2. Narcotic intolerant pain: The patient is unable to take an effective dose because of side-effects.

A similar classification could be used for the NSAIDs and the other non-narcotic analgesics.

Another significant part of the equation regarding the use of drugs to treat pain, is the patient's fear of problems, both short and long-term, as a result of taking them. It is possible to treat successfully without drugs some patients with chronic pain, but the commonly successful treatments of patients with chronic pain do revolve around drugs. Patients must be informed that the drugs are used to improve their quality of life and that if the drugs decrease their quality of life then they should stop taking them. An analogy that most patients understand is that patients with diabetes cannot survive without insulin but they all understand that insulin is a dangerous drug.

All patients with chronic pain should be considered for a trial with morphine as it is the best analgesic available. It is not, however, always effective for the reasons mentioned above. There are also medical and social reasons for not using morphine in some patients. There is no evidence that the medicinal use of narcotics leads to recreational addiction. Nevertheless, the German government has made the prescription of morphine so difficult that the medicinal use of the drug has decreased and at the same time the recreational (street) use has increased dramatically (Zenz & Weber-Stumpt 1993). If patients do become habituated, then it is possible to wean them off the narcotics. The medical profession does not have the right to withhold the most effective analgesic because of the fear of habituation, because the evidence to support this phobia is just not available. It is the perceived wisdom that narcotics are ineffective in patients with neuropathic pain. They are certainly less effective in these patients, but they are, nonetheless, effective in a significant proportion of cases (Jadad et al 1992).

The unconventional analgesics listed in Table 12.2 all have a place in the treatment of patients with chronic pain, both nociceptive and neuropathic (McQuay et al 1996). At the present time the rheumatological and the pain literature is littered with double-blind placebo controlled studies of the successful use of antidepressants in the treatment of patients with chronic pain (Max 1994). The scientific evidence is irrefutable; what is not clear is whether the therapy is better for the physical or the emotional component (Fig. 12.3). The evidence for the role of anticonvulsants in the treatment of chronic pain is now clear (McQuay et al 1995). There are many other unconventional analgesics prescribed for patients with chronic pain with varying success and little scientific evidence.

Injections

It is possible with injections to provide short-term relief for most patients with chronic pain, though the duration of this relief is very rarely predictable. Thus it is just as frustrating for the medical profession, knowing that they can predictably relieve most pains for a short time, as it is for the patient with chronic pain. The injections may be divided into (1) diagnostic, i.e. identifying where the pain is coming from and (2) therapeutic, i.e. providing long-term pain relief. It must be stressed that there are no permanent destructive procedures of nerves. The nervous system is designed to overcome any destructive procedure and all the so-called permanent destructive procedures for pain, be they injections or operations, are time-limited (White & Sweet 1969). Indeed the most common pain that results in medicolegal confrontation after surgery is due to lesions of nerves, i.e. neuropathic pain.

When planning treatment of patients with chronic pain, it is necessary to understand where the pain is arising. It is possible to use local anaesthetic to block most, if not all, peripheral nerves. If after successful blockade of the appropriate peripheral nerve or nerves, the patient does not obtain pain relief, one may infer that the pain is not coming via that nerve or nerves. The pain may be arising more centrally, i.e. at the spinal cord or higher, or alternatively the pain may be referred pain from adjacent nerves.

It is possible with the spinal application of drugs such as opioids and $alpha_2$ adrenergic agonists to provide relief for some patients with pain arising in the spinal cord (Glynn et al 1986). Implantations can be made around the spinal system which will deliver the drugs to the spinal cord and so provide longer-term pain relief. There are two basic systems, intrathecal and epidural, and these systems may give the drugs continuously or intermittently. These systems are in their infancy and their efficiency at the moment leaves a lot to be desired but they will eventually, it is hoped, be as reliable as the pacemakers which 20 years ago were plagued with technical problems.

The sympathetic nervous system may be blocked with injections either postganglionically or at the paravertebral ganglia (Fig. 12.6). The involvement of the sympathetic nervous system in chronic pain syndromes remains controversial (see later discussion of reflex sympathetic dystrophy). However, there is no doubt that this system is involved in some chronic pain syndromes and it behaves in a similar manner to the somatic system with blockade and destructive procedures.

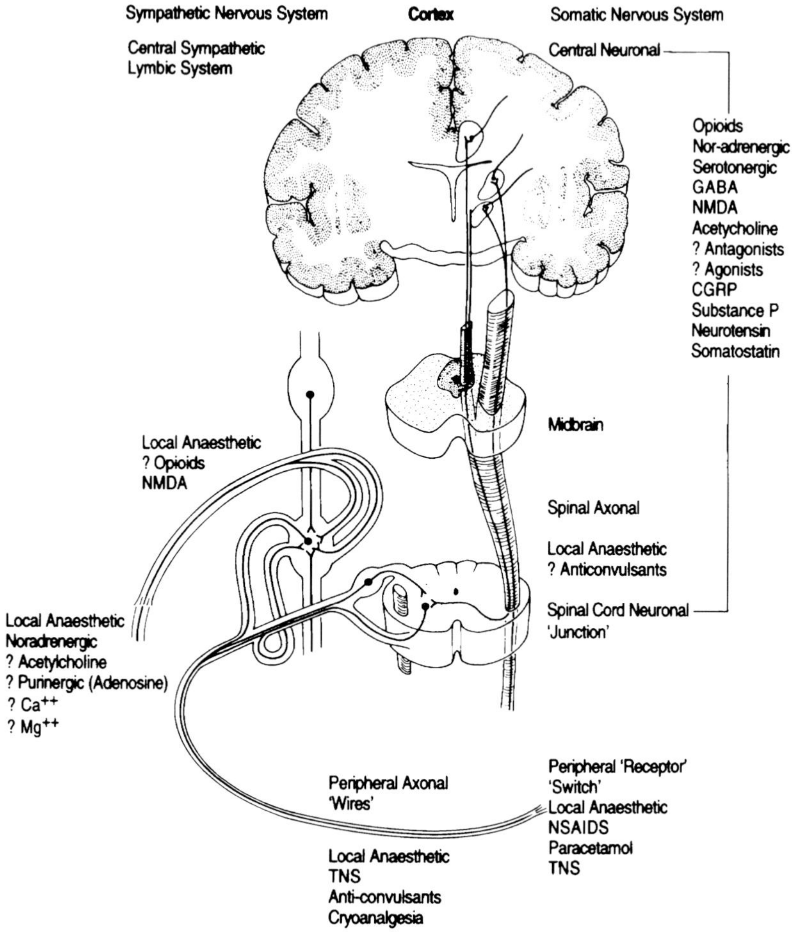

Fig. 12.6 Summary of the possible sites of action of the various therapeutic modalities used to treat the physical component of pain.

Surgery

Surgery for the relief of chronic pain may be divided into (1) operations for the cause of the pain and (2) operations for the symptomatic management of the pain (Table 12.2). A discussion of the definitive operations for the treatment of the cause of chronic pain is beyond the scope of this text. Symptomatic surgery for the relief of chronic pain is well reviewed by White & Sweet (1969). Surgical destructive procedures are time-limited for the reasons discussed above and so these are most often best reserved for patients with limited longevity. Dorsal root entry zone lesion (DREZ), an operation on the spinal cord which seems to have a role in the management of patients with pain following brachial plexus avulsion, may not be time-limited (Nashold & Ostdahl 1979). The difference between this operation and most of the other destructive procedures is that DREZ involves the destruction of neurons, whereas most of the other operations are on axons. The use of electrical stimulation of the spinal cord may have a place in the surgical management of chronic pain (North 1993).

In summary, surgery has a small but defined role in the symptomatic management of chronic pain.

Treatment of the emotional component (Table 12.3)

There is always an emotional component to chronic pain (Fig. 12.4), but this component does not always need therapy. The art of treating these patients successfully revolves around the identification of the problem(s); there are usually several factors involved. The most important single factor here is effective communication. Following the establishment of effective communication, these patients require a clear explanation of what the pain means and does not mean; and that chronic pain does not serve any useful protective function and is not an indication of progressive damage. The next stage should be education, so that patients understand that the emotional component is a normal concomitant of all chronic pain. Finally, the therapeutic options may be explained (Table 12.3).

Patient

The first option, of coping without any help, implies that an adequate explanation has been given by the medical therapist.

Table 12.3 Therapeutic modalities for the treatment of the emotional component of chronic pain

Patient *The patient can cope with the pain and the problems that the pain creates without support*
Pharmacological
Conventional
Antidepressants
Anticonvulsants
Unconventional
Narcotics
Professional
Conventional
Psychologist
Psychiatrist
Clerical
Unconventional
Faith healer
Alternative medicine

Pharmacological

The pharmacological option revolves around the use of the antidepressants, which have been shown in many retrospective control trials to be better than placebo in the treatment of patients with all varieties of chronic pain (McQuay et al 1996). Whether this effect is on the physical or the emotional component of a patient's pain is difficult to prove. It is interesting that the anxiolytics have not been shown to be of much benefit in patients with chronic pain.

Anticonvulsants are also useful in the treatment of many of the neuropathic pains (McQuay et al 1995); these drugs may have an effect on the emotional component as well as the physical. It is also worthwhile noting that morphine has been used to treat every known psychiatric problem. In the days of 'melancholia', when there were no other drugs in the armamentarium, laudanum was used successfully. All the opiates, therefore, have an effect on the emotional component as well as the physical. Thus far we have no pharmacological options for anger.

Professional

Professional counselling is always an option, but I believe that patients should make a positive decision to consult a counsellor. It is invariably a disaster to send a patient to a counsellor without his or her agreement. This usually results in an angry patient and a frustrated counsellor.

Once the patient has agreed to consult a counsellor, the next decision is which type of counsellor – psychologist, other paramedical counsellors or psychiatrist – the decision should be made in conjunction with the patient. Most importantly, the counsellor must have both an interest and an understanding of chronic pain.

There are many and varied pain management programmes, and where possible it should be tailored to the individual patient. All these programmes are to some degree successful, but, as with the physical component, there is no particular one that suits all patients.

Low back pain

Low back pain is very common and the medical profession does not have a clear understanding of its precise mechanisms (Cochrane 1979). Following surgery not involving the back low back pain is most likely to be due to positioning before, during or after surgery. A good example is the lithotomy position which may aggravate an underlying condition, or indeed provoke, back pain. Patients with pre-existing back pain should be warned that the pain may be aggravated by the surgery, particularly if the patient will be in an abnormal position during the operation. Low back pain following surgery is most likely to be due to the patient being moved while anaesthetised or still drowsy.

The same can be said of any back pain from the cervical spine to the coccyx, therefore it is necessary to document the pre-existing problem and to discuss with the patient the possibilities of that pain being aggravated by anaesthesia, surgery or position during surgery. It is worthwhile remembering that there is very little relationship between the imaging of the spine and pain (Jensen et al 1994, Deyo 1994).

Neuropathic pain

Neuropathic pain is defined as pain initiated, or caused by a primary lesion or dysfunction in the nervous system (Merskey & Bogduk 1994). The lesion or dysfunction may be in the peripheral nervous system i.e. outside the spinal cord, or in the central nervous system i.e. involving the spinal cord or brain. This is the type of pain most likely to follow surgical trauma and it is also the type of pain most likely to be associated with medicolegal confrontation. There are two main reasons for neuropathic pain being more likely to lead to litigation than others.

1. The pathophysiology of neuropathic pain is poorly understood and so there is a degree of argument within the medical profession as to whether the pain exists or whether it is purely fictitious.
2. It is uncommon following surgery (of the order of 1% or less) and so surgeons do not come across the problem very often.

This rarity means that surgeons are more likely to question patients' veracity, particularly as they believe they have performed the operation to the best of their ability; and in addition this type of pain has not followed other similar operations. This questioning of the patient's veracity is likely to irritate the patient and so provide the second reason for medicolegal confrontation.

There is no doubt that neuropathic pain is a distinct entity, as there are pains that may be clearly defined such as phantom limb pain, thalamic pain and pain that follows brachial plexus avulsion. Very few members of the medical profession would deny the existence of these syndromes. However, some of the other syndromes (pp 281–282) may be controversial.

The problem that the medical profession has with all neuropathic pain is understanding the mechanism of the pain. As doctors, we produce a name for a condition, which implies that we understand the condition. We do not understand the pathophysiology of all neuropathic pain. The origin of the pain may be defined as peripheral or central, which suggests the limitation of the treatment programme. Peripheral therapies are unlikely to be of any use in central pain, whereas central therapies may help peripheral pain. Indeed the response of neuropathic pains to treatment appears to be random, in that all therapies provide relief some of the time but no therapy provides relief all the time for any specific pain (Tables 12.2 & 12.3). If we are going to be able to produce a logical approach to the treatment of neuropathic pain we will need to involve Chaos Theory (Horton 1993).

Neuropathic pain following surgical trauma is unlikely to be a result of negligence. Phantom limb pain occurs randomly following amputation of a limb, i.e. there are no predictors of which patient will develop phantom limb pain following amputation. Studies conducted to try and prevent the occurrence of phantom limb pain have confirmed this absence of predictive factors. These studies have also confirmed that the pain diminishes with time (Jensen & Rasmussen 1989).

It is highly unlikely that phantom limb pain would form the basis for a medicolegal confrontation. If the other neuropathic pains which follow surgical trauma have a similar basis to that for phantom limb pain then it would suggest that these syndromes are also not a result of surgical negligence. These syndromes also seem to occur randomly. However, they do occur more commonly in the most common operations; for example, the operation most often performed in Oxford is coronary artery bypass grafting and this is the most common referral to our unit for post-surgical pain. This suggests that there is a definitive incidence.

Until there are data available from epidemiological studies, estimates of the incidence of neuropathic pain following surgery will be guesswork. In addition, the natural history seems to be for these pains to improve with time, but if the rate of improvement is exponential then some patients' pain will not resolve.

The most likely reason for a patient to seek legal redress because of neuropathic pain following surgical trauma, is the surgeon's lack of empathy with the patient and also the failure to refer for, or to provide appropriate treatment for, the pain. The therapeutic options available for both the physical and emotional components of the patient's pain are shown in Tables 12.2 & 12.3. The possible site of action of the various therapies is shown in Figure 12.6. The symptoms and signs and diagnostic criteria for certain neuropathic pains that could follow surgical trauma will be briefly discussed.

Painful neuromas

It is interesting that painful neuromas are not mentioned in the classification. They may be the cause of peripheral neuropathic pain.

Neuroma formation occurs whenever a nerve is cut. This means that neuromas form after all surgical trauma, though very few are painful. In animal models, neuromas are always supersensitive to pressure, temperature, and various neurotransmitters e.g. noradrenaline (Wall & Gutnick 1974). This highlights the problem of extrapolating from the animal models to man, particularly in respect to chronic pain. This is not to say that painful neuromas do not occur; they do, classically in stump pain following amputation, but they are thought to be an uncommon cause of neuropathic pain. Thus any surgical operation may result in a painful neuroma. This neuropathic pain is not generally, however, a result of surgical negligence. The onus is on the plaintiff to prove negligence rather than on the surgeon to prove the opposite.

Nerve root irritation

The pain associated with nerve root irritation is classically neuropathic pain. The nerve root may be irritated anywhere between the vertebral column to the peripheral receptor. Any irritation within the nerve is included in this discussion.

The problem with understanding the pain associated with nerve root irritation is similar to the problem of understanding the pain associated with neuromas. Not all nerves that are 'irritated' result in the complaint of, or perception of, pain. In addition, the pain from irritated nerves may be referred outside the anatomical distribution of that nerve (Basbaum & Wall 1976). In the latter way the pain from nerve irritation differs from that associated with painful neuromas. All the conditions listed on pages 281–282 could be the result of an irritable nerve – the classical nerve irritation is lumbar spinal or radicular pain after failed spinal surgery. The occurrence of this pain following spinal surgery cannot readily be equated with negligence as similar painful conditions are associated with all types of surgery, albeit less frequently (Christie & Chen 1993).

Reflex sympathetic dystrophy (complex regional pain syndromes I); causalgia (complex regional pain syndromes II)

Reflex sympathetic dystrophy and causalgia have recently been redefined (as above) by the taxonomy committee of the International Association for the Study of Pain (IASP), because of a general dissatisfaction that there are assumptions implied in the original names (Merskey & Bogduk 1994). This is an important step because not all patients with these syndromes obtain relief from blockade of the sympathetic nervous system; the sympathetic nervous system is not always a factor.

These new names and definitions are also limited, but their advantage is that they remove the necessary involvement of the sympathetic nervous system. They are an approach to a less restrictive understanding of the underlying pathophysiology of the pain in these syndromes. The new labels are by no means correct, but they are so generalised as not to imply any mechanism for the pain. I believe that this redefining has many more advantages than disadvantages, and until we have a better understanding of the cause of these types of pain these definitions should be accepted.

Recently there has been correspondence in the American literature about the occurrence of these syndromes following surgery (Rocco 1993, Reuben 1994). Long-term pain folowing regional nerve block for hand surgery has been recently estimated at 0.5% (Weeks et al 1994).

Reflex sympathetic dystrophy. Reflex sympathetic dystrophy has so many synonyms that it is almost impossible to compile a complete list. The reason for this is that the medical profession cannot agree on one name, which implies that they cannot agree on the cause.

The pathophysiology of this syndrome remains to be defined and it is unlikely that there will be one pathophysiological cause for the pain which accompanies it. It is a neuropathic pain and as such the cause of the pain may, again, be a random error in the system. The IASP have agreed on four diagnostic criteria, three of which (2–4) must be present to confirm the diagnosis:

- The presence of an initiating noxious event, or a cause of immobilisation.
- Continuing pain, allodynia or hyperalgesia the discomfort of which is disproportionate to the inciting event.
- Evidence at some time of oedema, changes in skin blood flow, or abnormal sudomotor activity in the region of the pain.
- This diagnosis is excluded by the existence of conditions that would otherwise account for the degree of pain and dysfunction.

Causalgia. The word causalgia was coined by Silas Weir-Mitchell in the American Civil War to describe the burning pain that followed a penetrating injury to a peripheral nerve, usually by a bullet (Mitchell 1872). Subsequently, any burning pain was called causalgia by the medical profession and so the term has by common usage come to mean a burning pain with or without the history or signs of a peripheral nerve injury. The IASP has agreed on three criteria, all of which must be present to confirm this diagnosis:

- The presence of continuing pain, allodynia, or hyperalgesia after nerve injury, not necessarily limited to the distribution of the injured nerve.
- Evidence at some time of oedema, changes in the skin blood flow, or abnormal sudomotor activity in the region of the pain.
- This diagnosis is excluded by the existence of conditions that would otherwise account for the degree of pain and dysfunction.

Arachnoiditis

Arachnoiditis was originally a result of infection and was endemic in the African and Indian subcontinents (Jenik et al 1981). It was not associated with pain but with motor weakness. In addition, the infective arachnoiditis was generally confined to the cervical and thoracic portions of the spinal cord. Iatrogenic arachnoiditis occurs most commonly in the lumbar spinal cord and is more commonly associated with pain than with motor weakness. Arachnoiditis has been reported after all penetrations of the dura, even after spinal anaesthesia (Rubin 1993), although it is very rare in the latter case. Any surgical trauma that penetrates the dura may be followed by arachnoiditis. The pathophysiology of arachnoiditis is not known but it is believed to be related to blood, trauma and/or foreign bodies, or infection.

The pain that patients complain of may vary from classical nerve compression pain to low back pain which may or may not be associated with clinical evidence of nerve root damage up to and including paralysis. Diagnosis is based on the history, clinical examination and imaging evidence of scarring within the theca. The imaging required to confirm the diagnosis may vary from plain X-ray to enhanced MRI scan.

Arachnoiditis following surgery is rare, the actual incidence or prevalence of arachnoiditis per se is not known. The medicolegal situation will be clarified when the myodil cases are completed, in which myodil was given to hundreds of thousands of patients, a number of whom have developed arachnoiditis. Some of these patients have had laminectomies, others have had only the myelogram and so it is difficult to know whether the patient should be warned of the possibility of arachnoiditis.

Some surgeons give epidural local anaesthetic and steroids; there are a number of current medicolegal cases claiming that these injections cause arachnoiditis (Dougherty & Fraser 1978). If they do cause arachnoiditis it is exceedingly rare. There is no doubt, however, that intrathecal steroids can cause arachnoiditis (Johnson et al 1991).

The incidence of symptomatic arachnoiditis following surgery to the spinal column is unknown but as it is an uncommon occurrence, whether or not it should be discussed with the patient prior to surgery depends on the indication for surgery. In this situation the alleged negligence may revolve around the discussion of arachnoiditis as a possible complication.

CONCLUSION

Chronic pain following surgery is uncommon and so the individual surgeon does not have to deal with it as a problem very often, which means that the surgeon is vulnerable. The individual patient's expectation of the operation is that there should be no complications and any deviation from this implies fault.

There are very few, if any, predictive factors as to which patients or which operations will be associated with chronic pain; the incidence appears to be random. Medicolegal confrontation should be precluded by being empathetic with the patient at the first post-operative consultation, and, if appropriate, arranging further investigations and consultations.

Acknowledgement

I should like to thank Dr Graham Burt for reading the manuscript and for his helpful comments.

REFERENCES

Basbaum A I, Wall P D 1976 Chronic changes in the response of cells in adult cat dorsal horn following partial deafferentation: the appearance of responding cells in a previously non-responsive region. Brain Research 116: 181–204

Brennan T A, Leape L L, Laird N M, Herbert L, Localio A R, Lawthers A G, Newhouse J P, Weiler P C, Hiatt H H 1991 Incidence of adverse events and negligence in hospitalized patients. Results of the Harvard medical practice study I. New England Journal of Medicine 342: 370–376

Caplan R A, Posner K L, Cheney F W 1994 Perioperative ulnar neuropathy: are we ready for shortcuts? Anesthesiology 81: 1321–1323

Christie J M, Chen G W 1993 Secondary hyperalgesia is not affected by wound infiltration with bupivacaine. Canadian Journal of Anaesthesia 40: 1034–1037

Cochrane A L, Baker M E, Crown S, Dixon A StJ, Edwards F C, Glass N J, Grieve G P, Hamblen D L, Hitchcock E R, Kelly R, Newman P H, Park W M, Pragnell C J, Price D J, Woods P H N, Wyke B D 1979 Working group on back pain. Her Majesty's Stationery Office, London

Commission on Provision of Surgical Services 1990 Report of the working party on pain after surgery. The Royal College of Surgeons and The College of Anaesthetists, London

Deyo R A 1994 Magnetic resonance imaging of the lumbar spine. New England Journal of Medicine 331: 115–116

Dougherty J H, Fraser R A R 1978 Complications following intraspinal injection of steroids. Journal of Neurosurgery 48: 1023–1025

Dush D M, Simons L E, Platt M, Nation P C, Ayres S Y 1994 Psychological profiles distinguishing litigating and non-litigating pain patients: subtle, and not so subtle. Journal of Personality Assessment 62: 299–313

Glynn C J, Jamous A, Teddy P J, Moore R A, Lloyd J W 1986 The role of the spinal noradrenergic system in the transmission of pain in patients with spinal cord injury. Lancet ii: 1249–1250

Glynn C J 1988 Clinical research into pain relief. In: Newton D E F, Wesbster N R (eds) Clinical research in anaesthesia. Bailliere Tindall, London, vol 2: 89–105

Glynn C J 1994 Pain. In: Walton J, Barondess J, Lock S (eds) New Oxford medical companion. Oxford University Press, Oxford, pp 631–635

Glynn C J, Smith S. The relationship between quality of life and pain relief. (in preparation)

Gould T M, Crosby D C, Harmer M, Lloyd S M, Lonn J N, Rees G A D, Roberts D E, Webster J A 1992 Policy for controlling pain after surgery: effects of sequential change in management. British Medical Journal 305: 1187–1193

Green R A 1987 Medico-legal aspects of anaesthesia. In: Kaufman L (ed) Anaesthesia review 4. Churchill Livingstone, Edinburgh, pp 147–158

Horton D, May R M 1993 The chaos of disease response and competition. In: Mullin T (ed) The nature of chaos. Clarendon Press, Oxford, pp 183–200

Jadad A R, Carroll D, Glynn C J, Moore R A, McQuay H J 1992 Morphine responsiveness of chronic pain: double-blind randomised cross-over study with patient-controlled analgesia. Lancet i: 1367–1371

Jenik F, Tekle-Haimanot R, Hamory B H 1981 Non-traumatic adhesive arachnoiditis as a cause of spinal cord syndromes. Investigation of 507 patients. Paraplegia 19: 140–154

Jensen T S, Rasmussen P 1989 Phantom pain and related phenomena after amputation. In: Wall P D, Melzack R (eds) Textbook of pain. Churchill Livingstone, Edinburgh, pp 508–521

Jensen M C, Brant-Zawadzki M N, Obuchowski N, Modic M T, Malkasian D, Ross J S 1994 Magnetic resonance imaging of the lumbar spine in people without back pain. New England Journal of Medicine 331: 69–73

Johnson A, Ryan M D, Roche J 1991 Depo-medrol and myelographic arachnoiditis. Medical Journal of Australia 155: 18–20

Jones J G 1989 Depth of anaesthesia. Bailliere Tindall, London, p 3

Laing R, Lam M, Owen H, Plummer J L 1993 Perceived risks of postoperative analgesia. Australian and New Zealand Surgery 63: 760–765

Leape L L, Brennan T A, Laird N M, Lawthers A G, Localio A R, Barnes B A, Herbert L, Newhouse J P, Weiler P C, Hiatt H 1991 The nature of adverse events in hospitalized patients. Results of the Harvard medical practice study II. New England Journal of Medicine 342: 377–384

Max M B 1994 Antidepressants as analgesics. In: Fields H L, Liebeskind J C (eds) Pharmacological approaches to the treatment of chronic pain: new concepts and critical issues. IASP Press, Seattle, p 229–246

McQuay H, Carroll D, Jadad A R, Wiffen P, Moore A 1995 Anticonvulsant drugs for the management of pain: a systematic review. British Medical Journal 311: 1047–1052
McQuay H J, Tramer M, Nye B A, Carroll D, Wiffen P J, Moore R A 1996 A systematic review of antidepressants in neuropathic pain. Pain (in press)
Mendelson G 1994 Chronic pain and compensation issues. In: Wall P D, Melzack R (eds) Textbook of pain. Churchill Livingstone, Edinburgh, pp 1387–1400
Merskey H, Bogduk N 1994 Classification of chronic pain. IASP Press, Seattle
Mitchell S W 1872 Injuries of nerves and their consequences. J B Lippincott, Philadelphia
Nashold B S, Ostdahl R H 1979 Dorsal root entry zone lesions for pain relief. Journal of Neurosurgery 51: 59–69
North R B 1993 Spinal cord stimulation for chronic intractable pain. In: Deninskey O, Beric A, Dogali M (eds) Electrical and magnetic stimulation of the brain and spinal cord. Raven Press, New York, pp 289–301
Pavlov I P 1960 Conditional reflexes. Oxford University Press, London
Powers M J 1987 A lawyer's view of the problem. In: Rosen M, Lunn J N (eds) Consciousness awareness and pain in general anaesthesia. Butterworths, London, pp 155–160
Puxon M 1987 Awareness under anaesthesia: a QC's view. In: Rosen M, Lunn J N (eds) Consciousness awareness and pain in general anaesthesia. Butterworths, London, pp 161–164
Reuben S S 1994 Sympathetically maintained pain and the use of regional anaesthesia. Anesthesiology 81: 1548
Rocco A G 1993 Sympathetically maintained pain may be rekindled by surgery under general anaesthesia. Anesthesiology 79: 865
Rubin A P 1993 Hazards of local and regional anaesthesia. In: Taylor T H, Major E (eds) Hazards and complications of anaesthesia. Churchill Livingstone, Edinburgh, pp 591–612
Thorwald J 1957 The century of the surgeon. Thames and Hudson, London
Walker J S 1994 Quality and safety in anaesthesia. British Medical Journal Publishing Group, London, p 9
Wall P D, Melzack R 1994 Textbook of pain. Churchill Livingstone, Edinburgh
Wall P D, Gutnick M 1974 Properties of afferent nerve impulses originating from a neuroma. Nature 248: 740–743
Warner M A, Warner M E, Martin J T 1994 Ulnar neuropathy: incidence, outcome and risk factors in sedated or anaesthetized patients. Anesthesiology 81: 1332–1340
Weeks L, Barry A, Wolfe T, Firrell J, Scheker L 1994 Regional anaesthesia and subsequent long-term pain. Journal of Hand Surgery 19B: 342–346
White J C, Sweet W H 1969 Pain and the neurosurgeon: a 40 year experience. Charles C Thomas, Springfield, Illinois
Wood P H N 1972 Radiology in the diagnosis of arthritis and rheumatism. Transactions of the Society of Occupational Medicine 22: 69–73
Zenz M, Weber-Stumpt W 1993 Opiophobia and cancer pain in Europe. Lancet 314: 1075–1076

Index